"Amazing Grace"
LYRICS BY JOHN NEWTON,
WORDS FROM THE APOSTLE PAUL...
BOTH MEN...

CAPTURED *by*

GRACE

*No One Is Beyond the Reach
of a Loving God*

WHEN
YOUR WORLD
FALLS APART

SEEING PAST THE PAIN OF THE PRESENT

DAVID JEREMIAH

THOMAS NELSON
Since 1798

NASHVILLE   DALLAS   MEXICO CITY   RIO DE JANEIRO

Praise for *Captured by Grace*

"If you want to be truly effective in every realm of your life, embrace the life-changing message within these pages. Let David Jeremiah inspire and encourage you."

—Ken Blanchard/Co-author of *The One Minute Manager* and *The Secret*

"Dr. Jeremiah has captured the subject of grace in a unique, practical and powerful way. When you read it, your heart, too, will be captured by grace."

—Dr. Tony Evans/Senior Pastor of Oak Cliff Bible Fellowship and President of The Urban Alternative

"I am really glad you picked up this book. *Captured by Grace* is the life-changing story of God's incredible favor and faithfulness. As always, David Jeremiah communicates with infectious joy and contagious faith. I promise that when you finish reading this book, you will say Grace really is amazing!"

—Dr. Jack Graham/Pastor of Prestonwood Baptist Church

"*Captured by Grace* is one of the most interesting and compelling books I have ever read. It is built on the foundation of Scripture and illustrated by the fascinating similarities between the first-century murderer Paul of Tarsus and the eighteenth-century slave trader John Newton. . . . Its unique writing style illustrates the author's incredible grasp of both Scripture and the lives of many who have been touched by the supernatural grace of God. Everyone can benefit by reading this enjoyable book."

—Tim LaHaye/Pastor and Author

"David Jeremiah is a modern-day treasure. With his emphasis on biblical truth and close watch on the pulse of contemporary culture, Dr. Jeremiah skillfully unfolds what the grace of God is and isn't in his newest book. This is must reading for anyone who wants to walk closely with the Lord and see lasting changes in their life. I highly recommend it."

—GREG LAURIE/Senior Pastor of
Harvest Christian Fellowship

"In *Captured by Grace*, David Jeremiah offers a fresh perspective on a familiar subject and has thrown a lifeline to those who can't seem to forgive themselves, laboring under a load of guilt because they just don't feel they 'deserve' God's forgiveness. Like the brilliance of a priceless jewel that appears even more glorious when displayed on black velvet, Dr. Jeremiah describes God's grace as most vividly revealed against the backdrop of a sin-blackened life. Using the stories of John Newton and the apostle Paul as the 'black velvet,' he unveils the timeless jewel of God's grace. Read this book, and be recaptured . . . *by Him*."

—ANNE GRAHAM LOTZ/Evangelist, Bible Teacher,
Founder of AnGeL Ministries, and Author

"It's not 'new' we need—it's fresh reminders of timeless truths. *Captured by Grace* is pure water for thirsty souls. Let David Jeremiah unplug the fountain of God's abundant grace 'til your soul is overflowing."

—JAMES MACDONALD/Pastor of Harvest Bible Fellowship
and Speaker on *Walk in the Word* Radio Program

"A compelling, vivid read—winsomely honest about how grace transforms us from victims to victors. *Captured by Grace* could just be the fresh experience of the love of God you've been waiting for."

—JOHN C. MAXWELL/Best-Selling Author

"David Jeremiah reminds us that God is on the offensive. He does not wait for us to come to Him. He pursues us until we are finally captured by His grace. If you're looking for a weak and passive God, you'll not find Him in this book."

—CHRIS MORTENSEN/ESPN Analyst and Reporter

"*Captured by Grace* makes it very clear that when we accept and then experience God's loving forgiveness in our lives, it produces harmony within our relationships and repairs the hurts of our past. Regardless of our individual journey, we all need this book and the true hope it offers."

—GARY SMALLEY/Founder and CEO of the
Smalley Relationship Center

"The song that I have been performing for years, and that we Americans have come to love, takes on even deeper meaning with this powerful book. You'll never hear 'Amazing Grace' in the same way again."

—JOHN TESH/Entertainer and TV Personality

"I have read every book David Jeremiah has written and assure you that this is the most compelling."

—PAT WILLIAMS/Author and Senior Vice
President of the Orlando Magic

"Rich in illustration, gentle in its touch and profound in its implications, David Jeremiah's *Captured by Grace* addresses a timeless theme with timely relevance."

—RAVI ZACHARIAS/Christian Apologist, Author, and Teacher

CAPTURED *by*
GRACE

To the people of Shadow Mountain,
who for twenty-five years have made our church a place of grace.

CONTENTS

PART TWO: GRACE FOR THE PRESENT

PART THREE: GRACE FOR THE FUTURE

ACKNOWLEDGMENTS

Captured by Grace is not just the title of this book. It is the phrase that best describes what has happened to all of us who have worked on this project.

The possibility of marrying the message of grace to the life stories of John Newton and the apostle Paul surfaced in a publishing meeting with Joey Paul and Byron Williamson of Integrity Publishers. Thank you, Joey and Bryon, for the belief you have had in this project. The fellowship we enjoy in publishing is a major blessing in my life.

Sealy Yates has been my literary agent for over twenty years. Sealy, you are the best at what you do, and you are constantly raising the bar for all of us who work with you! Thank you for your passionate commitment to the Captured by Grace campaign.

Cathy Lord took the responsibility of researching the life of John Newton, and I believe she may have read every book about him that has ever been published. Hardly a week went by that she did not drop something off at my desk that she had discovered about this remarkable man. In ways that only writers would understand, John Newton has become her personal friend. Thank you, Cathy, for the many hours you have invested in this book.

The most creative person I have ever met has an office just a few doors down from mine. Paul Joiner is just simply beyond description! Paul, it would be hard to point to any part of this project that you have not touched. You see everything in color! I wonder if your mind ever sleeps! I am so honored to have you as my friend and so blessed because of your imaginative input into all we do.

Rob Suggs has once again added his considerable gift to this project. Rob, your excellence in writing and editing is second to none. Thank you for making my writing assignments a high priority in your busy life.

Kevin Small has become an integral part of our publishing team. His understanding of marketing and distribution has dramatically changed the way we think about writing and publishing. Kevin, you stretch my mind and my faith, and I look forward to the times we spend together.

Because I pastor a large church and lead an international media ministry, writing can never be the first priority in my life. I write in the in-between hours of the day and night. I am able to do that because of the people of excellence God has placed around me. As my executive assistant at Turning Point Ministries, Diane Sutherland manages all my travel and my daily schedule. Diane, your commitment to details and your winsome, gracious personality make it possible for me to retreat from my busy world to study and write.

Barbara Boucher manages my office at Shadow Mountain and interacts daily with the many requests that come to my desk. Barbara, your heart for ministry is so evident. Thank you for your consistent and compassionate ministry.

My oldest son, David Michael Jeremiah, is a major player in just about everything I do. I love him deeply as my son, but I also respect him highly as a leader. He manages the priorities of a worldwide media ministry with an expertise beyond his years.

With the exception of my personal salvation, my wife Donna is the greatest blessing in my life. Without her encouragement, I would never have started to write. On those rare occasions when I have said

I was never going to write another book, she has just looked at me and smiled. She knows me better than I know myself, and she loves me anyway!

Finally, I want to express my love and adoration to Almighty God who has given me His Son, filled me with His love, and captured me by His grace.

David Jeremiah
San Diego, January 2006

The Hunters *and* *the* Hunted

The hooded figure climbs quietly from his mount, praying that his arrival has gone undetected. He soothes his horse as he hitches her to a post, perhaps one hundred feet from his target. The moonlight dances on the hilt of his sword as he approaches the building and turns to wait for his companions.

There are five of them in all, armed and prepared for any resistance. The men cluster tightly behind an old wall to review the situation and their plan. The target is an old potter's shop, seldom used today. The heretics obviously believe they can perform their illicit worship rituals here with impunity. They are about to learn otherwise.

"Wait for my signal," whispers the leader. "I will pound forcefully upon the door once; and when you hear my fist, you shout for all your lungs are worth. If we create shock and fear, these idiots are all the easier to overpower. Draw your swords and clubs, and don't hesitate to strike if anyone puts up a fight. But most of them are probably women and children and elderly fools who will only whimper as we lead them away."

The five of them creep to the door and the windows of the old shed. The leader places his ear to the door and hears the quiet cadences of prayer. They will be on their knees with eyes shut—the most perfect time imaginable. He throws his fist against the wood, almost splintering it, and five deep voices begin to roar and threaten and terrorize.

As the soldiers hurtle through the doorway, they see the little band of worshipers for the first time. They're screaming in surprise and fear, of course. One infant begins to shriek. Several women begin to cry and cower, assuming the worst is in store for them. Five young men leap to their feet defensively. Yet the fools have brought no weapons at all. They had to know this was going to happen to them. The women restrain their men, who quickly realize the futility of striking back.

The chaos quickly fades to silence now, other than the sobbing of the inconsolable child. The soldiers bring their chains and begin clanging and shackling. One of the older women weeps quietly. Another does something very odd: she smiles at the leader. "I understand what you're doing," she says. "You're serving God to the best of your knowledge. If you could only see . . ."

"Shut up!" yells the leader, just managing to hold back his fist. "Don't patronize me with your imbecilic faith. I have mastered the Law of God, and there is nothing you can teach me. Save it for the rats who have the run of your prison cell." The woman looks at the floor, but there is no anger in her demeanor. Only a kind of resigned sadness.

The leader lingers behind as the Christians are led outside, from where they will be marched before the Council. He examines a crude wooden cross at the front of the room. What manner of insane cult would select such an article of worship? The heritage of faith is purity, holiness—what could be more impure and polluted than an instrument of Roman torture for the dregs of society?

Their founder, the Nazarene, fully deserved His cross. But the Pharisee wonders why these eccentrics risk the arrests and beatings they will now receive, on behalf of an odd rabbi who has been dead for some time now (whatever wild claims they may make about his tomb).

Then the Pharisee stops and listens very carefully to the quiet night. What was that scurrying sound outside? A footstep? The others have been gone for several minutes, and no one else is in this area. He has checked it carefully.

Saul feels the beginning of a chill along his spine. This has happened before—more than once. He roots out the Christians; he does his job; he is reminded of their strange calmness, their—what is the word for it? Some kind of irrational mercy. And always, as Saul is reflecting over the oddity of it all, he hears—the footsteps.

In those moments, he experiences a strange inside-out feeling that *he* is the one who is pursued, and that someone or something else is doing the pursuing. It's irrational, of course. What possible sense could it make? He is God's champion, defender of the faith. All he can do is soldier on, keep doing his job, root out these infidels, capture them one by one. Capture their faith, capture their—yes, that's the word—their *grace*.

The captain strolls along the Charles Towne battery, on the coast of Carolina. He gazes out to sea and listens to the cry of the gulls, wiping the perspiration from his brow. What humid lands, these colonies—a kingdom of mud and mosquitoes. Already he is feeling restless, impatient; if only he could busy himself with gathering the crew and loading the ship for the home voyage.

But there is business still to be done. That is the master purpose of every voyage, after all. One hundred sixty, perhaps one hundred seventy dollars per head. The final sum will be a comfortable one, providing that a good majority of the captives come ashore alive. On the last trip, nearly one-half of these Africans expired. There was hardly a profit to be made.

Yet the captain is not insensitive to such things. He would rather not be in attendance when the cargo hold is opened and the tally is taken. This is the distasteful cost of doing business; the cargo must be packed tightly. It must be chained and disciplined. Some of the natives will die of various diseases, from whippings, or from the heat. Some will even refuse to take bread. It is an unpleasant state of affairs, but England must have its commerce; the colonies must have their workers for crops of rice and indigo.

Yesterday, the captain witnessed an auction at the slave mart. He could not help but be disturbed by the cries of despair as children were parted from their mothers. After no more than a few minutes of this, he found he had to leave, to take a walk among the quieter streets. Let others keep the accounts and do the dickering.

As he strolls now by the seaside, he hears them again: footfalls directly behind him. The captain whirls quickly to find no intruder but the ocean wind. Once more, he reassures himself that his imagination is overactive. His restlessness must be to blame. He hasn't been sleeping well; there have been strange and unpleasant dreams.

And yet Captain Newton has felt it more and more on these business trips: a sense of being followed, of being watched. Even as he has pursued the fortune of slave trading, he has been unable to escape the feeling that it is *he* who is being pursued. Some steady footstep always out of eyesight, some whispered voice just beyond his hearing . . .

"Something relentless," John Newton mumbles to himself. "Something is pursuing us all."

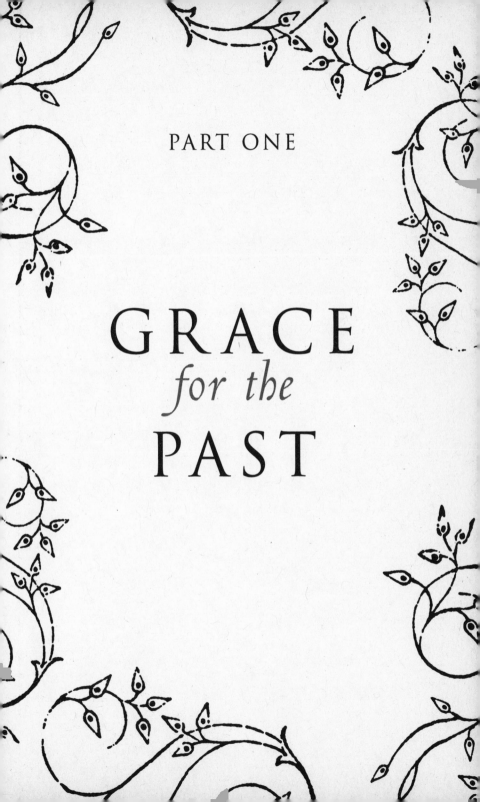

PART ONE

GRACE
for the
PAST

CHAPTER ONE

The Captivating Presence *of* Grace

Amazing Grace, How Sweet the Sound

It's autumn in New York. November 2004.
Freezing rain, weary drivers.
One carload of delinquents on a joyride.

Got the picture?

Their spree begins at the local cineplex. Bored with action flicks, the teenagers decide to act one out. They break into a car, grab a credit card, and proceed to a video store. There they charge four hundred dollars' worth of DVDs and video games.

Why not pick up a few groceries while they're at it? A surveillance tape catches the kids selecting a twenty-pound turkey.

Remember the turkey.

Pedal to the metal in a silver Nissan, the kids move along an irregular line intersecting with a Hyundai containing one Victoria Ruvolo. The two cars cross paths at approximately 12:30 a.m.

Victoria Ruvolo, forty-four, is heading for her Long Island home.

Having attended her fourteen-year-old niece's vocal recital, she looks forward to home and hearth—particularly hearth. She's ready to unravel the overcoat and scarves, burrow under an electric blanket, and rest her weary self.

Maybe the silver Nissan, approaching from the east, catches Victoria's eye—maybe not. Later, she won't be sure. She certainly won't recall the image of a teenage boy leaning out the window of the Nissan as the car approaches. Nor will she retain any memory of the bulky projectile taking flight from his hands.

This is the part about the turkey.

The twenty-pound bird crashes through Victoria's windshield. It bends the steering wheel inward, smashes into her face, and breaks every bone it encounters.

Victoria will remember none of this—frankly, a stroke of mercy. Eight hours of surgery and three weeks of recovery later, however, friends and family fill in the blanks. Victoria lies impassively in a bed in Stony Brook University Hospital and listens to every detail. Yet her emotions are difficult to discern, given the mask her face has become: shattered like pottery, now stapled together by titanium plates; an eye affixed by synthetic film; a wired jaw; a tracheotomy.

The public reaction is much more vigorous. The media has run with this story; weblogs follow every new detail of arrest and arraignment. Over Thanksgiving, New Yorkers whisper prayers of gratitude that they were not Victoria Ruvolo. Over Christmas, they cherish their health and their fortunes a little bit more than usual. Over the New Year, they cry out for justice.

Internet bloggers and TV pundits suggest what they'd do if they could be in a room for five minutes with those punks in the Nissan. They'd especially love to lay hands on Ryan Cushing, the eighteen-year-old who heaved the turkey. *His* face should be shattered. *His* life should lie in ruins. That's how the man in the street sees it.

But it's all in the hands of the justice system. On Monday, August 15, 2005, Ryan and Victoria meet face-to-restructured-face in the courtroom. Nine agonizing, titanium-bolted months have passed since the attack. Victoria manages to walk into the courtroom unaided, a victory in itself.

A trembling Ryan Cushing pleads guilty—to a lesser charge. Sentence: a trifling six months behind bars, five years probation, a bit of counseling, a dash of public service. People shake their heads in righteous indignation. Is that all the punishment we can dish out? When did this country become so soft on crime? Let's lock up all these criminals and throw away the key.

Who is responsible for this plea bargain anyway?

The victim. That's who. The victim requests leniency.

Ryan makes his plea and then turns to Victoria Ruvolo, all the essence of tough guy long since drained away. He is weeping with abandon. The attorney leads the assailant to the victim, and Victoria holds him tight, comforts him, strokes his hair, and offers reassuring words. "I forgive you," she whispers. "I want your life to be the best it can be." Tears mingle from mask of reconstruction and mask of remorse.

It takes quite an event to bring tears to the eyes of New York attorneys and magistrates. This is such an event. TV and radio reporters file their stories in voices that for once are hushed and respectful. The *New York Times* dubs it "a moment of grace."[1]

What do we do with such a story? It's beautiful, moving, inspiring—sure, all of those things. It's also *outrageous*. Why, it undermines every impulse of human nature, doesn't it? Let us be very honest. Would *you* have responded like Victoria Ruvolo? Surely you and I have been driven to a self-righteous frenzy over items far less dramatic. Some of us—some of the *best* of us—need one good incident on the expressway to bring out a snarl, a prolonged honking, a torrent of shouted invectives.

For that matter, remember when that fellow at work tried that little maneuver that really got your goat? You know the one—that petty little power play. How long did you seethe over that one? Or that woman at church who said that thing. Remember what she said and how you bristled? The look you gave her, and all that time you spent imagining what you'd like to say and do?

As for courtrooms, we've seen the opposite script play out. We've heard aggrieved families shouting at thugs as they stood to hear the verdict. And we've agreed with them, haven't we? It's just part of our constitution. Aren't we supposed to support justice and jeer at evil? Isn't it natural to affirm the process of punishing crime?

We're born that way. The smallest toddler retaliates to losing a toy to another child. She doesn't reclaim her toy calmly or dispassionately. She reacts in *outrage*. She seizes the plaything and shouts recriminations at its thief. It's all part of the human wiring. Work, church, playground—we're only human. We get mad *and* we get even.

Why, then, do we catch our breath upon observing behavior that precisely overturns these expectations?

Grace is shocking—something like the heavenly converse of a traffic accident. When love is returned for evil, we can't help stopping to rubberneck. Grace is the delivery of a jewel that nobody ordered, a burst of light in a room where everyone forgot it was dark.

Grace turns human politics on its head, right before our eyes. It renounces the entire conventional wisdom of social behavior. Grace suggests that human beings may be something more than honor graduates of the animal kingdom after all, that the rumors may be true that purity and goodness are real and alive.

Stories like that of Victoria Ruvolo transfix us for a moment. We find a smile, perhaps even shed a tear. It's like warming the soul at a hearth on a chilly night. Then it's right back to the struggle of the moment. We now resume our normal programming.

At least most of us do. Yet there are a rare few who find they cannot resume. The discovery of grace for them is like finding a knothole in the high gates of heaven. They cannot tear themselves away from peering into it. The light intoxicates their being. They wonder why, if this thing called grace is so magnificent—and if it is a standard option of every moment—why is it so rare and isolated? And urgently, pleadingly, the grace visionaries begin calling others to the knothole.

Such a man was the apostle Paul. He was once one of the seizers—the recriminators. These people, these Christians, had stolen his toy, and he was taking it back with a vengeance. They had laid hands on the faith of his fathers and polluted it. He would repay them with interest, galloping to far-flung regions just to torment them. That's when grace—or some Agent thereof—knocked him right out of the saddle, toppled his most precious assumptions, and took away his eyesight until he was ready to look hard at the thing he had refused to behold. And once his vision returned, that item was the only one he wished to see.

Paul changed his name and his person. He would write letter after letter to friends, to churches, to people he had never met—some who wouldn't be born for centuries. He spoke of many things in these letters, but he always came back around to the same theme: that moment of blinding grace on the Damascus Road, when sight came wrapped in blindness.

Our New Testament contains 155 references to grace; 130 of them come from the pen of Paul. The word opens, closes, and dominates every letter he wrote. It defines his teaching and his dearest hopes. Grace is the magnificent ideal by which he would measure his life and yours. The scourge of the martyrs has become the apostle of grace.

That's the startling power of one simple idea—the same power that transformed a ruthless slave trader to a timeless troubadour of liberation. John Newton shared Paul's obsession. In his elder years, he would sit by the fireplace in his former vicarage study at Olney. His once raging soul was now at peace. Just the same, he never wanted to forget the other John Newton—the one who traded in human cargo. Like Paul, his earthly eyesight was failing in latter years, but he could read the large letters he had painted on the wall over his fireplace:

> *Since thou wast precious in my sight,*
> *thou has been honorable (Isaiah 43:4)*
> *BUT*
> *Thou shalt remember that thou wast a*
> *bondman in the land of Egypt,*
> *and the Lord thy God redeemed thee (Deuteronomy 15:15).*

THE MELODY

It was John Newton's special joy as a pastor to craft sermons and hymns together. The Word and music were equally beloved to him, and he gave himself to both. For New Year's 1773, he turned his attention to 1 Chronicles 17:16–17: "Then King David went in and sat before the LORD; and he said: 'Who am I, O LORD God? And what is my house, that You have brought me this far? And yet this was a small thing in Your sight, O God; and You have also spoken of Your servant's house for a great while to come, and have regarded me according to the rank of a man of high degree, O LORD God.'"

The verses seemed to leap from the page before Newton's eye: *Who am I, Lord?* Why should King David, murderer and adulterer, receive the magnificent grace of God? Why should John Newton, trader of slaves? Such grace could only be described as amazing.

Yet the hymn that first emerged from Newton's pen might surprise the modern ear. For one thing, the melody was not the familiar one that has come down to the present day. It would be more than half a century before a man named William Walker would find just the right tune—a melody known as "New Britain." In Newton's time, as many as twenty different melodies might be used interchangeably. Even that immortal title had yet to assert itself. The hymn's original title? "Faith's Review and Expectation"—not exactly catchy enough for the pop charts, then or now.

There were more verses than we often recognize too. Many people claim to know all the verses of "Amazing Grace" by heart, but can they sing the lines below? These originally followed the present third verse:

> *The Lord has promised good to me,*
> *His word my hope secures;*
> *He will my shield and portion be,*
> *As long as life endures.*

> *Yes, when this flesh and heart shall fail,*
> *And mortal life shall cease,*
> *I shall possess, within the veil,*
> *A life of joy and peace.*

> *The earth shall soon dissolve like snow,*
> *The sun forbear to shine;*
> *But God, who call'd me here below,*
> *Will be forever mine.*

But a verse is missing, isn't it? The one that may be your favorite. What about "When we've been there ten thousand years"? The closing stanza you and I know and love first appeared in 1909. Edwin

Othello Excell, himself a prolific composer, inserted the final piece in the puzzle, completing the standard version of the hymn. Excell replaced verses four, five, and six with four lines that John Newton never wrote. How did it happen?

In the year 1852, antislavery sentiment had come to a boil in America. Newton would have heartily approved. Harriet Beecher Stowe's novel *Uncle Tom's Cabin* appeared that year, including a version of "Amazing Grace" that added these lines:

> *When we've been there ten thousand years*
> *Bright shining as the sun,*
> *We've no less days to sing God's praise,*
> *Than when we first begun.*

Excell admired this version excerpt with its vision set in eternal glory. He grafted these new lines to the existing ones, and we've sung it that way ever since.

The English used the song on occasion. Across the sea in South Carolina, the hymn was first published with a melody. That hymnal, *The Southern Harmony*, sold an amazing six hundred thousand copies in 1850—two years before Excell added his "ten thousand."

Years came and passed, and so did new hymnals and musical fashions. "Amazing Grace" was one nice hymn among many until, of all things, the age of acid rock.

In 1970, when electric guitars and angry lyrics ruled the charts, folk singer Judy Collins released an audacious track: an a capella rendition of the old hymn "Amazing Grace." Without the drums, without the backbeat, the result was a revelation to young ears. By early 1971, the song was a hit in England and America. Finally, three recorded minutes that the elderly and their flower-child grandkids could listen to together.

Then in 2004, Bill Moyers produced an entire documentary about the song for public television. He paid tribute to the mysterious power of a simple hymn that had traveled so far with so many adventures. Judy Collins, reprising her hit, told of its support during her bout with alcoholism. Opera singer Jessye Norman rendered a concert version. Country singer Johnny Cash used it to connect with imprisoned criminals. The song cast its spell in many worlds, whether sung by the Boys Choir of Harlem, shaped-note choruses in the Appalachian foothills, or among Japanese worshipers.

The hymn is heard at Olympic ceremonies and presidential inaugurations. It is considered essential in a time of disaster; a crisis such as the one of September 11, 2001; or at any moment of somber mood. It has become a de facto national anthem for events of magnitude.

Shoppers at Amazon.com may choose from among 3,832 separate recordings of John Newton's old hymn. It comes in every style, crosses every line, and reaches any and every ear. And when it is announced in a church service, people stand a little taller to sing it. They lift their voices a bit higher. Some of them feel that, just for a moment, they are catching a glimpse through the gates of heaven.

The Man

St. Augustine wrapped a powerful thought in vivid imagery when he said, "God always pours His grace into empty hands." The hands of John Newton could not have been emptier.

His father commanded a merchant ship and was always at sea. His mother raised him the best she could, schooling him in Scripture and sacred song. Mother and son attended a chapel near the Tower of London. In a nation in which 99 percent of the people were affiliated with the Church of England, Elizabeth Newton insisted upon an independent congregation.[2]

Just before his seventh birthday, John Newton lost his mother. It didn't take the old captain long to remarry and dispatch the boy to a boarding school. His was a childhood out of a Dickens novel. Unwanted children were often abandoned and abused at such schools. John left school and returned home. The elder Newton shrugged, put his young son on a ship, and began taking him along on his travels.

By the age of seventeen, John Newton's world was the open sea. The world of the Spirit, as lovingly taught by his mother, had vanished over his horizon. For seven years he declined into rebellion. Like some today, he mixed and matched convenient ideas to create his own religion, making "a shipwreck of faith, hope and conscience." In his own words, his "delight and habitual practice was wickedness," and he "neither feared God nor regarded men." In short, he was "a slave to doing wickedness and delighted in sinfulness."[3]

After a short stint in the wartime navy, Newton decided the regimented military life was not for him. He left in search of his father in the belief that his father could secure his release. It proved a futile move, as the deserter was quickly captured. He took a public beating, was stripped of his rank as midshipman, and was placed in shackles. Finally he managed to get on an Africa-bound freighter. There, in the shadow of the Dark Continent, John Newton sought to be lost where he could not be found. He could abandon himself to a life of dissolution.

Newton took up with a Portuguese slave trader on the island of Plantain, just off Sierra Leone on the western coast. The man's African wife was hostile to her husband's new friend and forced him to eat scraps from her plate like a dog. His life and fortunes had reached low ebb. Perhaps he remembered a story his mother once read him—something about another rebellious son far from home, eating among the pigs.

Finally, John Newton was taken aboard a slave ship, where he was quartered with the captain. Then, in March 1748, somewhere in the North Atlantic, grace arrived. The hand of God rescued a shipwrecked soul. If it could happen to Paul on the road to Damascus, it could come to Newton on the voyage to Britannia. In chapter 6, we'll hear more of his conversion story.

Two years later, Newton was married. But just as the storm seemed over, he began to be troubled by fits and seizures that precluded a life at sea. So he stayed home and worked as a tide surveyor at the docks of Liverpool. With plenty of time on his hands, he began to fill in the great gaps of a childhood that provided little formal education. He studied Greek, Hebrew, and Syriac. He read classic theological works in Latin, English, and French. More and more, he found himself drawn to that old book that brought memories of his mother—the Christian Scriptures.

Then the people wanted a pastor. In 1754, he accepted a calling in Olney, where he would serve for sixteen years. At the next church, this time in London, he served God and men for twenty-eight years. An aging but contented man, at the age of seventy-two he marveled that "such a wretch should not only be spared and pardoned, but reserved to the honor of preaching the gospel, which he blasphemed and renounced."[4] He preached the Gospel until the venerable age of eighty-one.

The melody, however, lingers on.

THE MESSAGE

Man and melody—each sailed quite a journey. Newton's hymn, of course, has easily outlived him. People wonder at the power of "Amazing Grace." What is so amazing about it? Like so many things, it defies the dissection we might give a frog in science class. We can't quite discover the secret, for the notes are the same as those on any piano. The words are transcendent, but no more so than the stanzas of any number of other hymns—"Holy, Holy, Holy," for example. No public relations firm has accounted for its influence. No pope or prelate has sanctified it. But there it is, a cherished piece of our lives.

Some have attempted to bottle its inspiration, filter its doctrine, and reduce it to an anthem of generic wellness. "Amazing Grace," to some, is simply "a greater sense of consciousness" or "the power of human potential," a "moment of intense awareness" or "experiencing the interconnectedness of all things." It is "being aware of the unity of which we are all a part" or "the unseen forces that are all around us." It is "relinquishing the ego," "achieving mental clarity," or "finding spiritual illumination."

For M. Scott Peck it is "hidden in the 95 percent of our consciousness of which we are unaware."[5] For Judy Collins, it is "letting go, bottoming out, seeing the light, turning it over, trusting the universe, breathing in, breathing out, going with the flow."[6] For folk singer Joan Baez, "it's a state I would like to be in for more than thirty seconds a day."[7] For Pete Seeger, "Grace means harmony . . . the law of gravity throughout the universe a kind of harmony . . . or the way that mathematics works."[8]

We can only imagine what John Newton would make of all this—perhaps express bewilderment over such nebulous metaphysical puffery. He would point out that his verses do no more, and no less, than tell the old, old story—the one that never grows old. They tell of the loving Father and the lost son. They speak of the incredible joy of salvation from the clutches of sin, of the amazingness of grace.

Perhaps it is not the song after all; perhaps it has never been the song but the idea—and the fact that this hymn is simply the one that best captures the lightning.

The lightning is grace. As Martyn Lloyd-Jones has written: "There is no more wonderful word than 'grace.' It means unmerited favor or kindness shown to one who is utterly undeserving. . . . It is not merely a free gift, but a free gift to those who deserve the exact opposite, and it is given to us while we are 'without hope and without God in the world.'"[9]

Someone has written that *grace* is a five-letter word that is often spelled J-E-S-U-S. For, if Newton's hymn was the melody that embodied the idea, Jesus was the Man. He was the once-and-for-all, perfect human image of grace, of love, of truth. "In the beginning was the Word, and the Word was with God, and the Word was God. . . . And the Word became flesh and dwelt among us, and we beheld His glory, the glory as of the only begotten of the Father, full of grace and truth. . . . For the law was given through Moses, but grace and truth came through Jesus Christ" (John 1:1, 14, 17).

In the Greek tongue of Paul's day, the word for "grace" was *charis.* It carried the connotation of graciousness or favor. But the term evolved in the Greek world until it meant the actual gift, the concrete expression of kindness. Grace happens. As Paul explained it, "The free gift is not like the offense. For if by the one man's offense many died, much more the grace of God and the gift by the grace of the one Man, Jesus Christ, abounded to many" (Romans 5:15).

Grace happens, and it acts. "For by grace you have been saved through faith, and that not of yourselves, it is the gift of God" (Ephesians 2:8).

Such grace can come only from God. It is the gift unsought, unmerited, unlimited. For no matter what we have done, no matter the depth of our transgression, the darkness of our hearts—grace overrules them all. God pursues us relentlessly, He will not give us up, and once He has captured us, He won't let us go.

These are the broad outlines of the great idea. Yet it is as if we are mapping an uncharted territory—surveying the bounds of heaven, if you will. We can never take in the whole expanse. Grace is too dazzling, too bright, for it is powered by the holy heart of God. Trying to comprehend it in whole is like staring directly into one thousand suns.

Grace is as infinite and transcendent as the God from whom it flows. He is "the God of all grace" (1 Peter 5:10), and He is abounding with mercy for the merciless, help for the helpless, redemption for anyone and everyone. There is no limit to the throng of guests invited to dine at the Master's overflowing table.

As Griffith Thomas has said, "All this in full measure and overflowing abundance, because of nothing in the object, and because of everything in the Giver, God himself."[10]

Grace is the bridge over a chasm that seemed infinite—the canyon between our depravity and His holiness. That bridge is wide and sturdy and sure, beckoning to us to cross over into a life too wonderful for us to imagine.

THE MERCY

At the heart of the mystery is an essential concept: the idea of mercy. We must understand grace, at least within the limits of our comprehension; we must understand mercy. And we must be clear on how the two ideas intersect.

We often use the words as if they are synonyms—one and the same. In fact, there are passages in the New Testament that make that appear to be so. A few scholars have put forward the neat and simple proposition that the Old Testament uses *mercy* while the New Testament speaks of *grace*.

The truth is more elusive, like the words themselves. Think of it this way: Mercy is God withholding the punishment we rightfully deserve. Grace is God not only withholding that punishment but offering the most precious of gifts instead.

Mercy withholds the knife from the heart of Isaac.
Grace provides a ram in the thicket.

Mercy runs to forgive the Prodigal Son.
Grace throws a party with every extravagance.

Mercy bandages the wounds of the man beaten by the robbers.
Grace covers the cost of his full recovery.

Mercy hears the cry of the thief on the cross.
Grace promises paradise that very day.

Mercy pays the penalty for our sin at the cross.
Grace substitutes the righteousness of Christ for our wickedness.

Mercy converts Paul on the road to Damascus.
Grace calls him to be an apostle.

Mercy saves John Newton from a life of rebellion and sin.
Grace makes him a pastor and author of a timeless hymn.

Mercy closes the door to hell.
Grace opens the door to heaven.

Mercy withholds what we have earned.
Grace provides blessings we have not earned.

In Victor Hugo's *Les Misérables,* Jean Valjean is a guileless, unassuming man until he is imprisoned during the French Revolution for stealing a loaf of bread in order to feed his starving family. After completing nineteen years of hard labor, he is bitter and angry toward both society and God.

Monseigneur Myriel, a seventy-four-year-old bishop in southeastern France, has also suffered greatly during the Revolution. All that remains of the bishop's aristocratic heritage are six knives and forks, a soup ladle, and two candlesticks. His experience has taught the bishop compassion for the indigent, and he ministers to them as a humble servant.

After four days of freedom, with repeated denials of food or shelter, the weary and hungry Valjean becomes a desperate man. He arrives at the door of the bishop's home. The hardened Valjean, mistaking it for an inn, brashly storms into the kitchen where he is confounded by the warm welcome he receives from the bishop. That night, while the household is asleep, Valjean leaves the first mattress and white sheets he has known in nineteen years and stealthily fills a knapsack with the bishop's treasured silverware and disappears into the darkness.

In the morning, the bishop corroborates the shackled Valjean's claim to the gendarmes that the silver has been given to him. The bishop asks them to release Valjean and says to him, "I'm glad to see you. But I gave you the candlesticks, too, which are silver like the rest and for which you can certainly get two hundred francs. Why did you not carry them away with your forks and spoons?"

Incredulously, Valjean asks the bishop, "Is it true that I am to be released?"

The bishop assures him that he is free and adds, "My friend, before you go, here are your candlesticks. Take them." Then he adds, "Do not forget, never forget, that you have promised to use this money in becoming an honest man. . . . Jean Valjean, my brother, you no longer belong to evil, but to good. It is your soul that I am buying for you. I withdraw it from [heinous] thoughts and from the spirit of perdition, and I give it to God."

Troubled by the grace offered to him, Valjean visualizes the contrast of the darkness in his own soul with the harsh light of love that has penetrated his bitterness. "A gentle light rested over this life and this soul. It seemed to him that he beheld Satan by the light of Paradise." It was certain indeed, "he was no longer the same man, that everything about him was changed." The bishop had "filled the whole soul of this wretched man with a magnificent radiance."

Twenty-four hours after his theft, Valjean returns to the scene of his crime and is observed "in the attitude of prayer, kneeling on the pavement in the shadow in front of the door of the gentle bishop.

A moment of grace can change a lifetime. In fact, a moment of grace can change an eternity.

Moments *of* Grace

If you're suffering from guilt or a slip-sliding self-image, skim back over chapter 1 and underline the phrases that most impress you, like: *I forgive you . . . God always pours His grace into empty hands . . . Unmerited favor . . . Unlimited . . . Grace is a five-letter word spelled J-E-S-U-S . . . Grace is a bridge over a chasm that seemed infinite . . .* Then choose one particular underlined statement and turn it into a prayer, asking God to make you a recipient of His amazing grace and a conveyer of it to others.

Ask yourself, "How can I be more like Victoria Ruvolo, who forgave her assailant and wanted his life to be the best it could be?" Is there someone you can forgive today? And as you close this chapter, don't forget to sing! Every time you close this book, walk away with a few bars of "Amazing Grace" playing in your mind or floating from your lips.

CHAPTER TWO

The Compassionate Plan *of* Grace

That Saved a Wretch Like Me

W hen was the last time you met a wretch strolling down the avenue? How about a transgressor? A miscreant? A worker of iniquity?

Look those words up in a dusty old dictionary, and you'll find an entire arsenal of powerful words for sin and its perpetrators. Yet many of these words are on the endangered vocabulary list today. They grow musty and unfamiliar from lack of use.

The question is, in a world such as ours, why would so many colorful and descriptive terms for wickedness go out of style? Sin is still in; only the names have changed. Debauchers have been replaced by "compulsive personality types." We don't hear much about iniquity, but we do make plenty of references to "unproductive personal habits." Nobody this side of the Grimm Brothers is actually *wicked* today—just a lot of people with "behavioral disorders," right? If anyone in our society does something socially unacceptable, just blame the chemistry and find the right prescription drug. If we can't eliminate sin in practice, we'll change its name and talk around it until nobody recognizes the problem.

A few years ago, the *Wall Street Journal* placed an advertisement in the *New York Times* observing that our generation has dismantled its old, sturdy frames of reference for personal behavior. The idea of guilt was swept away, leaving people to make their own judgment calls on moral issues. The ad concluded that "many wrecked people could have used a road map."[1]

Jettisoning the guilt trip sounds like a lot of fun at first—a real party. Only later, when it is too late, do we wander through the moral debris and wonder if our freedom was truly free. That's when the old terminology seems so much more descriptive—words such as *wickedness* and *wretch*. Throw in *remorse* and *penitence*.

We find the word *wretch*, of course, in "Amazing Grace." Let me ask you, how do you feel when you sing that phrase "a wretch like me"? Some of us belt out that line with a huge smile, as if we had no clue what we were proclaiming about ourselves! Others pay more attention, and they don't like that phrase one bit. Who is this song-book calling a wretch? There have been attempts to remove the W word from the standard hymnal.

Wretch. The term is often confused with *retch*, which is not even its distant cousin. At the risk of indelicacy, we'll simply point out that the one without the *w* descends from a Middle English term meaning to clear one's throat. *Wretch*, on the other hand, descends from a more ancient lineage—it comes from an Old English term meaning someone who is miserable, an exile. That's illuminating, for what are exiles but what the *Wall Street Journal* called "wrecked people who need a road map"?

A wretch is one miserable human being in a self-imposed exile.

Like the Prodigal Son. Like John Newton. As a matter of fact, your dictionary should carry a head shot of John Newton with its listing for *wretch*. Let's get back to his story.

A WRETCHED EXILE

To understand the wonder of grace through the eyes of Newton, you must have some idea of the wretchedness of his exile.

We rejoin Newton as a young man on the deck of one of his first sailing vessels. He is depressed, but Prozac won't be invented for centuries. He is raging, but there are no handy anger-management books around. Therefore he sits beneath the moon, stares into the restless sea, and weighs two options:

a) Maybe he will commit suicide;
b) Maybe he will murder the captain.

Perhaps by the restraining hand of God, he chooses

c) None of the above.

Newton wrote a letter in 1754 saying that before he had reached the age of twenty, he was never an hour in anyone's company without attempting to corrupt their character. He once said of himself, "My daily life was a course of the most terrible blasphemy and profaneness. I don't believe that I have ever since met so daring a blasphemer as myself. Not content with common profanities and cursing, I daily invented new ones . . ."[2]

His soul was deep in exile, farther away than any ship could have carried him.

In his book *Not the Way It's Supposed to Be: A Breviary of Sin,* theologian Cornelius Plantinga Jr. assures us that we can never arrive at any definition of *grace* without sin as our point of departure. Cheap grace, he says, trivializes the cross of Christ. How can we avert our eyes from a cross that is drenched in holy blood? It was for sin that God, clothed in flesh, writhed in agony on our behalf. It was for iniquity; for wickedness; for every manner of wretched, despicable evil that He submitted to beating and humiliation and finally the obscenity of death itself.

Grace can only shine in its ultimate brilliance because it emerges from ultimate darkness. Therefore, Plantinga points out, we load up on bland and inoffensive modern worship practices, "seeker-sensitive" though they may be, at our own peril. Catchy praise choruses and positive-thinking sermons are crowd pleasers, but sometimes the praise bands drown out the sobering reality of sin—not "unproductive habits," but *sin*—and the consequent demand for confession, repentance, and forgiveness.[3]

This is not to weigh in on all the issues that surround our modern worship but to question any gathering of the saints where sin is swept under the sanctuary carpet. That could happen against the background of a pipe organ or an electric guitar. The point is that we must confront the true enemy in clear terms.

Paul was the apostle of grace, but he never denied the apostasy of sin. In fact, it was his very honesty on that subject that caught John Newton's despairing eye. The exile was intrigued that a man like Paul could call himself the "chief" of sinners (1 Timothy 1:15), that God would pluck His champion from the roster of the enemy.

Newton read Paul's words in 1 Timothy 1:13–14 over and over: "I was formerly a blasphemer, a persecutor, and an insolent man; but I obtained mercy because I did it ignorantly in unbelief. And the grace of our Lord was exceedingly abundant, with faith and love which are in Christ Jesus."

Abundant grace for abundant sin. John Newton couldn't stop thinking about the implications of such an idea.

PRELUDE TO GRACE

Paul was not one to airbrush the scandal of his own past. His résumé, as it crops up in his writings, always includes the hard truth that he was the "least of the apostles," in his words, because he had the blood of the martyrs on his hands (1 Corinthians 15:9). He was "less than the least of all the saints" (Ephesians 3:8). He was the "chief" of sinners (1 Timothy 1:15).

But the truth of it, as Paul shows in Romans 3, is that none of us has clean hands. The apostle goes to the Old Testament to make his case—Ecclesiastes, five psalms, one citation from Isaiah. Five times he uses the words *none* or *all,* for none are righteous; all are ruined and helpless in the sight of God. We are a world of exiles. As it is written:

> *"There is none righteous, no, not one;*
> *There is none who understands;*
> *There is none who seeks after God.*
> *They have all turned aside;*
> *They have together become unprofitable;*
> *There is none who does good, no, not one."*
> *"Their throat is an open tomb;*
> *With their tongues they have practiced deceit;"*
> *"The poison of asps is under their lips;"*
> *"Whose mouth is full of cursing and bitterness."*
> *"Their feet are swift to shed blood;*
> *Destruction and misery are in their ways;*
> *And the way of peace they have not known."*
> *"There is no fear of God before their eyes." (Romans 3:10–18)*

The chorus to Paul's sorrowful song is "no one—not even one." He comes around to that refrain five times. Lest we cling to any shred of self-righteousness, Paul tells us again and again.

This is a message no one wants to hear, for the upshot of it is that you can be the most upright citizen of your town, and still, before the revealing light of heaven, you are a miserable wretch at the mercy of a holy God. You can have a crime-free record, perfect standing with the IRS, the works of Mother Teresa, the passion of Paul, and the conviction of Gandhi, and you still stand accused and convicted before the perfect standards of an infinitely righteous Judge.

Here are more words we'd rather not sing about ourselves: *total depravity*. We would prefer to reserve such a term for child abusers, pornographers, and terrorists. But Paul shakes his head sadly and says none of us is righteous. No, not one.

Our depravity doesn't come in half-doses: *total* means just that. Charles Swindoll has written that if depravity were blue, we'd be blue all over. We'd bleed blue, think blue thoughts, and have no possibility of a single fragment of a second when our heart, soul, and mind weren't flooded in blue. You could be as colorful a personality as you wish, but every tint of the rainbow would be overwhelmed by blue.[4]

Ivan Turgenev, the nineteenth-century Russian novelist and playwright, said, "I don't know what the heart of a bad man is like, but I do know what the heart of a good man is like and it is terrible."

And Aleksandr Solzhenitsyn writes, "If only there were evil people somewhere insidiously committing evil deeds; and it were necessary only to separate them from the rest of us and destroy them. But the line dividing good and evil cuts through the heart of every human being. And who is willing to destroy a piece of his own heart?"[6] Sin cuts its merciless swath through the entire human race, not missing a single heart.

On the other hand, there *is* some good news. Very significant good news! Total depravity meets its match in total grace; one infinite value cancels out another.

In the end, we must acknowledge the darkness within us and the light that comes only from God. Both are unrelenting, and both define every moment of our life. Every atom in our bodies is infected by the disease of sin, but every atom may likewise be covered by the grace of God. The vilest offender can reap the deepest joys of heaven.

The only requirement comes in two supreme realizations: first, that we are totally contaminated; second, that we are totally forgiven only through the love and grace and sacrifice of our Lord Jesus Christ.

Paul has shown us the first of those realities. Now, with great joy, he turns his attention to the second.

PRINCIPLES OF GRACE

Get ready, for we will look now at five of the most important verses in the Bible. This section of Romans may be possibly the most important single paragraph ever written.

John Bunyan, author of *Pilgrim's Progress*, attributed his conversion to these verses. Bible scholar Donald Grey Barnhouse drew a great heart across them in his Bible. He declared that they constitute the heart of Romans, the heart of the New Testament, the heart of the Word of God itself. Imagine: the whole galaxy of revelation from our Father revolving around this single point, the ground zero of our spiritual universe.[7]

Now as we stand upon this holy ground, Paul shows us seven components of the grace of God. Talk about your vocabulary! These words will never grow musty in the dictionary of heaven. They are words such as *grace, faith, justification, redemption, freely*—the antidote for *wretch, iniquity, depravity,* and the rest. Learn these verses, know the meanings of these words, and you have passed a master's course in salvation science.

Paul wrote this textbook of grace through the inspiration of the Holy Spirit. John Newton escaped his exile here. John Bunyan made his pilgrimage in this passage. This little site in your Bible is the missing link between life and death, flesh and spirit, creature and Creator. And every one of us must pass this spring and drink deeply if we are to understand who we are and how we may be rescued from ourselves.

Grace: Apart from Works

> *But now the righteousness of God apart from the law is revealed.*
> —ROMANS 3:21

In the entire world, only two religions may be found. The first of them might be called the religion of divine accomplishment. The second is the religion of human achievement. Paul sets these two conflicting ideas against one another.

The apostle knows from firsthand experience that human achievement is designed for failure. He has lived it both ways and found human achievement to be a dead end. He once surpassed every standard of excellence established for a Hebrew Pharisee, and it all came to nothing. And he will tell us over and over, in each of his epistles, that works can never suffice. We might as well try building a ladder to heaven.

> But to him who does not work but believes on Him who
> justifies the ungodly, his faith is accounted for righteousness.
> (Romans 4:5)

For by grace you have been saved through faith, and that not of yourselves; it is the gift of God, not of works, lest anyone should boast. (Ephesians 2:8–9)

[God] has saved us and called us with a holy calling, not according to our works, but according to His own purpose and grace which was given to us in Christ Jesus before time began. (2 Timothy 1:9)

Not by works of righteousness which we have done, but according to His mercy He saved us, through the washing of regeneration and renewing of the Holy Spirit. (Titus 3:5)

Knowing that a man is not justified by the works of the law but by faith in Jesus Christ. . . . I do not set aside the grace of God; for if righteousness comes through the law, then Christ died in vain. (Galatians 2:16, 21)

Grace: Accepted by Faith

> *Even the righteousness of God, through faith in Jesus Christ.*
> —ROMANS 3:22

Now we turn to the idea of faith. Listen to the frequency with which it comes through Paul's pen in Romans 3:

"God set forth as a propitiation by His blood, through faith" (v. 25).
"The justifier of the one who has faith in Jesus" (v. 26).
"A man is justified by faith" (v. 28).
"Justify the circumcised by faith" (v. 30).
"And the uncircumcised through faith" (v. 30).
"Do we then make void the law through faith?" (v. 31).

As noted British pastor Charles Spurgeon once said, faith is believing Christ is who He said He was and that He'll do what He promised to do—and then living accordingly. That way our faith is "accounted for righteousness" (Romans 4:5). And we have "peace with God through our Lord Jesus Christ" (Romans 5:1).

God's grace meets human faith, and peace is declared in the war between heaven and earth.

Grace: Available to All Who Believe

> . . . *to all and on all who believe. For there is no difference;*
> *for all have sinned and fall short of the glory of God.*
> —ROMANS 3:22–23

Key word: *all*. That is one immense three-letter word, for it measures the width of God's grace and the height of His love. God's net is as large as the number of people who are willing to fall into its safety. No one is outside the scope of His grace. There are no distinctions within the nation of the sinful, no pecking order within the league of the elect.

There are indeed degrees of sin. A jaywalker receives a lighter sentence than a murderer. But all of that is earthly reckoning—nitpicking by the standard of heaven. Because a millionth of a molecule of sin contaminates a soul, *all* are found guilty. And because grace cleanses us from sin just as absolutely, we find ourselves standing at the throne of grace without any human ranks or measurements. All are equally pure and clean before God. You and the apostle Paul will stand together, equally righteous in God's sight. The Father will look upon each of you and see only the purity of His own Son.

Grace: Attained by Justification

Being justified . . .
—ROMANS 3:24

At the center point of this centerpiece passage we find the concept of justification. Don't be fooled—the idea is more complex than you may suppose. I may forgive you for doing me some wrong, but I haven't justified you. The judge may throw your case out of court, but it doesn't affect your true guilt or innocence. Pardon simply takes away the punishment for a sin. Justification erases any record of your transgression.

Jesus infuriated the religious leaders by this very act. He forgave sins of which He was not even the victim! How could He, as a third party, forgive one person's transgression against another?

He can do so because He is God, because He is pure, and because He chooses to be a third party to every wrong act we can ever commit. Christ removes not only the penalty for our sin; He cleanses us completely from its slightest taint. You and I stand before God as if we lived a life of utter purity and perfection.

Forgiveness says, "I'm going to let you slide this time." Justification says, "I'm going to remove the offense from all memory, as if it never occurred." It forgives and forgets. The president can pardon, but he cannot reinstate the criminal to the position of one who has not broken the law. God does both—that's the key to justification.

John Stott writes that "justification is not a synonym for amnesty . . . [but] an act of justice, of gracious justice. . . . When God justifies sinners, he is not declaring bad people to be good, or saying that they are not sinners after all; he is pronouncing them legally righteous, free from any liability to the broken law, because he himself in his Son has borne the penalty of their law-breaking."[8]

Grace: Awarded Freely

> *Being justified freely . . .*
> —ROMANS 3:24

You already know the Latin word for "freely": *gratis*. Revelation 22:17 tells us that the water of life is *gratis* to anyone who wants it. Jesus says in Matthew 10:8 that *gratis* we have received, and *gratis* we should give.

A beggar presses his nose against a plate-glass window. The smells of the restaurant are intoxicating to him. He has no work, no shelter, and no hope. His stomach growls in protest as he watches the well-dressed, well-fed patrons enjoy their steak and lobster dinners. This is the finest restaurant in town. Who is he kidding by even looking upon the elegance of their feast? As a matter of fact, here comes the waiter to shoo him away, unappetizing scenery that he has become.

But the waiter's face bears no rebuke. Instead, compassion is written across it. "I've brought you our finest entrée," says the waiter, uncovering a sumptuous plate. The vagrant's eyes grow wide, and he reaches for the embarrassing pocket change that is all he can offer. "Put your coins away," laughs the waiter. "This one's on our owner, who spotted you from the window. He knows you could never afford such a meal, and he offers this one *freely*. Come back again when you're hungry."

You are an invited guest at the heavenly banquet, not a paying customer. *Gratis*—you have to like that word.

Grace: Acquired Through Redemption

Being justified freely by His grace through the redemption that is in Christ Jesus.
—ROMANS 3:24

Have you ever redeemed a coupon? Sure enough, we've come to the language of the marketplace.

Paul had walked through the streets of Rome and Corinth, where slaves were bought and sold like apples from a fruit stand. He knew that we are all slaves to sin and guilt, more helpless and humbled than the most shackled slave. Jesus steps into the street, produces payment, and sets us free.

But that illustration is lacking to say the least. In reality, Jesus used no coin but the precious exchange of His blood. It's not the same as a rich man reaching into his wallet for a few dollars when he has millions. Jesus puts up all that He has. He buys our liberation through His own suffering. He becomes the slave so that the real slave may go free.

That is why Christ is our *Redeemer*. Princeton theologian Benjamin Warfield loved applying that title to his Lord, because it reminds us not only of our precious gift but its ultimate price: "Whenever we pronounce it, the cross is placarded before our eyes and our hearts are filled with loving remembrance not only that Christ has given us salvation, but that he paid a mighty price for it."[9]

Grace: Accomplished Through Propitiation

Whom God set forth as a propitiation by His blood . . .
—ROMANS 3:25

Yet another beautiful word sadly lacking in current parlance is *propitiation*. It is one of the most powerful and profound terms in the biblical vocabulary. Yet it is used sparingly in the sacred Word of God. A mere four times we come across it in the New Testament. On each occasion, it provides a glimpse of our salvation through the eyes of God himself.

Its Old Testament usage provides a few clues to the mystery of propitiation. The ark of the covenant was a gold-covered wooden box about one yard long. The treasure it held was no less than the stone tablets of the Law, etched by the finger of God and borne from Mount Sinai in the hands of Moses. The box had a cover known as the mercy seat, which held two cherubim that faced one another from each end. The wings of these cherubim stretched upward then forward, nearly meeting in the middle over the ark.

The symbolism of the wings told everyone that God dwelled above the ark. Yet the ark provided a picture of judgment—a feeling of dread. For, as James Montgomery Boice points out, God looked down from heaven between the wings of those cherubim and saw the ark's cargo of commandments. They were as surely and injudiciously broken as the tablets themselves, which Moses had hurled in frustration. Disobedience called for judgment.

Ah, but there is that covering. What is it called? The *mercy* seat.

You see, once a year, on the Day of Atonement, the Jewish high priest entered the holy of holies to make atonement for the people's sins. He entered to make *propitiation*—the very word that comes down to us from Hebrew to Greek, translated as "mercy seat." The priest sprinkled the blood of an animal sacrifice upon the mercy seat.

This changed things. Now, as God looked down, He didn't immediately see those broken laws on shattered tablets. Instead He saw the blood of innocence, a humble offering of repentance. And forgiveness became possible—through propitiation.

How many herds of rams would it take to cover all our sins? How often must this ritual be repeated? The final answer, of course, was the blood of God's own Son.[10]

John writes, "He Himself is the propitiation for our sins, and not for ours only but also for the whole world" (1 John 2:2). There is enough room beneath those angels' wings for every one of us.

THE FOUNTAIN OF GRACE

In the dark background of John Newton's life, we come across a man by the name of William Cowper (pronounced *Cooper*).

Born in 1731, Cowper shared something in common with Newton. His mother died when he was small. And he, too, was abruptly shipped away to a boarding school. Cowper, small and shy, became the target of bullies and persecution. All the love and security of his life seemed to have been replaced by abandonment and victimization.

As Cowper grew, his studies became his refuge; he particularly enjoyed poetry and literature. His mother had been a Donne, coming from the family of the Christian poet John Donne, who wrote, "No man is an island." But his mother was dead, and Cowper felt very much like an island.

His father insisted that young William enter the legal field. When it came time for his final examination, the student suffered an emotional breakdown and attempted suicide. After this, he couldn't regain any emotional equilibrium. "I was a stricken deer that left the herd," he writes.[11]

By now, Cowper had decided that all life and all its agents were aligned against him; he had been born under a curse. He threw away his Bible in scorn, saying that God was one more bully out to get him. As a matter of fact, so was everyone else, for Cowper suffered from acute paranoia. The world was one great conspiracy against him. He had become a wretched exile with no road map home.

After his failed suicide attempt, Cowper was diagnosed with *hypochondrial melancholy.* That's when some of his few friends recommended a mental asylum. The grace of God here enters the story.

Dr. Nathaniel Cotton, poet and Christian, happened to be the physician in charge. For eighteen months, Cowper showed positive progress. Dr. Cotton helped Cowper recover his love for poetry and the written word. He patiently explained the infinite magnitude of God's grace, which was great enough to cover all His children, even William Cowper. Could it be that instead of all things being in league against him, all things worked for the good of those who loved this God? The patient listened, and he tried to believe. One day he succeeded.

Cowper picked up a Bible and read Romans 3, the heart of the Gospel. As it happened one day for Luther, for Wesley, for Newton, and for every desperate soul whose heart has ever despaired itself into the arms of God—Cowper succumbed to the holy pursuit of the Lord. The power of propitiation made it all come to life for him.

Later he would write, "Immediately I received strength to believe it, and the full beams of the Sun of Righteousness shone upon me. I saw the sufficiency of the atonement He had made, my pardon sealed in His blood, and all the fullness and completeness of His justification. In a moment I believed, and received the gospel."[12]

He would also claim, "Unless the almighty Arm had been under me I think I should have died with gratitude and joy. My eyes filled with tears and my voice was choked . . . I could only look up to heaven in silence, overwhelmed with love and wonder!"[13]

Cowper was thirty-three. Leaving the hospital to start life again, he met a family named Unwin. Around the fireside they would sit at prayer, and Cowper experienced a state of peace he had never thought possible. No man was an island; no man an exile.

When Mr. Unwin died, Cowper resettled with the rest of the family in the town of Olney. Does that name ring a bell? The local pastor happened to be John Newton. Quite naturally, the two men built a deep and abiding friendship. God had brought two stricken and stray sheep, two shipwrecked exiles, together. They were both willing captives of saving grace, and they both enjoyed pouring their devotion into hymns and poems. Cowper himself would go on to become one of England's greatest poets and men of letters. At one time he was considered for the position of England's poet laureate.

Together, William Cowper and John Newton produced the collection known as *Olney Hymns* in 1779. Of its 349 songs, sixty-seven were written by Cowper and all the rest by Newton. Grace abounds throughout the hymnal's pages, including in Cowper's well-known "God Moves in a Mysterious Way," and in the following familiar lines:

> *There is a fountain filled with blood*
> *Drawn from Immanuel's veins;*
> *And sinners, plunged beneath that flood,*
> *Lose all their guilty stains.*

> *The dying thief rejoiced to see*
> *That fountain in his day;*
> *And there have I, as vile as he,*
> *Washed all my sins away.*

E'er since by faith I saw the stream
Thy flowing wounds supply,
Redeeming love has been my theme,
And shall be till I die.

These men had found the fountain that is forever overflowing, the spring that wells up from eternity with everlasting life so that once men drink of it, they never thirst again. I hope you've found those waters and that you'll drink as deeply and gratefully of it today.

Moments *of* Grace

Have you been excusing a sin in your life by calling it another name? An unfortunate trait? A weakness? An unproductive habit? Before we can experience God's grace, we have to see ourselves as the sinners we really are in God's sight—as . . . well, as wretches. No, that's not the way society wants us to think of ourselves, but before we can experience abundant grace, we have to understand our total depravity and Christ's total love.

Consider writing out the words of 1 Timothy 1:13–14 and posting them where you can read them several times a day until they become personal to you: *I was formerly a blasphemer, a persecutor, and an insolent man [or woman]; but I obtained mercy. . . . And the grace of our Lord was exceedingly abundant . . .*

CHAPTER THREE

The Converting Power *of* Grace

I Once Was Lost but Now Am Found

A s Jesus sat down to teach, His eyes swept across the hodge-podge of humanity that was eagerly gathering around Him. As usual, it was neither the community's best nor its brightest who sought His wisdom today. Tax profiteers were here. Pleasure seekers were here. It was a representative assortment of the unwashed masses dismissively referred to as "sinners."

The religious leaders took their usual post on the periphery of the crowd—strategic placement for murmuring and whispering caustic commentary, also for avoiding dreaded physical contact with the ceremonially impure.

Then the world seemed to grow silent as the Master began to teach. Or rather to tell stories. The rabbi loved good narratives—long ones, short ones. This time He delivered His tales in a matching set, three variations on a theme. The subject might have been described as "lost and found."

First, there was a quick glimpse of a shepherd combing the rugged hills for a lost sheep, even to the point of neglecting ninety-nine others. Everyone could visualize the shepherd triumphantly bearing the bleating prize across his shoulders as his friends applauded.

Heaven, Jesus said, is something like those applauding shepherds. End of story.

Then He talked about a lost coin. This time the searcher was a frantic housekeeper, shaking every chair and pitcher to find that coin. Finally, with a little shriek of delight, the woman held high her prize. Like the shepherd, she couldn't help but call her friends and throw a party. There was a dash of humor in this story, and the crowd laughed appreciatively.

The angels, Jesus said, have such celebrations when even one sinner has a change of heart.

What must the Pharisees and scribes have made of all this— sheep and coins and clapping? What did misplaced possessions have to do with the Law of Moses? Purity—that was the issue, according to their Law! The only valid question was whether the shepherd or the woman were legally holy.

But Jesus wasn't finished for the day. Now He brought out the main course, to which the preceding dishes were mere appetizers. He told a story for the ages: one that echoes through history, that disarms every hearer, that no one ever tires of retelling. It is a story that loses nothing in any culture or setting, no matter where it is shared. Charles Dickens, the greatest of novelists in the English language, called this the greatest short story of all time.

This story concerned a lost son, but it was more than a quick sketch this time. With the skill of a masterful artist, Jesus painted the picture of the wealthy father of two young men, one of whom disgraces the family on an illicit spending spree. Each of the three main characters—father, elder son, lost son—will respond to the crisis in ways we would never quite have predicted. Yet when the story is complete, the hearer sits quietly and finally says, "Yes. The story is absolutely true. I know it is true because it is *my* story."

This is the power of the Prodigal. No one can help but see himself in the narrative. The painter Rembrandt was transfixed by the picture he found painted in the words of Luke 15. Early in his career, the artist was known to be an arrogant and pleasure-driven young man, and he painted himself into his version as the wandering son from the story, found in the shame of an Amsterdam brothel. Then, at the very end of his life, a wiser man but an ailing one, Rembrandt returned to the story again, this time painting himself into the parable as the loving father, embracing his child. Light emanates from the tender face of the father in a scene of raw emotional power.

The resulting masterpiece, *The Return of the Prodigal*, reached through the centuries to change the life of the Christian writer Henri Nouwen, who spent days silently meditating upon the spiritual resonance of the scene. As a result, Father Nouwen wrote a masterpiece of his own, a book named after the painting: *The Return of the Prodigal*.

Nouwen observes in his book that early in life, Rembrandt had responded, like many people, to the story of the son. As an older and wiser man, he sees the story in a new light. It has become for him a story not of the son who sins but of the father who forgives.

I believe Rembrandt and Nouwen were both on the right track.

FATHER OF MASTERPIECES

The story told by Jesus is a masterpiece that begets more masterpieces, in every medium. John Newton's "Amazing Grace" is one more in the list, because Newton saw himself as the world-wizened son who stumbled home. How could the words be chosen more simply or poignantly? *I once was lost but now am found.* He was that coin. He was that lamb. Above all, he was that wandering child who had brought shame to his birthright, who had committed acts his conscience would never turn loose. *Once lost; now found.* This is the story of all stories.

That other homeward-bound rebel, the apostle Paul, used the word *lost* only once in all his letters. But he, too, identified with the parable. Every sermon he preached in Acts and every epistle he wrote in our Bible echo with the themes of lost and found—of the helpless child captured by grace. Paul might well have seen himself everywhere in the story and even its setting: in the crowd that surrounded Jesus, among the scoffing Pharisees. He might have seen himself as the elder son, too proud of his own behavior to understand the grace he witnessed. In the end, of course, he had to join each one of us in identifying with the wandering, wasteful son. That identification is the needful step for every lost child in search of salvation.

We tend to focus on the player in this drama who carries the action—he who leaves, sins, and returns. Yet Rembrandt was absolutely right in placing the father at the center of the canvas. The Scriptures do no less, for the forgiving father is mentioned twelve times in twenty verses. He may go nowhere. He may "do" very little, at least visibly. But he is the true hero of this story, the true protagonist. We cannot understand any other character or any other development in this tale unless we see it through the eyes of that radiant father, without whom there is no story, no joy, no hope.

The Humiliation of the Father

A certain man had two sons. And the younger of them said to his father,
"Father, give me the portion of goods that falls to me." So he divided to them his livelihood.
—LUKE 15:11–12

There is nothing remarkable about the launch point of this parable: another restless young man with the cravings but not the capital. He lacks the maturity to respect the source of all that he has and all that he is. He simply wants what is coming to him.

Any young man would have known exactly where he stood. The Jewish Law made it clear and simple; you can read the fine print in Deuteronomy 21:17. In the case of two brothers, the older got two-thirds; the youngest got the rest. Either portion might be a nice fortune, but the catch was that the father needed to be dead first.

The second son's real message, then, is: "I can't wait for you to die, Dad."

Any normal father in that part of the world (or nearly any other part) would have slapped his son across the face and pushed him out on the doorstep—and he wouldn't have gotten any argument from the Jewish Law. But read between the lines of Luke, and you'll know very soon in the story that this is no common head of household. By the simple act of granting the insulting request, the father showed himself to be a man of grace.

This is a father who could see into the future. He knew the desolation and heartbreak that lay ahead for his son. He knew his own heartbreak. Yet he stood by the door and watched his son turn his back coldly and leave, taking with him one-third of the estate.

And what about that estate? We think in terms of stocks and bonds, the family silver, any real estate. The father in this story is clearly a man of means. We notice that his holdings included cattle and the acreage to keep them, servants and slaves, the ability to throw a great banquet at a moment's notice.

According to strict law, the father's land needn't be sold until his death. Again, a son late for distant parties would ignore such considerations. At the public sale of one-third of the land, every neighbor for miles would see into the family's shame.

In a small country with land at a premium, family inheritance was serious business. For the case of a young man who had lost his birthright among the Gentiles and dared to return home, a special ritual called the *kezazah* ("the cutting off") was established. According to Kenneth E. Bailey, the community would break a pot in front of the boy. They would cry out that the offender was cut off from his people and then turn their backs upon him forever.[2]

This wasn't a matter of sowing a few wild oats with the fallback plan of coming home later to take a place in the family business. This was a forever thing; a matter of drawing a line in the sand, insulting everyone on the other side, and disowning your people before they disown you. It was to say, "I invite you to ostracize me, and I don't care."

We place ourselves in the shoes of the father and wonder how we would respond. What emotions would dictate our actions? For many, the answer would be anger. Yet in this tale, the father's emotion is *disciplined love*. That kind of love has no strings, no conditions. It knowingly leaves every door open to hurt.

God's grace finds an expression infinitely repeated in His willingness to accept our insult. We stand before Him and say, "Give me what is mine," as if responsibility and obedience weren't part of the legacy. Who would want to take leave of His wonderful palace? Yet that's you and me. We go our way, to His heartbreak, until we have injured ourselves to our capacity of being injured.

God could take the stance of many parents and bar the doors, lock us in our rooms, and breed in us hearts of rebellion. Yet He stands and watches us set out on the path of misery, knowing it is the only way we will grow a heart of humble obedience. There is no limit to the mileage He will allow us to wander, no limit to the patience with which He awaits our return.

Paul the apostle and Newton the navigator understood just how far it was possible to travel before sailing off the edge of the world. For Paul, it was possible to take part in the murder of the saints. For

Newton, it was possible to assist in the enslavement of the innocent. For Paul, the far country was a few hidden rooms in Jerusalem. For Newton, the far country was the coast of Africa.

This particular distance is measured not in miles but in misery.

Separation from the Father

And not many days after, the younger son gathered all together, journeyed to a far country, and there wasted his possessions with prodigal living. But when he had spent all, there arose a severe famine in that land, and he began to be in want. Then he went and joined himself to a citizen of that country, and he sent him into his fields to feed swine. And he would gladly have filled his stomach with the pods that the swine ate, and no one gave him anything.

—LUKE 15:13–16

Cash in hand, the Prodigal sets out for the far country. Jesus gives it no name, because it's a place that is nowhere and everywhere. No matter who you are and where you live, there is a far country. No map is necessary. All you need is a sinful nature and a restless soul, and you are on your way.

For the son, that far country is all about sensuality, dissipation, and sexual adventurism—the cheapest bait Satan has to offer: "Eat, drink, and be merry." The problem with sensuality is that it fails to notice anything but the object of its lust. In this case, the Prodigal hasn't reckoned upon a local famine. Far earlier than he had imagined it (though he most likely never imagined it at all), his wallet runs dry.

Now he must turn from ceaseless partying to ceaseless labor. Poverty leaves him no choice. He finds himself working on the same sort of farm he has only recently liquidated. Every day he cannot help but see the true, enduring value of the land and the cattle.

But it is too late. He cannot bring back the estate he squandered—nor the love of the family he abandoned.

Manipulation of the Father

But when he came to himself, he said, "How many of my father's hired servants have bread enough and to spare, and I perish with hunger! I will arise and go to my father and will say to him, 'Father, I have sinned against heaven and before you, and I am no longer worthy to be called your son. Make me like one of your hired servants.' "

—LUKE 15:17–19

For as many years as I have read and reflected and preached and prayed over this parable, I have been drawn to three words in this passage. Those three words change the whole course of the story.

The three words come when the Prodigal *came to himself.*

What exactly happened when he "came to himself"? I've heard many sermons that fix upon that phrase as the moment of grace. We imagine that the Prodigal feels deep conviction for the sins he has committed, and we imagine him going to his knees to confess and repent.

Frankly, that's a stretch.

Read the passage again and look for any word such as *sorry* or *remorseful.* Is it all about his guilty soul, or is it actually about his empty stomach? Does he sincerely repent, or does he just have good common sense about getting a square meal?

We cannot be certain of the answer—or, more to the point, Jesus keeps it dark. For in a parable we see exactly what the Master desires us to see. And what He wants us to know for now is that the Prodigal knows he needs help. He surrenders. If there is any slim hope of his reinstatement at home, then at the very least he must repay every cent he has squandered. Working as a pig farmer, he knows he will never make it that far. As a matter of fact, he hasn't even been paid for his labor ("No one gave him anything" [v. 16]). He only thought that slopping hogs was reaching the bottom; slopping them for free—even lower.

So now he is desperate enough to consider slinking home. He sees himself at the very bottom of the pecking order, no longer a son but a servant. In time, maybe over a number of years, he could work off his debt.

It is essential that we, Jesus' listeners, understand that the Prodigal is still unprepared for grace. He is still running his own plans, only sadder and wiser in running them. Whether he realizes it or not, he is still securely within the borders of the far country, a self-chosen exile from the rescue of unconditional love.

We might prefer that the Prodigal "redeem himself," but that would be a misunderstanding of this parable and a misunderstanding of grace. No one on this planet has the ability to redeem him- or herself. Every one of us, like the Prodigal, must ultimately throw him- or herself on the mercy of the court.

But wait—are we *certain* the Prodigal isn't penitent? Listen to his speech he is preparing to give: "Father, I have sinned against heaven and before you, and I am no longer worthy to be called your son."

Again, Kenneth Bailey offers us a surprising glimpse behind the details. The Pharisees in Jesus' audience would recognize the son's speech as the words of Pharaoh when he tried to manipulate Moses into lifting the plagues (see Exodus 10:16). The Egyptian ruler certainly had no contrite heart; his words were simply damage control for the natural disasters that were ravaging his land. He would have said whatever Moses wanted him to say.[3]

Many a humble word has been spoken when someone is at the mercy of someone else. Words are cheap and inadmissible as evidence of a repentant heart. The Prodigal was simply seeking access to what he hadn't already consumed of his father's estate.

In other words, he is like you or me trying to save ourselves, completely on our own.

Reconciliation with the Father

And he arose and came to his father. But when he was still a great way off,
his father saw him and had compassion, and ran and fell on his neck and kissed him.
And the son said to him, "Father, I have sinned against heaven and in your sight,
and am no longer worthy to be called your son."

—LUKE 15:20–21

My mind's eye has always held a vivid image of this scene. I cannot imagine a picture more laden with emotion.

Here is the Prodigal, clad in shredded rags that had once been the high fashion of the moment. He is far thinner than anyone remembers him. His beard is clotted with dust, and his hair falls unkempt over his sagging shoulders. Like vagabonds everywhere, he clutches his meager possessions in a greasy sack, and he bears the odors of desperate alleys. Perhaps during the last few moments he has walked past old acquaintances, boyhood friends, and servants who failed to recognize him.

But the father doesn't even hesitate. He knows his boy immediately, because he has been watching, ever vigilant. His grieving imagination has already worked out how his son would appear on that glorious day of his return.

From the Greek text, we know that the father was not indoors when this storm-beaten scarecrow appeared on the horizon. The patriarch was out keeping watch, as a shepherd would do for a lost sheep, as a woman would do for the lost circle of silver. The father walks down this road each day, as far as he might safely venture from his estate, propelled only by hope for the reunion upon which he has set his heart. We know that he kept watch with all that was in him, for that is the essence of all three stories Jesus tells in Luke 15—a relentless pursuit of the lost treasure.

The father, then, sees the shell of his son from a distance, and he is consumed by compassion. He takes in the labored steps, the bent posture, the very picture of weary surrender, and there is no room in the father's heart for any substance but love. So joyful, so uncontrollable is the emotion within him that he begins to run toward the figure—even to "race," we are told. This would be unseemly for a Middle Eastern man of his estate. Everything was to be done with quiet dignity. To run means taking up his mantle in his hand, so that he won't stumble. It means exposing his bare legs. All of these things are beneath the pride of a patriarch. But true love is a powerful force. It erupts on occasion. It is totally unself-conscious.

If the sincerity of the son is ambiguous, there can be no mistake about the heart of the father. And that touches upon the very essence of this parable. The power comes from the father's grace, not the son's guilt.

There is still, however, the issue of public shame—for the boy and his clan. The father is more than aware of that. Therefore he humbles himself in running. He meets the boy in stride. He enfolds him in the full acceptance of his embrace, and he takes on his child's humiliation by his very body language.[4]

Try to imagine the story otherwise. We might yet have been moved if the son knocked at the door, went down on his knees, and had his apology gruffly accepted by the father. We might call it justice tempered by mercy. But nothing of the kind happens here. Instead, the father commits himself fully before a word can leave the mouth of his son, before the son can come across the property, before the son could even be recognized by anyone other than a parent who brought him into the world. The son's carefully prepared speech will be delivered as planned, but only after he has been showered in joy, grace, and kisses. By this time, the speech is neither rote nor rigid. The Prodigal is a helpless child again, secure in his father's arms with no need to plan or contrive. Only now is repentance genuine, when it floats upon a sea of grace.

There at the very edge of the village, a supernatural event has taken place. On this spot, grace has overwhelmed guilt. The Prodigal has come to that place as a lost person. He has not found himself any more than the sheep or the coin found themselves. In all cases, it took the obsessive love of the searcher for the lost thing to be redeemed.

The primary miracle is the insistence of grace. A secondary miracle is the thawing of a frozen heart. Even the selfish, calculating Prodigal cannot withstand the sight of his running, weeping father surrendering his high position to meet him at the edge of disgrace. In that moment grace takes him captive, and he sees what his rebellious soul has not until now allowed him to see: the beauty of his father's love, the absolute value of his acceptance, the sweet joys of loyalty and obedience. As far as his conscience goes, no one need tell him the depth of the pain he has brought to his home. He knows it now not simply with his mind but in the furthest depths of his heart.

That heart is broken, yet his soul is mended. Such is the supernatural event of grace.

Celebration of the Father

> But the father said to his servants, "Bring out the best robe and put it on him,
> and put a ring on his hand and sandals on his feet. And bring the fatted
> calf here and kill it, and let us eat and be merry; for this my son was dead
> and is alive again; he was lost and is found." And they began to be merry.
>
> —LUKE 15:22–24

Joy cares nothing for solitude. Somehow it always wants to invite a few friends.

There are so many things the Prodigal wants to say at this moment, so many things he *must* say to his father. Yet his father seems to be in no hurry to hear the lurid details of history or the fine print of confession. He is whirling in every direction, calling servants and grabbing slaves by the elbow. He sees in his mind a party such as never has been thrown in these parts.

Once it was the son who was so impatient for parties. The roles have reversed. The father wants the most expensive clothing in the house, the finest jewelry, the most elegant shoes. He insists upon the prime cut of the best beef that can be found on the ranch.

Every command is a meaningful expression of love to his son. The best robe would be the father's own, and that would signify the son's complete restoration to the family. The ring was a symbol of business, used to imprint wax and seal a deal. The ring said, "You are part of our daily operations. You may transact business on our behalf." The shoes squelched any possibility of the son returning as a servant. Only the family wore shoes. The fatted calf was simply an expression of deep joy—the best course for the happiest event.

As Jesus has said earlier, "There is joy in the presence of the angels of God over one sinner who repents" (Luke 15:10). Now we have the earthly picture of that joy.

Condemnation of the Father

> Now his older son was in the field. And as he came and drew near to the house,
> he heard music and dancing. So he called one of the servants and asked what these
> things meant. And he said to him, "Your brother has come, and because he has received
> him safe and sound, your father has killed the fatted calf." But he was angry
> and would not go in. Therefore his father came out and pleaded with him.
> So he answered and said to his father, "Lo, these many years I have been serving you;
> I never transgressed your commandment at any time; and yet you never gave me a

young goat, that I might make merry with my friends. But as soon as this son of
yours came, who has devoured your livelihood with harlots, you killed the fatted calf
for him." And he said to him, "Son, you are always with me, and all that I have is
yours. It was right that we should make merry and be glad, for your
brother was dead and is alive again, and was lost and is found."

—LUKE 15:25–32

So compelling is the interplay between this father and son that we are often taken by surprise when a third character walks onto the stage. As we knew from the beginning, there is an older son. He is the heir who stands to inherit two-thirds of the estate. He has bided his time and paid his dues in the family business.

When little brother came home, the older son was not there. We can only imagine him approaching the homestead after a long day of supervising the activities on a ranch. What is this music drifting across the lawn? What is the laughter and happy shouting coming from a habitually quiet estate?

A servant scurries by on some errand, and the older son takes him aside for questioning. The servant fills him in: "It's your brother—he's back, and your father is throwing the bash to end all bashes!"

The young fellow hurries on, and the brother stands there, trying to process what he has heard. *Can this be? My little brother is not dead after all? And why would our father throw a party for someone who destroyed our name and went through a third of our wealth?*

But for the most part, it's not really about *we*. It's about *me*. The more he thinks about it, the angrier and more self-righteous the older brother becomes. By the time he confronts his father, he is refusing to even call the guest of honor a brother. He is "this son of yours" (v. 30). And the message is, "Is this what you call justice? Rewarding a disgrace and ignoring loyalty?"

I have come to two conclusions about this older brother.

1. *He was a son who was living like a servant.* "Lo, these many years I have been serving you" (v. 29). Has he been doing it for love, or was it just good business? Go back to verse 12, and you might be surprised to discover that the father didn't just give the younger brother his share; he gave *both* sons what they had coming to them. When the father said, "All that I have is yours," he was simply stating what had become fact some time back. The older brother was a wealthy young man—not only in hard cash but in the love of his father. Unfortunately, somewhere along the line, he had *become* his work. He was all about earning, proving. Grace made no sense to him.

2. *The older brother was a sinner who thought he was a saint.* He says, "I never transgressed your commandment" (v. 29). Oh, really? That's a bit hard for us to imagine. There is no such thing as a perfect son. In some sense, every son or daughter among us is a prodigal. The older brother may have never left the estate, but he had still fled to the far country of pride and self-righteousness—much like Paul, who never left Jerusalem. Remember, prodigal distance is measured not in miles but in misery. The older son appears to be every bit as miserable as his brother. In fact, he refuses to enter the house where the party is in full swing (v. 28).

That's one of the saddest lines in Scripture. One son was so far from obedience, yet he basked in grace. The other was little *but* obedient, and he never received the priceless treasure that was within his reach all along.

How many of us share a frightening resemblance to that older brother? How about you? Could that gift be right there before you even now? Maybe you didn't travel to the Prodigal's den of sensuality. You might have taken the room right next door, where you found the dungeon of grim obedience. In this story, that was the harder one to escape.

These are two sides of the same coin: law and licentiousness. Either one makes slaves, and only in grace is liberation possible.

Lost and Found

Jesus finishes His trilogy and looks up at the crowd. Before Him are the so-called sinners—prodigals all. Many of them are visibly moved: faces wet or hidden in hands. More than a few are openly weeping. How could they *not* have identified with a character who broke every rule, spat in the face of all that was good and true, and somehow received love rather than condemnation? This is like no story they've ever heard. Could God really be like that father?

Beyond that layer of listeners, Jesus watches for the reaction of the older brothers—the scribes and Pharisees, grimly obedient laborers who pay endless dues on the ranches of Mosaic Law.

What Jesus sees does not surprise Him. Smugness. Smirking. Educated as they are, many of them probably don't identify with the character in the story who so clearly took their part. The self-righteous are like that—amazingly incapable of looking into the mirror of self-inspection.

Jesus has told these stories very deliberately. As He prepared to teach, He couldn't help but hear the mumbled criticisms about how He'd been spending His time—dining with sinners! Socializing with tax collectors! Imagine.

So He has told two stories that answer the question, "What is the value of the lost thing?"

First He has spoken of a sheep, which has reasonable value. The shepherd will go out of his way to find it.

Then He has spoken of a coin, with more buying power than a lamb. Therefore the woman will comb the house with proportionate urgency.

Then, after these sample problems, Jesus has brought the final exam. If a sheep has a value of x, and a silver coin has a value of, say, $10x$—then what value is carried by a misplaced soul? Is it $1,000x$?

1,000,000*x*? No mathematics can express such a sum. It would crash the theological computer.

That was one they didn't teach in Pharisee school. The value of Law they understood; the value of humanity was simply off topic.

Jesus said, in essence, "Here is the answer to the question. The rescue of one lost soul is worth more than the gold of a billion galaxies; therefore, it is cause for angelic celebration. The rescue of one lost soul brings the Creator of the universe Himself thundering down the path to embrace you. It sets off a celebration that never ends. It restores the lost soul to its family. It affords the soul the right to transact work for the kingdom. It invites the reign of love and grace, so that no sin you've ever committed even enters the equation. That is the value of one lost soul."

And Jesus might well have added, "You Pharisees have more facts about God than anyone. You are walking encyclopedias of holiness. You know what you need to do. As for Me, I'm here to keep watch on that lonely road, at the edge of the village, that highway to the far country. I know the name of every soul who wanders that road. I know the pain of every heartache they feel. And I am here to tell them what you will not tell them. I am here to put a robe of pure white upon their shoulders, to hide their sodden rags forever. And I am here to lay down My life and take on every stroke of punishment they have earned, because I can bear it and they cannot.

"After that, if you will but walk through this open door—we'll throw parties that put the far country to shame."

Moments *of* Grace

Which character in the story of the Prodigal Son is most like you? Are you a parent grieved over the sin of another? Are you yourself a backslider and a wayward soul? A responsible citizen yet filled with silent resentment like the older brother? Or is it possible you're a combination of all three?

Whatever your condition, remind yourself that you are worth more to God than the gold of a billion galaxies. He is seeking you, waiting for you, watching over you, and wanting to lead you to new levels of joy, peace, and strength. Today, begin your prayer to the Lord with these words: "Dear Lord, I am just like . . ." and name your character. Tell the Lord all about it, and feel the uplift of His loving grace.

CHAPTER FOUR

The Clear Perspective of Grace

Was Blind, but Now I See

I n an age of instant gratification, nearly everything has become available at rapid speed. You can receive an e-mail from the other side of the world only a second or two after it was composed, rather than waiting for an old-fashioned stamped letter to work its way through the world's labyrinthine postal system. You can shed those ugly pounds in seven days. You can see a photograph in the handy viewer *before* the lens snaps.

But a few things must still be brought to a slow simmer. Authentic, inside-out change is one of those things. Salvation is the ultimate version of a "new you." Having been told that you are a new creation, you expect to rise and walk in newness of life.

Why, then, do we have this creeping suspicion that nothing has really changed? Why do we still struggle with so many challenges in life: hasty words, compulsive habits, seductive temptations? Why don't we feel the moment-by-moment desire to be all the wonderful things Christ has promised us we can be?

Take heart. Every single one of us who answers to the name of Christian is a fellow struggler in this regard. There is no "microwave" serving of spiritual maturity. We all have to "work out [our] own salvation with fear and trembling" (Philippians 2:12).

Case in point: John Newton.

Those who love the story of Newton sometimes imagine him experiencing his moment of grace onboard his slave ship. They imagine the newly enlightened believer turning the ship back to return the slaves, as he quickly sits down to pen the verses to "Amazing Grace."

History tells another story: a story of the slave trader docking in Liverpool and then promptly signing himself on for another voyage to Africa. There he traveled from slave factory to slave factory, buying slaves and storing them in his ship, just like always. He sailed for the New World and studied his Bible as two hundred slaves were packed into shelving in the hold beneath him. On many voyages, as many as one-third of these men, women, and children died. Many others developed serious illnesses. Newton disembarked from the voyage and enjoyed the fresh air and outlying fields of Charleston, South Carolina, as the remaining slaves went to market and to their eventual destinies on rice plantations. Newton wouldn't write "Amazing Grace" until twenty-five years after his conversion.

Lest you find these facts shocking, it's important to understand the historical context. At the time, most believers did not see slavery as evil. The truth is that Newton spent ten years as a slave trader, and most of those came after his salvation.

Yet the committed believer begins to hear the voice of the Holy Spirit more clearly as time goes by. He begins to see the world as the Father sees it and to think with the mind of Christ. John Newton experienced a dawning horror about the true evil of his former vocation. His friends began to notice how often he discussed his qualms about the slave business.

The fact was that the old John Newton and the new one were two different men—and the new one was beginning to find his voice.

In 1788, Newton published a ten-thousand-word confessional pamphlet, *Thoughts upon the African Slave Trade.* Here he came clean as an opponent of the practice as old as humanity. He confessed his own part in years of the trade and realized there was nothing he could do now to repay the evil in which he had taken part. "I hope it will always be a subject of humiliating reflection to me," he wrote, "that I was once an active instrument in a business at which my heart now shudders."

As he approached death many years later, Newton would claim that much of his memory was fading. "But I remember two things," he wrote. "That I am a great sinner, and that Christ is a great Savior."[1] He held on to the two essential facts. Penitence is the prelude to the wonderful work of grace.

EYES WIDE SHUT

I remember planning an evening worship service several years ago. We would be coming to the Lord's table for Communion and then having the sermon. I realized with alarm that my text was Romans 1:29–32: twenty-one words cataloguing the corruption and depravity of humanity, perhaps the darkest pit to be found in Scripture. There was something terribly wrong about descending into this pit following the elevating moment of Communion.

The worst thing I could have done would have been to back away from the insistence of God's Word. Instead, I simply changed the order of service. I preached those troubling verses from Romans, and *then* we came to the table. As a result, there was a miracle within our fellowship. The experience of God's presence that evening was overwhelming. I saw the kind of tears I had rarely seen over the sharing of the elements. I certainly had to restrain my own emotions in order to preside.

How could a mere revamped order of worship make such a difference? On the next day I found out. It was Monday morning, and I happened to be reading a book called *Not the Way It's Supposed to Be: A Breviary of Sin.* The author, Cornelius Plantinga Jr., made the point that we seriously delude ourselves about the presence of evil in our lives. It's like purposefully removing all the black keys from the piano. Once you do that, the white keys no longer produce a melody. If we edit the sin out of our awareness, then grace no longer has any beauty or power for us. In due time we wonder why we need a Savior at all.[2]

In our worship service on the preceding evening, we happened to have gotten it right. We faced the reality of sin at full force, letting the Spirit of God do His gentle task of application within every soul present. When we came to the Lord's table, we experienced the most powerful working of His presence and grace we could have imagined. His body, broken for us; His blood, spilled for us—these were no longer theoretical concepts but realities that cut deep in the context of the very real sin that had been brought to our awareness.

Then again, I'm not naive enough to believe that everyone present shared in the experience. The voice of God himself may come in loud and clear, yet there are always those who aren't tuned in to the right frequency. I think of the struggler in the temple, pouring out his confession, as the Pharisee nearby observes him and prays, "Lord, I thank You that I am not like that sinner over there" (Luke 18:9–14). Surely there were those in our sanctuary who heard the menu of sins in Romans and applied them to everyone but themselves.

As Mark McMinn puts it, "Part of our mess is not knowing we are a mess."[3] We live quiet lives, never robbing a bank or committing a murder. None of us has been employed as a slave trader or held the robes of those throwing rocks at a martyr. We confuse calmness with holiness. It's been observed in surveys that the average person believes he is better than the average person.[4] We are blind to our own blindness.

It is the Pharisee in the temple, smug in his assumed righteousness, who concerns Paul in the second chapter of his letter to the Romans. He has known a lot of those; he had been one himself. He began his letter to the Romans with a powerful sermon against the clear-cut wickedness of the world. Any Jewish leader would have been standing and applauding, shouting "amen" to every sentence, every condemnation. They loved hearing him go after those worldly Gentiles.

But then they would have come to the next section—Romans 2. The amen corner would fall into shocked silence. For now, Paul was pointing an accusing finger at the "righteous." He used the same two words to sum up their position before God: "without excuse" (Romans 1:20).

The Jews of the time saw themselves walking proudly in the light of God's favoritism, while the blind Gentiles around them stumbled. No wonder they were no fans of Jesus when He told them that they, too, were blind—the blind leading the blind, as He described it. That combination, He said, ends up with everyone lying in the ditch (Luke 6:39).

EYES WIDE OPEN

The word that best describes Paul's opening to Romans 2 is *diatribe*. This was an argument presented through a lively debate with a heckler, real or imagined. Paul mastered the technique through his

travels, bringing new and unaccepted ideas into traditional synagogues. Someone might call out, "Ha! Here's the problem with your
theory . . ." And Paul would engage his challenger—a kind of show-
business technique for dealing with abstract ideas. Think of two
professional wrestlers on TV, hurling aggressive theological taunts.

Paul's stance was something like this: "So you think you're high
and mighty, that you're God's fair-haired boy? You'd better buy lightning insurance, and here's why."

The "why" turns out to be *judgment*. Paul uses some form of that
word seven times in three verses.

More important, in sixteen verses he presents six principles for
self-examination. Like Jonathan Edwards's classic sermon "Sinners in
the Hands of an Angry God," these verses refuse to candy-coat the
truth. They present the idea that your vision may be clouded, but
rest assured that God's eyesight is twenty-twenty. "And there is no
creature hidden from His sight, but all things are naked and open to
the eyes of Him to whom we must give account" (Hebrews 4:13).

God's Judgment Is According to Reality

> *Therefore you are inexcusable, O man, whoever you are who judge,*
> *for in whatever you judge another you condemn yourself;*
> *for you who judge practice the same things.*
>
> —ROMANS 2:1

That's how the New King James Version translates it. Donald Grey
Barnhouse created his own wording for this verse: "You dummy—
do you really figure that you have doped out an angle that will let
you go up against God and get away with it? You don't have a ghost
of a chance."[5]

That's what we mean by a diatribe, and it would get most preachers fired these days. But Paul brings such passion to this subject as one could only have when he has been there and done that himself. He assumes that if these folks are sight-impaired, he'd better write in big letters; if they are deaf, he'd better shout. As we read these verses in the Bible and really comprehend what is being said, our fingers almost feel singed by the page.

The hypocrite, Paul tells us, is totally intolerant of anyone's sins but his own. But what is most striking is the idea found in Shakespeare's *Hamlet*, "The lady doth protest too much, methinks." In other words, the louder you shout, the more likely it is that you are attempting to draw attention away from yourself. Your condemnations, according to Paul, really condemn *you*.

We call it hypocrisy. Paul is saying, "You're guilty of everything you criticize."

But surely that label wouldn't apply to you and me, would it? You watched those looters after the hurricanes and felt righteous indignation—and you're not guilty of looting. You saw a TV documentary about the spread of sexual permissiveness, and you were disgusted—and you haven't engaged in such licentiousness. You cheered when they caught that murderer—but you've resisted the temptation to kill anyone, even that neighbor down the street who really makes your blood boil! As a matter of fact, you'd like to . . .

Wait a minute: maybe *that's* what Paul is talking about.

Jesus told us during the Sermon on the Mount that our anger amounts to murder, that our lust amounts to adultery, and that basically we stand convicted upon our innermost thoughts.

Now there's a frightening idea. Imagine the crime-scene investigators combing your innermost thoughts for evidence. Who among us would be righteous? Therefore, yes, Paul can say, "You who judge practice the same things." And yes, it applies to you and to me and to the religious elite who were the targets of Paul's diatribe.

God's Judgment Is According to Integrity

But we know that the judgment of God is according to truth against those who
practice such things. And do you think this, O man, you who judge those practicing
such things, and doing the same, that you will escape the judgment of God?

—ROMANS 2:2–3

How many of us let John Newton off the hook for trading slaves? I know I did. After all (we remind ourselves), he lived in an unenlightened age. He simply fell in with the crowd.

How, then, do people living within the biases of their times manage to take two giant steps ahead of the crowd and proclaim something wrong, even when the world says it is right? Newton did it. So did a few others of his time. What is the source of that insistent voice that overrides the entire social conscience of our era? The mere whisper of the Holy Spirit can drown out the thundering noise of an entire world. Newton came to a place where he could dare to stand back and look upon his former livelihood and condemn it. How many of us would have had such courage? Probably none without the sustaining strength of that Spirit.

"For the LORD does not see as man sees; for man looks at the outward appearance, but the LORD looks at the heart" (1 Samuel 16:7). Paul has made this very point in Romans 1. In the words of Eugene Peterson's paraphrase, *The Message*, "By taking a long and thoughtful look at what God has created, people have always been able to see what their eyes as such can't see. . . . So nobody has a good excuse" (Romans 1:20).

For Christians, the voice of the Spirit takes precedence. But even for those who have never heard the Gospel, there is a conscience that is issued as standard equipment in the human engine.

The judgment of God takes the measure of our integrity, so no one can say, "Everybody was doing it." No soldier of the cross can say, "I was simply acting under orders," unless the orders in fact come from that voice of authority God has placed within His followers.

God's Judgment Is According to Opportunity

Or do you despise the riches of His goodness, forbearance, and longsuffering,
not knowing that the goodness of God leads you to repentance? But in accordance with
your hardness and your impenitent heart you are treasuring up for yourself wrath in
the day of wrath and revelation of the righteous judgment of God.
—ROMANS 2:4–5

"Listen," Paul says. "You upright, moral citizens have been enjoying the luxury of every possible advantage—and you dismiss them as if they were nothing by sinning against God."

What advantages? Paul names three: God's kindness, His forbearance, and His patience. These are all expressions of an infinite love that can never be deserved, could never be earned, and *certainly* should never be taken for granted.

Consider this world, teeming with people who lived and died without being told the first fact about Jesus Christ. The immeasurable wealth of His teachings and the liberating knowledge of His death and resurrection were unknown to them. They lived and died in darkness.

Meanwhile, we are those who live in the light. The full testimony of God's revelation and the full counsel of His kindness have been available to us all along, yet we dishonor Him. Unread Bibles collect dust on our shelves, when there are those in other countries who would give all that they own for one ragged New Testament.[6]

The kindness of God shed upon you and me is as unmistakable as the sun on a summer day, as prevalent as the oxygen in the air. How can we live as if we were utterly independent of His goodness?

Or how can we describe people so heedless of God's greatest favor? Paul calls their problem "hardness" or stubbornness (v. 5). The word in Greek is *sklerotes*, which is the source of our medical word *sclerosis*. Arteriosclerosis is the hardening of the arteries, in the case of the physical heart. But we speak of a spiritual heart; and it, too, has arteries that may harden. What can bring about such a condition? There would be many answers, but this much we can agree upon: anyone who is capable of ignoring God's kindness, patience, and forbearance is a chronic sufferer from that condition.

God's Judgment Is According to Morality

> Who "will render to each one according to his deeds": eternal life to those who by patient continuance in doing good seek for glory, honor, and immortality; but to those who are self-seeking and do not obey the truth, but obey unrighteousness—indignation and wrath, tribulation and anguish, on every soul of man who does evil, of the Jew first and also of the Greek; but glory, honor, and peace to everyone who works what is good, to the Jew first and also to the Greek.
>
> —ROMANS 2:6–10

Jesus said, "The Son of Man will come in the glory of His Father with His angels, and then He will reward each according to his works" (Matthew 16:27). As a matter of fact, your Bible is packed with reminders that an hour of accounting is coming. If your Bible were an appointment book (as in a way it is), it would have yellow Post-it notes falling from every page, reminding you to be ready for your appointment with destiny. If your Bible were a clock (as in a way it is), its alarm would be sounding every few minutes to remind you to start getting ready. But you and I tend to hit the snooze button. We mumble, "Just a few more moments to relax."

Paul's comment on that day of judgment is this: You get no

credit for the number of Bibles you own. The test of accountability will not be a "sword drill" in which we prove how many verses we have memorized. The test will instead be an inspection of how thoroughly those scriptures have permeated our lives. It will be a fruit inspection: what has blossomed from the buds of your allotted years on this planet?

It is obedience to God, not the knowledge of Him, that will make or break us. As a matter of fact, we could actually be worse off for being the sword-drill champion. For "disobeying the law which is being constantly dinned into one's ears will make condemnation so much more severe."[7]

God's Judgment Is According to Impartiality

For there is no partiality with God. For as many as have sinned without law will also perish without law, and as many as have sinned in the law will be judged by the law (for not the hearers of the law are just in the sight of God, but the doers of the law will be justified; for when Gentiles, who do not have the law, by nature do the things in the law, these, although not having the law, are a law to themselves, who show the work of the law written in their hearts, their conscience also bearing witness, and between themselves their thoughts accusing or else excusing them).

—ROMANS 2:11–15

In his book *Mere Christianity*, C. S. Lewis makes the same observation that Paul sets out in this passage. Isn't it interesting, Paul remarks, how all these Gentiles imitate so many aspects of the Hebrew Law, even though they've never heard it? They "show the work of the law written in their hearts, their conscience also bearing witness" (v. 15).

As for Lewis, he points out that in the midst of an argument, you will notice that people appeal to some standard of fairness. They say,

"How would you like that if someone did it to you?" Or, "I helped you, so you should help me." Take any atheist and he will appeal regularly to universal standards, the same as anyone else. Every time he says, "That's not fair," he has just condemned his own philosophy.

The revealing point is that when we make these appeals to standards, no one ever disputes their existence. They may try to find loopholes, but they never say, "There are no standards. There is no right or wrong." If we really believed there weren't rules, Lewis says, we would have no recourse but to pounce upon each other like beasts and thrash it out. Instead, we quarrel—and quarreling cannot occur unless someone has established rules to govern the dispute.[8]

Even the godless show "the work of the law written in their hearts" (v. 15). No matter how freethinking they may believe themselves to be, their consciences keep bearing witness.

God's Judgment Is According to Certainty

In the day when God will judge the secrets of men by Jesus Christ, according to my gospel.
—ROMANS 2:16

The Lord searches every heart and understands every intention, according to 1 Chronicles 28:9. How foolish must we be to bargain with Him, to posture before Him, or to speak to Him in any manner that is not absolute sincerity? The Spirit of God dwells among the file cabinets of your mind. He knows the inventory of the hairs on your head and the hours, minutes, and seconds of your life. Truly understanding the implications of that, we would be taken by uncontrollable fear if His character were not kind, patient, and forbearing. Who else could we trust with the contents of those file cabinets? Who else but someone with absolutely perfect, infinitely unconditional love?

Yet we go about the pretense of having any thought squirreled away from the eyes of God. Søren Kierkegaard, a Danish philosopher of the nineteenth century, watched a sixteen-year-old girl on her confirmation day. She was showered with gifts, among them a New Testament in a decorative binding.

Kierkegaard reflected upon the fact that no one really expected the girl to ever read the Bible; it was basically given as an ornament, a social prop. At the very best, the intention of the giver would be that if the girl ever found herself in emotional need, the Testament might come in handy. Yet within the bounds of such a life, the philosopher concluded, a true reading of those Scriptures would provide anything but comfort—they would suggest far greater terrors than whatever brought her to open the pages in the first place.

Kierkegaard's conclusion is that rather than live such a dangerous hypocrisy, we should walk through the town, take up every single Bible, and cart the whole load out to some mountaintop where we can say to God, "Take it back, this book! We are only capable of making ourselves miserable with it!"[9]

For the prophet Ezekiel, it is as if we sit in church with stupid grins and enjoy the cadence of the preacher's speaking, the lilt of his voice, and the fine sound of the Bible translation he has chosen. In other words, it has all become music without lyrics to us. It is the Word of God as elevator music, full of sound and fury and signifying nothing. As the prophet puts it, "Indeed you are to them as a very lovely song of one who has a pleasant voice and can play well on an instrument; for they hear your words, but they do not do them" (Ezekiel 33:32).

Lord, deliver us from such self-inflicted emptiness. Maybe Kierkegaard is right—maybe it would be better to give back our Bibles than to let them become frilly ornaments to unexamined lives. Help us to hear every eternal, inspired fragment of truth that issues from the revelation of the Word of God. Help us to look upon every detail of that which the Spirit would have us see. Otherwise we are blind indeed—one long procession of blind people, happily leading each other to a ditch as deep as the pits of fire.

We could be as blind as the characters in Hans Christian Anderson's tale "The Emperor's New Clothes." The king loved beautiful clothing, but he was as gullible as he was vain. Inevitably he became the prey of con men who promised to weave him a suit of thread so rare that only the pure in heart could see it. The emperor paid a fortune for his new suit, and the hucksters pretended to be weaving industriously. None of the royal advisers would admit that they couldn't see any thread on the loom. They gave glowing reports of the beauty of the clothing.

The whole charade culminated in the crafty weavers "dressing" the naked emperor in his brand-new attire. Then they skipped town with the proceeds. An announcement was made: There would be a royal parade, and only the pure in heart should attend. For only they could appreciate the special clothing the emperor would wear.

Attendance was high, since everyone believed him- or herself to fit the criteria. But who would give voice to the spectacle their eyes took in? It took a young child to blow the lid off the whole scam. He loudly proclaimed that the emperor had no clothes.[10]

In Romans 2, Paul has become that child. He goes to the fashion show of holiness and says that he sees nothing but naked moralists. But the message never goes over well. People would rather not be awakened from their illusion. We desperately want to *see* those beautiful threads. We want to hear soothing music when the Word of God is proclaimed. We want to look at our own chests and see them covered with medals for every achievement in spiritual purity, above and beyond the call of duty, so that there is no day of judgment at all; instead, the hosts of heaven will throw a testimonial banquet in our honor.

The scales fell away from John Newton's eyes, but only after years of inner struggle. He had to learn to see and to hear. He had to learn to think with the mind of Christ. Praise God that the day could come when he could sing out, "I once . . . was blind, but now I see."

Paul, too, rose from the ground after his incident on the road to Damascus. He dusted himself off and reflected on the words of Christ that had just thundered down upon him from heaven. Yet there was no instant sainthood delivered by angelic courier. To underscore his neediness, God struck him blind. He was utterly dependent upon a certain man in a certain town to care for him. For Paul, blindness was one of the requirements for sight.

The Holy Spirit will not let you be content in your blindness. He would not allow it for Paul, nor would He allow it for John Newton. Be assured He will not allow it for you. He longs to open the curtains and let in the light that will make your world sparkle with all the bright colors of paradise.

Only beware—it takes awhile for our eyes to become accustomed when the light floods into a darkened room. Even the beauty of pure light is painful at first. But even at that moment, even when our spiritual nakedness is laid painfully bare, we know that our shame is only momentary. We know that we are clothed in the grace that overwhelms every blemish.

In the words of Clara H. Scott's hymn:

> *Open my eyes, that I may see*
> *Glimpses of truth Thou hast for me;*
> *Place in my hands the wonderful key*
> *That shall unclasp and set me free.*
> *Silently now I wait for Thee,*
> *Ready, my God, Thy will to see;*
> *Open my eyes, illumine me, Spirit divine!*

Moments *of* Grace

This chapter warns that we seriously delude ourselves about the presence of evil in our lives. By nature we're not tuned to the divine frequency, and we're like the self-justifying Pharisee in Luke 18:9–14, not realizing the mess we're in.

As you conclude this chapter, pray earnestly—you might even kneel or take a moment to write out these words as a covenant to God—Psalm 139:23–24: "Search me, O God, and know my heart; try me, and know my anxieties; and see if there is any wicked way in me, and lead me in the way everlasting."

But beware! If you make that your earnest prayer before the Lord, be ready! God wants to shine the spotlight of His Spirit into your life to show you elements of attitude and behavior that need to be confessed and repented. It may be discouraging at first, but the result will be a richer life with a greater understanding of His astounding grace.

CHAPTER FIVE

The Comforting Provision of Grace

*'Twas Grace That Taught My Heart to Fear
and Grace My Fears Relieved*

E V. Hill was a gifted preacher of the Gospel. An African-American who was literally born in a log cabin, he started a church in the middle of the explosive Watts district of Los Angeles, and all his life he made a difference.

I'll never forget the day I heard him deliver a sermon at a conference at the Moody Bible Institute. The title was "What Do You Have if You Have Jesus?" Every one of his twelve sermon points came to life in the power of illustrations I could still produce from memory today. He held us spellbound.

As the pastor explained a particular point about blessings, he reached over to a little table stacked with award books to be handed out later. Dr. Hill was explaining that sometimes Jesus just reaches down to someone and blesses him for no reason at all.

The Lord says, "Here—take that!" And as Dr. Hill said those

words, he grabbed a book from the stack and threw it out into the audience. Then he said, "Or *you*—take that!" And he tossed out another volume.

At the bottom of the stack there happened to be a very fine Ryrie Study Bible. Dr. George Sweeting, then president of Moody, sprinted forward and rescued the Ryrie Bible before it could become the next blessing.

Twelve memorable points.

The next year, Dr. Hill returned to speak at the same conference. The very first words he said were, "Number thirteen!"

He was still preaching that same sermon.

It's true. Once you begin to talk about what you have if you have Jesus, prepare yourself for one long discussion. You could talk about it forever. And you could use Romans 5 as a jumping-off point. All the riches are cataloged here. First, however, you need to step back and realize the emotional range Paul has brought to this conversation.

The first chapter of Romans is downright terrifying: a widescreen documentary of the wickedness of the world.

The second chapter covers anyone left out by the first—that is, the "non-wicked" (at least any claimants to such). The religious elite have no excuse, Paul announces.

If the Pharisees stood and applauded during the first chapter, then sat in shocked silence during the second, Paul may well have been speaking to an empty room by chapter 5. That would be unfortunate, because there is a seismic shift in the change of tone here. Paul now delivers the most thrilling news in the history of the world.

It makes sense. The happy ending of a classic story is only powerful when the hero has struggled with deadly enemies. In Newton's terminology, our hearts must be taught to fear before those fears can be relieved. In the initial chapters of Romans, Paul has dimmed the spotlight and told a tale of fear until its blackness and bleakness became unbearable. The most terrible thing about this horror story is that we ourselves are the characters within it. Now Paul brings up the lights and tells the part of the story that we've been longing to hear—though it is far more wonderful, far more gratifying than our feeble imaginations could have painted it.

The Seven Wonders of Grace

Think of the opening of Romans as Paul's tale of a traveler, a treasure seeker. This adventurer has struggled down a dark road filled with misadventure. Through all his fighting and struggling he has become a guilty man. Every crime alluded to by Paul can be laid at the feet of this seeker. He has been caught in a vicious cycle of evil from which there would seem to be no escape.

The adventure was never supposed to go this way. When he first set out, the traveler thought of himself as a champion. He believed he could overcome any obstacle and defeat any enemy. Now he stands in humiliation and close to the point of defeat. He hears behind him the rustling of the enemy, drawing closer and closer. The enemy is Death itself, coming to serve its writ of execution for the many crimes of this fugitive. The traveler grows weaker and weaker as he tries to flee; his arms and legs become entangled in the jungle vines, and quicksand is everywhere.

The traveler knows he lacks the strength to keep running, to keep fighting, to keep raising himself from every pit. He is willing to surrender to his relentless, pursuing enemy.

Then, just before giving up, the despairing traveler comes across a startling sight. There is a sudden clearing, cut perfectly through the trees and the bush and the vines. The clearing seems like a long row until he discovers another long row that bisects it. The clearing is cut in the shape of a great cross.

The seeker steps into the clearing and feels immediately safe. Death cannot enter a place of such light. And at the center of the cross, he finds a table with seven items upon it: the seven wonders of grace. After his long quest, he has discovered the riches of Christ's inheritance. These are the ancient treasures that every soul has been seeking since the beginning of time—even those who never realized the object of their quest.

These treasures are the inheritance of anyone and everyone who might claim them. Yet so few have done so. Turning to survey them, the traveler sees these things: a parchment, a key, a music box, a cocoon, a bottle, a map, and a trumpet. Surely each has a special meaning and a special purpose.

To find the solution to each puzzle, we must read Romans 5:1–11.

First Treasure: A Parchment

Therefore, having been justified by faith, we have peace
with God through our Lord Jesus Christ.
—ROMANS 5:1

As the seven treasures are grouped, one is clearly set in front of the others. It is a parchment, rolled up and tied with a silk ribbon. As the traveler unrolls it and reads the text upon the document, he observes that this item is very old indeed.

The heading of the parchment reads: *Justified*—Declared Righteous. And just below this line, he finds his own name.

The holder of this document will hereby be absolved of all his guilt, absolutely and without exception. No past sin will be held against him. The Greek wording of this ancient document makes it clear that the traveler's justification is something that has already occurred—a completed action, a done deal! The seeker would judge that this parchment is some two thousand years old. But it is as durable and indestructible as eternity itself.

The ink is red. Only in the blood of God's own Son could such an order have been written and executed. When the Lord God issues a proclamation, it is irreversible. He does not change His mind. Can you imagine? The holder of such a proclamation need do nothing to earn or to maintain his or her innocence. It has been established and proclaimed once and for all.

Justification means that the war is over. Before the cross and before the love of Christ, we were the prisoners of our own self-destructive nature. There was nothing we could do to lift the charges of guilt that lay upon our heads.

The traveler feels an amazing sense of peace such as he has never felt. It begins to course through his whole being as he clutches the parchment to his chest. He realizes that his shoulders were stooped and weak from the invisible burden he had been carrying. Now the burden has fallen away, and his back feels young and strong again. *Peace*—a cease-fire in the holy war.

The fine print on the document reveals that this kind of peace is not about the easy life. On the contrary, the seeker knows there are many adventures and many exciting battles still to come. The peace is not a mere feeling but a state of reality. The word for it in Hebrew is *shalom*—the condition in which life can best be lived. This peace, according to the Jewish understanding, is salvation lived out right here on earth.

There is peace because the great enemy, Death, can no longer pursue him. He is at peace with God, free to walk in triumph rather than cower in fear. He is now God's servant rather than His prisoner. "And you, who once were alienated and enemies in your mind by wicked works, yet now He has reconciled in the body of His flesh through death" (Colossians 1:21–22).

This is the kind of peace Paul would describe again in another letter: "Be anxious for nothing, but in everything by prayer and supplication, with thanksgiving, let your requests be made known to God; and the peace of God, which surpasses all understanding, will guard your hearts and minds through Christ Jesus" (Philippians 4:6–7).

The traveler thrusts the document of peace into his shirt, where it will, as Paul says, guard his heart and mind in Christ Jesus. This treasure is the one that makes all the others possible. Without the parchment of justification, the traveler could never claim the other six that lie just beyond it.

Second Treasure: A Golden Key

Through whom also we have access by faith into this grace in which we stand.
—ROMANS 5:2

The traveler lifts a small golden key. Where is the door it unlocks?

As he holds it before him, he begins to *feel* the answer deep in his soul, and a startled gasp escapes his lips.

This is not the key to any earthly palace or storehouse. Through the cross, there is a new principle operating in his life and in ours. We now have free access to the grace of God—the same grace that has already declared us justified. It is as if the judge has signed the parchment and then invited us home with him rather than telling us to go on our way. The accuser is now a dear friend who wishes to share our company.

The word *access* is only used three times in the New Testament, and it always refers to the believer's access to God through Jesus Christ.

Grace is God's riches lavished upon those of us who, only moments before, stood accused. The prisoner on death row, of all people, has won the grand sweepstakes: the unsought, undeserved, and unconditional love of God. Like the traveler, we have been running through that jungle, always imagining the angry face of the Judge who will sentence us. We imagine Him to be in league with Death, our pursuer.

Yet it turns out that the Judge has been pursuing for love rather than vengeance. His face is compassionate rather than angry. And finally He pays the highest price imaginable so that He might provide that statement of justification that will allow restoration into His own family.

Once it has been accomplished, there is a new way to live. We have access to all the riches of grace. This key, in the hand of the traveler, represents the fact that the Father is saying, "Forget the past. All that I have is yours."

Grace must also be understood as a *standing*, just as Paul states it in Romans 5:2. It is a permanent condition rather than a sometime thing. As John Stott says, "We do not fall in and out of grace. . . . No, we stand in it, for that is the nature of grace. Nothing can separate us from God's love."[1]

Third Treasure: A Music Box

And rejoice in hope of the glory of God.
—ROMANS 5:2

As the traveler prepares to behold more of the seven wonders of grace, he reflects on the timeliness of these treasures:

The past: Justification for what we have done.
The present: Access to the glory of Christ.
The future: Promise of glory to come.

This third treasure is represented by a music box. Why such an odd choice for this wonder?

Paul is telling us that the promise of glory to come is a reason for celebration. It is like the father who throws a feast when the Prodigal returns. It is like John Newton deciding his emotions about grace can only find the right form in a triumphant hymn. It is Paul saying, "Rejoice in the Lord always. Again I will say, rejoice!" (Philippians 4:4). And is it even possible to rejoice without music slipping in?

Paul's word comes from the Greek *kaukaomia* which, interestingly enough, means to boast. This is not an in-your-face, braggadocio boasting but an uncontrolled jubilation. And we have permission to do this boasting, because it's all about God instead of us. We are celebrating a dream of the future that God has promised us will really come true. "But 'he who glories, let him glory in the Lord'" (2 Corinthians 10:17).

Oh, how much more often we would celebrate, and how jubilant our churches would be, if we paid more attention to the whispers of the future that lie on these biblical pages—whispers of hope about a glory that lies ahead. "To them God willed to make known what are the riches of the glory of this mystery among the Gentiles: which is Christ in you, the hope of glory" (Colossians 1:27).

Paul tells us, "When Christ who is our life appears, then you also will appear with Him in glory" (Colossians 3:4). The glory is in Christ alone, but we will share in its riches in an ultimate way. This will be the culmination of all our hopes and the joy to which our whole lives have pointed.

Have you noticed that the sweetest joys sometimes come in the anticipation of something? It's Christmas morning for a child, the wedding or future home for the young couple, even the simple anticipation of a hot bath when you're out shoveling snow in freezing temperatures. These are joys yet to come, and that sends a little shudder of pleasure through the frame.

It's like a music box that has the enticing melody of a far country, one that lies ahead. A music box is only a simple piece of machinery; it cannot suggest what the full orchestra can produce. But it is a reminder, and our imagination does the rest. This is a fine treasure indeed—a treasure that offers hope—and the traveler cherishes it.

Fourth Treasure: A Cocoon

And not only that, but we also glory in tribulations, knowing that tribulation produces perseverance; and perseverance, character; and character, hope.
—ROMANS 5:3–4

This next treasure is certainly the most curious yet. It is a cocoon!

The traveler wonders if it could really be a treasure at all. As he gently lifts it, he feels a slight tinge of pain in his hand. He knows immediately that this one is going to be quite different from the lovely music box. He looks more closely.

Paul has been telling us about glory. That's a terrific word. *Glory!* What could be more positive?

But here is Paul mixing it with *tribulations*. We don't like the sound of that. Isn't that the word that always goes around in the company of *trials*? Why would we "glory" in trials and tribulations? We're not gluttons for punishment. Where's the jubilation there?

The traveler has already realized that the peace received in the first treasure is no guarantee of an easy life. How could he have an adventure without a few dragons to slay? He lifts the cocoon again; and for the first time, as he gently squeezes it, he observes the miracle. An image of his face is there, like a reflection—but the reflection is changing.

As he applies light pressure, his face in the cocoon shows sadness. But the sadness begins changing into a kind of rugged strength: perseverance. That appearance, in turn, begins to show itself in a new, more admirable character in his features. As he looks even more closely at the image of his own face, he sees that it is taking on a powerful, confident look to it—a look of hope.

Like the odd little insect that becomes a butterfly, the child of God is constantly transforming into something more beautiful. It is the same process of development that Paul describes in these verses. The traveler remembers trying to slice his way through the jungle while only becoming weaker. Now, with this amazing treasure, he sees that the dragon's breath of fire can only make him stronger! Paul uses the Greek word *thlipsis* for "suffering," and the idea is a kind of pressure, as in squeezing grapes to extract the juice.

We don't go looking for trouble, but we certainly do make use of it. Bad times are our fuel for transformation. They make us stronger, nobler, wiser, and more worthy of serving God in ever-increasing capacity.

Take Paul, who gave us these words in Romans, through the inspiration of the Holy Spirit. Did he lead the life of luxury after he committed himself to God's service? Here is his own answer to that question:

> I speak as a fool—I am more: in labors more abundant, in stripes above measure, in prisons more frequently, in deaths often. From the Jews five times I received forty stripes minus one. Three times I was beaten with rods; once I was stoned; three times I was shipwrecked; a night and a day I have been in the deep; in journeys often, in perils of waters, in perils of robbers, in perils of my own countrymen, in perils of the Gentiles, in perils in the city, in perils in the wilderness, in perils in the sea, in perils among false brethren; in weariness and toil, in sleeplessness often, in hunger and thirst, in fastings often, in cold and nakedness—besides the other things, what comes upon me daily: my deep concern for all the churches. (2 Corinthians 11:23–28)

Now read Paul's letters—most of them written during and after all of these trials—and then answer this question. Has he become more positive or more discouraged? Is he wiser or more bitter? What has been the result of his constant tribulations? He sits in cramped prison cells awaiting his own execution and writes letters of joy and jubilation. For him, to live is Christ; to die is gain (Philippians 1:21). It's a win-win proposition when you understand your life as a cocoon.

Paul has come to realize that no matter how hard you squeeze him, all you can do is help the process along—the process of transforming him to the image of Christ. There is nothing the world can throw at us that God will not use for His glory and our eternal joy.

The traveler cradles the cocoon gently in his hands. He begins to realize that this treasure is every bit as precious, every bit as essential as those that came before it. He looks carefully into the little chamber of transformation again and begins to understand the process in three steps.

1. *From tribulation to perseverance.* It's the idea of tempering steel. The flames only make the iron stronger. Suffering without the hope of Christ leads to defeat and bitterness, but through the wonders of grace, we develop perseverance through our trials. We take the blow; and the next time it comes, we face it more squarely.

As the prophet phrased it, "I will bring the one-third through the fire, will refine them as silver is refined, and test them as gold is tested. They will call on My name, and I will answer them. I will say, 'This is My people'; and each one will say, 'The LORD is my God'" (Zechariah 13:9). Our suffering bonds us even closer with God.

John writes of these trials of faith in Revelation. Peter speaks of how intense heat purifies gold by burning away the dross. Jesus tells us in the Sermon on the Mount that we are blessed when we are persecuted. And Job, whose name is synonymous with suffering, says, "When He has tested me, I shall come forth as gold" (Job 23:10).

Do you catch the theme? Persevere, and your destiny is golden.

2. *From perseverance to character.* What exactly is character? Paul is referring to the idea of a character without impurities—a man or woman of integrity. James refers to this as the process of perfection: "My brethren, count it all joy when you fall into various trials, knowing that the testing of your faith produces patience. But let patience have its perfect work, that you may be perfect and complete, lacking nothing" (James 1:2–4).

When we endure, we begin to lose our fear. We develop the assurance of our own strength, knowing that the trial will not consume us. Such confidence gives us the character to act based on principles rather than out of desperation.

3. *From character to hope.* People of character are positive people. They live by the rules of righteousness, and they know it works. That positive pattern breeds hope and destroys the cynicism that is the mark of our age. How many truly hopeful people do you know? Hope springs from character, character from perseverance, and perseverance from tribulation—but only when we trust God to lead us through the fire.

Later in Romans, Paul writes, "For I consider that the sufferings of this present time are not worthy to be compared with the glory which shall be revealed in us" (Romans 8:18). Those are the words of a hopeful man. He is saying, "Do I have problems? Absolutely. But they're not worth talking about when we could be discussing the incredible things God has in store for us."

Read through your Bible for case study after case study. It is a book of godly men and women enduring the suffering that brought them godliness.

Lloyd John Ogilvie has written about the most difficult year of his life, a time when his wife underwent five major surgeries, radiation treatment, and chemotherapy, and when a host of other problems beset him all at the same time. He says, "Prayer was no longer a contemplative luxury, but the only way to survive. My own intercessions were multiplied by the prayers of others. Friendships were deepened as I was forced to allow people to assure me with the words I had preached for years. No day went by without a conversation, letter, or phone call giving me love and hope. The greatest discovery that I have made in the midst of all the difficulties is that I can have joy when I don't feel like it."[2]

We're all going to face problems. Wouldn't you rather face them as Dr. Ogilvie did, with an army of fellow believers and the counsel of the Holy Spirit encouraging you every step of the way? Don't you think joy makes a considerable difference? Yes, *joy*, in the midst of the worst that life has to offer. It all begins with the *knowledge* (Paul says "*knowing* that . . .") that life is not a cruel and random course of victimization. It is a cocoon: an orderly path toward the wonderful goal of being Christlike.

Fifth Treasure: A Bottle of Perfume

Now hope does not disappoint, because the love of God has been poured out in our hearts by the Holy Spirit who was given to us. For when we were still without strength, in due time Christ died for the ungodly. For scarcely for a righteous man will one die; yet perhaps for a good man someone would even dare to die. But God demonstrates His own love toward us, in that while we were still sinners, Christ died for us.

—ROMANS 5:5–8

The traveler is becoming more and more excited as he realizes the astounding worth of each new wonder. A small bottle now comes into his curious fingers. The label on the little bottle reads For Your Enrichment.

He carefully pulls out the stopper and curiously sniffs its contents.

Immediately, he feels as if he has stumbled into a dream of heaven. This is perfume, but not like any worldly cosmetic. As the traveler closes his eyes and concentrates on the rich aroma, what he feels is the fragrance of love captivating his whole being.

In these verses, Paul says that God's love has been poured out in our hearts by the Holy Spirit. He goes on to explain that this outpouring is particularly sweet and powerful because Christ died for the ungodly. This passage is John 3:16 expanded and expounded—Scripture's central message given its most vivid presentation.

Once the precious liquid in this bottle is poured upon the traveler's heart, the aroma will never become stale. The power is absolute and final: "Who shall separate us from the love of Christ? Shall tribulation, or distress, or persecution, or famine, or nakedness, or peril, or sword? . . . For I am persuaded that neither death nor life, nor angels nor principalities nor powers, nor things present nor things to come, nor height nor depth, nor any other created thing, shall be able to separate us from the love of God which is in Christ Jesus our Lord" (Romans 8:35, 38–39).

Real Christians have that essence about them. If you can't smell it on their breath, you can at least hear it in their words, feel it in their attitudes. The love of God seems to permeate their spirit, so that there is always enough love to spare. Who else could understand that the rude driver on the freeway probably just had a bad day? Who else could ask God to bless a completely intolerable boss? Who else walks into a room filled with quarreling church members and furthers peace through his or her very presence?

For these people, the love of God has become the supreme fact of life, because nothing can separate them from it. Nothing can take it away. It is greater and more potent than all the problems of the world, and it would wash these problems away like a springtime rain if enough of us were willing to let it happen through us.

Paul speaks of that love being poured out all over God's children, like a drink offering might have been poured on the altar in his time; like the blood of Christ flows over every one of our sins, washing them away forever. And we need to notice that it is the Holy Spirit who does this pouring, carefully directing every drop where it most needs to go.

Not that there is any careful rationing of those drops. The Lord God is not stingy. His love overflows us. It drenches us to the bone, to the heart. We will carry its aroma forever.

The traveler begins to pour the contents of the bottle upon his chest, hoping it will find his heart. He finds that no matter how long he pours, the sweet liquid just keeps coming. He can bathe freely in the abounding love of God.

Sixth Treasure: A Map

Much more then, having now been justified by His blood, we shall be saved from wrath through Him. For if when we were enemies we were reconciled to God through the death of His Son, much more, having been reconciled, we shall be saved by His life.

—ROMANS 5:9–10

The traveler finds another parchment, rolled up. Will it be a proclamation like the first one? No, he quickly discovers this one is a map. Everyone knows about treasure maps, but hasn't this seeker already found his treasure? Why would he need a map now?

The main idea behind these verses is that God has already achieved the more difficult task of dying for us when we were sinners. Why wouldn't He be able to perform the easier one, which is to live within us? Or as the early Christian John Chrysostom put it, "If God gave a great gift to enemies, will He give anything less to His friends?"

This is a map that works two ways. It shows the past and the future, and there is a great red cross in the very center that is marked You Are Here. He can see his own blackened sins quickly disappearing like invisible ink on one side. So much for the past. On the other side, beyond the red cross, his future steps are coming into focus. The details are not clear to him, but he sees that wherever he goes, that red cross will go with him to shelter and empower him.

Griffith Thomas writes, "If the death of Christ was the means of our reconciliation, the life of Christ will be the means of our preservation."[3]

This is not a map that tells us exactly where we will go; it is a promise that He will be our life and our Lord, that He will accompany us and empower us for every destination and every path.

The traveler realizes that in the center of the terrible jungle lies the cross that is a clearing, in the center of the clearing lie the treasures, and now in the center of his heart lies that cross; and wherever he goes, uncharted destinations or not, that cross will overshadow all, giving him the authority of Christ and His kingdom.

Seventh Treasure: A Trumpet

And not only that, but we also rejoice in God through our Lord Jesus Christ,
through whom we have now received the reconciliation.
—ROMANS 5:11

And what is the final wonder? A trumpet, of course!

A what? "I'm not a musician!" mumbles the traveler. "I have no idea how to blow this thing."

Just the same, he knows these are no ordinary, run-of-the-mill ancient treasures. These are the treasures of our riches in Christ Jesus.

So the traveler shyly lifts the trumpet to his lips and lightly breathes into it.

A ringing call to arms issues from the bell of the trumpet. It is as if an angel did the trumpeting! What a happy, victorious song it is.

Paul says, "We also rejoice." And it's just about as simple as that. This is the second treasure that has instructed us to rejoice, but this final one is all about joy. We once were lost and now are found. Our hearts were taught to fear, and now those fears are relieved. What can we do but rejoice? We sound the music, so that it is heard far and wide. When people hear that trumpet's call, and when they see us rejoicing, they, too, will yearn for these treasures. And they will find that everyone may share them. We will gather together and share the wealth that is the totality of our spiritual possessions in Christ. The deepest joy of all comes when we share the joy and introduce it to seekers and travelers yet to come this way.

It is fitting, then, that the final treasure is a call to worship. What else could it be? I defy you to read Romans 5:1–11 slowly, thoughtfully, and prayerfully, as you meditate upon each of the seven wonders in your own life, without experiencing a renewed urge for worship and praise of Christ. His riches continue to shower upon us year by year, day by day, and moment by moment. I dare you to contemplate the power and love and goodness of the living God, to let His love flow over you today, and not feel a soul-deep joy, an all-encompassing peace, and a rising courage to face the challenges that this week brings to your life. And finally, I urge you to consider deeply whether you can accept this glorious wealth without sharing it with as many other human beings as you possibly can.

The jungle of this world, you see, is filled with desperate, weary people who have come to the end of themselves. Their hands and their feet are entangled in the coils of the world and all its sin. Their path is obstructed by the cultural darkness that seems to grow deeper with each passing day. And all the time, there is the sound of Death stalking the forest, drawing ever nearer. At the lowest rung of spiritual maturity, you might have compassion upon them and perhaps understand when they offend you. At the higher rungs, you will begin to reach out a hand of love.

Your friends, your acquaintances, perhaps even your family members are desperate for the peace you have found. The price has been paid for their sins to be forgiven and their names to be written in Christ's blood upon that timeless parchment. All they need is a messenger to tell them the glorious news.

Can you think of any good reason not to be that messenger?

Moments of Grace

Which of the seven wonders of grace do you most need right now? Close chapter 5 of this book and open chapter 5 of Romans. Read the first eleven verses aloud to yourself, slowly, thoughtfully, and prayerfully.

Using a small card, make a list of the seven blessings contained in these verses. Beside each entry draw a simple picture that illustrates that blessing. You might use the images suggested in *Captured by Grace*—a parchment, a key, a music box, and so on; or you might picture each blessing with a unique item from your own imagination. Then slip the card into your purse or pocket, having it available to intentionally share with someone in need this week. Show your list to that person, describe the symbols, and pass along the comforting provision of God's grace.

CHAPTER SIX

The Connecting Point *of* Grace

How Precious Did That Grace Appear the Hour I First Believed

J ohn Newton's life had become a living metaphor: life as a tempest. His days merged into one long voyage through turbulent waters, his ship pounded by storms approaching from any and every point of the compass. He was a man without a country, a vessel wandering with no port.

On this night, March 21, 1748, the young slave trader dozed fitfully in his bunk, uncertain whether it was sea or soul that propelled him from nightmare to nightmare. Finally, rising to clear his head, he became aware of a storm rocking the ship. All hands were awake, and voices were shouting with urgency. Water was beginning to flood the hold.

Newton wondered if this was how it all ended: entombed on the ocean floor—no Christian burial for one who had lived no Christian life. Sailor's instinct set in, and he rushed for the deck and air to breathe. Just then he felt a rough hand on his shoulder. "Bring me a knife," yelled the captain, shouting to be heard above the chaos.

Newton returned below to run the errand. As he did so, the man who took his place on deck was washed overboard. *That wave was meant for me*, thought Newton as he worked the pumps. He threw all his strength into the task and stammered, almost without thinking, "If this will not do, the Lord have mercy upon us!"

Mercy. That word leaped out at him as if some other voice had uttered it. *Mercy* wasn't typical of the words found in his vocabulary over these recent years. But what of that? What mercy, what compassion, what favor had anyone ever shown him? God had stolen his mother, and men had stolen everything else.

From three in the morning until noon the next day, when he was physically spent, Newton pumped water. He claimed one precious hour of sleep and then steered the ship until midnight. The job required a certain concentration, but Newton found it possible to let his mind wander for the first time in many hours. Long-suppressed thoughts and emotions spilled over his soul. He reflected over the tempest of an angry life.

As hope of survival began to take hold among the crew, Newton felt something happening within him. He couldn't explain it. He couldn't give logical reasons. He only felt a rising certainty that no mere accident of fate spared his ship. Something more than a random throw of the cosmic dice had allowed him to see another day. For the first time since childhood, Newton could actually *feel* a purpose to the fabric of the universe.

But the Agent of that purpose remained mysterious to him. God was a mysterious benefactor whose acquaintance he had yet to make.

"I began to pray," he would recall in his later writings. "I could not utter the prayer of faith; I could not draw near to a reconciled God, and call him Father. . . . The comfortless principles of infidelity were deeply riveted. . . . The great question now was how to obtain faith."[1]

Newton continued to ponder these questions as his long watch on deck continued. When he was finally relieved at the wheel, he hurried to the supply cabin in search of a Bible. Paging through it, squinting at the lines, trying to remember the verses beloved by his mother—he came in time to Luke 11:13: "If you then, being evil, know how to give good gifts to your children, how much more will your heavenly Father give the Holy Spirit to those who ask Him!"

It seemed as if the verse was placed there especially for his eyes. *If you then, being evil . . .*

If the book were true (and his blessed mother had staked everything upon it), then this verse must also be trustworthy. And that would be the most wonderful of all possible truths, for what it offered was *help right now.* "I have need of that very Spirit, by which the whole was written, in order to understand it aright," he would write. "He has engaged here to give that Spirit to those who ask: I must therefore pray for it; and, if it be of God, He will make good on His own word."[2]

Newton was hardly aware of the movements of his ship as it completed its voyage. He was deep in thought, lost in prayer, buried in Scripture. Three weeks later, the boat anchored in Ireland—and the storm returned with a fury the very next day. With a chill, Newton realized there would have been no survival if the ship had been a day later in docking. It was as if a heavenly hand had restrained the wrath of nature just long enough for his crew to harbor safely.

Newton would later say that he had embraced the truth of the Gospels and the power of their Savior to rescue him from the hell he had fashioned of his own life. There in the pages of Matthew, Mark, Luke, and John, he found the one and only hope that his soul could be rescued from the anguish and despair that had become his permanent dwelling place. It was hard for him to believe: all his sins, blotted out in one moment; all that was wretched about him, forgiven.

There was powerful emotion in this feeling of absolute mercy that was vast enough and generous enough even for his miserable soul. He felt an earnest yearning to repent of the sins he could identify and to live now for that Savior of mercy. He even smiled as he felt deliverance from the lesser matter of swearing, so common to sailors. He was excited to know that his tongue would now reflect the kingdom of God rather than the sordid places of the world.

Newton later believed that at this point, his conversion was not yet accomplished. In his own judgment, his soul was still in the grip of unacknowledged sin. He had the knowledge but not the acquaintance of the Christ of the Scriptures. As he would later describe it, "I had no apprehension of . . . the hidden life of a Christian, as it consists in communion with God by Jesus Christ; a continual dependence upon him."[3]

Looking back, he would feel that many miles and many trials still lay before the younger Newton before he would finally enter the secure embrace of His Savior. In the late autumn of his years, at the age of eighty, he would find himself writing in his diary upon the fifty-seventh anniversary of the storm that could have claimed him yet helped to deliver him: "March 21, 1805. Not well able to write. But I endeavor to observe the return of this day with Humiliation, Prayer, and Praise." This had become a personal day of remembrance. For over half a century now, he had marked the anniversary with thanksgiving and reverence.[4]

Seventeen centuries earlier, another old man sat with pen in hand, lost in his own memories. His eyes were failing, but there were sometimes young friends to assist him. He thanked the God of heaven for those friends. He wrote them frequently: teaching, encouraging, pleading occasionally for visits and assistance. He found that he couldn't discuss the journey of the Christian faith without recounting his own voyage. In many ways, his passage had paralleled that of John Newton. We know it by reading his letters.

Yet it would be a traveling companion named Luke who would tell the apostle Paul's story in its fullest version. His conversion is well documented, being detailed three separate times in the book of Acts. The story occupies more space in the New Testament than any other record except those surrounding the crucifixion of Christ.

Why is so much importance attached to the conversion of Paul? Griffith Thomas replies that the future of the Christian church pivoted upon this one event. A singular conversion experience for a singular individual: Paul was a Jew by birth, a Roman by citizenship, a Greek by education, and eventually a Christian by grace; a missionary, a theologian, and evangelist; a pastor, an administrator, a philosopher, and a statesman.[5]

SAUL THE HUNTER

Then Saul, still breathing threats and murder against the disciples of the Lord, went to the high priest and asked letters from him to the synagogues of Damascus, so that if he found any who were of the Way, whether men or women, he might bring them bound to Jerusalem.

—ACTS 9:1–2

The man we know as the apostle Paul, who transformed his world more than anyone other than his beloved Master, first appears as an ambiguous face in the crowd. Saul, as he was then known, is the witness to an episode of mob violence. He is a passive young observer at the martyrdom of an early Christian leader. Stephen is that leader: a man described as having an angelic face; a rising star among the Jesus followers, just as Saul is a rising star among the enemies of Jesus.

These are volatile days in Jerusalem, for the Christian church is newly born. It is Stephen who captures the ire of the religious status quo. Its enforcers pursue him out of Jerusalem and stone him to death, laying their cloaks at the feet of "a young man named Saul" (Acts 7:58). The year is most likely AD 35.

The next time Saul is mentioned, we notice the word "consenting," as opposed to simply observing. Saul finds himself endorsing the violence (Acts 8:1). He is a young rabbi, quickly learning his way beside his elders. Mob fever is a highly potent contagion. It reaches out to infect and demonize bystanders. We have seen this in the streets of Munich in the early 1930s, in Paris in 1789, and even in Los Angeles in 1992.

There is something restless and highly flammable inside Saul of Tarsus. He was passive, then approving, then at the head of the line attacking the young church. By Acts 8:3, he is dragging away believers to imprisonment.

Finally, in Acts 9:1, Luke uses the Greek word *phonos* to describe the work of Saul. The translation is "murder." "Then Saul, still breathing threats and murder against the disciples of the Lord . . ." The young Pharisee now has the blood of the martyrs on his hands. The persecution of the church has completely taken possession of his soul. Saul of Tarsus has found his calling.

Compared to the Pharisees we meet in the Gospels—more critical and cynical than explosive—Saul has become somewhat of a hit man of the holy mob. He is breaking into home meetings, participating in scourgings, and attacking men and women alike.

Finally, when the Jerusalem church lies in ruins, he finds that he has not sacrificed enough blood to the demanding gods within himself. The cravings of sin can never satisfy but only demand larger offerings. Saul appears before the high priest and asks for permission to take his show on the road. By this time, Christians have fled Jerusalem in terror, seeking refuge in cities such as Damascus, the capital of Syria. Christians there have established an outpost and are already proselytizing Jews in the local synagogues. In the back of his mind, perhaps Saul wonders why these heretics cannot keep their mouths shut when it places their lives in danger. In any case, he wants to hunt them down, get them in shackles, and deliver them to Hebrew justice in Jerusalem.

Listen to his own confession. Here he refers to the church as The Way, as it has begun to describe itself: "I persecuted this Way to the death, binding and delivering into prisons both men and women, as also the high priest bears me witness, and all the council of the elders, from whom I also received letters to the brethren, and went to Damascus to bring in chains even those who were there to Jerusalem to be punished" (Acts 22:4–5).

This Way has become a difficult road because of the tireless attacks of Saul, who is now striking from a distance. "Being exceedingly enraged against them," he will later recall, "I persecuted them even to foreign cities" (Acts 26:11). He will describe himself as "a blasphemer, a persecutor, and an insolent man" (1 Timothy 1:13). Much like John Newton, he will struggle to find words to express the abhorrence he feels for his early life. He will view himself as the chief of all sinners (1 Timothy 1:15).

Self-righteous anger always feeds on some hidden fire. Something inside Saul made him unrelenting in the bloodiness of his attacks. He could have murdered every Christian alive and started on other sects and cults, and still the burning would have endured. Maybe he had a dawning realization of that fact in time and began to realize that some greater Power was trying to speak to him.

One way or the other, violent emotions can only be ratcheted so high. Sooner or later there would have to be a reckoning, not with the enemy in Damascus but with the true demon that lay within himself.

SAUL THE HUNTED

From the beginning of our faith, converted Christians have spoken of God not as a passive deity hiding in His throne room but as a relentless pursuer—a heavenly Shepherd gathering in every single lost sheep. The most compelling word picture may come from a poet named Francis Thompson.

Thompson was a homeless man on the streets of London, often earning a few pennies by selling matches. So ashamed was he that when he sent a few poems to a magazine, he would give only the return address of a chemist's shop. The editors, startled by the quality of the poetry, sought him there and found that place to be where Thompson fed his opium addiction.

Thompson went on to write a poem called "The Hound of Heaven," about the God who follows us until we become His own. The poem begins this way:

> *I fled Him, down the nights and down the days;*
> *I fled Him, down the arches of the years;*
> *I fled Him, down the labyrinthine ways*
> *Of my own mind; and in the mist of tears . . .*
>
> *From those strong Feet that followed,*
> *followed after,*
> *But with unhurrying chase,*
> *And unperturbed pace,*
> *Deliberate speed, majestic instancy,*
> *They beat—and a Voice beat*
> *More instant than the Feet—*
> *"All things betray thee, who betrayest Me."*

Finally, after fleeing and hiding in every possible false refuge,

Halts by me that footfall:
Is my gloom, after all,
Shade of His hand, outstreched caressingly?
"Ah, fondest, blindest, weakest,
I am He Whom thou seekest!"

Men and women who do the pursuing can only capture empty air. Nothing satisfies. This indeed is the definition of religion. What sets apart our Christian faith is the story told in reverse—one of a loving Father who pursues *us* because we are too foolish and too sin-stained to go to Him.

Read the thoughts of all the great people of faith through the ages, and you'll find that common denominator. God pursued them "down the nights and down the days." For example, C. S. Lewis writes, "I never had the experience of looking for God. It was the other way round: He was the hunter (or so it seemed to me) and I was the deer. He stalked me . . . took unerring aim, and fired. And I am very thankful that this is how the first (conscious) meeting occurred. It forearms one against subsequent fears that the whole thing was only wish fulfillment. Something one didn't wish for can hardly be that."[6]

Saul saw himself as the relentless hunter. Yet he must have begun to realize that he had become the hunted. "All things betray thee, who betrayest Me." Naturally the divine encounter finally occurred just where a tale of pursuit should: on a road.

Confrontation

What were the thoughts of Saul the merciless as his entourage traveled the Damascus Road? Perhaps he was imagining the violent scene that lay before him in a few hours. Perhaps he was savoring the anticipation of another city cleansed from the Christian disease.

But maybe not. Could it be that by now Saul was at war within himself? We can't know his precise thoughts when "As he journeyed he came near Damascus, and suddenly a light shone around him from heaven" (Acts 9:3).

The apostle will later tell this story and fill in several details. For instance, the event transpired at high noon (Acts 22:6; 26:13). We are assured it was no natural phenomenon, no heat-related stroke or hallucination, for the invading light was more brilliant than the noonday sun.

We also learn that the event was experienced by all of Saul's companions, but only Saul understood the voice that everyone heard. The others "stood speechless," recognizing the presence of a supernatural phenomenon but not understanding it (Acts 9:7).

Finally, we learn that it was Jesus Christ himself who met Saul along the road. It was His voice that spoke the words that would haunt the young man for the rest of his life.

Ever since that day, commentators have looked for a psychological or natural explanation for this idea of Jesus appearing to Saul. Maybe he fabricated the entire incident later as counterfeit credentials for his insistence upon apostleship.

These rationalizations simply don't square with any piece of evidence that we have. Saul saw Christ, and his traveling companions saw and heard *something*. Then the Lord spoke of it independently to a man named Ananias, who didn't even know Saul, except through his infamous reputation. We could no more credibly explain the event as "mass hallucination" than we could the Resurrection. History makes its case clearly. The best evidence of this miracle's authenticity is the undeniable effect it had on Saul—just as the best evidence for the Resurrection is what happened to those disciples who witnessed the supernatural power of God and were transformed instantaneously.

Paul holds the status of an apostle because he saw the risen Lord. He writes, "Am I not an apostle? Am I not free? Have I not seen Jesus Christ our Lord? Are you not my work in the Lord?" (1 Corinthians 9:1). The early church accepted his experience as a valid one and counted him the equal of Peter, James, John, and the rest.

As far as the revelation of Scripture is concerned, this was the first appearance of Christ since the martyrdom of Stephen. Christ has brought things full circle, appearing to an assassinated Christian leader and then to one of the killers—who in godly irony would succeed him.

Conviction

The words Christ spoke to Saul are serious and direct: "Then he fell to the ground, and heard a voice saying to him, 'Saul, Saul, why are you persecuting Me?'" (Acts 9:4).

These would be the words of a judge or a prosecuting attorney—except that their context is unmistakably personal. Saul's name is called twice, as if painfully: "Saul, Saul!" Then, "why are you persecuting Me?"

Saul might never have given a thought to whom he was persecuting, other than Jewish heretics, who, in his view, were spiritual blasphemers who threatened the venerable faith. He never considered that he would find himself kneeling in the dust before these disciples' Master.

In Saul's mind, he had been reforming. He had been cleansing. He had been investigating and arresting, and yes, applying sanctions: prison or physical torture. He had just been doing his job, giving it 100 percent. Nothing personal!

Until now.

The voice he hears is Aramaic, the authentic language of his fore-fathers—the language spoken, in fact, by Jesus. "Saul, Saul, why are you persecuting Me? It is hard for you to kick against the goads" (Acts 26:14).

Saul the zealous rabbi, blinded by an almost radioactive light, struggles with two new and shocking facts:

First, he is speaking to Jesus, who is *not dead.*

Second, Saul has been attacking Jesus himself and not simply His faceless followers.

Could it be that when we attack our fellow Christians in any way, by words or by church politics, we are attacking Jesus, who stands behind them and who is more alive and more present than we acknowledge? Could it be that what we dismiss as "fussing and feuding" in the church is not so harmless after all, because it drives yet more nails into those blessed wrists?

F. B. Meyer points out that in one agonizing moment Saul no longer sees himself as God's champion but as God's enemy. "By every blow he struck at the infant church, he was lacerating those hands and piercing that side. By every sigh and groan extorted from the members of the Body he had elicited from the Head in heaven the remonstrance, 'Saul! Saul! Why persecutest thou Me?'"[7]

Conversion

Saul's entire conception of God has been undermined in one fell swoop. Imagine discovering that the God you worship is Someone else entirely, Someone who bears radical differences to your most precious assumptions about Him. You would ask the very question Paul now asks: "And he said, 'Who are You, Lord?' Then the Lord

The Connecting Point of Grace 113

said, 'I am Jesus, whom you are persecuting. It is hard for you to kick against the goads'" (Acts 9:5).

Saul knows the answer to his own question—he just hasn't had the time to process the vast implications. *Who are You, Lord?* The answer to that question will force a new one: *Who am I?*

Just when Saul thought he knew all the answers, the questions have changed. What does he do with his deep reserves of anger? It all becomes fear, in one terrible instant.

It is hard for you to kick against the goads. Everyone in Saul's world knows about the ox driver and his long pole, the end of which carries a sharpened piece of iron. That point "goads" the ox to move where he is instructed. But the constant jabbing is painful, and every farmer knows there are times when the ox will turn on the goad stick and attack it—which of course only increases the pain.

For the ox known as Saul, what are the goads? Christ is saying that something has been pricking away at Saul, trying to guide him to proper plowing, but he has been bloodying himself by resisting.

The goading may have begun with the words that came from the mouth of Stephen, who accepted his cruel death with amazing grace. Stephen's face shined "as the face of an angel" (Acts 6:15). Perhaps Saul felt something tugging at his heart, and he pushed back.

Next, it may have been the behavior of the Christian believers who prayed for Saul even as he attacked their families. It may have been the persistence of the people of The Way who would leave all that they had in Jerusalem to keep following Christ elsewhere—and then would dangerously reveal their position by telling everyone within earshot about Jesus.

Saul was not getting the point—he was slamming his head against it. *All things betray thee, who betrayest Me.* The Hound of

Heaven has drawn nearer and nearer in His pursuit, finally corner-
ing him at high noon on the highway.

Consecration

Saul's first question has been, "Who are You, Lord?"

His second is the inevitable sequel: "So he, trembling and astonished, said, 'Lord, what do You want me to do?' Then the Lord said
to him, 'Arise and go into the city, and you will be told what you
must do.' And the men who journeyed with him stood speechless,
hearing a voice but seeing no one. Then Saul arose from the ground,
and when his eyes were opened he saw no one. But they led him by
the hand and brought him into Damascus" (Acts 9:6–8).

Saul's companions may be more fearful even than Saul. At least
he can understand what is being said to him. For their part, they see
a light, hear a voice, and discover that their leader, so reckless and
aggressive only moments ago, is now blind, trembling, and helpless.
He has led believers to their prison; now he must be led by hand to
his deliverance. Saul experiences the ultimate humility that physical
helplessness always brings. He has depended only upon himself, but
now he must learn to depend on the kindness of strangers.

Communion

Now comes the true agony. Saul must be left to deal with himself in
a lightless world. "And he was three days without sight, and neither
ate nor drank" (Acts 9:9).

These three days must have been the longest of Saul's life. What
does a man do for three days in utter darkness, after his very identity
and his convictions have been violently stripped away from him?

If he is a weak man, he flees into denial. He ignores his senses. Perhaps he even loses his mind.

But if he is a strong man—and Saul is one—he thinks. He processes. He tries to reconceptualize reality in the light of recent evidence.

There is so much to reconsider and relabel. We can imagine that his past life and career flash before him, as if they were the life and career of someone else entirely—some very evil person, drawing pleasure from the way he has destroyed lives, taking part in murder and torture, looking to new cities to persecute adherents of the Christian faith.

Even while blind, he sees more clearly than ever before. Perhaps in his dark world, that angelic countenance of Stephen looms again before him—a follower of this truly living Christ whom Saul has helped to destroy, even if passively. He sees face after face, sometimes of women and children, all people he has attacked without any provocation other than a difference in spiritual paradigms. And he wonders—what of his own spiritual paradigm now? How will these eruptions change him?

For three days, he refuses food or water. For three days, he faces the violence of his revelation squarely, without distraction, without subterfuge. This is simply the character of Saul, and surely one reason that God chose him. Saul is a man of powerful integrity and resolve. If he believes in the way of the Law, he will pursue it with all his strength. If he discovers that Jesus is real, he will face that truth with all his concentration and follow every implication to the action it demands. He is not given to half-measures.

The voice of Christ has said, "Why are you persecuting Me?" The voice has said his name twice, with emotion. The Man behind the voice has knocked him in the dirt and blinded him and left him among strangers. Why didn't this Lord of power kill him on the spot? Why has He brought him to this place?

Then Saul begins to see the faces again—Stephen and the rest of them. There is love in those faces. It is not like the serious, stodgy, often angry demeanor of Saul's own brand of faith. No, there is compassion, forgiveness, mercy—the true word for it would have to be *grace.*

Saul has impatiently listened to some facts about the Nazarene and His teaching. They are distortions of the words of Jesus for the most part, but still Saul can tell that the Lord was not one to call for violence or retribution. He was a man of grace. This must be why He did not knock the Pharisee from his horse and then finish him off. This is why the Lord obviously has the power to deal with *all* His persecutors, yet doesn't.

Grace—that must be the key to the whole enigma. Grace, a subject that might as well be foreign language to the Pharisees.

Saul saw Ananias in a vision. He heard the man's voice when Ananias came and found Saul at the street called Straight. Saul must have almost laughed, for this fellow was quaking with fear of the notorious Hebrew hunter. Yet Ananias trusted his Jesus so much that he obediently came in search of the one he always prayed wouldn't come in search of *him.* And there was a gentleness about Ananias as he laid his healing hands upon Saul of Tarsus. There was no anger or resentment, only *grace.*

All of these people, captured by grace.

Thirty years after the martyrdom of Stephen, the day will come when Paul bides his time in a Roman prison and awaits the same kind of fate as many of the people he once arrested. Perhaps he sees one more time the face of Stephen and of so many others since then, no longer enemies but brothers and sisters in the faith. By now he has lived and taught and served in the power of grace.

And he will face the executioner with no less love, no less compassion. He will go out with grace.

John Newton spent many hours thinking about that. He wrote a great deal about the life and career of the man who became better known as Paul. Newton always returned with fascination to the fact that God had selected the most terrible of His antagonists, not for special punishment but for special ministry.

A man like Newton, who had the blood of African slaves on his hands, could draw a lot of hope from a fact like that. He might have thought, *For God to pursue so seriously, so relentlessly, a child who has insulted His goodness in every way—there must be high purpose.*

C. S. Lewis, too, marveled at the Hound of Heaven, who never loses the scent:

> You must picture me alone in that room in Magdalen, night after night, feeling, whenever my mind lifted even for a second from my work, the steady, unrelenting approach of Him whom I so earnestly desired not to meet. That which I greatly feared had at last come upon me. In the Trinity Term of 1929, I gave in and admitted that God was God and knelt and prayed: perhaps that night, the most dejected and reluctant convert in all England. I did not then see what is now the most shining and obvious thing, the Divine humility which will accept a convert on even such terms. The prodigal son at least walked home on his own feet. But who can duly adore that Love which will open the high gates to a prodigal who is brought in kicking, struggling, resentful, and darting his eyes in every direction for a chance of escape? [8]

Do you think that Heavenly Pursuer is only after challenging game such as Paul, John Newton, or C. S. Lewis? I think you know better.

The love of Christ is on your trail, too, my friend. Even if you have already given in, "kicking, struggling, resentful" like Lewis, or "blindest, weakest" like Francis Thompson, He continues the pursuit. No, He does not wait impatiently for you to say the prayer of salvation and then turn on His heels to abandon you in favor of other sport. The truth is that the grand chase never ends—not until you totally resemble Him yourself. That is an eventuality none of us reaches in this life.

You can be certain there are parts of your identity, your hopes, and your dreams that are still on the run. You may harbor ambitions that need to be converted to godly ones. You may relate to your spouse or your parents or your coworkers in ways that Christ longs to bless with His love and grace, if you would only let Him.

What will it take? Being knocked down? Losing your sight? What must God do to captivate your attention and make you realize that He is alive, gloriously alive?

Perhaps you need several days of utterly focused fasting, such as Paul had, to work through the implication of His lordship on your personal world. Perhaps you need a long and thoughtful voyage by yourself, like Newton.

Even so, let the chase continue! We could have no more loving Pursuer. This is the story of your life: He will follow you until you follow Him. It will continue until your whole being has been captured by grace.

Moments of Grace

Perhaps the Hound of Heaven is pursuing you now. It's a love chase, as He seeks you for your own good. If this is true, how should you respond?

Think again of the startled words of Saul as Jesus appeared to him on the Damascus Road. Saul shouted two questions at the brilliant form whose glory had blinded his eyes and sent him reeling from his horse. Which of the two questions is most appropriate for you at this point in your life?

Who are You, Lord?
What do You want me to do?

Even if it takes several days of fasting and prayer, focus on those questions until Christ captures your heart with grace. If you've been a Christian many years, focus on that last question and reaffirm that you're doing what the Lord wants you to do, fulfilling the perfect will of the God of all grace.

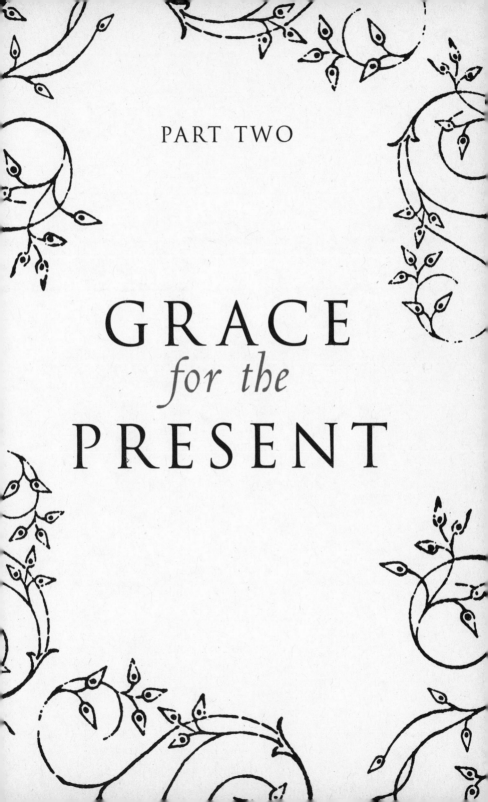

PART TWO

GRACE
for the
PRESENT

CHAPTER SEVEN

The Confusing Paradox of Grace

Through Many Dangers, Toils, and Snares I Have Already Come

By the time we get around to singing the third verse of John Newton's great hymn, we might be thinking several things:

Are we going to sing every single verse?

When is the part about being there ten thousand years? That's the coolest part.

These shoes aren't very comfortable.

I wonder if I could sing the alto part? I get tired of soprano sometimes.

Hmm, I wonder what these words are all about . . .

Every now and then, someone stumbles upon that last thought. What a nifty concept! You and I can actually pay attention to the words and ideas as they emerge from our lips. I've heard of Christians trying this and experiencing an immediate "worship upgrade," from business class to first class.

Sometimes I wonder what would happen if we slipped in some *different* lyrics one Sunday. Maybe we could sneak in a new verse to "Amazing Grace" that went:

> *I sing every hymn each week in church,*
> *I make every note sublime,*
> *I never pay attention to a single word,*
> *I'm thinking of dinnertime.*

Wouldn't it be fun to look out at the congregation and count how many singers noticed the change and how many just went on harmonizing?

That one is a verse you'll probably never sing, but I would venture that you've sung the following one:

> *Through many dangers, toils, and snares I have already come.*

As you sing those words, what do you usually think about? Do you reflect upon the dangers, toils, and snares through which you have already personally come?

John Newton didn't write those words because they sounded good or to give the organist an opportunity to play some effective minor chords. He wrote them because he had lived them. It's remarkable how many close encounters with death this man had. I visualize his office as having a file cabinet with three drawers: the top one labeled Dangers, the middle one Toils, and the bottom one Snares—all packed with files.

Consider a few of his highlights:

- At a shooting party, Newton almost killed himself by accidentally firing his shotgun while scrambling up a bank. The bullet singed the edge of his cap, missing his head by a couple of inches.
- During the storm described earlier, he was sent below deck while the man who took his place was washed overboard.
- Similarly, at the last minute, his captain oddly pulled him away from a river trip in Africa. That boat sank; and once again, the man who took his place drowned.
- Newton once tried to go overboard and retrieve his fallen hat. He was so intoxicated at the time that he nearly drowned. Even sober, he couldn't swim. Someone grabbed him and pulled him back.

Brushes with death have a way of making us consider great big questions about life and eternity. Newton's own close calls edged him closer and closer to his conversion experience. He regarded his survival as proof of the hand of Providence sustaining him over and over, when by any human reckoning he should have perished. Salvation meant more than the hope of heaven to him; it was a literal experience that he had many times, and the sum total of it persuaded him that God must have a particular purpose for his life.

Wouldn't you love to be in heaven when John Newton and Paul sit together and exchange war stories? Believe it or not, you would notice that Paul's were even more hair-raising than Newton's. And Paul's days of pursuing Christians were almost dull compared to his life *after* he became a believer. The book of Acts can be read as a kind of Spirit-filled James Bond movie from the first century. The apostle faces death every chapter or two, then he dusts himself off and proceeds to the next calamity.

Here are a few of Paul's action scenes:

- He survived a murder plot by the Jews first and then the Greeks (Acts 9:23, 29).
- He was stoned nearly to death then dragged out of a city. Left for dead, he later got on his feet and walked to a new city (Acts 14:5, 19–20).
- Having managed to get the entire city of Jerusalem in an uproar, he was dragged bodily from the temple and then pursued by Roman soldiers (Acts 21:30–32).

Even if John Newton talked about shipwrecks, Paul could say, "Been there, done that"—*three* of those, actually. He could talk about arguing the case for his life before rulers. He could tell about being lowered in a basket from an opening in the wall, to escape murder.

Perhaps it seems to you that your own life is fairly humdrum, not exactly Hollywood blockbuster material. You can imagine Paul and Newton looking up at you from that heavenly table and saying, "Now, what's *your* story?" And you'd begin to stammer, "Well, you see, I haven't had too many adventures really; I was a tax accountant" or, "I took care of the house."

But wait a minute. Think a little harder. We all have our portion of dangers, toils, and snares—dramatic or less dramatic, it really makes no difference. Have you ever lost a loved one and thought your heart would break? Have you experienced a painful divorce? Have you ever been out of work, unable to pay bills, and not certain what you were going to do in the immediate future? Or how about this one: have you ever been a parent? If the answer to that one question alone is yes, then you are an authority on dangers, toils, and snares. I know of no parent who hasn't lain awake nights worrying about his or her children for all kinds of reasons.

Trouble is like home. You're either there, coming from it, or on your way back to it. And I'm certain you've had your share of each of these:

Times of *danger* when you've been truly afraid.

Times of *toil* when you labored almost beyond endurance.

Times of *snare* when you've wrestled with temptation—sometimes winning, sometimes losing.

At this point, I'd like to suggest that you stop, put this book down for a few moments, and do some focused thinking. I urge you to make a list of your most important examples from each of Newton's categories.

Your Dangers:

Your Toils:

Your Snares:

Have you made your list? I'm serious about this. We're not in any hurry here. Let's go no further until you've thought carefully about your dangers, toils, and snares.

Got your list in hand? Good. You've reflected deeply at that pressure point where truth meets experience. Now you're in the right frame of mind to experience a blessing, because in the next few pages, Paul is going to offer us a theology of hope in times of crisis. If you can hold those personal experiences of yours with one hand and take hold of the Bible's guidance with the other, you'll undergo not only a worship upgrade but an everything-in-life upgrade.

One word of warning: if you get into the habit of *thinking* about these words rather than simply reading them, your life may be in significant danger of being changed for the better!

The Requirement of Grace
for the Christian Life

*But we have this treasure in earthen vessels, that the excellence of the power may be of
God and not of us. We are hard-pressed on every side, yet not crushed; we are perplexed,
but not in despair; persecuted, but not forsaken; struck down, but not destroyed.*
—2 Corinthians 4:7–9

Imagine a business traveler who is constantly on the go from one city
to another, his appointment calendar packed. His clients always have
some new crisis that he is expected to handle personally. It's one
petty squabble after another, and he's always laboring to make peace
between petty factions. His business is thriving, but there are plenty
of headaches and no time for rest.

That was life two thousand years ago—at least for the apostle
Paul. His business was church planting, and every new church
brought new joy and new crises. Since Paul was the founder of so
many congregations, he found himself in the middle of one contro-
versy after another. Corinth was a problem church. There always
seemed to be disruptions there: public immorality, divisions, and
now a problem with false prophets. Some of them were challenging
Paul's authority, and he wrote the letter that we know as 2 Corinthians to defend his credentials and to help the church members think
spiritually about the problems they were encountering.

In 2 Corinthians 4:7, we find Paul trying to help his readers see
the glory of our heavenly Father in the dust of everyday experience.
That's what makes the difference in this life: seeing things from
God's perspective. Paul is showing that it can be done, because God
has been revealed in human form through Jesus Christ, the ultimate
treasure in an earthly vessel—flesh and blood. All the eternal and
infinite glory of God shined through the humanity of His Son, who

was fully human and yet fully divine. Jesus' enemies saw Him as just another man, but behind those eyes dwelt the one true God.

That's fine. But what does it have to do with your problems or those of the Corinthians? Here comes the part that should send a chill up your spine, as it does mine. If we are ministers of Christ—and I don't mean paid ministers of a church, but the kind of minister every single Christian is by appointment—then we share in that eternal glory. As the Father dwelt in the Son, the Son dwells within us through the Spirit. We have this treasure, the ministry of Christ, in our "earthly vessels," our frail and imperfect human bodies.

This is a difficult concept to understand, but Paul always has a handy word picture available. This time he uses the idea of a clay jar. If there was one absolutely ordinary, run-of-the-mill object that everyone in the Middle East could understand, it was a clay jar. Cheap pottery was everywhere and used for everything. The jars were breakable, but it didn't matter because it was so easy to get another one. Clay earthenware was as common as—well, as the clay beneath one's feet.

A clay pot had absolutely no value in itself. Everyone knew that. On the other hand, it could hold a priceless pearl, a gold piece, a bite of bread to fend off hunger, a day's drink of water, a wedding ring, even a sleeping newborn baby. It wasn't the jar but the treasure inside that counted.

I know people who carry Bibles that look as if they've been through several shipwrecks with Newton. The covers are wrinkled and torn. The pages are nearly falling out. But the worn-out container holds the eternal Word of God.

It's not the vessel but its contents. A lowly clam hides a pearl; a lump of coal compresses into a diamond. We fall for one of the devil's greatest lies when we assume that our human limitations make any difference to the workings of God through us.

There will certainly be problems. Clay has its cracks, its heat limit, its fragility. But it still does the job and holds its precious cargo. "Just think about all that I've gone through," Paul is saying. "Is God any less real because I've been beaten and had rocks thrown at me? No—*more* so to us, because He bears testimony through all these things."

Dangers, toils, and snares. They just come with the territory. Paul tells Timothy he might as well expect to be mistreated, because the godly in Christ Jesus are always persecuted (2 Timothy 3:12). And in 2 Corinthians 12:7, Paul mentions his "thorn in the flesh." That one makes for an interesting story.

THE RESOURCE OF GRACE
FOR THE CHRISTIAN LIFE

It happened that Paul was once raised to the heavens by God to see glories no man had ever previously beheld. For the Lord's purposes, this vision was necessary for Paul. On the other hand, so was an infirmity of some kind. Why? Because Paul's supernatural experience would tend to breed pride. It could ruin him for ministry. Therefore God allowed a "thorn," literally a stake driven into the flesh. And "a messenger of Satan" was allowed to "buffet" or beat him. In 2 Corinthians 12:7, Paul speaks in language descriptive but not precise. He doesn't tell the precise nature of the suffering he endured, but he does tell us all we need to know: trials are allowed by God to help us keep perspective and to enable us to grow spiritually.

And it's interesting, isn't it? The greater the Lord's plans for us, the more we generally need to be tried. The more critical an army's mission, the harder the army needs to be drilled. The more significant the lesson you're teaching your children, the more discipline you'll need to employ. We think it strange when James tells us to consider it joy to endure a trial (James 1:2–3), but in truth, nothing could make more sense.

If you're involved in tough times right now, congratulations! God loves you, and He has great things ahead for you. Sometimes His earthen vessels simply need to be heat-treated.

Paul says of his suffering, "Concerning this thing I pleaded with the Lord three times that it might depart from me. And He said to me, 'My grace is sufficient for you, for My strength is made perfect in weakness'" (2 Corinthians 12:8–9).

It's good advice to consider our sufferings a joy, but no one is very good at that. Even Paul asked God to take away his trouble—his "thorn"—three times. The result? God turned him down three times.

Question: Is there any such thing as an "unanswered prayer"? Or would it be wiser to call them "unwanted answers"?

Yes, there are times when God doesn't give us what we want. But in those cases, He speaks to us in ways that are just as valuable as the thing we prayed for. The question is whether we are listening. In the case of Paul, for example, God gives this answer to the prayer: "My grace is sufficient for you" (v. 9). There is very rich, very practical wisdom in that answer—much more than a blunt "no."

It's as if God is saying to us, "I will not take away the trial, but I will give you the power to endure it." Here's another way of putting it: "I won't give you what you want, but I'll give you what you need. If I took away the trial, you would grow no stronger—in fact, you would be just a little weaker and more helpless, like a pampered child. But if I allow the trial and help you endure it, you will be stronger, wiser, and more useful to Me."

Another long truth in God's short answer: there is power in the grace of God. The verb translated "is sufficient" is in the present tense—as is God's grace, which is always present. In every situation, we can rely on Him to provide strength and courage. He will never give us all that we want, but He will always give us all that we need.

Compare our Lord to the gods of all the world's religions and you'll find that grace is the difference maker. It is the x-factor that radically sets Him apart. Our God is "the God of all grace" (1 Peter 5:10). He is kind, benevolent, and longsuffering. We need not beg Him, bribe Him, or appease Him. He actually longs to bless us every single moment, every single day. He comes down to us rather than demanding that we climb the impossible ladder to infinity to reach Him. Grace is God taking the initiative.

In this same letter, Paul will explain, "God is able to make all grace abound toward you, that you, always having all sufficiency in all things, may have an abundance for every good work" (2 Corinthians 9:8).

Notice the repetition of the word *all*. *All* grace abounds toward us so that we are *all* sufficient in *all* things. He is all we need in all we face, so that for all we do, we can overflow with His grace and power. Did you know it was possible to live like that?

One Friday morning, British pastor Charles Haddon Spurgeon was challenging his ministerial students. He said:

There are many passages of Scripture which you will never understand until some trying experience shall interpret them to you. The other evening I was riding home after a heavy day's work; I was wearied and depressed; and swiftly and suddenly as a lightning flash, this text laid hold on me: "My grace is sufficient for you!" When I got home, I looked it up in the original, and finally it dawned upon me what the text was saying, MY grace is sufficient for THEE. "Why," I said to myself, "I should think it is!" and I burst out laughing. It seemed to make unbelief so absurd. It was as though some little fish, being very thirsty, was troubled about drinking the river dry; and Father River said; "Drink away, little fish, my stream is sufficient for you!" Or as if a little mouse in the granaries of Egypt, after seven years of plenty, feared lest it should die of famine, and Joseph said, "Cheer up, little mouse, my granaries are sufficient for you!" Again I imagined a man way up on the mountain saying to himself, "I fear I shall exhaust all the oxygen in the atmosphere." But the earth cries, "Breathe away, O man, and fill your lungs; my atmosphere is sufficient for you!" [1]

Think of it this way. When you have a big problem, ask yourself, "How big is the problem?" Then ask yourself, "How big is God?" I tremendously doubt the time will ever come when you find that the problem is the larger of the two. Kenneth Wuest says it this way:

There is enough grace in God's heart of love to save and keep saved for time and eternity, every sinner that ever has or ever will live, and then enough left over to save a million more universes full of sinners, were there such, and then some more. There is enough grace available to give every saint constant victory over sin, and then some more. There is enough grace to meet and cope with all the sorrows, heartaches, difficulties, temptations, testings, and trials of human existence, and more added to that. God's salvation is an oversize salvation. It is shock proof, stain proof, unbreakable, all-sufficient. It is equal to every emergency, for it flows from the heart of an infinite God freely bestowed and righteously given through the all-sufficient sacrifice of our Lord on the Cross. Salvation is all of grace. Trust God's grace. It is superabounding grace.[2]

THE RESULTS OF GRACE IN THE CHRISTIAN LIFE

We agree that we are just ordinary clay pots to be used to display God's power. We even accept that we will be prodded by painful experiences in order to learn that grace provides all we need. Now the good news! Here's the upshot of our humbling and our thorns—the result of trials is strength.

The Grace of God Produces Power

And He said to me, "My grace is sufficient for you, for My strength is made perfect in weakness." Therefore most gladly I will rather boast in my infirmities, that the power of Christ may rest upon me. Therefore I take pleasure in infirmities, in reproaches, in needs, in persecutions, in distresses, for Christ's sake. For when I am weak, then I am strong.

—2 CORINTHIANS 12:9–10

Paul hated the thorn that plagued him. But in time, he accepted it. He knew there could be no ministry if there were no trial, because this life wasn't about Paul's strength but God's. The weaker Paul appeared, the greater the Lord would be glorified. Let me ask you: if you were the most talented person in the world, would that help or hinder your witness? People would say, "You can believe what you want when you have that much natural ability." But when we see absolutely ordinary individuals change the world for Christ—and our history is absolutely filled with those—we can have no doubt of the presence of God in this world.

The next time you think it's all about your strength or talents, remember the following:

• God used an uneducated fisherman to be the church's first great leader. His name was Peter.

- God used a fix-it man sitting in jail to write *Pilgrim's Progress*, one of the greatest classics in the English language. His name was John Bunyan.
- God used a shy, obscure monk to set off the greatest Christian reformation in history. His name was Martin Luther.
- God used a Bible college dropout to preach the Gospel to more people than anyone in history. His name is Billy Graham.
- God used an ordinary shoe salesman to create revivals and new ministries all over the world. His name was Dwight L. Moody.

It was Moody who said, "If this world is going to be reached, I am convinced that it must be done by men and women of average talent." The story is told of an occasion when he was preaching in London. Members of the royal family and other VIPs were present. When Moody came to the name Eliseus in Luke 4:27 (KJV), he couldn't seem to get the word out of his mouth. He began reading the verse again from the beginning, but he still stammered over the *E* word. A third time: same results. Deeply troubled, he closed his Bible and said, "Oh, God, use this stammering tongue to preach Christ crucified to these people." From that moment he preached with a power his closest followers had never heard. The crowd was awed by the presence of God that evening.[3]

This is among the deepest of spiritual truths. Remember that the ultimate treasure in an earthly vessel is God's own Son, whom the establishment believed it could kill. Because He was composed of flesh and bone, they assumed He was simply one more man who could be squashed beneath the thumb of the Roman Empire. He was simply a peasant carpenter from Nazareth, or so they thought.

What if God had chosen instead to save the world as His chosen people wanted it saved, through the military genius of a fabulous leader? What would that say of God, if anything at all?

Instead, countless people have come to Christ through concluding that only one kind of power could possibly turn the world upside down as it did within decades. The weakness of humanity is the proper container to glorify God.

The Grace of God Provides Perspective

For our light affliction, which is but for a moment, is working for us a far more exceeding and eternal weight of glory, while we do not look at the things which are seen, but at the things which are not seen. For the things which are seen are temporary, but the things which are not seen are eternal.

—2 Corinthians 4:17–18

When you struggle with some trial, your first question might be, "Why is this happening?" A better one would be, "What is God teaching me?"

It's difficult for us to remember that God's great desire is for us to see things as they really are, rather than as they appear to be. As Paul says, we see in a mirror dimly right now. He is always working to remove the fog so that we might share His heavenly perspective. Have you ever met a child who was given her every desire? What is the result of that kind of parenting? It creates spoiled, undisciplined children who believe the world will always serve their requests on a silver platter when they snap their fingers.

I'm sure you'll agree that good parents don't raise their children that way. Instead they deny their children certain demands when it is appropriate to do so. Effective parents are always using the moment for an object lesson. They let their children know that love is not the same as pampering. Would your Father in heaven be any less wise in His parenting? He refuses to solve all our problems, but He gives us all the sustaining grace we need for toughing it out.

Can you remember taking your child to a new Sunday school class when she was three years old? She may have cried. She may have clung to your legs and begged you not to desert her until the situation tugged at your heart. you may have experienced every impulse to simply give in and take your child to the adult class with you or stay with her in the child's class. You would have then failed to help your child learn how to adjust to a new environment. Instead, you would have taught her that a pathetic demeanor will manipulate desired results.

Now consider that time when you were in an adult-sized version of that situation: you were unemployed or grieving over a lost relationship, perhaps. As you cried out to God, don't you think it tugged at His loving heart? Don't you think He longed to gather you up in His arms and give you everything you wanted? But He loved you enough not to give in. He knew how much wiser and stronger you would become through learning to depend upon His grace in a time of storm. Once your pleading was over and you had calmed down—just as the child does in a new Sunday school classroom—you were able to hear God say entirely new things to you. You could feel yourself growing. You said, "I made it through this trial by trusting God, and next time I won't be knocked down so easily."

Let's consider the remarkable ways God nurtures us through our struggles, according to this passage of Scripture.

1. *Afflictions help us to anticipate glory.* Reigning with Christ requires suffering with Him—no cross, no crown. But holding the hand of Christ through the darkness gives us a glimpse of the glorious nature of deliverance that is to come.

2. *Light things help us appreciate heavy things.* Paul calls it "light affliction," and frankly, that's what most of our sufferings are. These are like smaller models of the "higher" suffering called death, and the higher glory of eternal life. God teaches powerful truth through lesser mediums.

3. *Temporary things help us appropriate eternal things.* "For the things which are seen are temporary, but the things which are not seen are eternal" (2 Corinthians 4:18). The hope of wearing Olympic gold drives athletes to persevere through, and even to value, the pain of dedication. Comparing the value of temporary pleasures with potential glory, they press on. Gold medals are of fleeting value. Some even turn up in pawn shops to be exchanged for a different metal. The goal before us also requires rigorous perseverance through pain. Unlike the hopeful competitor, we can have confidence that every trial, every struggle, has a particular purpose to produce in us some eternal value.

4. *Outward pain helps us accelerate inward progress.* "Therefore we do not lose heart. Even though our outward man is perishing, yet the inward man is being renewed day by day" (2 Corinthians 4:16). Isn't it exciting that modern-day science is only now beginning to affirm what the Bible has said all along? There is a close relationship between body, mind, and soul. This is why you've met people with physical challenges who have extra layers of wisdom that few others have attained. Bodily suffering drives us deeper. We find God at the broken places, teaching and encouraging.

John Newton wrote, "We will look back upon the experiences through which the Lord led us and be overwhelmed by adoration and love for Him! We will then see and acknowledge that mercy and goodness directed every step. We shall see that what we once mistakenly called afflictions and misfortune were in reality blessings without which we would not have grown in faith."[4]

We can't wish away our problems, and we're unlikely to put on a fake smile and pretend we're enjoying them. What we can do is meet them squarely and soberly, refusing to view them as random shots from an unkind world. Instead, we know they are necessary challenges for the positive growth we're intent on experiencing. Who wants to remain a child forever? We know we need a good workout. We know it's necessary to build our spiritual muscles. There are no muscles of any kind that strengthen without resistance.

When you're at the gym, sometimes you can get through a grueling cycle on some machine by thinking about the muscles that machine is helping. I suggest you do that very thing during times of struggle. Where can you "feel the burn"? What part of your character is going to be that much more godly tomorrow? My friend, perspective will completely change the way you approach challenges.

In one of his books, my friend Ron Mehl wrote these words: "Storms always leave us with a list of things to clean up and fix. They are times when God restores to us the things we lose through negligence, ignorance, rebellion, or sin. For the Christian, storms are a no-lose proposition. They help me to see and acknowledge the loose shutters, missing shingles, and rotten fence posts in my life while turning me back to the only One who can make the necessary repairs."[5]

The Grace of God Promotes Perseverance

We are hard-pressed on every side, yet not crushed; we are perplexed,
but not in despair; persecuted, but not forsaken; struck down, but not destroyed.
—2 CORINTHIANS 4:8–9

In 2 Corinthians 6:4–5, Paul lists his personal struggles as tribulations, needs, distresses, stripes, imprisonments, tumults, labors, sleeplessness, and fastings. Remember his authority was under attack at this church. Consider the fact that he chooses his *problems* as his credentials. Can you imagine a pastor offering such problems to a church as his résumé today? Paul would suggest sleeplessness and prison time as two of the reasons he would make a good pastor. And of course he would be right.

Notice also the four "gauges" Paul uses to demonstrate the difference the grace of God has made in his life (and will make in yours). Each of these gauges takes some particular measure of the emotional state. Imagine the first gauge. At one end of the gauge is the word Victorious, at the other end, Defeated. Because of grace, the needle keeps hovering near the victorious end of the meter, and that means that in spite of the pressure, you can keep going. The second gauge shows Confident and Despairing as the extremes, and, while we may often be more perplexed than confident, because of grace, we are never despairing. No need to slow down.

These gauges are the difference in an empty fuel tank and one that is simply low. Grace makes that difference: you proceed with caution, but you're not out of gas on the side of the road. Here are the four gauges:

1. *He was pressured, but not defeated.* Paul is saying he feels the pinch, but he isn't crushed. The term means being pushed into a narrow place. Paul was a man who spent time in some very small prison cells. As you know if you've read his prison letters, his joy could not be compacted by lack of space; it only became greater. Grace moved that needle.

2. *He was perplexed, but not despairing.* Church problems left Paul at his wit's end sometimes. But he never gave up, and he always found the right answer. Grace kept him moving toward the right solution.

3. *He was persecuted, but not deserted.* The word for "persecuted" derives from the idea of being pursued or chased. As we've seen, Paul knew something about that kind of hunting, and he also knew about being hunted. Even when it seemed that his enemies vastly outnumbered his friends, he never felt deserted, because Almighty God was always with him with sufficient grace for his every need.

4. *He was pounded, but not destroyed.* The verb here means "to be struck down." Paul was often knocked down but he was never knocked out. He was sometimes left for dead, but he did not die. He kept getting back up to preach the Gospel of God's grace. When he was in prison, his work seemed to flourish. To the very end of his life, he was planning on new destinations and new churches. The kind of hope Paul had cannot be suppressed no matter how you pound it. Grace renders it eternal.

The Grace of God Promotes Praise

Sometimes we can gather hidden jewels simply by taking a closer look at Paul's sentence structure.

For example, notice the three phrases in these passages that begin with the word *that.* It may seem to you like an insignificant word, but Paul actually uses it as a bridge from human action to godly destiny. *That* means "in order to" or "so that."

Here are the three statements:

2 Corinthians 4:7	*"that the excellence of the power may be of God and not of us"*
2 Corinthians 4:11	*"that the life of Jesus also may be manifested in our mortal flesh"*
2 Corinthians 12:9	*"that the power of Christ may rest upon me"*

Reading them together, we see a pattern emerge.
We do what we do:
• that *God's power* will be present in us.
• that *Jesus' life* may be manifest in us.
• that *Christ's power* may rest upon us.

Again, Paul is pointing us to a bridge that Christ has built. On this side of the river, you experience dangers, toils, and snares. It's so easy to be discouraged and to develop a negative and cynical attitude. Then our friend Paul beckons to us. He points to these bridges that seem to disappear into the fog that lies upon the river. We decide to cross those bridges, because things can't be any worse than they are on this side. On the other side, we find the limitless power of God and the rejuvenating life of Christ.

But what precisely are those bridges? They are *attitudes* about our lives and our trials. The attitudes of the world lead to a dead end. The attitude on these bridges takes us to a whole new world. We realize that there is a purpose to our pain. God is up to something, and it's always something very good, something worth cherishing hope for. We begin to trust, putting our eyes on Him rather than on our struggles. And having done that, we find ourselves walking— first one tentative step, then another. We hear the echo of our footsteps beneath the bridge. We move into that mist. And then we begin to make out the shapes that lie on the other side: shapes of maturity, of wisdom, of new strength and new service for God.

Before we know it, we're not thinking of our infirmities at all.

John Newton lost his wife on this side of the bridge. This was surely the ultimate test of his faith, for he had an abiding love for her after many years of marriage. Having been married for twenty-two years, he wrote her a letter that said, "Every room where you are not present looks unfurnished."[6]

But one day he began to face the prospect of living out his life in unfurnished rooms. He had hoped, with all of his heart, that he would precede his wife to the grave. But now it was clear that his beloved Mary was becoming weaker every day. Newton's friends worried about him; they couldn't imagine how he would handle life without Mary by his side.

The Christian should be "hard-pressed, yet not crushed; perplexed, but not in despair." Would Newton have that demanding level of spiritual maturity?

On the day of Mary's death, John Newton preached at the regular service time. The next day he visited parishioners, and finally he preached the sermon at her funeral. Did he grieve? Of course he did—powerfully. He would later write, "The Bank of England is too poor to compensate for such a loss as mine. But the Lord, the all-sufficient God, speaks, and it is done. Let those who know Him, and trust Him, be of good courage. He can give them strength according to their day. He can increase their strength as their trials increase . . . and what He can do He has promised that He will do."[7]

John Newton had tried that bridge and found it would bear his weight. As a matter of fact, the grace of God has limitless strength. Every single one of us can trust our very lives to it. It has never failed, and it never will.

His grace is sufficient, no matter what you may be facing right now. His grace will lead us through every trial imaginable, until we begin to look upon one another and see not ourselves but the image of Christ himself, our hope, our refuge, and our goal. On that day, you and I will look back upon these earthly anxieties with hearts of loving gratitude. Troubles are very real, but in the light of His shadow, they somehow fade into the mist.

Moments *of* Grace

Look back over the lists you made of your own dangers, toils, and snares. Are you beat up or upbeat? Are you drawing on His storehouse of grace?

Your daily interaction with God's Word is a barometer of your capacity to access God's grace for each day's needs. Glance at your Bible for a moment. Does it show the wear and tear of heavy use, or does it appear to have just come out of the box? Are its verses underlined and well marked? Have you claimed specific promises for specific needs? What individual verses are you leaning on right now?

If you need to do better in this area and aren't sure where to turn, try reading through 2 Corinthians, the book in which Paul talks openly about his own struggles. This book contains many "victory verses." Find one or two, draw boxes around them in your Bible, and use them in claiming God's all-sufficient grace for your situation right now.

CHAPTER EIGHT

The Confident Promise of Grace

'Tis Grace Hath Brought Me Safe Thus Far,
and Grace Will Lead Me Home

There are times when we feel we've wrestled life into a shape that feels comfortable. We hope the time has come to reap some enjoyment from the daily pace. Life makes sense, and we feel a quiet sense of satisfaction.

In these times, we begin to savor those patterns of life that help us navigate the passage of time: the familiar arrival of the seasons, the rhythms of honest work and daily life, the subtle transitions of aging.

Then, like a thief in the night, some uninvited event breaks into our lives. In the flicker of a moment, the work of years comes undone. The dependable pattern is destroyed, and life as we know it seems to be threatened. Suddenly the world doesn't seem so orderly and natural but random and even heartless.

John Newton may have harbored a few of these reflections during the mid-1750s, when his own life was torn by crisis.

Everything had been going so well, right up to that afternoon in November 1754. On that day he was sitting at tea with his wife, enjoying the warmth of the drink and the fire in the hearth, chasing away the autumn chill. His mind happily moved among all the last-minute details of preparing for a new adventure at sea. In only two days, he would be the captain, piloting a brand-new ship on its maiden voyage—the *Bee*.

Seafaring men enjoy the anticipation of that next journey: assembling the crew, taking inventory, dipping pen in ink to inscribe that first entry in the ship's log. Surely Newton's mind was as busy as the bee that was his craft's namesake.

And then, just like that, his body toppled unconscious to the floor.

Mary screamed in panic. Her husband had passed out without warning. Only the regularity of his breathing showed any evidence of life. After that, he slowly woke to a terrible headache that would not depart, as well as a dizziness that would never do for a ship's captain. He was left no choice but to resign from the only career he knew. John Newton would never sail again.

His heart was broken as he followed the news of another man's appointment as captain of the *Bee*. As the ship vanished over the horizon, Newton felt he was watching his life's work fade with it. He could only settle into his own recuperation period and begin thinking about what to do with the rest of his life.

It wasn't long before more news arrived concerning the *Bee*. There had been a revolt onboard. The slaves had seized control, killing Newton's replacement, along with two other men.

What thoughts went through the retired captain's mind? *It could have been me. There but for the grace of God go I . . .*

Imagine yourself escaping death only through a strange and

sudden illness at the last moment. What would be your thoughts? How might it affect your outlook?

On the one hand, you'd surely be grateful that God had intervened to spare you. On the other, you might ask, "Lord, what plans do You have for me now? Sailing is all I know."

But more calamity was yet to come. Just as Newton was recovering from his attack, his wife fell into an illness of her own. For eleven months he cared for her, praying that God would not take her away—that in His providence He would spare the wife as He had spared the husband.

Doctors had to be paid. The cupboard had to be stocked. While Mary was still ill, Newton accepted a position as a tide surveyor in distant Liverpool. It was a good job, but one that required sacrifice. He had to leave his beloved Mary behind, in the care of others. At this point her survival was in question; the doctors had done all they could do. How agonizing to try learning the skills of a new trade while wondering if his soul mate still clung to life—or whether he would ever see her again.

God is good. Newton wept for joy and thanksgiving when the Lord healed his wife at the very threshold of death's door. It was a miracle! Now the couple could be together again. As they sat again by the fire, they puzzled over the mysteries of providence. Why had God called home another captain, yet, with the other hand, taken away Newton's career? Why had He so nearly called Mary home, only to relent at the last fateful instant?

It was a question of those patterns.

Viewed from one direction, it appeared that the pleasant patterns of life had been torn apart. Then one could turn the picture around and perceive there were other patterns at work—deeper ones, the complex workings of almighty God. His intervening hand was unmistakable. John and Mary agreed that the Lord worked in mysterious ways, His wonders to perform. He had His own timetables and His own purposes that formed an intricate web that no mortal could disentangle in this life.

The patterns of God were more mysterious than the depths of uncharted seas, yet His grace was clear as the driven snow. That grace was no mystery. It was absolute, all encompassing, as vast as the sky on a starry night above deck.

The conclusion of the matter was that life was strange, but God was good. John and Mary Newton must give Him their trust and harbor no anxieties about it. When Someone loves you, you count on Him.

THE FOUNDATION STONE OF ROMANS 8:28

Newton's mind returned again and again to grapple with that profound sentence at the heart of the book of Romans, at the heart of God's Word, at the heart of God's character and every single person's life. Romans 8:28 is the foundation stone of the very workings of your destiny and mine. It is probably the most well-known line the apostle ever wrote—surely one of the most oft-quoted and memorized. Christians cling to it during the tempests of their lives like a wooden beam adrift in the sea.

Here it is, perhaps as familiar as your house address: "And we know that all things work together for good to those who love God, to those who are the called according to His purpose" (Romans 8:28).

John MacArthur describes Romans 8:28 as "breathtaking in its magnitude, encompassing absolutely everything that pertains to a believer's life."[1]

John Phillips observes that "like the cogs in an intricate piece of machinery, all things work together for good to the called of God for the simple reason that God's purposes cannot be thwarted."[2]

Maybe these patterns are like the cogs of a machine. But they're much more like a tremendous rock beneath your feet. When all the earth seems to tremble, and when nothing seems secure anymore, you can stand boldly on this rock, for no fault lines can dislodge it. No tremor can unsettle it. No, for this rock is set like a fine jewel within the shorelines of eternity, so that it is the tool of neither time nor space but only of the loving hand of God.

Let's explore five incredible truths from this awesome verse.

Romans 8:28 Is a Certain Promise

And we know . . .

Five times in the book of Romans, Paul will stand upon the assurance of *we know*. The apostle is really saying, "everyone knows" or, at least, "Christians know." It's a matter of common knowledge, a fact upon which everyone agrees.

Paul is not speculating that perhaps God is in control. He is reminding us that we know this for a certainty. Donald Barnhouse points out that "we know" may be the most excellent part of the verse. Finding out after the fact that everything was in the firm hand of God—well, that would be a wonderful thing. But God gives us that assurance *right now*. "To lay hold of that fact is to calm the turbulence of life and to bring quiet and confidence into the whole of life. Nothing can touch me unless it passes through the will of God."[3]

It is as if we are all characters in a suspense novel, when suddenly the apostle Paul sneaks in to whisper a word from the author. "The Novelist came up with an amazingly intricate plot," he says. "Everything comes out all right, though it gets a bit hairy for you in some of the chapters. When it all washes out, you're going to live happily ever after, and the villain will be punished."

It's a nice feeling to operate with inside information. Now all we have to do is get on with our scenes in the novel and a sly smile on our faces—a smile that says *we know.*

We know! But what *don't* we know?

"We do not know what we should pray for as we ought, but the Spirit Himself makes intercession for us with groanings which cannot be uttered" (Romans 8:26).

Can you see the pattern of verses 26–28? Paul is telling us there are things we can know, and things we cannot.

We can feel very good about the big picture (v. 28), but the little details are a mystery, for we don't know exactly what to pray for (v. 26). One of the greatest ironies of the Christian life is that we often have certainty about the ultimate and uncertainty about the immediate.

The truth is this: God is saying, "I want you to know right now that all of history, including the portion constituting your life, is completely under My control. No matter how things may appear, every little detail is part of a very beautiful picture. But I'm leaving those details as challenges of faith to prepare you for the world we will share one day. You must trust Me in those smaller things, knowing that the larger things are all established."

As we explore the many implications of this verse, let's say a word here about what it *does not* say:

- It does not say that everything will work out the way you'd like, if you'll only wait.
- It does not say that you can make things work out through positive thinking.
- It does not say that there's no point in what we do, because God pulls all the strings.

It *does* say that God is in control, but that He will intervene in this world to use every event as part of His comprehensive plan—His plan, but your ultimate good. He is working all the time, in all events, for the good of all believers: "For I am God, and there is no other; I am God, and there is none like Me, declaring the end from the beginning, and from ancient times things that are not yet done, saying, 'My counsel shall stand, and I will do all My pleasure.' . . . Indeed, I have spoken it; I will also bring it to pass. I have purposed it; I will also do it" (Isaiah 46:9–11).

Romans 8:28 Is a Comprehensive Promise

That all things . . .

Your Bible might translate these words as "all things" or "everything." Just as we discovered that "you know" is a blockbuster of a fact carried in only two words, the same thing happens here.

All things is our assurance that there are no limits. The offer is comprehensive and unconditional. No fine print. All sales are final. Or as we might say to the skeptic, "What part of 'all things' do you not understand?"

Please don't suspect Paul of being a cockeyed optimist, only considering the things in life that are already favorable. In this letter, as well as others, he discusses his many trials. In 2 Corinthians, as we saw in the last chapter, he offered an entire résumé of hard knocks. These were presented as his credentials for ministry. As recently as Romans 8:17, Paul has spoken of his "sufferings." We also hear of "groanings" in verse 23. But these miseries, too, are all part of that great plan that God is carrying out. Negative events have positive purposes.

But is Paul saying, "It's all good"? Is he claiming there's no such thing as evil, because of the final results?

Not at all. The death of a loved one is never a good thing, and the Spirit of God weeps beside us at the funeral. The terrible day you had yesterday is simply a terrible day. It felt bad; it *was* bad. The Romans 8:28 difference is that these are bad things that God *uses*. They are pieces of a great jigsaw puzzle that are ugly when considered on their own; but in the final picture, they will play a part that brings glory to God and works for the good of the believer.

Bad things, then, remain bad. But God remains good, and He is the Lord of those bad things. He is fully capable of using them in ways that will shine with a beauty we will see one day, either in this life or the next.

Paul uses the phrase *all things* several times in his letters. In each case, we come to understand that we serve a God of all things. There is nothing before us, nothing within us or outside us, nothing we can even imagine that is not His thing and usable within His plan.

We do well to look out upon this world from time to time and remind ourselves that we serve a sovereign God. He is the Lord of *all*. Everything in creation is no more, no less than the work of His hand. We have His promise "that in the dispensation of the fullness of the times He might gather together in one *all things* in Christ, both which are in heaven and which are on earth—in Him" (Ephesians 1:10, emphasis added).

Romans 8:28 Is a Complex Promise

. . . work together . . .

Paul looks out upon this shifting, changing, complex world and tells us that all things are working together.

This expression uses the Greek word *sunergeo*, from which we get our English word *synergism*: the working together of various elements to produce an effect greater than, and often completely different from, the sum of each element acting separately.

In the physical world, the right combination of otherwise harmful chemicals can produce substances that are of wonderfully positive use to us. For example, ordinary table salt is composed of two poisons: sodium and chlorine. Synergistically speaking, the final product is *much* better than the sum of its parts.

In the divine synergism, God mixes bitter herbs and spices with other tastier ingredients to create the perfect soup. Or, as Annie Johnson Flint has expressed it so beautifully in verse:

In a factory building there are wheels and gearings,
There are cranks and pulleys, beltings tight or slack—
Some are whirling swiftly, some are turning slowly,
Some are thrusting forward, some are pulling back;
Some are smooth and silent, some are rough and noisy,
Pounding, rattling, clanking, moving with a jerk;
In a wild confusion, in a seeming chaos,
Lifting, pushing, driving—but they do their work.
From the mightiest lever to the tiniest pinion,
All things move together for the purpose planned;
And behind the working is a mind controlling,
And a force directing, and a guiding hand.
So all things are working for the Lord's beloved;
Some things might be hurtful if alone they stood;
Some might seem to hinder; some might draw us backward;
But they work together, and they work for good,
All the thwarted longings, all the stern denials,
All the contradictions, hard to understand.

And the force that holds them, speeds them and retards them,
Stops and starts and guides them—is our Father's hand.[4]

Is our universe simply a finely tuned machine, and are we no better than its minor nuts and bolts? No, that is a gross, if common,
misunderstanding of the beautiful doctrine of God's providence. We
already know the beauty of the "machine" God has created: the rising and setting of the sun, the four seasons, the times of life. We
observe the way we interact with one another as people—in marriage, in parenting, in friendship. All of these are the subtle workings
of God's instrumentation. But the most beautiful part of all is that,
unlike the machines we ourselves construct, this one has parts that
act as free agents. The greatness of God is that He gives us freedom
even within the delicate movements of a universe preset to accomplish His final purposes.

Romans 8:28 Is a Comforting Promise

. . . for good . . .

It's a wonderful thing to turn through the pages of our Bible and simply enjoy the promises that fill its pages. Throughout the Scriptures,
God is telling us of all the good things He desires to give us, simply
because He loves us so devotedly. The promises of God are good,
because *He* is good—infinitely good. "Every good gift and every perfect gift is from above, and comes down from the Father of lights,
with whom there is no variation or shadow of turning" (James 1:17).

When it comes to "good things," you and I see before us an
embarrassment of riches. Try this experiment. Tomorrow morning,
when you rise, take a pen and a small notepad in hand. As you move
along, jot down every good thing in your life, whether it is some

event or some thought or just something you see. If you need to get to work, I predict you'll never even get out of the house—you'll be too busy writing. God has loaded down your life and mine with the goodness of family, security, necessities, friends, interests, a beautiful world, and—well, if we start the list here, we'll never make it out of this chapter. See what I mean?

If you were to try that experiment, I think you would be forced to abandon it rather quickly. The thoughts would begin to come more and more quickly as you turned your heart in gratitude toward the Giver of these gifts. There is only one Giver, of course. It all comes from Him.

The problem is that we are so burdened with good gifts that when anything at all comes our way that isn't pleasant—so much as a traffic delay or a trip to the dentist—we throw our arms toward the sky and ask, "Why me?"

I'm not certain I've ever seen someone receive wonderful news— a job promotion or an accepted marriage proposal—and say, "Why me?" We take all these good gifts right in stride, as if we fully deserve them. Ask yourself these painful questions: Given the way we live our lives and the extent of our obedience to God, how many of these good things are we really earning? How many of the bad things are really unfair?

The point is not to feel guilty about our unworthiness. This is a book about grace! God has found a way to bless us despite our unworthiness. No, the point is that as much as God has showered us with good things, shouldn't we trust Him with the ones that seem questionable? If your dearest human friend always does nice things for you, you trust that person. How much greater trust does God deserve when He promises us that all things will eventually find their place in the machinery that brings forth what is best for us as we draw nearer and nearer to heaven?

There is also great encouragement in realizing that nothing is wasted. That's the testimony of this verse. God creates no waste, and He allows no waste. My friend Rob Suggs struggled through two disappointing careers before he found his calling as a writer at midlife. He knew that finally he was doing exactly what God had wanted him to do, but he felt deep regret that he hadn't found that path sooner. One day he was explaining his feelings to a friend. "All those years there was a Christian publishing company two miles from my house," he said. "I could have been working there for years, honing my skills, learning to do more for God. If only I had those years back—my twenties and my thirties."

His wise friend replied, "Don't you think that if God were in a hurry, He could have directed you two miles down the road several years earlier? The Lord had His timetable. He was using all your experiences, good and bad. Without them, you wouldn't be precisely the writer that you have become along your path."

And it's true. I have known many people who looked back upon their lives with regret. It brightens our hearts to know that God uses every last iota of every experience to move us toward the goal He has in mind.

And that goal is a good one. We can trust Him on that.

Romans 8:28 Is a Conditional Promise

> *. . . to those who love God to those who are the called according to His purpose.*

So what have we learned from Romans 8:28?

We know. We have inside knowledge.

All things. Everything, no exceptions.

Work together. It's all part of one perfect plan.

For good. We absolutely cannot lose.

This is one of the most *absolute* verses in all of Scripture. We absolutely know that absolutely all things work absolutely together for absolute good. It's absolutely wonderful! But now comes the part that is *not* absolute.

This promise does not apply to absolutely everyone. This is a highly significant consideration: the Romans 8:28 difference works exclusively for those who love God and are called for His purposes.

There are promises in Scripture that are unconditional, and some that have conditions. John 3:16, for example, holds one of each. "God so loved the world." That is an unconditional promise. He loves every single one of the children He created. We need to do nothing at all for Him to love us. "Whoever believes in Him should not perish but have everlasting life." That part is conditional. We will receive eternal life *if* we believe in Him.

His love, then, is unconditional. His gift of salvation has the one condition that we must believe.

In the same way, the promise of Romans 8:28 turns upon a condition. If we love God, then this wonderful, absolute principle takes effect for our lives. If we reject God, the events of life add up to a different conclusion altogether.

But you may have noticed there is an additional qualifier that describes those for whom this promise applies. It is for:

• Those who love God.
• Those who are the called according to His purpose.

Why does Paul set out that distinction? Aren't they the same people? Yes. Paul is describing the recipients of this blessing from two perspectives. The human angle is "those who love God." The divine angle is "those who are the called according to His purpose."

"Those who love God" are the ones who have chosen to identify with Him in this world. Paul shares another beautiful promise about those people: "Eye has not seen, nor ear heard, nor have entered into the heart of man the things which God has prepared for those who love Him" (1 Corinthians 2:9). We cannot imagine the wonderful gifts God has prepared for us. James 1:12 also tells us that God has prepared a "crown of life" to those who love Him.

"Those who are the called" are the same people, seen from God's perspective. There is a reminder here for us that, as wonderful as God's gifts are, we don't simply sit back in a recliner to selfishly enjoy them. In the instant of salvation, we receive our marching orders. We are on the move as we do our enjoying. We are called and appointed according to His purpose. He has work for us to do, and we are to be doing it all the days of our lives.

So Romans 8:28, like John 3:16, ends with a sobering reminder. There is one small item that qualifies us for the treasure that is described. We must believe in Him. We must love Him and receive His call.

The Romans 8:28 promise doesn't apply universally. But we should look at it this way: God himself excludes no one from receiving the benefits of any of His promises. It is people who tragically exclude themselves by failing to do the most natural thing in the world: to believe in and love the Lord, who is the source of every good thing. I can't imagine that any reasonable, clear-sighted person could help but love the God that you and I know, for to know Him is to love Him.

Therefore it's up to you and me to help those people know Him the way we do.

We know that God is good. We know He is working in this world. We know He is using all things for His purposes and for our good. And we know that someday we will stand beside His throne and see all of this world's events, and all the moments of our lives, from outside of time. We will see our birth, our death, and everything that came in between them as if it existed in one comprehensive mural. In that moment, all of the pieces of the puzzle will be seen in their true places and true functions. We'll know exactly what God had in mind and why He allowed the worst moments of our lives.

At that time, having been released once and for all from the blindness of self-absorption, we'll be able to look beyond ourselves. I think you and I will marvel at the interconnectedness of one human life to another, so that for the first time we'll be able to perceive how God affected us through other people, and how He used us in the lives of others.

We'll see that many things in this world were truly evil. We will have experienced a great deal of it ourselves. We will understand that He was never once the author of evil. But when we stand beside Him and look back at this world, seeing just how delicately and how wisely He put those evil elements to His own purpose—we will have no recourse but to fall on our knees and sing praises to Him.

We know this. We expect this. But what about now? Can we allow ourselves to be such total captives of His grace that we trust Him completely with life's most terrible moments?

Helen Roseveare was a British medical missionary in the Congo. She stayed at her post during some of the worst turmoil in the country's history in 1964. Many Westerners fled, but Helen believed she should be willing to make any sacrifice for a Savior who had made the ultimate sacrifice for her.

Someone tried to poison her, but her dog ate the food and the attempt failed. Still she stayed on. Female missionaries and medical personnel were often raped by rebel armies, but still she stayed on. Even when her house was looted of every item within it, she refused to leave her post.

It's not as if Helen had no fear. She rarely slept well, knowing that at any moment someone could enter her home and take her life. But she concentrated on learning to trust God more absolutely.

On Saturday, August 15, 1964, a truckload of soldiers comman-
deered her hospital. Helen would later recall, "They were brutal and
coarse, rough and domineering. Their language was threatening and
obscene. All of us were cowed. We did exactly what they demanded,
mostly without argument." They caught the local chief, flayed him
alive, and ate him.[5]

Eventually, Helen Roseveare was beaten, raped, and humiliated.
Barely alive, she finally had to be taken from the country. During her
long and painful days of recovery, she found herself closer to God
than she had ever been before. She even loved the Congo more
deeply than ever. There was no bitterness within her, though Helen
had experienced terrible, mindless evil. It would have been so easy to
demand of God why He allowed these atrocities, when she had been
so faithful to His service. But in her heart of hearts, she felt that
God's question would be, "Can you thank Me for trusting you with
this experience, even if I never tell you why?"[6]

That question penetrates to the depth of our commitment to
Christ. Yes, *we know* God is working all things for our good. Sometimes in this life we have the rare privilege of seeing just how God
used this setback or that disappointment. We can feel the wisdom
and strength that came through the basic trials of normal living. But
can we trust Him even when we don't know the answers?

Paul sat in a prison cell and prayed fervently, hour after hour.
There was so much work to be done. He had planted his share of
churches, but most cities had still never heard the Gospel. He longed
to go to Spain; surely it was God who placed that burden within his
soul. And he needed to be with his brothers and sisters in the
churches that were struggling. He loved them so deeply, and he
longed to minister to them.

Yet God, who had shown He could easily crumble prison walls,
would not effect Paul's release. Time was running out. Eventually

he knew he would be executed. Surely God would rather have him on the front lines of the mission field, sharing the Gospel, rather than awaiting execution. Paul longed for freedom, but he simply trusted God.

John and Mary Newton longed for a family. For years they waited, trying to be patient, trying to conceive a child. Finally, after they had been married twenty-four years, the Lord sent them Elizabeth and Eliza in a very touching way. Mary Newton had lost a sister and a brother to tuberculosis, a deadly disease in that era. Each left behind one young daughter, and these became John and Mary Newton's adopted children.

Eliza, who was twelve when she joined the family, was often ill. The summer before her fifteenth birthday, Mary took her to Southampton, where the ocean air was thought to be healthier. Her husband wrote an encouraging letter, comparing the Southampton waters to the Pool of Bethesda in the Gospels. Maybe the Lord would work a healing miracle in Eliza's life.

But six weeks brought no improvement. Three weeks after returning to London with her mother, Eliza was dead.

Her grieving adoptive father prepared a little memorial book for the girl he had awaited for so long. In it he wrote: "If we know and trust Him . . . He chooses better for us than we can for ourselves . . . but now I can praise and adore Him for . . . His plan. I not only can bow . . . to His sovereignty, but I admire His wisdom and goodness, and can say from my heart, He has done all things well."[7]

Can you say that about your walk with God? Can you praise and adore Him even when your heart is breaking and you feel overwhelmed by disappointment? It could be that you're struggling with some trial at this very moment. If you can place your trust totally in His love and His promise to work all things for your good, then you will have taken a step toward embracing the mysteries of His grace.

You will bear a slightly closer resemblance to the Savior who gave His life to save you.

Then God will look upon your life, smile, and say, "Yes, My child. How you've grown since you first came to know Me! You're becoming wiser and stronger every day. There was a time when you could rejoice only when the sun was shining. But now your soul is taking on real substance. Now you are becoming sturdy and strong. I have trusted you with this burden, and you have honored Me through the stubbornness of your faith.

"Though your eyes are presently filled with tears, My child, and though your shoulders sag with unhappiness, I want you to know something. I want you to be assured that our adventure together is only beginning. Trials remain for you to face, but behind each one rests a greater glory. Beyond each obstacle there lies a greater joy. And all along the way, I have paved your road with blessings to remind you of the inheritance that is yours as My child. Walk on, now, in the joy that will not be slowed even by sadness. Walk on toward the crown of glory that has your name on it.

"Walk on, My child. And let us walk together."

Moments of Grace

Romans 8:28 is breathtaking in its magnitude and encompasses absolutely everything that could possibly happen to us. Every life event is turned inside out as part of God's comprehensive plan for the ultimate good of those who love Him. Even our sins, mistakes, and missteps. As a result of the total sweep of this promise, our hearts should be light as feathers and our joy should be boundless, grounded by faith in that all-pervasive promise.

If you've had a drooping attitude, try smiling right now—a big, face-wide grin. Tell your heart to cheer up. Command your emotions to soar to new, joyful levels. Take control of your feelings, and rejoice in Christ. Take it as a given that your current set of burdens will work out for good. Remember that discouragement is always from the devil, and make a choice to rejoice in the Lord "always"— and "always" means today!

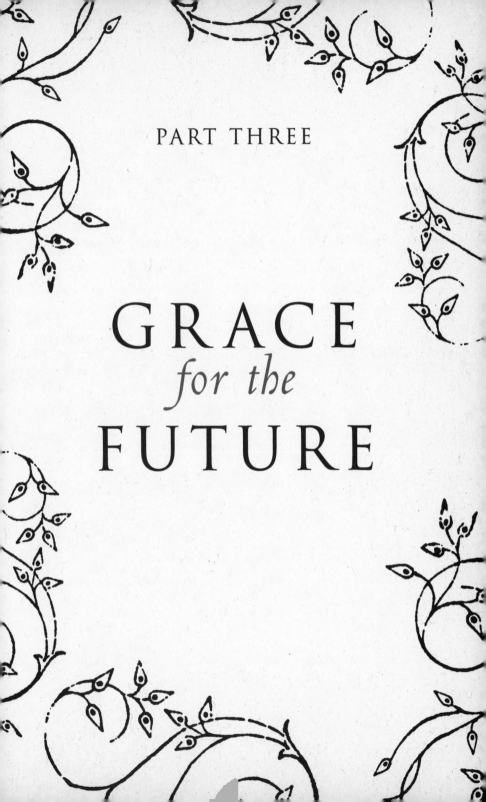

PART THREE

GRACE
for the
FUTURE

CHAPTER NINE

The Compelling Prospect of Grace

*When We've Been There Ten Thousand Years,
Bright Shining As the Sun*

John Newton had no problem with the idea of death. But retirement? He was opposed to the very thought of such a thing.

After all, who were these younger men who were coming around now, patting him on the shoulder as if he were an ancient relic? Bringing their not-so-subtle hints about slowing down, preaching more infrequently, allowing others to help him with his pastoral calls—why, he was at the height of his fruitfulness in the Gospel ministry. The Lord had lavished upon his heart a zeal that was still overflowing. Retire? He declined to entertain any consideration of the matter.

Even a dear old friend like Richard Cecil was working on him. It was Cecil's opinion that Newton should give up the pulpit entirely. "John, old boy," he said with a quiet voice and the usual pat on the shoulder. "Your sight is failing. Your hearing is nearly gone. I know you think you can be brave and cover it all up, but we are your friends. We have your best interests at heart. All things have their times and seasons under the sun, my friend—even old sea dogs in holy vestments. What will it take to slow you down? The Lord God sending Elijah to gather you up in His golden chariot?"

To which Newton could only snort with disdain and a raised voice, "What! Shall the old African blasphemer stop while he can speak?" And who would dare to answer that one?

Retirement—bah!

On the other hand, *death*: now, there was a subject worth talking about. Newton's letters and diary entries looked more and more to the hope of paradise that lay just over the horizon of his lifelong voyage. "The day of opportunity wears away, and the night is approaching," he wrote in 1802. Two years later, after signing a letter, he added: "Time, how short! Eternity, how long."[1]

His friends noticed in him a growing tendency toward morbid humor. He told one colleague that he was "packed, sealed, and waiting for the post."

While John Newton still possessed life and breath, however, he tended to his beloved sermons and hymns—"Amazing Grace" among the latter. Its final verse, as we've seen, would be filled in much later by another hand. But Newton did supply three verses we seldom use, and these provide a fine commentary on our present closing verse. They also demonstrate the extent to which Newton was eager for the comforts of the next world, even as a ship's captain watches anxiously for the farther shore through his spyglass:

The Lord has promised good to me,
His word my hope secures;
He will my shield and portion be,
As long as life endures.

Yes, when this flesh and heart shall fail,
And mortal life shall cease,
I shall possess, within the veil,
A life of joy and peace.

The earth shall soon dissolve like snow,
The sun forbear to shine;
But God, who call'd me here below,
Will be forever mine.

John Newton understood that life was, after all, a voyage from a familiar port to one unknown. He would no more dread the next world than he would resist steering his ship into the harbor toward which it was chartered.

When Newton finally passed on, he was given a Christian burial and a fitting epitaph upon the stone that marked his grave. But his loved ones might well have used the words of Paul to describe the life of John Newton: "For the grace of God that brings salvation has appeared to all men, teaching us that, denying ungodliness and worldly lusts, we should live soberly, righteously, and godly in the present age, looking for the blessed hope and glorious appearing of our great God and Savior Jesus Christ, who gave Himself for us, that He might redeem us from every lawless deed and purify for Himself His own special people, zealous for good works" (Titus 2:11–14).

It's uncertain whether Newton ever preached from this passage, but he surely cherished this thorough description of the work of God's grace. These verses demonstrate how that grace is with us in the past, the present, and the future:

• It has appeared to all men.
• It appears now for teaching.
• It will appear again in the return of Christ.

John Newton and Paul the apostle were both captured by the timelessness of that grace. Neither ever lost sight of how Christ had intercepted their self-destructive courses in the past. Both men found His redemptive grace in every aspect of their present, and both men actively awaited a future in which the grace of the Lord would find its final and ultimate culmination.

Paul might have spoken for both men when he wrote, "By the grace of God I am what I am, and His grace toward me was not in vain" (1 Corinthians 15:10). Grace was no isolated theme; it was the whole story. These men understood themselves completely through the lens of God's redemptive grace.

Grace Teaches Us

Paul explains to Titus that the grace of God has *appeared.* The Greek word translated "appeared" gives us our modern word *epiphany*—a wonderful word. We use it in a secular way to describe a sudden and intense realization of truth. An epiphany is that proverbial light bulb appearing over your head, but lit by solar power!

When the Greeks spoke of an epiphany, they were referring to the breathtaking view of sunlight bursting in power over the edge of the world to illuminate the darkened earth. The grace of God, Paul tells us, has suddenly brought light to our world after thousands of years of darkness. It explodes upon the world with awesome power, providing humanity with an intense realization of the nature of God.

In several other passages (particularly in the three pastoral epistles, 1 and 2 Timothy and Titus), Paul returns to this idea of the bright epiphany of our Savior. A lovely comparison: before the rising sun or the risen Son, we are humbled and grateful. Both are miracles completely outside our control; our physical and spiritual survival, respectively, depend upon them. God's grace is His gift to a helpless and dying planet.

That "epiphany," for Paul, is the birth of Christ in Bethlehem. There is ultimate grace in God appearing in flesh among the poor. There is breathtaking grace in God becoming a helpless child, entering the world in a cattle shed with shepherds to greet His coming. From there, every aspect of the life of Jesus communicates grace: Jesus healing the sick; Jesus befriending sinners; Jesus teaching love and forgiveness, rather than playing on the public's anger and rebellion against Roman authority. Finally Jesus submits to a shameful death and forgives His very executioners from the cross. But the best is yet to come. In the Resurrection, we find the culmination of the gift of grace—victory over death is God's ultimate gift of grace to His undeserving children.

In Christ, the grace of God is made manifest. If love is the attribute that describes God the best, grace is the one that makes that love obtainable for us. Grace is the most radical concept ever to be introduced into this world. It is counterintuitive to human nature, challenging every human tendency and providing the solution for every human problem.

Grace changes people as nothing else can do. It cleanses the sins of the past. It enables righteousness in the present. And one thing it does for certain: it constantly surprises us. For the essence of grace is surprise. There is nothing shocking about giving people exactly what they deserve. Grace subverts the rules and gives people what they *don't* deserve. It is motivated by the warmth of love rather than by cold calculation. Therefore, grace is always doing something we didn't expect.

For example, what does grace do in the present? It walks to the blackboard and begins to teach: "For the grace of God that brings salvation has appeared to all men, teaching us" (Titus 2:11–12).

Paul tells us that the grace of God appears to all men and then instantly begins the lesson. After all, we find ourselves living here in the present. We look backward at the first appearance of grace, when Christ was born in Bethlehem in the darkness of a sinful world; we look forward to the glorious appearing of Christ at the end of time, when we will be made perfect. But what about now? We need to know how to live in the interim. Grace, through the power and guidance of the Holy Spirit, is here to help us live. It therefore clears its throat and begins our education.

Let's discover what lessons are included in the curriculum of Grace University.

Grace Teaches Us to Renounce Sin

Denying ungodliness and worldly lusts . . .
—Titus 2:12

The first lesson of grace is about denial. Grace wants to usher us toward a new life, one of purity and righteousness. The first consideration is dealing with the problems of the old life that cannot accompany us on that journey. Our word for *denial* comes from the Greek word for *disown*. It is as if you are grabbing an old habit by its ear, taking it to the front door, and depositing it outdoors to be picked up with the trash. To disown is to detach completely. It is to say, "I will not own any problem that begins to own me."

But let's allow Paul to explain it for us. This concept of denying ungodliness carries over to the next chapter of Paul's letter to Titus:

> For we ourselves were also once foolish, disobedient, deceived, serving various lusts and pleasures, living in malice and envy, hateful and hating one another. But when the kindness and love of God our Savior toward man appeared, not by works of righteousness

which we have done, but according to His mercy He saved us,
through the washing of regeneration and renewing of the Holy
Spirit, whom He poured out on us abundantly through Jesus
Christ our Savior, that having been justified by His grace we should
become heirs according to the hope of eternal life. This is a faithful
saying, and these things I want you to affirm constantly, that those
who have believed in God should be careful to maintain good
works. These things are good and profitable to men. (Titus 3:3–8)

In summary, it's as if to say the wealthiest man in the province
has come to the city and seen the worst social reprobates imaginable,
luxuriating in dark alleys like pigs in a trough. These are vagrants
guilty of every offense. He has gone down into the grime, getting
their filth all over himself, in order to pull them out of the alley and
escort them home to his palatial manor. There he has washed them
by his own hand, fed them, clothed them, and whispered words of
hope and a future to them. Then he has told them they were adopted
as his children. Everything he has is theirs.

Those adopted sons and daughters would surely be moved to the
depths of their souls. You wouldn't expect to find them sneaking
back to their sordid dens of corruption, would you? Not when the
glorious riches and friendship of the master are available.

Needless to say, it is you and I who have been cleaned, fed,
clothed, and adopted. Why in creation would we wish to live by the
decadent trappings of the old life? Grace, having cleansed us, should
now live within us, giving us new desires and values.

When I watched Mel Gibson's movie *The Passion of the Christ*, I
was astounded by the emotions that rose up within me. The most
powerful and least expected of all, however—and the one that had
the most lasting influence upon me—was this thought: *Because of
what Christ did for me, I don't want to ever do anything to bring shame*

or hurt to Him. Watching with my own eyes an approximation of His suffering on my behalf provided a new and more powerful motivation to live a holy life.

Many of us forget what has been done for us. We forget the pain He accepted on our behalf, and we forget that we are delivered to the possibility of a new life, one so much more joyful and rewarding.

Grace Teaches Us to Rule Self

> *We should live soberly . . .*
> —Titus 2:12

In our new life in the Master's house, we will want to deny "ungodliness and worldly lust." How then shall we live? *Soberly.*

This is a very crucial New Testament concept that many of us need to study more closely. A good translation of that word would be "with self-control." Spiritual sobriety is the maturity to exercise sound mind and judgment. It is inner self-government that reins in all the passions and desires that war against us. The grace-driven believer disciplines his passions as a military leader would discipline his troops. And what passions? Eating, sleeping, talking, playing. The Spirit of God will point you to the specific issues of your own life. The idea is that the poor, rescued reprobate will not only give up the old, worthless pursuits; he will exercise wisdom and restraint in the new choices he makes of his time.

Throughout his letters to Timothy and Titus, Paul mentions this sobriety as a character trait required of pastors as well as men and women, young and old. In other words, every Christian should be showing constant growth in the area of sober living. Remember that self-control is a fruit of the Spirit. Are you seeing the fruit in your own life?

The Jews of New Testament times had a wonderful word picture that accompanied the concept of sobriety. It was to "gird up the loins of your mind." Remember how the father of the Prodigal had to run to meet his son? Gym shorts were not available, so the runner had to gather up his robe about him to allow his legs to move forward with power. Sobriety is gathering our wits, getting the impediments out of the way, and moving forward much more rapidly. Your life and mine should follow the model.

Let's also take a look at three situations calling for sober-mindedness:

1. *In anticipation of Christ's revelation.* "Therefore gird up the loins of your mind, be sober, and rest your hope fully upon the grace that is to be brought to you at the revelation of Jesus Christ" (1 Peter 1:13).

2. *In preparation for Satan's temptation.* "Be sober, be vigilant; because your adversary the devil walks about like a roaring lion, seeking whom he may devour" (1 Peter 5:8).

3. *In evaluation of our place in fellowship.* "For I say, through the grace given to me, to everyone who is among you, not to think of himself more highly than he ought to think, but to think soberly, as God has dealt to each one a measure of faith" (Romans 12:3).

We are called, therefore, to be serious and disciplined in mind and spirit, to wait on the Lord, to fight off temptation, and to serve the church. Imagine what your life could be if you became strategic about girding up the loins of your mind. How fast would you run?

Grace Teaches Us to Respect Others

We should live . . . righteously . . .
—TITUS 2:12

Grace, by its very essence, is unselfish. It follows Paul's guidance in Philippians 2:3 to "let nothing be done through selfish ambition or conceit, but in lowliness of mind let each esteem others better than himself."

Can you imagine a world where respectful behavior is normal? The loss of simple, civil respect is one of the symptoms of how far we have fallen as a society. We see the loss of respect for figures of authority, for elders, and for sacred matters of faith (whether our own belief or the beliefs of others). Our children watch television programs that encourage them to speak their mind, to have an attitude, and to do whatever they want to do. We notice that nothing is ever said about basic respect.

The grace life respects not only elders and people of authority but everyone it encounters. It respects those with whom we disagree. It respects strangers. In work situations, it respects subordinates. When we live by grace, we see through the eyes of grace. Suddenly that other person appears to us as a child of God, someone to whom Christ is reaching out, just as He is reaching to us. We hear His voice whispering to us, "Will you help Me get through to that one? Will you serve this person? She cannot hear my voice now, but she will respond to your gentleness."

Respect is the key that opens the door to any relationship. If you want to connect with someone hard to reach, take time to express words that demonstrate respect. If you want to end an argument very quickly, show respect.

Try the power of the respect principle with an elementary-level child sometime. Children feel very small. When you stop to speak to them and address them not in condescending grownup talk, but as you would talk to anyone else, you will make a friend forever. Jesus insisted on giving children love and time even when His disciples tried to push them away. The grace of Christ respects everyone. He focused on what they had that was special (in their case, childlike faith). Grace does that well. It finds what is worthy and respectable in every human being and honors it.

You can learn to relate to people this way. Let grace be your teacher.

Grace Teaches Us to Reverence God

> *We should live [in a manner that is] godly in the present age . . .*
> —Titus 2:12

Paul is always very logical in the procession of his ideas. He has told us to live soberly (the inward life). He has told us to live righteously (the outward life). Now he tells us to live in a way that is godly (the upward life).

The Greek word translated "godliness" is *eusebeia*. It is used frequently in the letters to Timothy and Titus. "Godliness" in these verses means piety and reverence toward God. We devote ourselves to Him and to His will in our hearts, our heads, and with our hands.

We've all known godly men and women, and immediately we admire them. How did they get to be that way? Were they godly at birth?

The answer is that the grace of God teaches godliness. Every day, as we listen to His voice, as He convicts us of sin and encourages us toward service, as He brings out the fruit promised in Galatians 5:22–23, as He molds us to the image of Christ—all this time we are growing in godliness. Of course, not everyone has the same growth rate. There are those who stop right at the gate of salvation and never go more than a step or two deeper into Christian maturity. This is like being adopted into the Master's family and insisting on sleeping in the garage and eating from the garbage can. A feast has been set for us, and the Spirit feeds it to us bite by bite.

I used to think that godliness was an impossible goal, if not for everyone, at least for me. And then I read these words in 2 Peter: "His divine power has given to us all things that pertain to life and godliness, through the knowledge of Him who called us by glory and virtue, by which have been given to us exceedingly great and precious promises, that through these you may be partakers of the divine nature, having escaped the corruption that is in the world through lust" (1:3–4).

Not only is godliness within reach, but everything we need to achieve it has already been given to us in the "exceedingly great and precious promises" of God's Word.

So what is holding us back? What keeps us from the goal of godliness? The disconnect is not God's but ours. Paul tells us that becoming godly is hard work, that it requires our disciplined effort. "Exercise yourself toward godliness. For bodily exercise profits a little, but godliness is profitable for all things, having promise of the life that now is and of that which is to come" (1 Timothy 4:7–8).

I believe this is what Paul is talking about when he tells the Philippians to work out their own salvation with fear and trembling (Philippians 2:12).

Grace Teaches Us to Respond Diligently

Zealous for good works . . .
—TITUS 2:14

God's grace always results in good works. Once again, imagine coming to live in that wonderful mansion. The Master is with you always, but He is constantly asking you to run "errands" with Him. What are these errands? He's constantly paying little visits of service to other people. He saves other lives like your own. He continues to give gifts and loving friendship to you. He does everything He can to make the world a better place.

Now imagine living within the scope of that influence and failing to have it rub off on you. No one but someone with the hardest of hearts could avoid falling right into step with the Master and helping Him to do all that can be done. Why, after a while, you might have the idea of getting organized about it. You'd call together all the former reprobates from the dark alleys and say, "Let's fan out and get as much done in this city as we can. Some of us will work nearby, feeding and clothing and helping; others will go out of town and get to work. Think of how much we can get done!"

Yet inevitably there would be someone who says, "Go ahead, knock yourself out, my friend. I'm not much on that service stuff. I'm going to hang around the mansion and watch television."

Now I ask you, could that person be in touch with his inner grace? Especially since the others would be discovering that service was the greatest gift of all from their Master. Service completes our joy. It uses the spiritual gifts that we were made to use, so that nothing else can provide so much fulfillment. That's called being "zealous for good works."

Isn't it interesting that Paul gives the strongest statement in the Bible concerning the nature of salvation by grace through faith: "For by grace you have been saved through faith, and that not of yourselves" (Ephesians 2:8). Then, in the very next breath, he adds: "For we are His workmanship, created in Christ Jesus for good works, which God prepared beforehand that we should walk in them" (Ephesians 2:10).

He has been making the powerful point that our own works cannot save us. Only His grace can do that. But what were we created for? Works! He does the saving, and we do the serving. That's how it was meant to be.

Paul bears testimony of this principle in his own life: "But by the grace of God I am what I am, and His grace toward me was not in vain; but I labored more abundantly than they all, yet not I, but the grace of God which was with me" (1 Corinthians 15:10).

Watching for the Blessed Hope

Looking for the blessed hope and glorious appearing of our
great God and Savior Jesus Christ.

—Titus 2:13

Paul gives us the picture of someone keeping watch, like the father of the Prodigal Son. The grace life keeps hope alive in the human heart. We begin to see more and more through the eyes of heaven, just as John Newton did as he grew older. Retirement seems distasteful, for God's work is never done and we were created for good works. Death, on the other hand, means heaven. To live is Christ; to die is gain. In their old age, these two men, Paul the apostle and Newton the navigator, began to look more and more alike—just as all of us begin to show the family resemblance after years of being daily molded more and more to His image.

Meanwhile, through the eyes of heaven there is always hope. We realize that our actions now can bear fruit years, generations, even centuries after our lives. Newton's most famous fruit, of course, is "Amazing Grace." But I believe he would have been even more satisfied with an influence he had that is less widely known.

In the year 1759, as John Newton was beginning to adapt to life after sailing, a man was born by the name of William Wilberforce. He was born wealthy and had a winning personality. As he grew to manhood, he was attracted to the political life. But he could find no peace within himself. He gradually became more and more certain that God had a higher calling for him. When he was twenty-one years old and still processing what the future might hold for him, he was a member of Parliament. Wilberforce began to attend a church in London, St. Mary Woolnoth. The rector there was a man by the name of John Newton.

It was impossible to know Newton without knowing about the past that still plagued his memories. He would preach about his days as a slave trader, and about how God had come to show him the inhumanity of buying and selling human beings. At this time, in 1780, many agreed that slavery was a problem, but most people doubted that anything could be done about it.

Newton spoke the conscience of God on the subject. The young Wilberforce listened carefully. There was a new friendship between the old captain and the young idealist. Newton fanned Wilberforce's gifts into flame and convinced him that his political life could be used for the service of God's kingdom. More and more, the passion for the abolition of slavery took hold of William Wilberforce. As he grew older, he became England's leader in the movement to abolish British slavery. After a battle that lasted eighteen years, the slave trade itself was abolished.

Then, three days before Wilberforce's death in 1833, the House of Commons passed the law that emancipated all slaves in British colonies. Within twenty years, the influence had become so powerful in America that slavery was abolished there too.

Newton was right—there is nothing more amazing than grace. It isn't content to take hold of our lives and change us from the inside out. It then reaches through us to change everyone in the world that it can.

Even as John Newton anticipated the joys of heaven, God was using him to spread good works in this world. His legacy today is both song and freedom—two things that match quite well. His last recorded words were "I am satisfied with the Lord's will."[2]

His epitaph reads as follows:

JOHN NEWTON
Clerk
Once an infidel and libertine,
a servant of slaves in Africa,
was, by the rich mercy of our Lord and Savior,
JESUS CHRIST,
preserved, restored, pardoned,
and appointed to preach the faith,
he had long labored to destroy.
He ministered near sixteen years as curate and vicar,
Of Olney in Bucks
and twenty-eight years as rector of these united parishes.
On February 1, 1750, he married
MARY,
daughter of the late George Catlett,
of Chatham, Kent,
whom he resigned to the Lord who gave her,
on December 15, 1790

John Newton hasn't been there ten thousand years, by our reckoning. But then again, in the new home he has found, there is no measurement of years or of moments. We know that time and space are creations of God only for this world. When we go to the mansions Christ has prepared for us, one moment will be as a thousand years, and a thousand years as a moment (2 Peter 3:8).

I imagine that two men, the personal subjects of this book, are beloved friends in that world. What conversations they must have together!

Newton's epitaph above includes the words:

appointed to preach the faith,
he had long labored to destroy.

It's easy to imagine Paul asking him about those words. "You could have done no more toward being an enemy of the faith than I did," Paul might say.

And perhaps Newton, as overflowing with grace as ever, would reply, "All of us were equally enemies of the faith who were well-deserving of our death, but for the love and mercy of God. I pursued free men to imprison them in slavery. You pursued believers to imprison them in Jerusalem. Praise God that He pursued us more relentlessly, more devotedly, more lovingly. Praise God that we were captured by grace. And let us worship His name that He freed us from the slavery we had imposed upon ourselves."

And upon those words, I'm quite certain that the two men, the two brothers, the two eternal children in Christ would turn again to the throne where sits the King of kings, the Lord of creation. And they would add their voices to the song of the angels, exalting the One whose grace is deep enough and wide enough to rescue every single one of us.

Moments of Grace

Think of the self-control aspect of grace—the grace of God teaches us to deny ungodliness and worldly lusts and to live self-controlled in this present world. What one single habit in your life most needs to be captured by the grace of God? Is it overeating? Swearing? Lust? A short temper?

To practice self-control in this area, use the Six-C Method: Determine to bring every thought and habit under *captivity* to Christ. *Confess* it to God in a specific prayer of repentance. *Claim* the victory from God on the basis of His great and precious promises. *Confide* this matter to a friend who will serve as your accountability partner. And *continue*, no matter what—don't give in or give up, even if you have failures along the way. God's grace is stronger than your weakness, and His blood not only forgives you; it *cleanses* from all sin (1 John 1:9).

CHAPTER TEN

The Continual Praise *of* Grace

We've No Less Days to Sing God's Praise Than When We First Begun

E *ternity.*

It excites hope and defies understanding.

Maybe if we could envision—just a little—what that world will be like, we would no longer fear death. Perhaps if our limited minds could manage to hold the briefest glimpse of paradise, the conception would change everything about the way we live now.

But that would be like a teacup trying to hold the Pacific Ocean. We might as well try wrapping our arms around the Milky Way galaxy, and a grasshopper might as well try to understand quantum physics. No matter how much we try, we cannot begin to comprehend the nature of that final blessed destination, when all the obstacles of our fallen human nature will finally be removed. We see now in a mirror darkly, but then we will see face to Face.

What will it be like to experience "forever"? *When we've been there ten thousand years.* Even as those words thrill us, we recognize their limitations. Time is a creation of God, like stars or starfish. When we take our first eager step into that next and higher world, time will be no more. A moment will be as ten thousand years, and ten thousand years as a moment.

But of course the poet understands that, for the following line expresses the idea of eternity superbly: "We've no less days to sing God's praise than when we first begun." We will have the bounds of eternity to praise and worship the Name that is above all names. But even that solid biblical truth creates a challenge of comprehension for many of us. There are some who hesitantly ask, "Will we really be singing for all of eternity? Couldn't it get—um, tiresome?

The reason we stumble over that one is that we can no more understand perfect gratitude than we can understand the perfect love that inspires it. We were created to exalt the Lord. In the act of worship we find our ultimate fulfillment, as a horse finds its place in running or an eagle in flight. Perhaps the idea of eternal praise giving is such a foreign one because wholehearted worship in *this* world is equally strange to us.

But if you want that briefest glimpse of eternity; if you want the foretaste of glory divine—then worship is the one channel for approaching the throne of God. And it comes at that still point where grace meets gratitude.

After all, what is Newton's great hymn but a song of grace wrapped in gratitude? How do you respond when you receive an unexpected, unmerited, and beautiful gift? You feel humbled. You feel uplifted. You feel that more than anything else, you want to express your thanks in the most profound way you can find. Placing the matter in mathematical terms, if the response of gratitude is proportional to the value of grace, then we are thankful when someone brings us a cup of cold water, we are overjoyed to receive a gift of unexpected wealth, and we are infinitely and eternally grateful when someone rescues us from death and despair.

The idea of ingratitude, in the light of what we have received, is worse than unthinkable.

Consider that Paul lists ingratitude as a hallmark of the world's last days. Do you recognize the following description of a culture on the verge of collapse? "But know this, that in the last days perilous times will come: For men will be lovers of themselves, lovers of money, boasters, proud, blasphemers, disobedient to parents, unthankful, unholy" (2 Timothy 3:1–2).

I think we can all agree that complaining is a contagion of our times. My friend James MacDonald undertook a study of Internet sites that have been set up just for complainers. One of them is The Complaint Station, which claims to have served five million whiners. Another site seems to understand griping as one of life's greatest joys:

Complain about anything. The whole world is here to listen.
Complain about your neighbor. Complain about the airlines.
Complain about trains. Complain about noise. Complain about
your mother-in-law. Complain about high prices. About getting
ripped off. About potholes. About police. Complain about wel-
fare. Complain about work. Complain about your boss. Complain to us. We'll listen and tell everyone. No exceptions! [1]

There are even Christian complaint sites, believe it or not. You can complain that Bible college is too expensive or that nonbelievers curse too much. You can vent about those pastors and church staff members who really bother you. It's difficult to imagine how any follower of Jesus Christ would believe that complaining was a worthwhile or edifying pursuit.

Would you rather be around people who are hateful or grateful? Consider a recent scholarly study on the results of gratitude. It's a bit more difficult to find Web sites devoted to thankfulness than those given to complaining. Yet this 2003 research concluded that grateful people receive a wide range of benefits simply because of their perspective on life. They sleep better and enjoy better physical health. Their social relationships are enhanced. They have a deeper and rewarding sense of spirituality. "Gratitude not only makes people feel good in the present, but it also increases the likelihood that people will function optimally and feel good in the future."[2] Gratitude is one heaping helping of wellness—something more beneficial than ten thousand vitamins or ten years of workouts at the gym.

Grace should create gratitude. And gratitude simply makes the world a far more positive place. It's not surprising to find that the apostle of grace has a great deal to say about the spirit of gratitude.

Praise Priority

In everything give thanks; for this is the will of God in Christ Jesus for you.
—I Thessalonians 5:18

The word *joy* occurs 181 times in the Bible, and the word *thanksgiving*, which appears in one of its various forms some 136 times, is woven tightly throughout the fabric of Scripture.

In the Old Testament, the grace of gratitude was given such prominence that certain members of the priesthood were assigned the sole task of leading the congregation in expressing it. For example, when Nehemiah's workers finally completed rebuilding the wall around Jerusalem, they recognized the moment with a service of thanksgiving: "Now at the dedication of the wall of Jerusalem they sought out the Levites in all their places, to bring them to Jerusalem

- If you have food in your refrigerator, clothes on your back, a roof over your head, and a place to sleep, you are richer than 75 percent of this world.
- If you have money in the bank, in your wallet, and spare change in a dish somewhere, you are among the top 8 percent of the world's wealthy.
- If you prayed yesterday and today, you are in the minority because you believe in God's willingness to hear and answer prayer.
- If you have the ability to choose between churches where you may freely worship, you have a blessing many people in this world do not.
- If you are a devoted follower of Jesus Christ, you live with the daily assurance that you will have eternal life, and that your Savior has gone to prepare a mansion for you in glory. Millions of people believe this sad life is all there is.[3]

Helen Keller made a compelling observation: "I have often thought it would be a blessing if each human being were stricken blind and deaf for a few days at some time early in adult life. Darkness would make him more appreciative of sight and silence would teach him the joys of sound."[4]

Imagine your life devoid of gratitude. It would be a life completely lacking any healthy perspective. It would be capable of seeing only problems. It would be dominated by fear, anxiety, stress, and ultimately the dark cloak of depression. In short, a life without gratitude would be a kind of living death.

Praise God that His grace has broken through to us. The death and resurrection of His Son have rescued us from that darkness, and His Holy Spirit has come to live within us, encouraging our hearts each day toward every positive emotion. The benefits of being a serious disciple create a spiral of gratitude that should break out of the

to celebrate the dedication with gladness, both with thanksgivi
and singing, with cymbals and stringed instruments and ha
(Nehemiah 12:27).

On at least two occasions, the Bible links the spirit of grat
praise with the victorious Christian life: "Now thanks be to C
who always leads us in triumph in Christ" (2 Corinthians 2:1
"But thanks be to God, who gives us the victory through our L
Jesus Christ" (1 Corinthians 15:57).

William Law, writing centuries ago, said, "Would you know w
is the greatest saint in the world? It is not he who prays most or fa
most, it is not he who gives alms most,…but it is he who is alwa
thankful to God,…who receives everything as an instance of Go
goodness and has a heart always ready to praise God for it."

PRAISE PERSPECTIVE

In the Old Testament, the prophet Samuel exhorted the people
God with these words: "Only fear the LORD, and serve Him in tru
with all your heart; for consider what great things He has done f
you" (1 Samuel 12:24).

Shouldn't each one of us be instituting a personal service
thanksgiving on a daily basis? Consider these gifts of grace for whic
we rarely take time to be grateful:

- If you own just one Bible, you are abundantly blessed. Most
  people in the world do not.
- If you awoke this morning more healthy than ill, you are more
  blessed than one million people who will not survive the week.
- If you have never experienced the danger of battle, the loneliness of imprisonment, the agony of torture, or the pangs of
  starvation, you are ahead of more than five hundred million
  people around the world.

shells of our lives and flood the surrounding landscape with eternal light.

The more we think of God, the more we thank Him. Those two verbs come from the same root, by the way. Right thinking leads to bright thanking ("bright shining as the sun").

PRAISE POSSIBILITIES

Giving thanks always for all things to God the Father in the name of our Lord Jesus Christ.
—EPHESIANS 5:20

Whatever you do in word or deed, do all in the name of the Lord Jesus,
giving thanks to God the Father through Him.
—COLOSSIANS 3:17

In Ephesians, Paul instructs us to give thanks to God for all things. In Colossians, he tells us what he means by "all things": every act and every word.

If you want the model for how to live that way, look no further than Paul himself. He had a gratitude that followed him to his last days of imprisonment, illness, and even criticism by other Christians of his time. It's impossible to write the word *thanksgiving* over and over when it isn't engraved in your mind-set. Paul wrote four of his letters from prison, and every one of them carries the word *thanksgiving*. He mentions gratitude ten times in all.

Now consider that model for personal comparison. If we could see a transcript of all the words you have spoken over the past month, what would that verbiage reveal about your character? And what would happen if you were suddenly thrown into prison unfairly? What is your honest feeling about where your words and letters would fall on the positive/negative continuum? The words that proceed from our mouths say a great deal about who we are and what mind-set we carry through life; the setting from which we say those words says even more.

People tell me, "I agree that I should count my blessings. But if you only knew what my life was like right now—I've had a really down year. I've been victimized by all kinds of people and circumstances."

Paul and many, many other men and women from the early church suffered far more deeply than we have in those times we perceive to be tough. Perspective makes a great deal of difference, doesn't it? In our country, there are countless people who enjoy three meals a day with shelter over their heads yet spend their lives believing they're not well off. They see the mansions on the other side of town and feel deprived for being in the top 97 percent of the world's affluent and not the top 99.

Paul was stoned at Lystra, driven out of Thessalonica, rejected by the Athenians, jailed by the Philippians, apprehended by the Caesareans, carried in chains to Rome, and shipwrecked on the way. He was released and imprisoned again, thrown in a dungeon, and martyred for his faith. He lived with a daily infirmity of some kind (his "thorn in the flesh") that brought regular misery. And not a bit of any of it dampened his gratitude to God. Should we be surprised? Only if we make the tremendous error of connecting gratitude and joy to mere circumstances. Faith, hope, love, and gratitude are faith attributes we hold regardless of circumstances.

The most powerful expression of that idea once again comes from Paul. He offered the Romans a list of negative experiences that Christians could and did encounter: tribulation, distress, persecution, famine, nakedness, peril, and sword. Then he concluded: "Yet in all these things we are more than conquerors through Him who loved us" (Romans 8:37).

Paul takes his stand at the very crosshairs of the devil's target and says, "I'm here. Let the world, the flesh, and the devil hurl every possible weapon at me. Remove every luxury I have, as happened to Job. Try me to the point of distress, as happened to Abraham. Let me stumble on the impediments of my own sinful appetites, as happened to David. I could even deny the Lord as Peter denied Him, and still the Lord would never deny me. For nothing, and I mean *nothing*, can separate me from the love of Christ. Nothing will deny me from being the conqueror that Christ has made me to be through the power and redemption of His love. For that reason, I can be strong. I can be courageous. I can stand against anything that stands against me, because I have the advantage of knowing I will win in the end through the victorious blood of my Savior; that no matter what happens to me here on earth, I will come before Him in the day of judgment and be declared *justified* because the Son has stood in my place. Therefore I will laugh and sing with the joy of heaven through the worst of storms, and just try to stop me! I will live every moment in the abundance of gratitude that flows from the power of grace."

Dr. Lee Salk was an eminent child and family authority who died in 1992. He loved to speak of his mother's experiences growing up in Russia. As a girl, she was driven from her home by Cossacks. As the attacking mob burned the village to the ground, she fled for her life, hiding in hay wagons and huddling in ditches. Eventually, crowded in a ship's hold, she crossed the sea to America.

Several years ago, a story in *Guideposts* magazine related the story behind Dr. Salk's famous quote: "Even after my mother married and her sons were born . . . it was still a struggle to keep food on the table. . . . But my mother urged us to think about what we had, not what we didn't have. She taught us that in hardship you develop a capacity to appreciate the beauty that exists in the simplest elements of life. The attitude that she so fiercely conveyed to us was this: When it gets dark enough, you can see the stars."

Praise Perfection

I will sing of the mercies of the LORD forever.
—Psalm 89:1

We can imagine two very similar figures, separated only by the centuries and the miles: John Newton dozing by his fire, Paul leaning against the cold wall of his cell. We can imagine both men allowing their thoughts to escape the confines of their aging bodies and drift to heaven, where the culmination of their lives and hopes would finally arrive. Since the day of rebirth for each—one tossed from a horse, one tossed by a storm at sea—these two had offered continuous praise and thanksgiving to the One who sent grace in pursuit of them. Both men could imagine what it would be like to finally say thank you face to Face, from within the veil of holiness rather than beyond this veil of tears. They could see themselves in the guise of the apostle John, standing there at the doorway to heaven in the beloved disciple's apocalyptic vision in Revelation 11:16–17:

And the twenty-four elders who sat before God on their thrones fell
on their faces and worshiped God, saying:

"We give You thanks, O Lord God Almighty,
The One who is and who was and who is to come,
Because You have taken Your great power and reigned."

My friend, do you ever daydream about that eventuality? Do you ever allow your heart to roam beyond the shackles of this dark world, into the realm of pure light, bright shining as the sun, where our Savior dwells? It is no idle dream but our firm destiny. It is the end result to which every moment and every activity of this life should point like a neon signpost in the desert.

In the meantime, however, this earth will have to do. We are called to live in a fallen world, but His grace is sufficient—as it was for Paul, as it was for John Newton. Each found joy, peace, and new life in the love of Christ that covered the shame of their pasts. I wonder if you have experienced that level of victory over your own history of struggles. I wonder if the grace of Christ is proving sufficient to you in those current challenges that threaten to bring you anxiety and rob you of sleep.

What a tragedy if a single one of us lived within arm's reach of the grace of God and never took it in hand to experience its tremendous power. I have experienced the sufficiency of God's grace over and over in my own life, including those moments when I battled cancer through chemotherapy. What I discovered is that Paul is absolutely correct: nothing can separate us from the love of Christ. Nothing can even come close. The extent of our challenge defines the extent to which God is glorified, and you are blessed as you cling more tightly to Him through the storm.

Grace is a powerful force whose path can be traced through this world. It cuts a swath through the heaviest fortifications of the devil, when Christians merely wake up and begin to trust in the power of their Savior. I would offer the most fitting example to close a book that has followed the journeys of Paul and Newton by land, sea, and spirit.

The story begins at the foot of the cross, where grace covered all of humanity's sin and began to travel its path of redemption through our world.

The story continues as grace pursues Paul until he is radically changed inside. It inspires him to write the most hopeful letters ever written—powerful epistles of grace.

We follow the path of grace into the eighteenth century, where it overtakes a slave trader at the depth of despair. First he finds grace for his own sins, and eventually he understands that grace applies also to the African slaves who are being bought and sold.

Only a few years pass before we find a young man named William Wilberforce, who is captured by grace himself. John Newton, in the fullness of his years, can do little to make a difference in the English slave trade. But Wilberforce, a rising star in Parliament, will finally see the blot of slavery erased from British practice.

Finally we follow the path of grace across the sea. The story of the hymn will find its culmination in word and influence simultaneously. The path leads to the door of a young lady in Cincinnati, Ohio, at the middle of the nineteenth century. New surprises await us there, and we can only shake our heads and offer our gratitude one more time to the God of all surprises, and for the grace that is His instrument.

Here is that story.

The Woman Who Started the War

Harriet Beecher Stowe wanted to be a writer, and she was off to a reasonable start. She and her sister published a children's book that enjoyed modest success. But Harriet wanted to write novels like Dickens and Hawthorne. What she needed most was a subject worthy of a writer's passion.

Harriet lived with her husband in Cincinnati, Ohio, where her father was the president of Lane Theological Seminary. Cincinnati was an interesting town in 1850—a frontier town, really. It thrived on the characters and commerce of the Ohio River.

It was in this setting that Harriet began to meet fugitive slaves who had escaped captivity in the South. Cincinnati was an important stop on the Underground Railroad, by which many African-Americans were able to come northward to freedom.

Harriet met some of the former slaves, saw their scars, and heard their stories. With her husband, she also visited a few Southern towns and witnessed the ugly realities of plantation life with her own eyes. She couldn't cleanse those sights from her mind even after the Stowes moved to Maine. To add even greater drama to the situation, the Fugitive Slave Law was passed in 1850, making it a crime to harbor a runaway slave. Harriet Beecher Stowe felt more and more indignant over the injustice of this whole establishment. So did many other people. Slavery was America's great burning issue.

Yet it was the loss of her son Charley that finally provided the spark that moved Harriet's pen. Her baby died of cholera, and she grieved miserably. Now she understood what it was like when slave women had their newborn children ripped from their arms and taken away from them forever. Now she felt an emotional link to the American slave.

Her novel *Uncle Tom's Cabin* was published in 1852. More than any mere speech or tract, it would be this sensational book that would personalize the issue of slavery for many Americans. Readers knew Uncle Tom and Simon Legree as if they were real people. Many folks had simply thought the existence of the industry was unfortunate; now they were moved and impassioned.

The antislavery movement had grown in power from its origins in England, where men like John Newton had lit the candles that would grow into flame under William Wilberforce and his associates. In America, Harriet Beecher Stowe's novel spread the same fire. Within a few years, the American Civil War would be fought over this issue. Abraham Lincoln would later meet the author, who was now a celebrity, and joke, "So you're the little woman who wrote the book that started this great war."

One other factor lay behind the phenomenal success of *Uncle Tom's Cabin*. "I could not control the story; the Lord himself wrote it," she would say later. "I was but an instrument in His hands, and to Him should be given all the praise." Even in the emotional devastation of losing her child, she found that God's grace was sufficient. She channeled her mourning into heartfelt writing and allowed the Lord to use her gifts.

Harriet Beecher Stowe's novel tells the story of a Christian slave who is sold to Simon Legree. He has taught himself to read the Bible, but his new master allows no free time for his slaves. Legree demands that Tom deny his faith and live for the devil. Tom replies, "I'll hold on. The Lord may help me, or not help me; but I'll hold to Him and believe Him to the last."

This determination inspires Legree to new levels of cruelty. Tom weakens under the constant barrage of his master but holds on to his faith with his last reserves of courage. Then one night he sits at a dying fire, deep in despair, when a vision rises before him: "One crowned with thorns, buffeted, bleeding." The suffering slave looks into the eyes of his true Master and draws strength from the grace and power of the vision. Before his eyes, the thorns are transformed into rays of heavenly glory. The figure bends closer to Tom and encourages him with the promise of heaven for those who overcome as He, the Lord, has overcome.

The vision fades and Tom is suddenly awake, and "the triumphant words of a hymn" fill the silence of the night. He remembers the song from happier days and begins to sing. His melody happens to be three verses of "Amazing Grace." The first two come from Newton's "lost verses," the ones we seldom use today.

The slave's third verse, however, is the charm:

When we've been there ten thousand years,
Bright shining as the sun . . .

Tom is a changed man now. He gives up any idea of physical freedom and embraces the eternal freedom that is his legacy as a follower of Christ. He devotes himself wholeheartedly to sharing this hope in Christ with his fellow slaves. The outcome is not hard to foresee. Simon Legree has Tom whipped to death, and the slave joins His Savior in the ultimate fellowship, where a crown of glory awaits those who finish the race.

There has always been power in the idea of martyrdom, even when the martyr is a fictional character like Uncle Tom. Every reader knew that Harriet Beecher Stowe's Uncle Tom represented many thousands of genuine slaves who were not fictional at all. In the early church, it was said that "the blood of the martyrs is seed." What grows from that seed? Faith—passionate faith. And a faith that gets to work. A decade after the publication of Stowe's novel, slavery was outlawed and Christian activism had taken the lead in its defeat.

This is the first use of the final verse of "Amazing Grace" that can be found. Most scholars believe that it was *Uncle Tom's Cabin*, therefore, that finished the work that John Newton had done; it was the book that inspired America to take a stand against slavery, just as Newton, through Wilberforce, had done in England. This is the triumphant path of grace that begins at the foot of the cross and leads to the present day, and to *you*.

What path will grace follow now, through your commitment and your gratitude?

The Fragrance of Grace

Amazing grace is the thread that ties together the powerful, righteous work of outlawing slavery in two great nations: amazing grace as the miraculous work of the Spirit, and "Amazing Grace" as an enduring hymn of gratitude for the love and mercy of God, given freely to those who might have died without hope.

Grace taught Newton's heart to fear, and grace his fears relieved. Grace taught his heart to see the reality of justice beyond the social conventions of his day. It inspired him to write words that for many generations would perfectly capture that grace as it had first captured him.

Grace taught Harriet Beecher Stowe's heart to grieve for the weary, abused human beings she met in Cincinnati. It strengthened her to survive her own grieving over an infant son taken by disease and to glorify God regardless of circumstances. Finally, that same grace inspired her to write a classic novel that would complement Newton's classic hymn—which she ended in a new way, to complete the circle of God's providence.

In her book *Radical Gratitude*, Ellen Vaughn tells about an incident that took place on the Washington subway system. The crowded train had stalled on an underground track. Harried commuters were beside themselves. No one had been speaking to anyone, but now they burst into mutual, frenzied bouts of accusation against the driver, the Metro authorities, the federal government, or anyone else they could blame for this terrible inconvenience.

Somewhere in the midst of all this invective, a woman with a number of bulky shopping bags dropped and shattered a new bottle of perfume. Within a few minutes, the pure, luxurious fragrance had wafted the length of the crowded car. It was as if the fresh smell released people from a dark spell. They breathed in, grinned with pleasure, relaxed, and began laughing with each other.[5]

This world, filled with complaints, threats, and cries of despair, could use a whiff of the aroma of paradise. The darkness may seem impermeable, yet it flees before the light of God's grace. All we need is to find our own voice. Grace will make use of the letters of Paul, the lyrics of Newton, the literature of Mrs. Stowe, or the love that is yours exclusively to express. His grace can take any and every form. It can burst out in any hopeless or desperate situation. It has traveled its mysterious path for two thousand years, and this present darkness can do nothing but afford it a greater opportunity for God's greater glory.

I pray that you are even now following the path of God's fragrant and beautiful grace, that it is filling your heart with a peace and joy that stand defiant against the worst attacks of the evil one, that your relationships are constantly becoming more and more Christlike, so that those who know you cannot help but be touched by grace and cannot help but ask about its source. I pray that even as you have been captured by grace, you will be its vessel for helping it capture more and more of a world desperate to know it; so that one day, when we stand before the Source of amazing grace, you'll have even greater reason for joy and gratitude, for in the end you became part of the story yourself.

Freely you have received, freely give.

—JESUS (MATTHEW 10:8)

Moments of Grace

Here are four ideas for cultivating thankfulness. First, count your blessings—literally. The hymnist Frances Ridley Havergal (author of "Take My Life and Let It Be") kept a daily thanksgiving list along with her prayer list, and each day she recorded new blessings for which to be thankful. Why not give that a try? You might use your daily calendar or handheld computer. Have you ever thanked God for the small, overlooked blessings? Hot water in the mornings? A warm pair of socks? Your shoes?

Second, ask a close friend to tell you when you complain. Most of us gripe and complain so frequently it's become a habit of which we're unaware. Appoint a friend as an attitude spotter.

Third, begin using biblical terminology when thanking others. Instead of saying, "Thank you," try, "I thank God for you."

Fourth, make it a habit to go to sleep every night with thanksgiving on your mind. When you turn out the lights, find three or four blessings and let your last waking thoughts be contented thanksgiving prayers of praise to God.

Captured Forever

I f you've read this far, my friend, then you and I have become travel companions of a sort.

Together we've come through the storms with John Newton and then sat beside him at the hearth and marveled at the transformation of his spirit. We've wondered how it is that a person who begins life as a social castaway—bereft of mother, abandoned by father, and abused by his fellow men—can become so loving and find such inexhaustibly gracious resources to offer the world.

You and I have also walked a few miles with a man once known as Saul. We have watched as he rooted Christians out of their homes. We have observed his ironclad views of religious purity—and seen all of it disappear into the dust of one Damascus Road. Maybe there were times when you placed the book aside just to sit and contemplate the impossibility of these things: a man with gold-plated credentials as a Hebrew rabbi, a Greek scholar, and a Roman citizen, pushing all of it aside for a life of hardship, telling everyone about the crucified carpenter from Nazareth, knowing it could only lead to his own execution. Why?

If it were only about John Newton or Paul the apostle, perhaps we could dismiss these things as freak occurrences of history. But we know better than that, don't we? We know that their living church has conquered million-to-one odds to survive and topple the Roman Empire in those first years. It has withstood political suppression, intellectual attack, and social upheaval on every populated continent. It begins with a crucified peasant and a handful of unimpressive followers; it ends with hundreds of millions of devout believers alive today. How?

And now, at this very moment, that living faith has found its way to the doorway of your own heart.

You and I have navigated these pages together, it's true. But there was always a Third Party in our presence. You sensed it, didn't you? John Newton knew He was there. Paul knew He was there. And now He stands before you and asks about your own acknowledgment.

This is where my personal part of your journey ends. Our paths diverge here, for there is only One who can make that final leg of the journey—the one that leads into your soul. I know that's what He longs to do today. As in Francis Thompson's poem, the tracks of the Hound of Heaven have followed you to the present moment, the present situation, the present point of decision. Jesus Christ, the very personification of grace, loves you deeply. He has loved you since before you were born. According to the Bible, He has anticipated this moment with longing, ever since the foundation of time. He has been anxious to know you as His friend. That's how much you mean to Him.

I want to be certain you know exactly what is involved in saying yes to that love and that grace. There's nothing complicated about it, believe me. There are no requirements you need to go out into the world and fulfill. There's not a cent that you need to pay. It's all about grace, remember?

You simply need to agree with Jesus Christ that only He can calm the storms of life. You need only to take your stand beside Him as He stands beside you, to let *Him* answer for every sin and failing in your life.

Then begins the life of joy that He has always wanted for you. As we discussed, it's not a life free of pain or struggle. But it's a life with Him by your side, Him giving you hope, Him giving you all that you need to come through any storm. It also means an eternity of enjoying His presence. Think of that, my friend—an eternity in which there will be no more pain, no more tears, and you will finally be all that He created you to be.

The reward is unfathomable; the requirement is simple. How, then, can you say yes to Jesus Christ right here and now?

1. *Acknowledge* that you are a helpless sinner, like every one of us in this world. As Paul writes, "There is none righteous, no, not one" (Romans 3:10).

2. *Affirm* that Jesus Christ, being God's perfect and sinless Son, accepted your own penalty by dying for you. "But God demonstrates His own love toward us, in that while we were still sinners, Christ died for us" (Romans 5:8).

3. *Ask* Him to save you right now. "If you confess with your mouth the Lord Jesus and believe in your heart that God has raised Him from the dead, you will be saved" (Romans 10:9).

4. *Always* serve Jesus Christ as Lord and Master, every day. "But you are not in the flesh but in the Spirit, if indeed the Spirit of God dwells in you" (Romans 8:9).

Yes, this decision will totally transform your life. From that very moment when you accept the salvation and lordship of Christ, He will begin to transform you a bit more every day to resemble Himself. You will become wiser, stronger, more of a blessing to others. But all of it begins with that one simple statement—that one sincere *yes*, from your heart to the heart of Christ.

If you're not sure exactly how to go about it, I would suggest that you imagine Jesus Christ right there in your presence, as He most certainly is. Then say a simple prayer, which means nothing more than talking to Him. Your words might be like these:

Lord Jesus, I'm like everyone else—I can't make it through life on my own. I'm imperfect. I'm prone to sin. I have come to realize that there's nothing in the world I can do to make myself acceptable to You. But I know that You loved me so much that You were willing to submit to the cross on my behalf. That's a grace so amazing I cannot understand it; I can only accept it. And I do. I accept Your free gift, and I know that from this moment on, I am saved. I am a child of heaven. And I give the rest of my life to serving You and experiencing the joy that only You offer. Fill me now, dear Lord, and raise me to walk in newness of life. I thank You and praise You! Amen.

If you have become a child of Christ through this book, I congratulate you and welcome you with all my heart! Life for you truly begins right now—could anything be more exciting? I hope the first thing you do is to let someone know about your wonderful decision. Find a good church where Christ is preached and where your fellow believers will care for you and help you grow.

I would love to hear about your experience too. It would add joy to my day. You can get in touch with me by writing to:

Turning Point Ministries
P.O. Box 3838
San Diego, CA 92163

My friend, may your life reflect the grace that is too marvelous for words. May you begin now to partake of it wholeheartedly, from this moment until we arrive together at that final destination, where you and I will bow before the Author of grace, and where all of His love and all of His mercy will reach their ultimate expression.

SELECT BIBLIOGRAPHY

Bull, Josiah. *"But Now I See": The Life of John Newton*. Carlisle, PA: Banner of Truth Trust, 1998.

Cecil, Richard. *The Life of John Newton*, ed. Marylynn Rouse. Fearn, Ross-shire: Christian Focus, 2000.

Hindmarsh, D. Bruce. *John Newton and the English Evangelical Tradition*. Grand Rapids: Eerdmans, 2000.

Newton, John. *The Journal of a Slave Trader: 1750-1754*. ed. with introduction by Bernard Martin and Mark Spurrell. London: Epworth, n.d.

—————. *Letters*. Carlisle, PA: Banner of Truth Trust, 1960.

—————. *Letters and Reflections to My Adopted Daughters*. Comp. Jody Moreen. Enumclaw, WA: Pleasant Word, 2005.

—————. *The Life and Spirituality of John Newton*, introduction by D. Bruce Hindmarsh. Vancouver, B.C.: Regent College Publishing, 2003.

—————. *Out of the Depths*. Revised for Today's Readers by Dennis R. Hillman. Grand Rapids: Kregel, 2003.

—————. *The Searcher of Hearts*. Fearn, Ross-shire; Christian Focus, 1997.

—————. *Thoughts upon the African Slave Trade*. London: 1883.

Turner, Steve. *Amazing Grace*. New York: HarperCollins, 2002.

NOTES

Chapter 1: The Captivating Presence of Grace

1. "A Moment of Grace." www.nytimes.com./2005/08/17/opinion.
2. D. Bruce Hindmarsh, *John Newton and the English Evangelical Tradition* (Grand Rapids: Eerdmans, 1996), 51.
3. John Newton, *Out of the Depths*, revised by Dennis R. Hillman (Grand Rapids: Kregel, 2003), 28, 33, 41, 66.
4. Richard Cecil, *The Life of John Newton*, ed. Marylynn Rouse (Fearn, Ross-shire: Christian Focus, 2000), 162.
5. Quoted in Steve Turner, *Amazing Grace* (New York: Harper-Collins, 2002), 215.
6. Ibid., 217.
7. Ibid.
8. Ibid., 218.
9. D. M. Lloyd-Jones, *Romans: An Exposition of Chapters 3:20–4:25, Atonement and Justification* (Grand Rapids: Zondervan, 1970), 57.
10. W. H. Griffith Thomas, *Outline Studies in the Acts of the Apostles* (Grand Rapids: Eerdmans, 1956).
11. Victor Hugo, *Les Miserablés,* Trans. Isabel Florence Hapgood. In the public domain. www.gutenberg.org/etext/135.

Chapter 2: The Compassionate Plan of Grace

1. Thomas G. Long, "God Be Merciful to Me, a Miscalculator," *Theology Today*, vol. 50, no. 2 (July 1993), 165–68.

2. John Newton, *The Life and Spirituality of John Newton*, introduction by D. Bruce Hindmarsh (Vancouver, B.C.: Regent College Publishing, 2003), 50.

3. Cornelius Plantinga Jr., *Not The Way It's Supposed to Be: A Breviary of Sin* (Grand Rapids: Eerdmans, 1995), 199.

4. Charles R. Swindoll, *Growing Deep in the Christian Life* (Portland: Multnomah, 1986), 207.

5. Kent Hughes, *Romans—Righteousness from Heaven* (Wheaton, IL: Crossway, 1991), 76.

6. Aleksandr Solzhenitsyn, *The Gulag Archipelago 1918–1956: An Experiment in Literary Investigation* (Boulder, CO: Westview, 1973), 168.

7. Donald Grey Barnhouse, *God's Remedy, God's River—Romans*, vol. II (Grand Rapids: Eerdmans, 1953), 5–6.

8. John R. W. Stott, *The Cross of Christ* (Downer's Grove, IL: InterVarsity, 1986), 189–92.

9. Benjamin Breckinridge Warfield, "Redeemer, Redemption" in *The Person and Work of Christ* (Philadelphia: Presbyterian and Reformed Publishing, 1950), 325–48.

10. James Montgomery Boice, *Romans, Vol. I—Justification by Faith: Romans 1–4* (Grand Rapids: Baker, 1991), 375–76.

11. William Cowper, *The Works of William Cowper* (London: H. G. Bohn, 1853), 101.

12. Richard Cecil, *The Life of John Newton*, ed. Marylynn Rouse (Fearn, Ross-shire: Christian Focus, 2000), 119.

13. John Piper, "Insanity and Spiritual Songs in the Soul of the Saint: Reflections on the Life of William Cowper," Bethlehem Conference for Pastors, 29 January 1992. http://www.desiring god.org/library/biographies/92cowper.html.

Chapter 3: The Converting Power of Grace

1. Henri J. M. Nouwen, *The Return of the Prodigal: A Story of Homecoming* (New York: Doubleday, 1992).
2. Kenneth E. Bailey, *The Cross and the Prodigal* (Downers Grove, IL: InterVarsity, 2005), 52–53.
3. Ibid., 67.
4. Ibid.

Chapter 4: The Clear Perspective of Grace

1. Josiah Bull, *"But Now I See": The Life of John Newton* (Carlisle, PA: Banner of Truth Trust, 1998), 62, 358.
2. Cornelius Plantinga Jr., *Not the Way It's Supposed to Be: A Breviary of Sin* (Grand Rapids: Eerdmans, 1995), xiii.
3. Mark R. McMinn, *Why Sin Matters: The Surprising Relationship Between Our Sin and God's Grace* (Wheaton, IL: Tyndale, 2004), 21.
4. Ibid., 50.
5. Donald Grey Barnhouse, *Man's Ruin, God's Wrath—Romans*, vol. I (Grand Rapids: Eerdmans. 1959), 18.
6. Adapted from Charles Haddon Spurgeon, *Earnest Expostulations in Metropolitan Tabernacle Pulpit*, vol. 29 (Carlisle, PA: The Banner of Truth Trust, 1971), 196.
7. William Hendriksen, *New Testament Commentary: Exposition of Paul's Epistle to the Romans* (Grand Rapids: Baker, 1980), 95.
8. C. S. Lewis, *Mere Christianity* (New York: Macmillan, 1958), 4–5.
9. John Warwick Montgomery, *Damned Through the Church* (Minneapolis: Bethany Fellowship, 1970), 62–63.

10. Adapted from Kent Hughes, *Romans—Righteousness from Heaven* (Wheaton, IL: Crossway, 1991), 71–72.

Chapter 5: The Comforting Provision of Grace

1. John R. W. Stott, *Romans: God's Good News for the World* (Downers Grove, IL: InterVarsity, 1994), 140.
2. Lloyd Ogilvie, *Drumbeat of Love* (Waco, TX: Word, 1978), 176–77.
3. W. H. Griffith Thomas, *Outline Studies in the Acts of the Apostles* (Grand Rapids: Eerdmans, 1956), 150.

Chapter 6: The Connecting Point of Grace

1. John Newton, *The Life and Spirituality of John Newton*, introduction by D. Bruce Hindmarsh (Vancouver, B.C.: Regent College Publishing, 2003), 54.
2. Ibid., 57.
3. Ibid., 63.
4. D. Bruce Hindmarsh, *John Newton and the English Evangelical Tradition* (Grand Rapids: Eerdmans, 2000), 13.
5. W. H. Griffith Thomas, *Outline Studies in the Acts of the Apostles* (Grand Rapids: Eerdmans, 1956), 163.
6. C. S. Lewis, *Christian Reflections* (San Diego: Harcourt Brace, 1956), 228.
7. F. B. Meyer, *Paul: A Servant of Jesus Christ* (Fort Washington, PA: Christian Literature Crusade, 1978), 42.
8. C. S. Lewis, *Surprised by Joy* (San Diego: Harcourt Brace, 1956), 228.

Chapter 7: The Confusing Paradox of Grace

1. Mrs. Charles Cowman, *Streams in the Desert* (Grand Rapids: Zondervan, 1965), 90.
2. Kenneth Wuest, *Wuest's Word Studies from the Greek New Testament*, vol. 3 (Grand Rapids: Eerdmans, 1973), 82.
3. Paul Lee Tan, *Encyclopedia of 7000 Illustrations: A Treasury of Illustrations, Anecdotes, Facts, and Quotations for Pastors, Teachers, and Christian Workers,* electronic ed. (Garland, TX: Bible Communications, 1979). Published in electronic form by Logos Research Systems, 1997.
4. John Newton, *Out of the Depths*, revised by Dennis R. Hillman (Grand Rapids: Kregel, 2003), 12.
5. "August 15, 1964—Congo Rebels Reached Helen Roseveare," Christian History Institute. http://chi/gospelcom.net/DAILYF/2002/08/daily-08-15-2002.shtml.
6. "Digging Ditches: Evangelicals Now Interviews Legendary Missionary Helen Roseveare." www.e-n.org.uk/2005-09/3132-Digging-ditches.htm.
7. Josiah Bull, *"But Now I See": The Life of John Newton* (Carlisle, PA: Banner of Truth Trust, 1998), 304.

Chapter 8: The Confident Promise of Grace

1. John MacArthur, *The MacArthur New Testament Commentary: Romans 1–8* (Chicago: Moody, 1991), 471.
2. John Phillips, *Exploring Romans* (Chicago: Moody, 1969), 134.
3. Donald Grey Barnhouse, *Romans, God's Heirs: Romans 8:1–39* (Grand Rapids: Eerdmans, 1959), 153.

4. Annie Johnson Flint, quoted in Mrs. Charles Cowman, *Streams in the Desert* (Grand Rapids: Zondervan, 1965), 110–11.

5. chi/gospelcom.net/DAILYF/2002/08.

6. www.e-n.org.uk/2005-09/3132-DiggingDitches.htm.

7. John Newton, *Letters and Reflections to My Adopted Daughters*, comp. Jody Moreen (Enumclaw, WA: Pleasant Word, 2005), 105.

Chapter 9: The Compelling Prospect of Grace

1. Steve Turner, *Amazing Grace* (New York: Harper Collins, 2002), 107.

2. Josiah Bull, *"But Now I See": The Life of John Newton* (Carlisle: Banner of Truth Trust, 1998), 359.

Chapter 10: The Continual Praise of Grace

1. James MacDonald, *Lord, Change My Attitude (Before It's Too Late)* (Chicago: Moody, 2001), 35.

2. Robert A. Emmons and Michael E. McCullough, "Highlights from the Research Project on Gratitude and Thankfulness." http://psychology.ucdavis.edu/labs/emmons/.

3. www.sermonillustrator.org/illustrator/sermon2/blessed.htm.

4. James S. Spiegel, *How to Be Good in a World Gone Bad: Living a Life of Christian Virtue* (Grand Rapids: Kregel, 2004), 174.

5. Ellen Vaughn, *Radical Gratitude* (Grand Rapids: Zondervan, 2005), 48.

Praise for *When Your World Falls Apart*

This moving book reveals how one man of God who had preached biblical principles for years stared death in the face—and found that God is faithful to those who put their trust in Him. David, his family, and his great church rose to the challenge of one of life's greatest bends in the road and let it enrich their lives.

TIM LAHAYE
author, pastor, teacher

David Jeremiah lifts the plumbline of God's word so high that we can more accurately measure the truth, so clear that we can more easily see the truth, and so relevant that we can more faithfully obey the truth.
Praise God for him!

ANN GRAHAM LOTZ
author of *Just Give Me Jesus*

From the vantage point of his own battle with cancer, David Jeremiah opens up the biblical pharmacy to dispense the divine radiation that cures the soul of the sufferer. He does so with the insight and sensitivity that can come only from one who has a deep understanding both of Scripture and sickness.

JOHN MACARTHUR
pastor, teacher, author

For those times when life overwhelms us . . . When Your World Falls Apart *will be a balm of healing.*

BARBARA JOHNSON
author, inspirational speaker

WHEN
YOUR WORLD
FALLS APART

*This book is dedicated to the faithful members of the
Shadow Mountain Community Church.
Their prayers carried me through my bend in the road
and continue to sustain me to this day!*

Contents

Acknowledgments

When I first encountered my bend in the road in the fall of 1994, I did not think I would write a book about my experience. But the lessons I learned have been too valuable to keep to myself. This is not primarily a story about me; it is a record of God's dealings with me during these traumatic years. As always, He works best through the people He brings next to us at such crucial times.

I cannot say enough about the medical professionals who ministered to me during the crucial days of my illness. Dr. Thomas Witzig was part of the diagnostic team at the Mayo Clinic that walked me through the first stages of lymphoma. His Christian faith and his encouraging words helped me over the first hurdle.

When I returned to San Diego, I was placed in the capable care of Dr. Alan Saven at the Scripps Clinic. He directed the first chemical treatments and diagnosed the disease when it returned in 1998. Dr. Saven is a highly regarded oncologist who takes an aggressive approach to the treatment of cancer and a gentle approach to the treatment of his patients. Dr. James Mason, also of the Scripps Clinic, took me through the stem cell transplant. His upbeat approach to healing and health was a great encouragement to me. I am also indebted to Dr. Richard Furman, a thoracic surgeon from Boone, North Carolina.

His friendship and counsel have been a source of great strength, and his love for the Word of God has been a great example.

When I was released from the Scripps Clinic in March 1999, I was made aware of the importance of taking better care of my body. After some research into the options, I signed on with Mike Douglas, a former NFL prayer, who is now a physical trainer. I began working out every day under Mike's guidance and have gradually begun to implement some of the nutritional advice that he tries to pound into my head every morning. Mike has given me a new appreciation for the importance of physical fitness, even at the age of fifty-nine.

During the days that I was recovering from the stem cell transplant, several Christian leaders took time out of their busy schedules to call me repeatedly, sharing their love and concern. I want to thank especially Tim LaHaye, Jim Cymbala, John MacArthur, and John Maxwell for their prayers and encouragement.

Several friends provided tremendous assistance as I began to pull together the notes in preparation for this book. Helen Barnhart helped to administrate the project, keeping everything in proper order in the computer. Brenda Josee organized the material, and Rob Suggs produced the final manuscript. As always, my literary agent, Sealy Yates, walked with me through the entire process. He visited me in the hospital and helped me formulate the strategy for this book. I respect Sealy as a professional, and I love him as my friend.

I also want to express my deep appreciation to the people who allowed their stories to be told in this book: Helen Barnhart, Carole Carlson, John Hovey, Marv Eastlund, Sharon Paul, Glenda Palmer, and Steve Garrison.

The leaders who surround me at Shadow Mountain Community Church have demonstrated their love and support from the very beginning of this episode in my life. Thanks to Ken Nichols, Gary Coombs, Steve Caudill, Brian Rickard, Max Baumgartner, Ray Benton, Vance Yoder, and Roger Wiles. A special thanks to Glenda Parker, my administrative assistant, who spent many hours during my illness and recovery coordinating things between my family, the church, and *Turning Point*.

All of my children have ministered to me in a special way during the journey around the bend in the road. David and Cami, John and Jan, Daniel and Merae, and Jennifer and Emmanuel have found creative and expressive ways to encourage me.

Finally, I want to express my love for my wife, Donna. Together we have negotiated several bends in life's road. The closeness we experienced during those times will never be forgotten. Our love for each other has grown deeper, and our faith in Almighty God has been strengthened. I think you will capture something of the special relationship we enjoy as you read her foreword to this book.

—David Jeremiah
El Cajon, California

Foreword

Being married to David Jeremiah has been quite an adventure. Our journey together these past thirty-seven years has brought us both great joy and pain. But no matter what the circumstances of our lives, we have always been grateful for the abundant grace of God, even during our darkest hours. Today, as I listen to Dave preach, see him playing with our grandchildren, or watch him jump with excitement at a ball game, my heart is filled with gratitude for the mercy of God.

Jesus Christ became my personal Savior when I was nine years old. Only when Dave considered becoming the pastor of Shadow Mountain Community Church in El Cajon, California, did I discover that the evangelist who preached the message during which I accepted the Lord once served as pastor in the pulpit that Dave now fills.

Cheerleading for Cedarville College positioned me close to the court and to a tall, lanky player named David Jeremiah. Dave and I shared an interest in radio, and along with Paul Gathany, we launched WCDR radio for Cedarville College. I love to tell people I was a disc jockey for a one-hour music program—I just don't tell them the limited scope of the radio station.

My decision to accept Dave's marriage proposal involved a lot of heart searching. I knew Dave planned to be a minister, and I had great reservations about being a pastor's wife. When I accepted the reality that God's plan for me could include the role of a pastor's wife, Dave and I launched into married life with eager anticipation for what God had in store for us.

Dave is an optimistic person who grasps every situation with confidence. Through the years, his optimism has influenced me, and I have learned to choose hope no matter the circumstances. That has been the single most important factor as we have faced each bend in the road the last few years.

Pastoring our first small church required a large amount of faith and provided many opportunities to choose hope. Moving to California from the Midwest with our little family filled our lives with excitement. Being part of a growing church and launching a broadcast ministry kept us facing each new day with a curious anticipation. The launching of *Turning Point* also brought an opportunity for me to work alongside Dave and motivated me with the joy of seeing his ministry's extended impact on so many lives.

I realize there is never a good time for bad news; however, the timing of the discovery of Dave's cancer forced both of us to internalize many of our emotions. Our oldest son, David Michael, was a newlywed and living on the East Coast; Jennifer was in her first year at Cedarville College and suffering from homesickness; and Daniel, our youngest son, had major decisions to make regarding his upcoming college plans. Only our daughter Jan was close by in Coronado!

Dave was strong and gave me the courage to choose hope rather than despair. I knew all the Bible passages about faith and trust, yet when the man I loved, my husband, the father of my children, the man who preached boldly about faith, could be dying, I wasn't sure that I could find the faith to carry on.

I wish I could tell you there is an easy way to survive any bend in the road of life, but that would not be true. I can tell you that each day held its own level of anxiety and that each day the Lord provided just enough strength and hope for that day.

As a wife and mother, I attempted to keep life as normal as possible. Celebrating holidays and birthdays, attending sports events, and mingling with our church family kept me hopeful. On the few days when I felt completely overwhelmed, I would drive up into the mountains east of our home. Getting out by myself gave me time to gain perspective alone with the Lord and realize that the choice I made to hope was not a once-for-all choice, but a moment-by-moment choice.

During these times, I discovered that hope, as the writer of Hebrews said, is the "anchor of the soul" (6:19). Hope was the anchor that brought me back to the God I had trusted with my life as a child. Now I had to trust God with the life of my husband.

In our private moments, Dave and I would draw strength from each other. Over the years, I have prayed for many people and circumstances. But how could I hold the man I loved in my arms and pray for God to spare his life without giving in to a sense of quiet desperation? Dave could sense when I was feeling down and knew what to say to lift my spirits and to help me regain a sense of hope.

Today, our journey together is continuing. In the course of Dave's recovery, two of our children have married, more grandchildren have been born, and *Turning Point* has launched a television program. We have discovered that looking forward is the only way to live.

No matter what your circumstances may be, please read this book with the awareness that the man who wrote it is a living testimony to the sustaining power of hope found only in the Lord Jesus Christ. The prophet Jeremiah's confession of faith is recorded in Lamentations 3:21–24:

> *This I recall to my mind,*
> *Therefore I have hope.*
> *Through the LORD'S mercies we are not consumed,*
> *Because His compassions fail not.*
> *They are new every morning;*
> *Great is Your faithfulness.*
> *"The LORD is my portion," says my soul,*
> *"Therefore I hope in Him!"*

Living with hope,
Donna Jeremiah

1

A Bend in the Road

Sometimes we come to life's crossroads
And we view what we think is the end.
But God has a much wider vision
And He knows that it's only a bend—
The road will go on and get smoother
And after we've stopped for a rest,
The path that lies hidden beyond us
Is often the path that is best.
So rest and relax and grow stronger,
Let go and let God share your load
And have faith in a brighter tomorrow.
You've just come to a bend in the road.

It all began on an ordinary Monday morning.

I pulled the van out of my garage, turned onto the road, and drove toward the highway, where I merged into the familiar flow of traffic. How many times in my life had I performed this simple action—thousands? Tens of thousands?

I had no particularly pressing concerns during the forty-minute drive to La Jolla, California. I glided by the trees and shops and traffic lights that formed the reassuring backdrop of my world. I was thinking typical Monday-morning thoughts, reflecting on how tired I was.

How had I let myself get roped into this excursion to be poked and prodded by doctors? Mondays were good for many things: getting a jump-start into a new week, collecting my thoughts, reviewing another Lord's day, and catching my breath before thinking about the next one. Physical examinations weren't on my list of preferred Monday-morning activities. (To be honest, I have yet to find a suitable day for visiting the doctor.) But on this particular bright morning—September 26, 1994—I was thinking about Sunday's three sermons and the toll they had taken on my tired blood. I was reflecting dolefully on the rest and rehabilitation I could have been enjoying at that moment, instead of a forty-minute drive to Scripps Clinic for a full physical.

Those were my idle thoughts during a mundane drive on a Monday morning. But the clock was ticking: Forty minutes of peace and contentment were draining away before chaos struck.

On this day, the road of life on which I was traveling led to a sudden, sharp turn for which I was completely unprepared. I had no dark premonitions, no particular reason to cherish the simple securities and comforts that would be stripped away from me at the end of this journey. I was blissfully unaware of the rapid approach of a bend in the road.

It was still early as I arrived at the Center for Executive Health in La Jolla. The exam got underway at 7:45 A.M. with the interview, and I handled the usual barrage of questions from the nurses armed with their clipboards. Then I was ushered over into another part of the clinic for an EKG stress test. It went smoothly, and I could tell my numbers were good ones.

So far, so good. I smiled with satisfaction as the doctors nodded and made little checks on their notepads. They stroked their chins and admitted that I was in pretty fair shape for a grizzled fifty-three-year-old veteran of life's trenches. Better still, the physical exam was downhill all the way after the EKG. I had been through all this before, and it was easy to tell that I was checking out fine on the remaining tests. The men in the white coats gave me the thumbs-up at every point; I was beginning to think that maybe this was a smart way to spend a Monday after all.

Late in the morning, I was taken to an examining room, where I met the head physician. He asked me to lie faceup on the table, and I complied. The doctor began to go over my body from head to toe.

Soon I'll have this whole thing behind me, I thought. *It will feel good to have another successful physical in the books. The white-coats will hand me the bill and show me the door. I'll be free to climb into my van, drive back down the highway, and get on with my crowded agenda. And I'll have a little extra spring in my step, knowing that for one more round, I've come out victorious in the battle against time and corruption.*

Those were my thoughts.

That's when the bomb fell.

As the doctor probed the left side of my abdomen, he said, "Dr. Jeremiah, you have a mass here in your abdomen that causes me some concern. It feels to me as if your spleen is greatly enlarged."

I felt my heart skip a beat. "What do you think it is?" I asked.

"I can't say," he replied quietly, "until we see a CAT scan of that part of your body."

That's it. Two sentences—a handful of words—brought a crowded, thriving life to a screeching halt. As I sat up and dressed myself, I struggled to absorb the doctor's words. My mind launched into "spin-control" mode, searching for positive angles.

I had my scan late that afternoon in the radiology center across the street and was informed that results would be available the following day. At least the suspense wouldn't be prolonged; within hours I would be given words of comfort—or something else.

I was shell-shocked that afternoon as I went through the motions of the scan and closed out my business with the clinic. I was still in a daze as I made my way back to my home in El Cajon.

How was I going to handle this news bulletin there? This was something I needed to handle carefully—it was, after all, a bomb. I knew that Donna, my wife, planned to leave the next day to visit her mother in New Hampshire. She would be scrambling around the house, packing suitcases and orchestrating last-minute arrangements. She'd have that happy, busy glow about her, energized by the anticipation of her trip.

That's why I decided to keep silent. Why rain on her parade? At this point, everything was preliminary and tentative. I decided to let this evening be a bright one for at least one of us. I refused to ruin a pleasant trip for my loving wife.

So I kept the curtains tightly shut on the black clouds inside me. I smiled and made the best I could of the situation. The next morning, I drove Donna to the airport and watched her plane disappear into the blue, trouble-free sky that still existed for other people. Then I headed to my office, where I sat and watched my telephone, waiting for the call that would reveal my earthly fate. The moments ticked by slowly, and every ring was a false alarm.

Finally that afternoon, I picked up the receiver and heard the doctor's calm voice on the other end of the line. I listened desperately for a victorious affirmation—words about tests that came back negative, about lumps that were less than they seemed. I wanted those words desperately, and I poured out my soul praying for them.

But those words were not available to me. Instead, the doctor's fears were confirmed—I had a mass on my spleen.

The doctor carefully explained to me that three radiologists examined the scan and shared the firm opinion that I had lymphoma, a cancer that attacks the lymphatic system, of which the spleen is the center. We talked for a few minutes, then I returned the receiver to the cradle of the telephone. The most terrible phone call of my life was over. I felt emptiness and despair rising up inside me.

It was Tuesday, the day for staff meeting at our church—another difficult hurdle in my current state of turmoil. I kept the meeting short, dismissing it after a brief time of prayer. Then I sought out my close friend and staff member Dr. Ken Nichols and beckoned him into my office. I closed the door carefully, sat down beside him, and shared with him the details of my physical and the prognosis. He was the first person with whom I shared the crisis. We cried, embraced, and prayed. Then we pulled ourselves together and began to think about what to do.

Ken had an idea. He remembered a longtime friend of mine—Dr. Marv Eastlund of Fort Wayne, Indiana. I've known him since I was a pastor there many years ago. Dr. Eastlund is not only a knowledgeable physician, but he is also an experienced sufferer who spent six weeks in Mayo Clinic for a pancreatic disorder. (I'll give you his story in greater detail in chapter 9.)

Ken thought Dr. Eastlund might be able to help, and that sounded good to me. I made the call, and Dr. Eastlund didn't hesitate before issuing a directive: Go to Mayo Clinic immediately. My kind friend promised to make a phone call to expedite things for me. And in a matter of hours, I had an appointment at the Mayo Clinic.

On Thursday morning of that same week, I boarded a plane heading eastward. I was traveling on business—I was scheduled to speak at rallies in New Hampshire and Maine to support our *Turning Point* radio ministry. My friends Steve and Susan Caudill were flying with me. The plan was for Donna to meet us in Manchester, New Hampshire, at the first rally. As so often happens with air travel, the connections were perilously tight; we arrived at the rally with just enough time for me to kiss Donna hello and hurry to the platform.

The event was thrilling, and it lifted my spirits. The building was packed with fifteen hundred excited listeners. Several of them gave their hearts to Christ that night, securing their eternal destinies. Just at the time I was having a close encounter with death, these wonderful souls were having their first encounters with eternal life. I shook hands, chatted with folks, and signed books and Bibles until the last of the crowd went home.

When God permits His children to go through the furnace,
He keeps His eye on the clock and His hand on the thermostat.
His loving heart knows how much and how long (1 Peter 1:6–7).

—Warren Wiersbe

On the way back to the hotel, Donna and I stopped for a late dinner. That's where the thrill of the evening wore off. I became pensive over my plate because I knew that the time had come to level with my wife about the week's events.

We found our hotel and settled into the room, unpacking our things and turning down the sheets. Then I sat down on the bed and opened to Donna those dark curtains of my soul. I told her the whole story of three days of despair. When I finished, we cried and prayed and held each other through most of the night.

A bend in the road took us to that room. There, far from our home, on the other side of the continent—there, in a strange hotel—we huddled together to face the most challenging moment of thirty-plus years of marriage.

"You're Going to the Mayo Clinic!"

The rallies came to an end, and Donna and I returned home at last. There were more doctors' examinations and troublesome hours of sorting out insurance questions. Our ministry had begun a new insurance plan at the beginning of October, and that coverage would not extend to a trip to Mayo. It looked as if we'd have to settle for surgery in San Diego. I had a date with the doctors for Tuesday morning at Sharp Hospital, at which time my spleen would be removed.

My condition was no longer a secret; I'd begun to call some of my network of ministry friends around the country. I coveted their prayers. One of these men was Lowell Davey, president of the Bible Broadcasting Network. When I called him and described my situation, he responded without hesitation, "David, you are going to Mayo Clinic! If your insurance will not cover it, I'll raise the money myself."

I think you'll understand that by this time, Donna and I were spent. The emotional roller coaster had left us dizzy and exhausted. I told Lowell that my surgery was scheduled for Tuesday morning at 7:45—only five days from now. I set a condition. "If you can get me into Mayo Clinic on Monday morning," I said, "then I'll go."

Two hours later, I received a phone call from a doctor at Mayo Clinic, calling to confirm my appointment at 7:45 Monday morning. I was astounded, to put it mildly. True friendship is a powerful force for strength and encouragement.

With our minds finally set on a course of action, I began to prepare myself for the weekend. I was scheduled to officiate at a wedding for the daughter of my administrative secretary on Saturday afternoon at 3:00. Once again, I was mindful of my personal situation casting a pall over someone else's joyful occasion—particularly in the case of a wedding. I asked for the couple to be kept in the dark about my crisis until after the ceremony. This was their once-in-a-lifetime day, and it should be filled with joy.

The next morning, I preached at both services. The Lord once again honored His Word. But this was not just another Sunday for me. Afterward, I told Donna that in twenty-five years of preaching, I'd never felt the presence of the Lord as I did that day. Other preachers know this feeling—at times it was almost as if I were sitting on a pew in the back of my mind, listening to someone else preach. I was deeply aware of Paul's statement, "When I am weak, then I am strong" (2 Cor. 12:10). I'd never been so weak, and He'd never seemed so strong.

That afternoon, we flew east, this time toward Mayo Clinic.

During my first appointment, there were rounds of blood tests, physical examinations, and more questions. Finally I met with the first doctor. She went over the results and confirmed the diagnosis of lymphoma. She also made the arrangements for my next appointment, in the department of hematology.

When she called hematology, she was told that no opening would be available until Thursday. My heart sank. This was Monday! Three days seemed like an eternity, and I had work to do back home. How could we wait here for seventy-two hours? The doctor sensed my desperation. She considered quietly for a minute and finally said, "I know one of the doctors in that department. Let me call him."

The doctor called her friend, and I heard her say into the phone, "He's a pastor from San Diego. His name is David Jeremiah." Then a look of surprise splashed across her face. She put her hand over the mouthpiece and turned to me. "He knows you!" she said. Speaking into the phone, she said, "Does that mean you'll see him this afternoon?"

It did. I was instructed to head right over.

My doctor had been speaking to a colleague named Dr. Thomas Witzig, who had once heard me speak at Moody Founder's Week. Dr. Witzig is a wonderful Christ-follower, and it pleased me greatly to discover that he would be the lead physician. When we sat down to talk, he walked me through the procedures to come during the next few days. Dr. Witzig agreed that surgery was required, and it was scheduled for Tuesday morning at the Methodist Hospital in the Mayo Clinic complex.

That's where I went the next morning. The surgery lasted about two hours and revealed that the lymphoma was centered in the area immediately around my spleen. The surgeons decided to leave the spleen in place; it was actually not as diseased as they had anticipated. This was the first tentatively hopeful medical news we'd received, and you can imagine our gratitude.

The doctors patiently educated Donna and me about my condition. They explained that lymphoma is a treatable form of cancer. There are never any guarantees with this dreaded enemy, but we at least had the possibility for recovery through chemotherapy—and that made hope possible.

We held tightly to that hope. Our spirits basked in the prayers, support, and encouragement of our church family and friends; we fed on their support and felt strengthened for the battle ahead. But in the midst of all the love and affirmation, it was the Lord, "a stronghold in the day of trouble" (Nah. 1:7), who knew the needs of my body and soul most deeply. It was He who walked with me through the valley of the shadow, He who lavished upon me a deeper, more personal experience of His presence than I'd ever known before. As I sought refuge in His Word, I found consolation beyond description for my troubled spirit.

Again and again I was reminded of the words of the apostle Paul. Long ago he was confronted with death and fear, and perhaps he experienced emotions a bit like my own. Paul was so gifted and had a heart eager to minister, yet he was forced to bide his time in a dark prison. I know Paul asked God the same questions I have asked, and I'm grateful he recorded God's answers: "And He said to me, 'My grace is sufficient for you, for My strength is made perfect in weakness.' Therefore most gladly I will rather boast in my infirmities, that the power of Christ may rest upon me" (2 Cor. 12:9).

God's grace is sufficient—I can tell you it's true.

Life Is Difficult

Somewhere along your own path, you've likely encountered a bend in the road too. Suddenly you faced circumstances you never expected or wished to encounter. I hope you've found it helpful, as I have, to read encouraging words from fellow strugglers.

Gordon MacDonald is a friend and fellow struggler. His fine book *The Life God Blesses* has ministered to me more richly than I can tell you. Gordon writes with wonderful insight about the methods God uses to bring blessing into the lives of His servants. In one chapter, he coins a term to describe one of those tools. He calls them "disruptive moments." According to Gordon, disruptive moments are "those unanticipated events, most of which one would usually have chosen to avoid had it been possible."

He adds, "We don't like disruptive moments; they are too often associated with pain and inconvenience, failure and humiliation. Not that they have to be, but that seems the way of the human condition."[1]

Few of us ever fully grasp that simple but painful biblical truth—the heat of suffering is a refiner's fire, purifying the gold of godly character and wisdom. Wouldn't we rather it be a simpler, more comfortable process? But we know life simply doesn't play out that way. Everything worthy in this world comes at a price.

The Russian writer Aleksandr Solzhenitsyn understood the fullest implications of that idea. The point was driven home for him during long years of solitude and suffering in prison, the price he paid for writing a few words of truth about his government. He knew something of disruptive moments and wrote, "It was only when I lay there on rotting prison straw that I sensed within myself the first stirrings of good. Gradually it was disclosed to me that the line separating good and evil passes, not through states, nor between classes, nor between political parties either, but right through every human heart, and through all human hearts. So bless you, prison, for having been in my life."[2]

Can I say, "Bless you, prison," about my deepest trials? Can you bless the prisons that loom in the bend of your road? It takes a deep

---

Tried for a season, pure for eternity.

—Warren Wiersbe

---

spiritual wisdom to cultivate that ability—a profound faith that God loves us and that His purposes are truly right for us.

M. Scott Peck begins his bestseller *The Road Less Traveled* with three simple, indisputable words: "Life is difficult." Who will argue with that? Life *is* difficult.

My cancer diagnosis confirmed Peck's words. It was a profoundly disruptive moment in my life. This was no mere bump in the road; it felt like a gigantic and bottomless pothole. It opened up in my road quite suddenly, with no highway markers to warn me, and I plunged into its darkness. I had not been offered alternate routes or given a vote on the matter.

Life is difficult, and difficulty is the only path to wisdom.

One Great Challenge, Two Indispensable Passages

None of us enjoy suffering, but we can know one thing for certain: Disruptive moments are occasions for comforting one another. For example, I cherish the hope that my own disruptive moments will enable me to comfort you in yours. Perhaps I can pass along some nuggets of wisdom that came at the price of suffering in my own life.

Pain draws me to God's Word, and in the midst of my trials, I've spent countless hours in deep personal reflection upon Scripture.

I've been drawn repeatedly to two passages of Scripture: 2 Corinthians 12:7–10 and Hebrews 12:5–11. I invite you to take a few moments to reflect upon these passages with me; I think you'll see a recurring pattern in both texts.

Let's first look at 2 Corinthians 12:7–10:

> And lest I should be exalted above measure by the abundance of the revelations, a thorn in the flesh was given to me, a messenger of Satan to buffet me, lest I be exalted above measure. Concerning this thing I pleaded with the Lord three times that it might depart from me. And He said to me, "My grace is sufficient for you, for My strength is made perfect in weakness." Therefore most gladly I will rather boast in my infirmities, that the power of Christ may rest upon me. Therefore I take pleasure in infirmities, in reproaches, in needs, in persecutions, in distresses, for Christ's sake. For when I am weak, then I am strong.

This passage of Scripture describes a disruptive moment in the life of the apostle Paul. As we will see, Paul outlines for us the purpose, pain, provision, product, and perspective of this disruptive moment.

The Purpose of the Disruptive Moment

"Lest I should be exalted above measure by the abundance of the revelations . . ." (v. 7).

Paul clearly states that the purpose of his suffering was to protect him from the sin of pride. In the preceding verses, Paul described a time in the past when he had been granted an opportunity to be caught up into the very heavens with God. Now that's certainly a remarkable opportunity! Such an experience had been granted to no other person, and Paul could have easily been filled with pride over his unique privilege. If Paul had a press agent, he would have most certainly billed Paul as the only man who had visited heaven and lived to tell about it. But God uses disruptive moments to help us keep things in perspective.

The Pain of the Disruptive Moment

"A thorn in the flesh was given to me, a messenger of Satan to buffet me" (v. 7).

Scholars have spent untold hours speculating on the nature of Paul's problem. What was the affliction he was referring to? Some have suggested that Paul had developed eye problems, since we know that he began to dictate his letters to others. Another theory is that Paul was suffering from epileptic seizures. Sir William Ramsey even suggested that Paul had some recurring strain of malaria. You could fill a medical encyclopedia with other ideas that have been advanced: hysteria, hypochondria, gallstones, gout, rheumatism, sciatica, gastritis, leprosy, lice, deafness, dental infection, or remorse. Remorse? Don't forget that Paul had persecuted and tortured many Christians prior to his conversion.

Although we cannot be sure about Paul's "thorn," we can say this: The word used for *thorn* carries the literal meaning of *stake*. So what Paul wants to suggest to us is that he'd had a stake driven into his flesh—quite a disruptive moment, wouldn't you agree?

We're not told the specific nature of Paul's suffering, so we must conclude that the details are beside the point. What matters is that Paul did suffer in such a way that he compared it to the pain of a stake being pounded through his flesh. If we'd been told the exact nature of his affliction, this passage might have just seemed to be a story about Paul. We wouldn't be able to fill in the blank with our own personal afflictions, and our own "thorns" might seem outside the reach of God's grace. Instead, we're invited by 2 Corinthians 12:7–10 to identify with Paul's suffering. We're given the opportunity to realize that if God's grace was sufficient for him—whatever the nature of his suffering—it is sufficient for us as well.

The Provision in the Disruptive Moment

"My grace is sufficient for you, for My strength is made perfect in weakness" (v. 9).

Paul didn't relish painful experiences any more than you or I do. In fact, he asked God three times to remove the thorn from his flesh. But God refused his request. He would not remove the thorn, but He would do something else—in the midst of the ordeal, He would give Paul all the grace he needed to continue his work. He also told Paul that His strength would be made perfect in this time of weakness.

Think of that: strength enshrined in weakness, power in pain. It completely defies and undermines the human approach to things—and that's why it glorifies God.

The Product of the Disruptive Moment

"That the power of Christ may rest upon me. . . . For when I am weak, then I am strong" (vv. 9–10).

What God told Paul was merely this: "You won't lack the grace to do your job. You won't lack the strength to be my ambassador. But the creative difference will be this: Your weakness will serve to magnify the glory of My power in such a way that no one will ever again be able to explain your experience in human terms."

The weaker we are, the stronger His grace is revealed.

Or to put it another way: When "this little light of mine" becomes dimmer, His great floodlight shines all the more brightly.

The Perspective of the Disruptive Moment

"Therefore most gladly I will rather boast in my infirmities, that the power of Christ may rest upon me" (v. 9).

What a perspective! Paul sees himself in the midst of this disruptive moment and says, "I'm not the same man that I used to be. I've suffered, and I've felt my share of pain, yet now I find within myself an inner depth, a spiritual dynamic I've never known before. I've entered into the deepest mystery of life—the fellowship of Christ's sufferings. And now that I see the meaning of it all, I wouldn't trade a moment of misery for pure gold. In the end, you see, our pain offers us a far greater wealth. I've had a thorn in my flesh, and I claim it as a badge of honor."

So the apostle Paul has told us all about his weakness. Was he simply a passive person? Don't even consider it! The briefest study of his life demonstrates that there was nothing passive about Paul. This was the man who had scoured the countryside in search of Christians to intimidate. This was the man who had successfully debated the apostles on the question of Gentile salvation. This was the man who had faced stonings and beatings for the sake of the gospel.

Paul chose the most hostile settings in which to preach the gospel and plant churches. He scattered seeds of the gospel throughout Asia Minor and along the Aegean Sea. As the seeds grew, he trained the first pastors and elders in all the new churches. And then, in his spare time, he wrote half the New Testament!

So please don't call him "passive." Paul was a mover and a shaker, a human dynamo. How, then, do we reconcile that with his claim to weakness? How can a man be both weak and strong?

The answer lies in the phrase, "when I am weak, then I am strong." That statement bears careful scrutiny. Listen well to Charles Stanley's eloquent paraphrase: "When I, Paul, in and of my own strength, am weak, then I, Paul, relying on the power of Christ in me, become strong, capable of whatever the Lord requires of me, full of energy and zeal to accomplish His will."[3]

Keep these principles in mind as we move to our second passage, Hebrews 12:5-11:

And you have forgotten the exhortation which speaks to you as to sons:

"My son, do not despise the chastening of the LORD,
Nor be discouraged when you are rebuked by Him;
For whom the LORD loves He chastens,
And scourges every son whom He receives."

If you endure chastening, God deals with you as with sons; for what son is there whom a father does not chasten? But if you are without

chastening, of which all have become partakers, then you are illegiti-
mate and not sons. Furthermore, we have had human fathers who corrected us, and we paid them respect. Shall we not much more readily be
in subjection to the Father of spirits and live? For they indeed for a few
days chastened us as seemed best to them, but He for our profit, that we
may be partakers of His holiness. Now no chastening seems to be joyful for the present, but grevious; nevertheless, afterward it yields the
peaceable fruit of righteousness to those who have been trained by it.

The Purpose of the Disruptive Moment

"God deals with you as sons" (v. 7).

Can you remember facing a disruptive moment as a child? Perhaps
you fell from your bicycle and skinned your knee. What was your first
impulse? To call for help, of course. And perhaps when you did that,
your mother or father called out, "Stay right where you are—I'm coming to help you!"

That's precisely what God says to us: *Stay where you are. I'll be there with
you.* When life wounds us and we're in deep pain, we instinctively cry
out to God. And it is then that we hear Him and feel His presence so
clearly. In the midst of tragic circumstances, we can have the richest
fellowship with Christ afforded to us. That's when our faith becomes
fully real, and we experience the assurance of things we've hoped for.
We have confirmation in our hearts for what we've always believed
with our minds. We may have talked for a lifetime about being a child
of the Father, but now, as helpless creatures who have stumbled and
been wounded, it becomes true for us: *I am a child; He is my Father.*

He is your Father. You'll find it out at the bend in the road. At the
point of your own disruptive event, remember this truth. Engrave it
on your mind, and hold fast to it: *He is there for His children. He has always
been there, and He always will be there.* Can there be any doubt He will be
there in this place, and in this moment, for you?

The purpose of the disruptive moment is to demonstrate that we
are truly the children of God. There is no training and learning

without pain in the process. As we take our first steps as children, we stumble and fall. And every child that the Father loves will experience His training methods. No discipline, no growth—it's as simple as that. "Whom the LORD loves," He disciplines, chastens, and trains.

The Pain of the Disruptive Moment

"He chastens, and scourges . . ." (v. 6).

Let's be clear: God's Word never claims that times of pain and suffering should be eagerly anticipated. These are not times we have chosen. At the point of suffering, we don't feel joy; we feel genuine human pain. But that's not the end of the story.

The Provision of the Disruptive Moment

"For whom the LORD loves He chastens" (v. 6).

We find comfort in knowing the Father is watching over us. He sees us walk through the bend in the road, and though we don't anticipate the disruptive moment, He does. He is attentive, but He does more than watch us; He walks with us. And never does He walk closer to His children than those times when we're experiencing deep pain and misery.

The Product of the Disruptive Moment

"He [disciplines us] for our profit, that we may be partakers of His holiness" (v. 10).

God's discipline is "for our profit," although it seems anything but profitable at the time. Just as earthly parents discipline their children so they will grow up to be well-adjusted and successful, our heavenly Father disciplines us so that we will "grow up" to "be partakers of His holiness."

The Perspective of the Disruptive Moment

The writer of Hebrews offers three possible choices we can make in response to the disruptive moments we face.

1. We can despise the moment and rail against it (v. 5)."Why did this happen to me? Why am I going through this? Why would God allow me to have this experience?" How quickly we're prone to strike out against God when we come to a bend in the road. Those who choose this course of action, of course, are shortsighted. They have probably forgotten all about God on those occasions when there were nice surprises around the bend. But now, disaster strikes. They don't know what else to do, so they curse God. The writer of Hebrews tells us not to do that. He says, "Do not despise the chastening of the LORD."

2.We can become discouraged by the event, lose heart, and give up (v. 5). The writer of Hebrews instructs us not to be discouraged when we are rebuked. That's far too easy a response. Discouragement makes us want to give up, to throw in the towel and surrender to despair. That's not the spirit God wants in us. His goal is our perseverance, for it leads to growth and maturity, as we shall see.

3.We can endure it and be trained by it (vv. 7, 11). Finally—the right response. The Scriptures show us so clearly that nothing in life is wasted if we love and serve God. No matter how sharp the bend in the road, no matter how disruptive the moment, *everything* that happens to us is for the eternal purposes of God. He is training us through the process. Like any worthy parent, He wants to teach us what we cannot learn in any other way.

British journalist Malcolm Muggeridge wisely explained this concept to William F. Buckley: "As an old man, Bill, looking back on one's life, it's one of the things that strikes you most forcibly—that the only thing that's taught one anything is suffering. Not success, not happiness, not anything like that. The only thing that really teaches one what life's about—the joy of understanding, the joy of coming in contact with what life really signifies—is suffering, affliction."[4]

The only road that leads to the destination God desires for us has its sharp bends. All attempted shortcuts lead into wilderness.

Where are you, traveler? Perhaps you're facing a disruptive moment in your life, one you could never have anticipated. Perhaps your road has led to a divorce, a death, a financial disaster, a physical or mental sickness, or the heartbreak of seeing a fellow traveler wander away from the path. Maybe the bend in your road is something so disappointing and devastating that you can hardly bear to acknowledge

---

I bear willing witness that I owe more to the fire, and the hammer, and the file, than to anything else in my Lord's workshop. I sometimes question whether I have ever learned anything except through the rod. When my schoolroom is darkened, I see most.

—Charles Spurgeon

---

it. You could be standing by the side of your path, so overcome by pain that you believe you can't move on.

Please remember this: Your crisis is important to God. Could it be that you're looking at it from your own perspective? That's not the way our Father behaves toward us. Whatever struggle or setback you face is intended to empower and purify you. Your situation is important to Him, because He is using it to make you a more valuable servant in His kingdom.

Having lived through some very disruptive moments of my own, I want to give you five principles to remember. They've helped me, and I trust they'll be just as valuable in your own travels down that long and winding road.

Five Principles to Remember

Principle #1: Disruptive Moments Are Often Divine Appointments

Second Corinthians 12 identifies Satan as the messenger sent to test and torment Paul. But the devil wasn't given free rein; he couldn't do anything to Paul that God wouldn't allow. Remember Job? Satan was allowed to test him, but only with the permission and conditions pre-scribed by God. Paul and Job always remembered that God was ulti-mately in control.

The Father is the One who disciplines His sons—Hebrews 12 makes that very clear. Every trial we face, difficult as it may be, comes from the hand of God, who loves us and wants us to grow. If we're wise enough, we will see that disruptive moments are really divine appointments.

That perspective will make all the difference for you. It will keep you from lashing out at God in despair. It will keep you from giving in to discouragement. You will say, "God, You are in control—You have a plan, and that's why You have allowed this to happen in my life."

Some years ago I was given a copy of a letter that I can imagine being written by God to someone going through a disruptive mo-ment. It remains as poignant and pertinent now as it did then.

My child, I have a message for you today; let Me whisper it in your ear, that it may gild with glory any storm clouds which may arise, and smooth the rough places upon which you may have to tread. It is short—only five words—but let them sink into your inmost soul; use them as a pillow upon which to rest your weary head:

THIS THING IS FROM ME

Have you ever thought of it, that all that concerns you, concerns Me, too? for "he that touches you, touches the apple of His eye" (Zechariah 2:8).

I would have you learn, when temptations assail you, and the "enemy comes in like a flood," that this thing is from Me; that your weakness needs My might, and your safety lies in letting Me fight for you.

You are very "precious in My sight" (Isaiah 43:4). Therefore it is My special delight to educate you.

Are you in money difficulties? Is it hard to make both ends meet? This thing is from Me, for I am your purse-bearer, and would have you draw from and depend upon Me. My supplies are limitless

(Philippians 4:19). I would have you prove My promises. Let it not be said of you, "you did not believe the LORD your God" (Deuteronomy 1:32).

Are you in difficult circumstances, surrounded by people who do not understand you, who never consult your taste, who put you in the background? This thing is from Me. I am the God of circumstances. You came not to this place by accident; it is the very place God meant for you. Have you not asked to be made humble? See, then, I have placed you in the very school where this lesson is taught; your surroundings and companions are only working out My will.

Are you passing through a night of sorrow? This thing is from Me. I am the "Man of Sorrows, and acquainted with grief." I have let earthly comforters fail you, that, by turning to Me, you may obtain everlasting consolation (2 Thessalonians 2:16, 17).

Has some friend disappointed you? One to whom you opened out your heart? This thing is from Me. I have allowed this disappointment to come, that you may learn.

I want to be your Confidant. Has someone repeated things about you that are untrue? Leave them to Me, and draw closer to Me, thy shelter out of reach of "the strife of tongues," for I "shall bring forth My righteousness as the light, and My judgment as the noonday" (Psalm 37:6).

Have your plans been upset? Are you bowed down and weary? This thing is from Me. You made your plans, then came asking Me to bless them; but I would have you let Me plan for you, and then I take the responsibility; for "this thing is too much for you, you are not able to perform it by yourself" (Exodus 18:18). You are only an instrument, not an agent.

Have you longed to do some great work for Me, and instead been laid aside on a bed of pain and weakness? This thing is from Me. I could not get your attention in your busy days, and I want to teach you some of My deepest lessons. "They also serve who only stand and wait." Some of My greatest workers are those shut out from active service, that they may learn to wield the weapon of prayer.

Are you suddenly called upon to occupy a difficult and responsible position? Launch out on Me. I am trusting you with the possession of difficulties. "For this thing the LORD your God will bless you in all your works and in all to which you put your hand" (Deuteronomy 15:10).

This day I place in your hands this pot of holy oil; make use of it freely, My child. Let every circumstance as it arises, every word that pains you, every interruption that would make you impatient, every revelation of your own weakness, be anointed with it! Remember, interruptions are divine instructions. The sting will go as you learn to see Me in all things.

Therefore "set your hearts on all the words which I testify among you today . . . for it is not a futile thing for you, because it is your life, and by this word you shall prolong your days in the land" (Deuteronomy 32:46, 47).[5]

The moment we accept the fact that our ordeal has been permitted, even intended by God, our perspective on disruptive moments will totally change. We will find ourselves saying, "God, You have allowed this in my life. I don't understand it, but I know that it couldn't have happened to me unless it was filtered through Your loving hands. So, this thing is from You."

Principle #2: Progress without Pain Is Usually Not Possible

We live in a skin-deep world. Our culture glorifies clothing, fashion, makeup, tummy tucks, and nose jobs. There may be nothing wrong with any of these, but in the end they are only cosmetic. Character and substance are shaped in the crucible of adversity. Show me someone who lives a carefree life with no problems or trials or dark nights of the soul, and I'll show you a shallow person.

Ron Mehl, another pastor who has battled cancer, summarizes this point succinctly: "[Disruptive moments] always leave us with a list of things to clean up and fix. They are times when God restores to us the things we lose through negligence, ignorance, rebellion, or sin. For the Christian, [disruptive moments] are no-lose propositions. They help us to see and acknowledge the loose shutters, missing shingles, and rotten fence posts in our lives while turning us back to the only One who can make the necessary repairs."[6]

Unless there is pain in the formula, we will never stop to listen carefully to what He is saying. We'll be moving along happily, thinking we're going somewhere—but in reality, we're only spinning our wheels. We're not making any progress at all toward the deeper things our Father longs to show us. Sometimes He must allow us to stumble along the everyday journey. We're wounded and filled with pain, yet our disaster is just the opposite of what it seems; it's the demonstration of God's "tough love"—His determination to teach us and to make us wiser and stronger.

Life, then, brings all of us disruptions. It's up to us to choose our response. It can make us bitter, or it can make us better.

If we choose to let the disruptive moment make us better, we will toughen up. We will face the bend in the road with courage. Listen again to Gordon MacDonald: "The spiritual masters have taught us . . . that the one who would get in touch with his soul must do so with diligence and determination. One must overcome feelings, fatigue, distractions, errant appetites, and popular opinion. One must not be afraid of silence, of stillness, or of entering the overpowering presence of divinity with a humble spirit."[7]

Principle #3: The Promise of God Is the Provision of Grace

As we've delved into these two strategic biblical passages, we've seen one urgent theme that seems to stand out in bold letters. It is the voice of God saying to us over and over, "My grace is sufficient. My strength is made perfect in weakness. You are My son, and I will deal with you as My son." I'd like to direct you to one more snapshot from Scripture that completes the picture of God's provision in times of pain. You'll find it in John 15:1–8. In this passage, Jesus borrows a word picture from the plant kingdom. He explains that because He loves us, He must do some pruning in order for us to thrive and blossom. Do you understand how this principle works in gardening? Even with green things, God's concept of discipline holds true.

But the Gardener is loving and devoted. Someone has said, "The Father is never closer to the vine than when He is pruning it." That statement is right on the mark. You will find this truth consistently affirmed in the lives of wise, godly people who have faced disruptive moments. They will look at you and say without hesitation, "Never in all my life have I sensed the closeness and provision of God as I did when I came to the bend in the road. Never before have I been more fruitful than I've been since I came through the bend in the road."

Principle #4: Disruptive Moments Produce Dynamic Growth

We've looked at three Scripture passages together. They've yielded for us three specific products of adversity in the Christian life:

2 Corinthians 12:7–10	More Power
Hebrews 12:5–11	More Holiness
John 15:1–8	More Fruit

You can struggle against the disruptive moment, shake your fist at the heavens, and find yourself exhausted, defeated, and in despair—or you can accept the moment and let it train and strengthen you. The three passages above tell us that if you take the latter course, you'll discover on the other side more power, more holiness, and more fruit. Those are precious gifts that cannot be purchased with any coin other than tears. When you possess them, you'll comprehend with joy what God wanted so much for you to experience in your life.

God allows no pain without purpose. Instead, He uses pain to dispense power. His power can rest upon you only when you've abandoned the idea that you're big enough to go it alone. You're not big enough; you'll never make it without depending utterly upon Him and going in His strength. You're destined to fail without righteousness and holiness. And some pruning must take place, with sharpened shears, to cut away those things that would prevent righteousness and

---

Those who navigate little streams and shallow creeks, know but little of the God of tempests; but those who "do business in great waters"' these see His "wonders in the deep." Among the huge Atlantic waves of bereavement, poverty, temptation, and reproach, we learn the power of Jehovah, because we feel the littleness of man.

—Charles Spurgeon

---

holiness in your life. But how liberated you will be, how free to grow toward the heavens, after that pruning is accomplished!

Every plant, of course, must weather a storm every now and then. Ron Mehl has written, "Someone once told me that the times when plants grow the most are not necessarily during the warm, gentle rains or beautiful summer days. In fact, during fierce winds and raging storms come times of the most growth. Botanists tell us that if you were to take a cross-section of the earth during a vicious storm, you could literally observe the roots reaching further down into the soil."[8]

Can you feel it when the heavens open up and the wind and the rains thrash you? Can you feel your roots reaching ever deeper into His loving care?

Principle #5: What We Receive from Disruptive Moments Depends upon How We Respond

I remember so well the time when I came to my bend in the road. Everything God had given me to do was growing and thriving. The size of our church had doubled. The number of listeners to our *Turning Point* nationwide radio ministry had doubled. The books I had written were finding larger audiences. People were responding to our ministry. All of this was for the glory of God. And then, right in the midst of all these blessings came the disruptive moment. On the face of things, it seemed to make so little sense.

Have you had that kind of experience? Just when you had everything lined up in your life exactly as you wanted things to be, you experienced an unwelcome and unanticipated disaster that spoiled everything. And you asked many questions, all beginning with the word *why*.

"Why this, Lord?" you might ask. "Why now? Why not later? Why not someone else?"

We all ask the "why" questions. They're a natural part of being human. But we can ask better questions—we can ask "what" questions: "What, Lord? What would You have me do? What are You trying to teach me?"

I've faced pain, disappointment, doubt, and despair. In the midst of my trials, I've stopped asking the "why" questions and begun to focus on the "what" questions. I've told you the story of my terrifying medical diagnosis in 1994. But God wasn't through with me yet. I faced one more bend in the road; you'll read about it later in the book. In each of the following chapters, you'll hear from fellow strugglers and consider the deep message of hope that flows from the beautiful poetry of the psalms. You and I will share together the lessons the Lord offers so graciously to those who stumble and struggle.

I pray that the words of hope you'll find in this book will uplift and comfort you as they have me. And I hope my prayer becomes your prayer too:

> *Lord, what do You want to teach me to make me a better person? What are Your plans to make me more effective? Lead me and guide me through this process, O Lord. Be my teacher; show me Your ways. And don't let me miss any lesson You've prepared for me.*

Psalm 71

1 In You, O LORD, I put my trust;
  Let me never be put to shame.
2 Deliver me in Your righteousness, and cause me to escape;
  Incline Your ear to me, and save me.
3 Be my strong habitation,
  To which I may resort continually;
  You have given the commandment to save me,
  For You are my rock and my fortress.
4 Deliver me, O my God, out of the hand of the wicked,
  Out of the hand of the unrighteous and cruel man.
5 For You are my hope, O Lord GOD;
  You are my trust from my youth.
6 By You I have been upheld from my birth;
  You are He who took me out of my mother's womb.
  My praise shall be continually of You.
7 I have become as a wonder to many,
  But You are my strong refuge.
8 Let my mouth be filled with Your praise
  And with Your glory all the day.
9 Do not cast me off in the time of old age;
  Do not forsake me when my strength fails.
10 For my enemies speak against me;
  And those who lie in wait for my life take counsel together,
11 Saying, "God has forsaken him;
  Pursue and take him, for there is none to deliver him."
12 O God, do not be far from me;
  O my God, make haste to help me!
13 Let them be confounded and consumed
  Who are adversaries of my life;

Let them be covered with reproach and dishonor
Who seek my hurt.

14 But I will hope continually,
And will praise You yet more and more.

15 My mouth shall tell of Your righteousness
And Your salvation all the day,
For I do not know their limits.

16 I will go in the strength of the Lord GOD;
I will make mention of Your righteousness, of Yours only.

17 O God, You have taught me from my youth;
And to this day I declare Your wondrous works.

18 Now also when I am old and grayheaded,
O God, do not forsake me,
Until I declare Your strength to this generation,
Your power to everyone who is to come.

19 Also Your righteousness, O God, is very high,
You who have done great things;
O God, who is like You?

20 You, who have shown me great and severe troubles,
Shall revive me again,
And bring me up again from the depths of the earth.

21 You shall increase my greatness,
And comfort me on every side.

22 Also with the lute I will praise you—
And Your faithfulness, O my God!
To You I will sing with the harp,
O Holy One of Israel.

23 My lips shall greatly rejoice when I sing to You,
And my soul, which You have redeemed.

24 My tongue also shall talk of Your righteousness all the day long;
For they are confounded,
For they are brought to shame
Who seek my hurt.

2

Psalm for a Dark Night

Lord, Just today I read
That Paul and Silas were
Stripped and beaten
With wooden whips.
"Again and again the rods
Slashed across their bared backs"
But in their desolate dungeon
Their feet clamped in stocks
They prayed.
They sang.
They praised.
In this musty midnight of my life
Imprisoned in the dungeon of confusion
Bound by chains of anguish
Help me, please help me
To pray
To sing
To praise
Until the foundation shakes
Until the gates fling open
Until the chains fall off
Until I am free
To share the Good News
With other chain-bound prisoners.

—RUTH HARMS CALKIN,

TELL ME AGAIN, LORD, I FORGET

Three o'clock in the morning.

At that darkest and most dismal of hours, there may be no silence deeper than the silence of a hospital corridor. During my stay at Green Hospital, I became closely acquainted with the time and the desolate feeling of it.

I also became acquainted with the feeling of morphine. When you reach a point at which you must be involved with such a terrifying medication, you are desperate indeed. My morphine drip was a distinctly uncomfortable all-day, all-night arrangement. Those of you who have experienced this medication know that morphine is a powerful and frightening narcotic, one that causes unpredictable reactions for different people.

My reaction to the drug was a waking nightmare of confusion and disorientation. I could only manage short periods of sleep punctuated by sudden, startled consciousness—like being shaken violently awake. After this jarring sensation, I would be unsure where I was, what day it might be, or what was happening to me. That was the pattern of my life: moments of sleep, moments of confusion. It lasted for about five days that all blurred together like an unpleasant dream.

The nights were worst, of course; they were long and dark and lonely. I remember waking abruptly one night, looking around with grogginess at the bed and the darkened room, and doing the best I could to get my bearings. There was nothing on my mind, with the exception of a Scripture passage that seemed to be lingering in wait for me. How had that biblical passage lodged in my mind?

I slowly began to remember. A friend had been talking to me about those verses. He had a sense of urgency about my need to read Psalm 71. "This is a psalm you've got to read, pastor!" he had said. And now, wide awake at 3:00 A.M., I decided this was a pretty good time to take his suggestion.

A Light Shining in Darkness

Beneath the fluorescent light from my headboard, I reached for my Bible and turned to the psalm. Was this a good time to be reading the

Bible, with my mind addled by morphine? I knew in my heart it was indeed the right moment. I understood that God's power is greater than morphine, and He proved it once more in the stillness of a hospital ward. God's Spirit reached out to my soul through the inspired words of Psalm 71 and brought me comfort and assurance. Once again, like so many times before, His hand gathered me up through the Scriptures and pulled me into His powerful embrace. In the late-night loneliness and lack of a sound mind, I found blessed hope.

It doesn't matter how deep is the pit we've stumbled into—we can always grasp at that ray of heavenly hope. For example, consider the plight of Lawrence Hanratty. Here is how the media covered it:

Jolted, jilted, hammered in a car crash and robbed, Lawrence Hanratty was named Friday as the unluckiest man in New York.

Nearly electrocuted in a construction site accident in 1984 that put him in a coma for weeks, Hanratty lost the lawyers fighting for his liability claim—one was disbarred, two died—and his wife ran off with her lawyer.

Hanratty, who spent years fighting heart and liver disease, had his car wrecked in a crash last year. When police left the scene of the accident, he was held up and robbed.

"I say to myself, 'How much more am I going to be tested in life to see how much I can endure?'" Hanratty told the *New York Daily News* in a description of more than 10 years of agony.

As if he hasn't tolerated enough hardship, 38-year-old Hanratty of Mt. Vernon, N.Y., said an insurance company now wants to cut off his worker's compensation benefits and his landlord has threatened to kick him out of his apartment.

Depressed and suffering from agoraphobia, a fear of open spaces, Hanratty uses a canister of oxygen and takes 42 pills a day for his heart and liver ailments. But with help from neighbors and a New York state assemblyman, he is not giving up yet.

"There's always hope," he said.[1]

"There's always hope," Mr. Hanratty was able to say, despite how little evidence life had given him to believe it. Have you ever been at the threshold of surrender? Have you been at the point of discarding your faith by the side of the road or requesting an extended sick leave from God's army? I've been there. And someone else has too. He recorded his feelings in Psalm 71.

Who wrote this psalm? We usually find the author's name inscribed at the top of the psalm. Turn to Psalm 23 and you'll read, "A Psalm of David." But Psalm 71 is interesting: The author has chosen to remain anonymous. All the same, I feel confident that it was written by David, who is giving us a kind of sequel to Psalm 70, the preceding one. These verses take up right where the previous ones leave off. And there's a fascinating and quite tragic story to be found in the background if we peek behind the curtains.

There was a time in King David's life when one of his sons, a young man named Adonijah, tried to usurp his father's throne. David had promised the title to another of his sons, Solomon. So political turmoil and family warfare were all entangled. Some scholars feel that David wrote these psalms during that heartrending time of family discord.

Can you imagine it? Here is elderly King David, nearing the end of his amazing life. He has brought the young nation of Israel to its greatest peak of power and stability. In the midst of building a dynasty, he has already survived a previous family insurrection. Absalom, his heir, had turned on his father and attempted to seize the throne. The cost to King David of his son's insurrection was horrendously heavy, including the life of Absalom and the unity of his people. Now his son Adonijah is attempting to steal what has been promised to Solomon. The whole nightmare seems to be coming to pass again. When you read about David's life, you realize you've only *thought* you had family turmoil.

David's aging heart was burdened with a deep grief you and I are probably incapable of beginning to comprehend. Had he served God so long for such a reward as this? David knew he'd made serious mistakes in his younger years, and he understood that his sin would bring consequences to be worked out in turmoil for both his family and his kingdom. Even so, this was a heavy price for a father who deeply loved his sons and the godly nation that had been entrusted to him. No pain exceeds that of an anguished and heartbroken parent, and David was suffering to the very core of his being.

Psalm 71 is an incredible jewel in the Scriptures. It's not lengthy—a mere twenty-four verses. And yet hidden within these double-dozen lines are at least fifty quotations or allusions to other psalms. The psalmist brought all of these references together in his troubled mind, considered them from the lens of a lifetime of godly wisdom, and pieced them all together in a mosaic masterpiece of heartfelt poetry. As you read it, you may begin to understand the amazing comfort and healing it brought to me at 3:00 A.M. in a silent hospital room. My mind began to take leave of my own troubles recalling the sorrows of an ancient king in a faraway land and the message of peace and liberation that came out of his despair.

The Reality of Trials in the Believer's Life

There is a strange idea going around in churches today. Some Christians have the odd impression that being a believer will exempt them from all problems. Somehow they feel that, upon conversion, they're

---

There is nothing, no circumstance, no trouble, no testing that can ever touch me until, first of all, it has come past God and past Christ, right through to me. If it has come that far, it has come with a great purpose.

—Alan Redpath

---

issued the spiritual equivalent of ID cards that say, "This absolves the holder from any kind of pain or trouble while living on this planet."

It simply doesn't work that way. We Christians have no immunity whatsoever to pain or suffering. It matters not whether you're a new convert or a wise spiritual giant, you're still an imperfect human creature living in a fallen world; you struggle with all the blessings and burdens being a member of the family of man entails. When we become part of God's own family, what sets us apart is not any difference in the sin environment around us, but in how we deal with it.

Peter wrote, "Beloved, do not think it strange concerning the fiery trial which is to try you, as though some strange thing happened to you" (1 Pet. 4:12). In other words, don't be surprised if you give your life to Jesus Christ and you still stumble and take a fall the next day. You've gained no special right to bypass the human condition of suffering.

In Psalm 71 we find a poet who knew something about suffering. He saw his life as a pathway moving steeply uphill and filled with treacherous obstacles—a hill to be climbed in a lifetime of diligence and humility. He describes for us in passionate phrasing the view he sees as he looks upward to the horizon. Like any inspired poet, he compels us to look through his eyes, see that hill in every detail, and recognize it as our own. Then it becomes possible for us to begin to understand why we must climb that steep hill and why we face obstacles.

Trials Because of Ungodly Foes

"Deliver me, O my God, out of the hand of *the wicked*, out of the hand of the *unrighteous and cruel man*" (v. 4; emphasis added).

David had some very dangerous enemies, and they were creating tremendous anxiety in his life. The word *cruel* comes from the same Hebrew word that is sometimes translated "leaven." It means this enemy was not only wicked, but he was also spreading his wickedness every way he could, as leaven spreads outward in the rising of bread dough. His evil was permeating the layers around itself like a contagion, infecting all that it touched.

This is a problem that is very simple: We have enemies to contend with. You may not have soldiers hunting you down, as David did, but someone may be angry with you at work. Perhaps he is angry with God, and because he knows about your faith, he focuses all the heat of his rage on you. You, as a believer, become the symbol of everything in life that has confused and infuriated him, so he tries to make your life miserable. I know Christians whose lives have been turned upside down because of another individual's unprovoked attack. It can happen, and it can happen to you.

Trials Because of an Uncertain Future

"Do not cast me off in the time of old age; do not forsake me when my strength fails" (v. 9).

Sometimes the enemy is a bit more subtle. For example, could your enemy be a faceless foe such as aging? David answers in the affirmative in Psalm 71:9.

May I share something with you? At 3:00 A.M., all alone in my hospital room during a morphine drip, I did see aging as my enemy. I was reading this psalm, and I knew exactly what the psalmist meant. The very passage of time itself can become a trial to us. It seems as if the years have coldly discarded us by the side of the road while younger, stronger, and livelier feet sprint past us on the path. We hear the youthful laughter and feel the weight of our years. David pleads with God, "Do not cast me off in the time of old age; do not forsake me when my strength fails." That was my prayer, too, while hooked up to machines in a silent and lonely hospital wing.

Aging, of course, will bring illness, as much as we may choose to live in denial of the fact. I remember my self-satisfied feelings about my sunny health as I progressed through my physical examination in 1994. The last word I expected to hear was *cancer*. But as with any member of the human race, the more the aging process encroached on me, the greater became the possibilities I might encounter that disease. When the reality of it came to pass, I simply had to face it. I didn't vote for it; I didn't receive a notice in the mail from the surgeon general. Cancer is no respecter of persons. One of the facts about humanity is aging and all that comes with it. It's a trial we all must face.

Trials Because of Unfaithful Friends

"For my *enemies* speak against me; and *those who lie in wait for my life* take counsel together, saying, 'God has forsaken him; pursue and take him, for there is none to deliver him.' O God, do not be far from me; O my God, make haste to help me! Let them be confounded and consumed who are *adversaries of my life;* let them be covered with reproach and dishonor *who seek my hurt*" (vv. 10–13; emphasis added).

Some trials come from those who aren't even enemies in the truest sense. We can be hurt by the very people who are closest to us. The coalition causing the trouble in this particular passage was not made up of Philistines or other foreign tribe. No, David's enemies were people within his own circle, from his own family. Among them were his sons, Absalom and Adonijah. These two beloved sons had each tried to usurp the throne. In this case, Adonijah sought to turn his own father's advancing years against him. He saw his elderly father as a ripe target for a power play. I urge you to think about that for a moment and to try to imagine how it must have broken a father's heart.

Sometimes the deepest cut is inflicted from the closest range. No wound is quite so painful as the one inflicted by someone we love and trust. Families are experiencing discord all over our country today. How tragic it is when people turn against their most basic social unit. My friends in the legal profession tell me that the bitterest and most painful scenes they ever encounter are in divorce courts. Men and women who were once bound to each other by vows of faithfulness and undying love have now become the fiercest of enemies intent on striking out at each other and inflicting pain.

A house divided against itself is a terrible trial indeed.

Trials Because of an Unparalleled Heavenly Father

"Also Your righteousness, O God, is very high. You who have done great things; O God, who is like You? You . . . have shown me great and severe troubles" (vv. 19–20).

There is another way to look at trials, one that will require you to see them through a completely different lens. Trials can come through friends or enemies or aging, but they can also come from God Himself. Does that idea shock you?

Parents are less likely to be shocked. They can remember times when they had to allow their children to experience hardships they might easily have removed. Fathers and mothers are tempted to hover over a child, swooping in to deflect any temptation or threat that comes into the child's path. But something called love prevents them from doing that. Wise parents love their children enough to allow them to experience pain, for that shocking pain can teach things the wisest words of parents can't. As much as parents suffer when their children are hurting, they would suffer more if their children were never allowed to grow into all the wisdom and maturity intended for them.

Some things can't be learned through lectures; they must come at the cost of burned fingers or skinned knees. Parents know that, and they're able to comprehend the fact that God is another Parent—a perfect one—who must allow suffering in His own children to facilitate their growth. It's important to understand that God doesn't coldly stand aside during the trials we experience any more than you are aloof during your own children's episodes of poor decisions and unwanted consequences. Loving parents find themselves pacing the floor and praying intently as they watch the struggles of their children. They know deep in their hearts that their beloved children will come out of it wiser and more mature, but those parents hurt with their children just the same.

God sends trouble into our lives to strengthen us and to make us better children in His family. David recognizes this and, in essence, says, "God, You did it. You have shown me severe troubles." Doesn't that seem like a strange thing to thank God for?

No, because the psalmist realizes God loves us. As we saw in the last chapter, those whom the Lord loves, He chastens.

The Result of Trials in the Believer's Life

We could imagine an infinite number of different kinds of trials. And the number of potential responses to these trials are also limitless. Anything can happen to us; many roads can be chosen by us. Our choices will determine what kind of people we turn out to be.

I've often been asked how it felt to learn I had cancer. "Were you afraid?" people ask. Absolutely! I was *desperately* afraid. There's no disputing that. Was I afraid to die? No. I'm not afraid to leave this life, although I'm not eager to do so either. A good bit of my fear focused on losing precious years with the people I love. Some of it was simply about pain. Some of it was about the unknown. How would you respond to the news that you were suffering from a possibly fatal disease? Imagine the thoughts and feelings that might flood your heart at such a time, and you'll know the same things I experienced.

Let's examine a few of those feelings:

Vulnerability

Most of us live under the illusion of invulnerability; particularly when we're young; particularly, too, I think, when we're male. Men enjoy the delicious illusion of controlling their own destiny. We determine our own fate (or perceive we're doing so) by acting and taking things into our own hands. We feel we've got it all figured out, and everything is under control. Look us up fifty years from now—we'll be playing with our great-grandchildren. We'll live forever! We live in the illusion of invulnerability.

The first thing a serious crisis does is burst that pleasant bubble. Suddenly everything we've believed about life seems to be shattered. Our lives are in chaos just when everything seemed to be in such fine order.

Psalm 71:7 says it this way: "I have become as a wonder to many, but You are my strong refuge." What was David talking about?

David was a king. He knew that everyone was watching him to see what he'd do. If you happen to be a Christian leader, you know how absolutely true this is. When I announced that I had cancer, I knew exactly what people were saying: "David Jeremiah has been preaching all this 'faith in God' stuff for thirty years now. He's been 'talking the talk' just fine. But now he's living it out. How is he going to handle it? Can he 'walk the walk'?"

That's the position David found himself in. Everyone knew the awful details of his dysfunctional family. He was not only the king, but also the man who talked to everyone about God. Now he seemed to have feet of clay. What was he going to do?

David didn't know what to do, but he knew enough to watch God to find out what God would do. The king didn't have all the answers, but he knew Someone who did. He was wise enough to know the limits of his own wisdom.

If you're lacking in that ability, a sense of vulnerability will enhance it for you. You'll be painfully aware of your limitations. And you'll turn in abject humility to the only One in the entire universe who is indeed invulnerable.

Insecurity

In Psalm 71:2, David cries out, "Deliver me in Your righteousness, and cause me to escape!"

Can you identify with that? It's the most basic cry the soul can release: *Lord, I want out!* Stop the world; I want to get off! Oh, how we'd love to simply wake up tomorrow morning and find that God has miraculously removed us from the crisis. Where do we go to reclaim the security and confidence we had so recently? We want things the way they were.

We've already heard David's words, "Do not cast me off in the time of old age; do not forsake me when my strength fails" (v. 9). Can you see the insecurity and loss expressed in those words? Remember the bold and courageous kind of man David was. But time and circumstances and failure have removed any illusions he had of being in control of his own destiny. He no longer buys into the illusion of invulnerability.

And that's not a bad thing. One commentator has called Psalm 71 "a psalm for a godly old man." I like the "godly" part, don't you? The "old man" part, well, that will have to grow on me. But this psalm does lay out a path for those who have traveled a great distance on the trail of life, progressed in years, and entered some of the wastelands. This psalm shows how to crown our mature years with godliness.

As we age, our natural defenses against life's injuries begin to erode. Perhaps we've retired and no longer have that cherished career to lean upon. Our income is no longer disposable. Our eyes are weaker, our joints are fragile, and our energy is fleeting. And we begin to see the names of our friends in the morning paper, no longer as the movers and shakers who dominate the business page, but in the section that gives the details of funeral services. What a humbling passage of life that is. Little by little, we're stripped of all the things in life that have lent us security. It's a season of slowly developing anxiety.

If we choose the right path, we find ourselves hurrying into the presence of God for true security and ultimate comfort. We've seen the worst of life. Now we're capable of understanding just how much we really depend on Him. We finally believe that indeed life is a vapor, as the Scriptures say. We have nothing to count on but our loving Father.

David wrote many psalms about hurrying into God's presence in fear and trembling. It's certainly one of the great themes of the psalms, and I've always found it interesting that he uses three key metaphors: "God, You are my strong *refuge* . . . You are my *rock* and my *fortress*" (emphasis added).

David was under attack from his own children. He had spent a lifetime building a strong and secure kingdom, and now he could feel it drifting out of his grasp. In the midst of his insecurity, he found that God was his refuge, his rock, and his fortress. And he fled into the comfort and safety of those walls.

Perhaps you've seen the film *Lawrence of Arabia*. The real T. E. Lawrence, who was a secret agent during the First World War, often engaged in desert guerrilla warfare against the Turks. The enemy forces who chased Lawrence constantly often felt they had him hemmed in and trapped. But he would ride to his hidden desert fortress. He was never too far away from it, and if worse came to worst, he could flee there, find safety, and strengthen himself on the ample provisions of food and water. Lawrence had a refuge, a rock, and a fortress in the dangers of the wilderness. But God provides a much better one for you and me.

In those times when we feel the hostile forces of the world pursuing us, we long for a strong refuge. As we feel suddenly exposed and vulnerable and our feet are unsteady in the shifting sands beneath us, we yearn for a rock and a fortress—the kind of security found only in God.

Dependency

A powerful leader is invariably self-reliant and independent. It simply comes with the territory. He charts his own course and depends on his own resources. But sooner or later, he reaches his limit. Whether age or enemies overtake him, he finds he's not self-reliant after all. When trials come, the greatest leaders of all, the wisest ones, will then turn their eyes toward heaven. When their power hits its limit, they'll

---

As I lift up my eyes to Him, and accept it as coming from the throne of God for some great purpose of blessing for my own heart, no sorrow will ever disturb me, no trial will ever disarm me, no circumstance will ever cause me to fret, for I shall rest in the joy of what my Lord is.

—Alan Redpath

---

seek a power higher than themselves and begin to experience a feeling of dependency.

In that moment of transformation, we suddenly realize, "I don't control my world after all! I could become a victim, no matter how smart or sly or strong or elusive I may be. Lord, I have nowhere to turn. I have no more ideas and nowhere to run or hide. Dear God, if You don't stand firm and strong for me, then all is lost and I have no hope. Only You can rescue me."

Now you may be thinking, *This is true, but I've still got a ways to go. I'm fairly young. These are all things that don't need to concern me right now.* Think again. Your clock is ticking, and your time will come far more quickly than you ever felt possible. No one has ever said, "I thought I would never grow old. My youth seemed endless!" Every human clock ticks off the moments toward vulnerability, insecurity, and dependency.

Emergency

David says, "Make haste to help me!" (v. 12). In other words, "Lord, can You speed it up just a little bit? Yes, I've been told that You have Your own timetable, and I know that's reasonable, but can You scratch some things out and move my appointment up just a little bit? I promise not to ask again. This is an emergency!"

Isn't that the way we all feel when we make the heavenly 911 call?

I have a lot of reasons to love the psalms. I could spend eternity detailing them for you. Among the greatest of all my reasons is that they were written by genuine, historical people who faced trials no different from the ones you and I face. And these ordinary people expressed themselves accordingly. The psalmists made no attempt to put a spin on things. There were no editors with red pencils marking out the really tough expressions of emotions. They just told it like it was and let the words fly. Their tough, painful, and starkly honest words are there for you and me as part of God's Word.

David could certainly let the words fly when he felt a sense of urgency. He felt all the despair and panic of any man in pain. But he also leads us, time after time, to an understanding that completely changes our attitudes. This understanding is expressed in these questions: Are there truly such things as emergencies from the heavenly viewpoint? Is God ever taken by surprise? Is He ever alarmed? Does He panic? For each of these questions, the answer can only be an emphatic, "No!"

This is a tremendously difficult perspective for us to master and maintain: *We move in time, but God operates in eternity.* He sees the end from the beginning. He cannot be taken by surprise, for our past, present, and future are before Him and in His grip all at once. An emergency to you or me is an opportunity in the great mosaic of His purposes, a useful occasion for building our trust, stretching our faith, teaching us to hope, and nurturing our patience. As Paul wrote, "Hope that is seen is no hope at all. Who hopes for what he already has? But if we hope for what we do not yet have, we wait for it patiently" (Rom. 8:24–25 NIV). This is known as perspective, the lens through which you choose to look at the things that matter in life.

How will you choose to deal with your personal crisis—as an emergency or an opportunity? A stumbling block or a steppingstone? The moment you and I can begin to see things through the heavenly lens, the picture becomes bearable—and we find new strength.

We've discussed the reality of trials. We've explored their results. But where do we go from here? What should be our response to trials? We'll take on the implications of that question in the next few pages.

The Response to Trials in the Believer's Life

Someone has said that Psalm 71 is filled with great praise and great complaining all at once. I'm not certain I would characterize this wonderful psalm in quite that way. I do know this: David brings us low then lifts us up. He takes us on a tour of the deep pit to which his own road has brought him then points us to the high road we should take when we come into those low places. As in so many of the psalms, David's pilgrimage embodies both human defeat and godly victory.

That's no insignificant footnote, for we tend to lack a theology of adversity in the church these days. A so-called prosperity gospel has so permeated our church life that we're constantly hearing a bit too much of the word *positive.* We're told to practice "positive thinking." We're assured that if we practice "positive confession," positive things will happen to us. Above all, we're exhorted to keep a positive attitude and look on the bright side.

Positive is a perfectly good word, and optimism is a fine thing. Unfortunately, life isn't always positive. Sometimes things go wrong. And if our minds are set on being relentlessly positive, the time will come when we may be living in fantasy. I like to be positive, and I count myself as a very positive thinker. But here's something I also believe: If you don't have a realistic view of adversity, the outcome won't be very positive when it's your turn to face it.

David wasn't much for fantasy worlds. When his life went wrong, he refused to ignore what was negative in his life. He was a realist, and he had a godly perspective. Let's follow David in his plan of operation.

Remember the Character of God

When David saw the worst life had to dish out for him, he could still remember the perfection and faithfulness of God: "In You, O LORD, I put my trust; let me never be put to shame. Deliver me in Your righteousness, and cause me to escape; incline Your ear to me, and save me. Be my strong habitation, to which I may resort continually; You have given the commandment to save me, for You are my rock and my fortress" (vv. 1–3).

Whenever we face trials, we need to remember who God is. Sometimes we get so focused on our trials we forget to focus on Him. If you take your pen in hand and mark your Bible carefully as you go through this psalm, you'll see that throughout his prayer David made references to God's character:

- He remembers God's glory in verse 8.
- He acknowledges God's power and strength in verse 18.
- He remembers God's faithfulness in verse 22.

Five different times in Psalm 71—verses 2, 15, 16, 19, and 24—David mentions the righteousness of God. The reason is clear. David understood that there was one thing he must do when trials were swirling around his head, when his own children were not honoring him. *He must never forget that God is righteous and good, that He is a God who can be trusted.* Things may be bad, and they can always be worse, but God never changes. He is never any less in control. He never has a smaller portion of love for us, and His plan for us does not deviate in the tiniest detail. All else changes but God. As the poet said, He is the still point of the turning world. David knew that he must never allow these thoughts to leave his mind, so over and over again he spoke about the righteousness of God.

We're not dealing in naive, rosy sentiment, my friend. I've looked in the face of death, and you may have done the same. If you've made that dark journey, I've been there too, and I'm here to assure you that we have a God who is trustworthy. I may not fathom every twist and turn in my journey. Many things have happened for which I can't give a rational human explanation. I'm sure it's the same way for you. But I can lay it all at the feet of God and say with all my heart, "I don't know the meaning, but He does. He knows what He is doing. Our God makes no mistakes!"

When we go through hard times, everybody on the street has an opinion about why it is happening, where we should go for help, and what's going on. Isn't it confusing? People have told me about every alternative cancer therapy dreamed up within or outside the world of science. And yes, at first I wanted to read every word of every brochure placed in my hands by concerned friends. If there was any hope contained in any one of them, I was going to find out about it. If there was any way for me to take my healing into my own hands, I was ready to do anything and everything.

But after awhile, we reach a new mind-set in which we push aside all the dreams and schemes and contrivances, and we fall on our knees to say, "My Lord and my God, my hope is in *You*. All the rest is too much for my limited and distressed mind, and it amounts to little account anyway. I look to no one, and nothing, but You, and I await Your guidance."

Review the Compassion of God

David said, "Deliver me, O my God, out of the hand of the wicked, out of the hand of the unrighteous and cruel man. For You are my hope, O Lord GOD; You are my trust from my youth. By You I have been upheld from my birth; You are He who took me out of my mother's womb. My praise shall be continually of You" (vv. 4–6).

What did David do in his moment of despair? He simply went back into his memory and reviewed the many pieces of wisdom about God he had learned over time. He reminded himself that God had proved faithful to him throughout all his life. David had confronted a giant. He had faced a jealous king with murder on the mind and an army of assassins. He had faced the legions of challenging nations. Somehow Israel and its king had survived and prospered. In all these things, God had been faithful. The Lord had brought him through.

And what was true for that David has been true for me.

I can look back and say, "God, You have blessed me every day of my life in some new and surprising way. You have satisfied the deepest longings of my soul. You have guarded me and guided me through every crisis I've faced. You blessed me with godly parents. From the very moment I was born, I was nurtured on Your Word as if it were my mother's milk. And You delivered me out of the chaos of my troubled teenage years. You watched over me through college and through seminary. You sustained me through my early days of ministry when I could have become so discouraged that I might finally have just thrown in the towel and abandoned Your work. God, as I look back over the years and see the height and depth and breadth of Your great compassion, I can only say that indeed, great is Your faithfulness."

What about you? What is your testimony of God's grace and goodness? Even if you have walked with the Lord for only a few weeks, God has been good to you. And the faithfulness of God that has been extended to you up to this point is simply a reminder that God is good, that He is compassionate, and that He cares. He is not going to change in the middle of your life what He has been doing faithfully throughout all eternity.

Rejoice in Celebration to God

Here is where we find the central miracle at the heart of the psalm. This is when we know it's time to take off our shoes, for we're on holy ground. David is pouring out his heart to God over excruciating family troubles. He cries out to God because of the terrible pain he feels. This would be for you, for me, for nearly any member of the human race a time of deep self-pity and anger toward God. Yet somehow, in the midst of David's wounds and suffering, his prayer is filled with worship and praise. Knowing all that you do of the troubled world of King David, I challenge you to listen closely to his words and see if you can come away unmoved:

- "My praise shall be continually of You" (v. 6).
- "Let my mouth be filled with Your praise and with Your glory all the day" (v. 8).
- "But I will hope continually, and will praise You yet more and more. My mouth shall tell of Your righteousness and Your salvation all the day, for I do not know their limits" (vv. 14–15).
- "Also with the lute I will praise You—and Your faithfulness, O my God! To You I will sing with the harp, O Holy One of Israel. My lips shall greatly rejoice when I sing to You, and my soul, which You have redeemed. My tongue also shall talk of Your righteousness all the day long; for they are confounded, for they are brought to shame who seek my hurt" (vv. 22–24).

This is the mark of the truly godly: In the very midst of life's deepest misery, their voices are lifted in praise of God. In a shattered family, from the rubble of a ruined business career, out of the tragic loss of a loved one—in all of these places, a tear-choked voice lifts itself toward heaven in unrestrained worship. In the obscene cruelties of a prison camp, in a totalitarian nation where God's people are hunted and imprisoned, in a life of failed health in which death is the only certainty—there is somehow, against all odds, the sound of singing in the darkness. It occurs in the life of David. Perhaps it will occur in your life as well, in that moment in which your faith comes shining through its steepest challenge.

Such a response defies every expectation. How can we account for it without naming the name of Almighty God? Watch and wait, and you'll find it to be true. You'll be faced with a trial, and God will give you two gifts: a scripture for your mind and a song for your heart. And the song He gives you will burst forth in lovely melody in the midst of the darkest night. I don't apologize for the fact that in my hospital room, in the middle of the night and a morphine drip, I was in my uncomfortable bed praising God with my hands lifted up to the Lord. I was celebrating Him, thanking Him for life, for health, for family, for friends—all that He is and all that He does. It was the most joyful song that hospital ever heard.

Perhaps it sounds a little less than real to you. "I've suffered before," you say, "and I wasn't singing anything but the blues. The Bible was the last book I felt like reading, and the last thing I was in the mood for was worship."

You may have a point. In most cases, we don't *feel* like praising God in the oncology ward of a hospital. But it happens when we look deeply into His truth, when we step just far enough outside our own entrenched emotional defenses to take a good look at where God has been in the past and where we know Him to be in the present. We do it out of sheer obedience. And we also sing the song because perhaps we've had experience with praise. We've praised Him in the midst of the crisis then been astounded at what He did for us. Praise not only benefits God, but also the one who offers it.

When you're under attack by the armies of suffering, don't think you have no weapons to raise. Lift a song in worship and praise. They're powerful weapons in the hands of God's children.

Renew Your Consecration to God

Above every element of the psalm I read that night, this was the thought that stoked my fire. I was at a point where it was more than reasonable to wonder, "Is this the end of my ministry? Have I gotten to the end of my business here? Is God finished with me?"

This is what David says: "When I am old and gray-headed, O God, do not forsake me, *until I declare Your strength to this generation, Your power to everyone who is to come*" (v. 18; emphasis added). That sentence forestalls me from asking those questions. I take David's verse as my marching orders for the rest of my life, to declare God's strength to this generation. Never assume God is through with you. Gray hair means nothing. In God's way of doing things, the best is always yet to come!

He isn't finished with you or me. He never forgets or neglects us, though it does happen the other way around. It may be hard for you to believe, but God can be set aside and forgotten in church. We can go to church every Sunday and never hear anything about God. May I never enter the doors of God's house and neglect to tell people that He is strong and awesome. I want to praise His name and proclaim His power, not only to our generation, but also to our children, and to every generation that is to come.

Reclaim Your Confidence in God and the Future

Have you found yourself taking a bleak view of things and giving in to cynicism? Have you gradually bought into a world-view based on Murphy's Law: Whatever can go wrong will go wrong? Psalm 71 takes you down a road that leads precisely in the opposite direction. Your cynicism is replaced by faith: Whatever can go wrong can—and will—be used by God. Instead of a future of good things constantly bent in the wrong direction, you see a godly future in which God bends the world's distorted hopes into His beautiful plan.

David has confidence in the future because he has confidence in the One holding it. He writes, "You shall increase my greatness, and comfort [encourage] me on every side" (v. 21). We need to understand the wording in this verse, particularly the word *greatness*. You and I have no greatness in ourselves for God to increase. David refers to his sphere of influence and his opportunity to make a difference.

Trials put us in place for that to happen. They are for our benefit, as unwelcome as they are at the time. They make us better men and women, which makes us more influential men and women who can make a difference for God's purposes. When you have walked through the fire, people begin to listen to you. When you have the wisdom

---

"You must learn to live with the insecurities and the ambiguities of life. But know this: I am secure. I am certain. I am not ambiguous. In the storm, I am your Rock that cannot be moved. I am your God."

---

borne of suffering, you begin to have the tools to accomplish something in the world.

Remember Peter, Jesus' disciple? He knew something about being tested. He wrote about the purpose of trials in 1 Peter 1:7: "That the genuineness of your faith, being much more precious than gold that perishes, though it is tested by fire, may be found to praise, honor, and glory at the revelation of Jesus Christ." Peter joins David in affirming that fire tempers the steel in your character. After it has burned its impression into you, you can burn your impression into the world.

The psalmist said in Psalm 119:67 and 71, "Before I was afflicted I went astray, but now I keep Your word. . . . It is good for me that I have been afflicted, that I may learn Your statutes." Testing makes you walk the straight path, while the untested go astray.

James, too, wants us to hear this same message. He says, "Consider it all joy, my brethren, when you encounter various trials, knowing that the testing of your faith produces endurance" (James 1:2–3 NASB). Testing gives you the fortitude to go the distance.

Peter leaves us with the blessing of those who will feel the heat of the oven and feel the grace of God in it: "But may the God of all grace, who called us to His eternal glory by Christ Jesus, after you have suffered a while, perfect, establish, strengthen, and settle you" (1 Pet. 5:10). There is the hope, my friends, of maturing, of strengthening, of settling after the fires of our crisis have burned out. We find ourselves wiser and better, and we can thank God for the worst we've been through.

Suffering and strength are two sides of the same coin. When I was younger, I heard that God doesn't greatly use someone until He crushes him. I never liked the sound of that, and I used to pray that I might be the exception. I used to say, "Lord, let me go straight to the heart of ministry without feeling the pain." But God doesn't make any exceptions.

You would be well advised to read a biography of the great preacher Charles Haddon Spurgeon. I always knew he was a great man, but when I looked more deeply into the details of his life, I learned that Spurgeon accomplished more in his one lifetime than most people could accomplish in two, even though he died at the age of fifty-seven. Spurgeon suffered with prolonged bouts of depression and anxiety, and his psychological and physical ailments were so crippling that he frequently was confined to bed for weeks.

Spurgeon came to see these problems as part of God's work in his life. His sufferings enabled him to comfort and encourage the many hurting people who were touched by his ministry. And he found a pattern to his life: His periods of depression invariably preceded seasons of God's special blessings on his ministry. He knew he did not suffer without reason.

The depression actually became, as Spurgeon described it, a sort of "John the Baptist" for him, heralding a new and mighty outpouring of God's Spirit. Here are his own words: "This depression comes over me whenever the Lord is preparing a larger blessing for my ministry; the cloud is black before it breaks. . . . The scouring of the vessel has fitted it for the Master's use. . . . Fasting gives an appetite for the banquet. . . . The Lord is revealed in the backside of the desert, while his servant keeps the sheep and waits in solitary."

Charles Haddon Spurgeon, this psychologically frail man, published more than 3,500 sermons, authored 135 books, and is still regarded today as the "Prince of Preachers."[2]

God is up to something when He sends difficulty our way.

Life is not going to be easy. But I do believe that it can be victorious. When you know Almighty God and His Son Jesus Christ, you can endure whatever is placed before you with strength that the world can't comprehend. If you don't know Christ, you must enter the battle without weapons or armor. You fight in your own strength, and you fall on your face.

Why? Because God is the only One who can help us when trials come into our lives. And He does more than help us. He is our rock, our fortress, our hope, and our confidence. As David wrote so many centuries ago, "Who, O God, is like You?" (Ps. 71:9 NIV).

The answer is, *no one.* God will send His rain on the just and the unjust, but His children, who recognize and embrace His ways, will know that the rain is cool, refreshing water from heaven. It makes us grow. It gives us joy. And it makes life—real life—possible in this dry and dusty world.

Psalm 121

A Song of Ascents.

1 I will lift up my eyes to the hills—
   From whence comes my help?
2 My help comes from the LORD,
   Who made heaven and earth.
3 He will not allow your foot to be moved;
   He who keeps you will not slumber.
4 Behold, He who keeps Israel
   Shall neither slumber nor sleep.
5 The LORD is your keeper;
   The LORD is your shade at your right hand.
6 The sun shall not strike you by day,
   Nor the moon by night.
7 The LORD shall preserve you from all evil;
   He shall preserve your soul.
8 The LORD shall preserve your going out and your coming in
   From this time forth, and even forevermore.

3

I Need Your Help, Lord

Day by day and with each passing moment,
Strength I find to meet my trials here;
Trusting in my father's wise bestowment,
I've no cause for worry or for fear.
He whose heart is kind beyond all measure
Gives unto each day what he deems best—
Lovingly, its part of pain and pleasure,
Mingling toil with peace and rest.

—CAROLINA SANDELL BERG

Many travelers, many roads.

For every pilgrim in this journey of life, the road will bend in a different direction. We can never know in advance which way it will turn, for the map doesn't display that kind of detail for us. We must walk on until we meet the bend or the dip or the steep, uphill climb that has been set in the path for each of us. And we look to God for the grace to meet that defining moment.

The bend in my road, of course, has been cancer. I can't say what yours will be or has been, but it will be equally challenging. And in time you'll want to tell others your story, just as I'm telling mine. That's a predictable quality of those of us who are survivors—we swap our war stories. My good friend Dr. John Hovey shared his narrative with me. In his case the foe wasn't cancer—but I'll let him tell you the story in his own words. Listen to the history of the bend in another traveler's road, and how it transformed forever the way he would see his God, himself, and those he loves.

⌐⌐

It was three years ago that my life took a fateful turn.

As a family, we love to take long walks on the California beaches. One particularly lovely day, we were taking such a walk and enjoying the sea and the wind and everything that goes with the beauty of the seashore. My wife, Mary, had noticed something that struck her as strange. It seemed to her that I wasn't swinging my left arm in a natural, fluid motion—and she was right. Now I'm a surgeon, as you know, and I began to notice a poor motor response as I transferred surgical instruments into and out of my left hand. You can imagine how such a thing would affect my work. In time, it influenced my surgical schedule, my suture technique, and my overall office practice as I increasingly struggled with simple manual dexterity.

During those weeks and months, I began to spend more and more time in reflection—crisis have that effect on us. I realized what the onslaught of this disability had begun to do to me. My surgical practice had become more and more demanding. And now, even the more simple activities of daily living became difficult. Getting ready for work in the morning took so much longer that even my quiet time began to be affected. Mary pointed out that my long, hard hours at the office not only kept me in a state of physical exhaustion, but they had been stealing more and more precious time way from the family who loved me.

All this work disruption and soul-searching culminated in a confrontation with reality. A few professional colleagues examined me, and their diagnosis was early Parkinson's disease. I had come to my own bend in the road.

I had put in twenty-five years of school and twenty-five years of exhausting and devoted work in the medical field; I had paid fifty years' worth of dues, the way I saw it. After all this time, I'd finally reached the peak years of my professional career. I was ready to enjoy the fruits of the harvest, but instead it seemed as if everything I had trained for was slipping away.

experience. But somehow people get that mistaken idea, and when they eventually face trouble—as they always do—they come to the irrational conclusion that the presence of trouble implies the absence of God. A greater mistake cannot be imagined.

God's Word reminds us that we are pilgrims and strangers in a foreign land whose roads are filled with hazards. The road is long, weary, and dangerous. It winds through veils of tears and Bunyan's Slough of Despond, but the long and winding road finally comes to the City of God, the place of joy and feasting. Simply stated, that's the biblical view of life in the world.

So where can we go to find traveler's assistance?

The Possibilities for Help on Our Journey

We Can Look Around for Help
The psalmist says, "I will lift up mine eyes to the hills" (v. 1). He has prepared for his journey through the mountains to Jerusalem. As he enters the road, he takes a moment to gaze up to the horizon. He thinks of the miles ahead, the twists and turns and surprises, the old friends and new ones whose acquaintances he will make. He thinks of the dust and the heat, the darkness and the thirsty miles. He admires the graceful line where the mountains embrace the sky.

I've always been intrigued by the prominence of mountains in the Bible. Many great things happened on mountaintops: the sacrifice of Isaac on Mount Moriah, the giving of the Law on Mount Sinai, the Transfiguration of Christ, the message on Mount Olivet, Elijah's prophetic showdown on Mount Carmel (more on that one later)— and, of course, all of history turns on a crucifixion one dark Friday on Mount Calvary. Climactic moments in the biblical narrative always seem to seek higher ground.

You may not live anywhere near the mountains, and you may even prefer the beach as a vacation destination. I must confess that I'm a "mountain man" at heart. I boast with pride to all my friends around the country that I'm twenty minutes away from the mountains and twenty minutes away from the ocean. On a couple of occasions, as I'm quick to point out, I've partaken of sea and slope in the same day! Some of us like to show off, you see. I know people who water-ski and snow ski on the same day, just for bragging purposes to impress their friends back east.

But there's something grand and majestic about mountains. They set the landscape and the people in context. Nothing calms my spirit

---

Blessed are those whose strength is in you,
who have set their hearts on pilgrimage.

—Psalm 84:5 (NIV)

---

or helps me to get things in perspective more effectively than a visit to the highest hills. I drive up into the Laguna Mountains and find a special place where I can survey the natural grandeur and reflect on my Creator. If I've lost Him in the confinement of the city, I can find Him in the immensity of the peaks. Something about the majesty of mountains invokes the majesty of God.

That happens in the Scriptures too. Listen to Isaiah 55:12: "For you shall go out with joy, and be led out with peace; the mountains and the hills shall break forth into singing before you."

Psalm 125:1–2 captures the same idea: "Those who trust in the LORD are like Mount Zion, which cannot be moved, but abides forever. As the mountains surround Jerusalem, so the LORD surrounds His people from this time forth and forever."

There are many passages in the Old Testament that describe the mountains as a place of blessing, but we know all too well that mountains can also be a place of danger. Rarely does a winter go by that we don't hear of someone being lost in the mountain terrain. The snow cover cuts off the navigation of outdoorsmen, who cannot retrace their steps out of the wilderness.

In ancient times, mountains were sites of danger and hardship. Their rocks and caves hid wild animals and bloodthirsty bandits. Pagan cultures built their temples in the mountains. Godly pilgrims found a sense of majesty in the high country, but they also found a sense of danger and a fear of the unknown. It was a place of fear and of hope, of danger and salvation. The Lord God could be sought there, but pagan gods were enshrined as well.

The psalmist must have thought of these things, reflecting on the many meanings of mountains. He gazed upward at the outset of the journey and said, "I will look to the hills."

We Can Look Within for Help

I must confess to falling victim to a widespread misconception about this psalm. Maybe you've experienced it too. We were raised with the traditional King James Version and its time-honored punctuation. It can be misleading in this particular instance.

Take a good look at the first verse of Psalm 121. The psalmist says, "I will lift up my eyes to the hills—from whence comes my help?" The New King James Version, which we use in this book, has corrected the punctuation, but I used to misread the two phrases as one: "I will lift up my eyes unto the hills from whence cometh my help." I used to conclude that we look for help from the mountains.

But that's not what the psalm says at all. The writer makes a statement: "I will lift up my eyes to the hills." He breaks off and asks a question: "From whence comes my help?" What a difference a dash makes! The traveler looks to the hills, then he looks inward. And as he looks inward, he asks himself the question, "Where am I going to find help?" He feels all the hesitancy and concern many of us do before we set out on a long journey. Traveling has a measure of insecurity about it, because we're out of our comfort zones. *What if something terrible happens while I'm out of town? Who can I turn to?*

This is what writers call an "internal monologue"—and what you and I call "talking to ourselves." Is that a healthy thing to do? Well, the fact is we do it all the time. Our Psalm 121 traveler is talking to himself. He feels a little anxiety about getting through the high hills to arrive at his faraway destination of Jerusalem. And he naturally thinks, *Will anyone help me if I get sick or I'm attacked or I run out of money?*

He looks around.

Then he looks within.

Finally, he looks above.

We Can Look Above for Help

In the second verse, we find the solid foundation of this psalm: "My help comes from the LORD, who made heaven and earth." At last the psalmist comes to the point that provides the essence of his song. He is telling himself, "I've looked up to the mountains, and I find no help. I've looked within, and I find no guidance. But finally I've looked up, and I've realized the source of my help. It comes from no one but God."

What a lesson for life's travelers on this earth: *My help comes from the Lord.*

The Lord is described here as the God who made heaven and earth. Do you think these words are window dressing, perhaps a flowery poetic device? Not at all. These words are chosen quite deliberately. The idea of being loved by a Creator who hung the stars in space and set the earth upon its course is a powerful source of encouragement. If He can guide the planets, surely He can guide our little steps. That's why we find this phrase so frequently used in blessings the Hebrews granted each other. Look at the following examples (emphasis added):

- "May you be blessed by the LORD, *who made heaven and earth*" (Ps. 115:15).
- "The LORD *who made heaven and earth* bless you from Zion!" (Ps. 134:3).

- "Happy is he who has the God of Jacob for his help,
  whose hope is in the LORD his God, *who made heaven and earth*"
  (Ps. 146:5–6).

The power of this statement is wrapped up in the idea that since God is the Creator of all things, and since all things are His handiwork, His power is not to be questioned. The Creator has made everything we can see or touch or imagine; when we cast our hopes on Him, we're not only coming to a God who *cares*, but a God who *can*.

God is not merely the Creator of all things, but He is the Sustainer of all things as well. In writing to the Colossians, Paul writes: "By Him all things are created." And he goes on to say, "He is before all things, and in Him all things consist" (Col. 1:16–17). This is very important, for at some times during history God has been characterized by philosophers as a "cosmic watchmaker" who has created the world and then abandoned it to its own devices to tick away the moments until it runs out of time. That's not the God of the Bible. After creation, He is intimately involved with the work of His hands, holding it all together. If, even for a moment, He were to remove His hand from this universe, it wouldn't tick happily away like a watch in the grass; it would all fly apart into oblivion. But our God doesn't do that. Instead, He continues to sustain us. He creates and He sustains.

On that day when your journey brings you to a bend in the road, you'll be filled with an unaccustomed sense of helplessness. You'll cry out, "Lord, I need help!" In your moment of deep anxiety, remember this: The One to whom you are praying is the One who made heaven and earth. He is the Creator God. I don't know what kind of problem you may be facing—in the weariness of the journey, I'm certain it can seem all but insurmountable. But take a deep breath and a new look, in the perspective of the One who created and sustains every atom of the universe. He's up to the challenge, don't you think?

That thought renews our strength to carry on.

The Promises of Help on Our Journey

We notice something slightly odd as we come to the third verse of this psalm. If we're reading through it quickly, we may not even notice. The writer's perspective changes from first person ("I") to second person ("you"). This may seem like so much grammatical wrangling to you, and you may be tempted to leave this one to your high-school English teacher to worry about. But it's actually a rather significant point. For example, some have made the case that an entirely new character has walked onstage and begins to speak in this verse. They suggest that in the first couple of verses, the psalmist asked the questions; now someone else, perhaps a priest, has come along to provide the answers.

I don't buy into that particular interpretation. I believe what we have here is an internal dialogue in the heart of the psalmist—if you'll remember, we detected an internal monologue in the opening of the psalm; now a dialogue is suggested as the traveler frames answers to his own questions. He has chosen to write it all down, of course, so the "you" really refers to himself and ourselves as well. "Who will help me?" he asks. He concludes, "Here is what God will do for you and for me."

In the process of answering his question for our benefit, the psalmist uses eight small verses to make three immense points invaluable to our journey toward those hills. You'll stand, as he did, looking down that road and up those mountains. Your heart will cry out to God, and here is what you'll need to remember.

The Lord Perceives You

We can't see God, but you need to know that He sees you—*always*. He knows you. Aren't you glad that God knows who you are? Isn't it unbelievable? The God who made heaven and earth knows you by name!

He knows the very hairs on your head *by number*. Jesus assured us of that (see Matt. 10:30). That's a very intimate kind of knowledge. Believe me, I've been up close and personal with the issue of hair quantity. Chemotherapy, as you know, is involved with cancer treatment, and hair loss is inevitable with chemotherapy. I had to brace myself for the loss of my silvery locks! I had the pleasure of looking in the mirror every day and remembering that He numbers the hairs on my head. I was glad Someone was keeping inventory. I numbered those hairs myself, sadly watching them fall out. But He knew the exact number. He knows us intimately.

If God numbers the hairs on your head, don't you think He's up-to-date on the larger issues of your life? Don't you think He knows exactly how you feel—and cares deeply? When you say, "God, I need Your help," you need to know that He knows you. He perceives you.

Notice what the text says next: "He will not allow your foot to be moved; He who keeps you will not slumber. Behold, He who keeps Israel shall neither slumber nor sleep" (vv. 3–4).

Lloyd John Ogilvie tells a story about Bishop Quayle, who was a leader in the Methodist church years ago. One night, the bishop worked into the early morning hours trying to finish his work and solve his various problems. It happened that the Bible on his desk was open to Psalm 121. At a moment of intense pressure, Quayle was feeling tired and frustrated and annoyed. Suddenly his eye fell on the startling words that told him God never slumbers, that our Lord watches over us on a twenty-four-hour vigil.

Here was Bishop Quayle burning the midnight oil, worrying over so many things—and God watching over him as he worried. Here was Bishop Quayle working for God rather than allowing God to work through him. It came home to the minister, with great impact, that such a life was exhausting and ultimately a losing battle.

In his inner being he heard the Lord say, "Quayle, there's no need for both of us to stay up all night. I'm going to stay up anyway. You go to bed and get a good sleep."[1]

Have you ever paced the floor at night because of your kids, a financial problem for which you didn't know the answer, a sickness, or other problem in your life? If you're like me, you worry and wonder who is taking care of things. Then you read in the Bible that the God in whom you have trusted, the One you ask for help, never sleeps. He never takes a day off, and He's never out of town. You don't even need a secret cell phone number or e-mail address. God is right there, watching you, so close to you that you don't even need to call out to Him. He's watching over you, even as you sleep, because He loves you.

My friend Ron Mehl has written a book entitled *God Works the Night Shift*. That's one of the best titles I've heard in a long time. Isn't it a great thought? God is always there, no matter when it is that you need Him. In the loneliest, darkest hour of the night, He is there because He doesn't slumber or sleep.

I have always loved the story of Elijah, the Old Testament prophet. Maybe it's because he's another mountain man. He called that great showdown with the prophets of Baal on Mount Carmel, as recorded in 1 Kings 18:1–40. On one side were all the prophets of the false god, Baal; on the other side was Elijah, all by himself, representing the God of Abraham, Isaac, and Jacob. It was a contest to determine who the real God was, and Elijah threw down the gauntlet. He said, "Here's how we'll play. You put a sacrifice on your altar, and I'll put one on mine. We'll each call on our respective gods to consume our sacrifice with fire. May the best God win."

God versus Baal—the sacrifice of the century! Elijah let the other side go first. From morning until noon, the prophets of Baal cried out to their god to send the fire—but the heavens were silent. How embarrassing for these prophets when their god was a no-show! You can imagine the increasing panic in their voices. They cried aloud, leaped about, wept, rolled on the ground, and even cut themselves to let the blood flow. Nothing helped.

Just about noon, the prophets were about to run out of time. It was a shutout, bottom of the ninth, and things were looking bleak for all the Baal believers. That's when Elijah did something that no preacher should ever do.

Sarcasm, to be sure, is a quality I don't admire; I've always said there's no place for it in the life of a godly man or woman. But to be honest,

Elijah had an unmistakable little mean streak in him. He was looking at all those leaping, wailing Baal prophets with their unlit sacrifice, and he simply couldn't resist: "Elijah mocked them and said, 'Cry aloud, for

---

Go in where thou wilt, He sees thee: light thy lamp, He sees thee;
quench its light, He sees thee. Fear Him who ever beholds thee.

—Saint Augustine

---

he is a god; either he is meditating, or he is busy, or he is on a journey, or perhaps he is sleeping and must be awakened.'"

Can you hear the taunting? Elijah was clearly enjoying the failure of his corrupt, pagan competitors. But he had to be confident to take that approach, for now it was *his* turn to demonstrate the power of his God. The rest, as they say, is history—as well as more proof that our Creator never goes to sleep. He is never too busy. Our Lord is attentive to all our needs, and Elijah put an exclamation point on that statement before the king, the Baal backers, and the entire crowd who had flocked to Mount Carmel to take in the show. Elijah prayed, and God answered him in no uncertain terms by sending fire to consume his sacrifice.

Alexander the Great was once asked how he could sleep so soundly while constantly surrounded with danger. He replied that he lost no sleep at all: Parmenio, his faithful guard, kept watch so he could rest. If a general can sleep because a mere man is watching over him by night, how much more should we sleep, knowing our eternal God is keeping watch? He never slumbers. He never sleeps. He perceives you, and I hope your sleep is deep and refreshing in the knowledge of it.

The Lord Protects You

"The LORD is your keeper; the LORD is your shade at your right hand. The sun shall not strike you by day, nor the moon by night" (vv. 5–6).

Now we come to another promise, and we remember the traveler whose eyes have looked up toward the horizon before his dangerous journey. He feels reassurance that God is keeping watch over him by night and shading him during the noon heat. Can you imagine a more devoted Master than that?

God is the pilgrim's shade on his right hand. The word *shade* is very important. Travelers along the ancient roads in this part of the world felt deep anxiety about the desert heat. Sunstroke was a serious issue. If you've ever visited Israel and traveled up the long road to Masada, you know how stifling the heat can be—dry and oppressive enough to drain away every ounce of your vitality.

"The LORD is your shade at your right hand," and again it's worth taking a close look at the particular phrase chosen to drive home the point. The phrase "right hand" suggests a wonderful truth about the place we hold in the heart of God. Psalm 98:1 says, "Oh sing to the LORD a new song! For He has done marvelous things. His right hand and His holy arm have gained Him the victory." The Scriptures consistently speak of the right hand of the Lord as indicative of His power. He has given you shade in His right hand, we're told. He protects you around the clock, with mighty power. That should bolster your courage.

He protects us by day. "The sun shall not strike you by day," the traveler proclaims. The forceful words *beat* or *hit* or *smite* or *kill* help us fully appreciate the deadly assault of the Mediterranean sun and the safety of the shade available only in our loving God.

Then, when the day is over, He will protect us by night. Verse 6 continues, "Nor the moon by night." Have you ever heard of being "moonstruck"? In the period of time when this psalm was written, there were all kinds of superstitions circulating concerning the moon. In fact, Matthew 17:15 records a story about a man who begged Jesus to heal his son. He described his deranged son in these terms: "For he is an epileptic and suffers severely; for he often falls into the fire and often into the water." And if you dig just a bit deeper into the background of this word *epileptic*, you'll discover that in most translations the word is actually *moonstruck*. People believed that the moonlight brought dangers, and the moon could be as deadly as the sun. You could be "struck" by both.

Needless to say, we're a bit beyond primitive lunar superstition. We don't lose any sleep over the prospect of being struck by the moon. And far be it from our sophisticated culture to fall prey to that kind of craziness—right? Not so fast: Such ideas about the moon linger on. When we say somebody is crazy, we call him or her a *lunatic*. Craziness is *lunacy*. Both these words come from the word *lunar*, or *moon*. Maybe we aren't as sophisticated as we think.

In any case, many people suffer from night fears. Nearly every child has begged for a night-light. Aging people often come to fear the night as well. The darkness and loneliness of it hold special terrors for them. Some suffer from insomnia and the long, dark night becomes even longer—a difficult time for them to endure.

For all of us who have struggled or been struck by fear, whether of the sun or the moon or anything else on the horizon, the message is this: *God is great. He will provide safety for you in the heat of the day, and in the terrors of the night He will never leave your side.*

The Lord Preserves You

"The LORD shall preserve you from all evil; He shall preserve your soul. The LORD shall preserve your going out and your coming in from this time forth, and even forevermore" (vv. 7–8).

This wonderful promise contains four precious truths.

1. **The Lord preserves us from evil.** God will help us make it through when evil and danger rear their heads. Think about the worst that can happen, the most evil thing that could befall you. Nothing is outside His control. Think about every kind of disaster that terrifies humanity. Every one you can name is subject to the God who preserves. Bad things do happen, but they happen within His supervision and long-term purposes. It's foolish to believe things have gotten out of His control; it simply cannot happen.

2. **The Lord preserves our existence.** "He shall preserve your soul," says the seventh verse. As our pilgrim narrator reassures us that God will keep our souls from all harm, he uses a particular word for *soul*. Hebrew writings usually reach for this word when the meaning is

life. In other words, God is going to *keep your life.* It doesn't end when you breathe your last breath. There is much more to the idea of life than the womb-to-tomb understanding to which we limit ourselves.

As we grieve at a funeral, we know we've come to a punctuation mark in someone's life. And that's what it is—but that mark is not a period, as we assume, but merely a comma. We need put no question mark on that one! You are an eternal creature. And He is the keeper of your existence, guarding your soul through earthly life and eternity as well.

The traveler looks at the long road before him, the hills above him, and reminds himself that this is one short journey in the world, set within a joyful journey in God's eternal world. That context lifts his spirits.

3. The Lord preserves us every day. I love this phrase: "The LORD shall preserve your going out and your coming in" (v. 8).

Sometimes when I rise in the morning and take a good look at the schedule blaring at me from my daily planner, I sigh deeply and feel like a slave to the world's demands. Do you ever feel that way? Go out, come in; go out, come in. The days begin to look alike as they entangle themselves into urgent appointments—this meeting, then the next one. Yet God promises to preserve us even as we go out and come in—which is, by the way, a wonderful Old Testament idiom that expresses the regular routines of life.

This promise extends even deeper into the world of everyday responsibilities. Maybe you have small children at home. You look at the day and think, *Boy, this is just like yesterday. And yesterday was like the day before. All I do is get up in the morning, take care of kids, wash clothes, clean up their messes, prepare them for school, run errands all over town, come home, make dinner, and fall in bed too tired even to sleep. Then I get up the next morning and start all over again.* In your darker moments you begin to wonder, *Is God involved in all of this? Does He care at all about the endless treadmill of my life?*

Let me assure you that He does care. He watches over you and preserves you in your going out and in your coming in. This is a promise that God's Word repeats over and over, so that there may be no question about it. He cares.

In his commentary on the Gospel of Luke, William Barclay quotes a little poem about the routines of life that was obviously written by a woman who was working at home:

> Lord of all pots and pans and things,
> Since I have no time to be
> A saint by doing lovely things
> Or watching late with Thee,
> Or dreaming in the dawnlight,
> Or storming heaven's gates,
> Make me a saint by getting meals
> And washing up the plates.[2]

God uses the kitchen filled with pots and pans, or the desk filled with business memos, as laboratories for sainthood. He watches over the routines of life. He watches our going out and our coming in.

4. The Lord preserves us eternally. The psalmist proclaims that the Lord will preserve us "from this time forth, and even forevermore" (v. 8).

God's care extends not only to every place and to every setting, but it also spans all of time and eternity. Time plays tricks on us, doesn't it? For the child anticipating Christmas morning, it moves like molasses, and a week might as well be a year. For an adult, the years seem to fly, and we can't believe how quickly each succeeding one whirls by us.

We begin to see time as our enemy. Its accelerating pace frightens and discourages us. If time is cold and uncaring, we think, then God must be too—but don't ever think such a terrible thought, for it's not so. God cares for us in time and eternity. Time is only His tool to bring us wisdom and perspective.

The Keeper of Our Lives

A pious Jew in today's world keeps certain elements in his home in keeping with the traditions of his faith. If you were to visit such a man, you'd come to his door and notice a small metal container on the outside doorway and also on the inside. He calls this little metal container a *mezuzah*. It enshrines for him, in a physical way, the words of Deuteronomy chapters 6 and 11, which tell us that we are to train up our children in the way they should go and that we are to teach them as they go out and as they come in.

So there at the doorway is the *mezuzah*. As the pious Jew leaves his home to travel to his place of work, he touches this little metal box with his right hand and repeats aloud a few of the words contained within it, asking God to preserve him as he goes out and comes in. His final words will always be, "The Lord keep you both now and forevermore."

Whether we "go out" to travel around the block or around the world, the Lord is our keeper. Eugene Peterson writes about God's watchful care over us:

> The Christian life is not a quiet escape to a garden where we can walk and talk uninterruptedly with our Lord; nor a fantasy trip to a heavenly city where we can compare blue ribbons and gold medals with others who have made it to the winners' circle. . . . The Christian life is going to God. In going to God, Christians travel the same ground that everyone else walks on, breathe the same air, drink the same water, shop in the same stores, read the same newspapers, are citizens under the same governments, pay the same prices for groceries and gasoline, fear the same dangers, are subject to the same pressures, get the same distresses, are buried in the same ground.
>
> The difference is that each step we walk, each breath we breathe, we know we are preserved by God, we know we are accompanied by God, we know we are ruled by God; and therefore, no matter what doubts we endure or what accidents we experience, the Lord will preserve us from evil, he will keep our life.[3]

I must return to my dear friend Dr. John Hovey, who has shared with you the bend in his road—a diagnosis of Parkinson's disease. I'm happy to give Dr. Hovey the last word on this topic. He says, "My family, like so many others, enjoys a fabulous turkey dinner on Thanksgiving Day. We enjoy the delicious feast set before us, and then we indulge in a family tradition that has become an established

---

Thou hast granted me many blessings;
Now let me accept tribulation from Thy hand.
Thou wilt not lay on me more than I can bear.
Thou makest all things work together
for good for Thy children.

—Dietrich Bonhoeffer

---

part of our celebration over the years. And I'm certain many other families do something similar. We take turns around the table sharing aloud what we're thankful for this particular year."

Dr. Hovey continues, "We always seem to have guests at our Thanksgiving feast, and they don't know what to expect. So I usually go first to break the ice. On the year I've told you about, the year of my diagnosis, I began by saying I was eternally grateful that God chose me as His child. I expressed how deeply thankful I was to have a loving family. Then I went on to say I was thankful for Parkinson's disease.

"Why? Because God used Parkinson's disease to bring me closer to Himself, to His Word, and to my family."

When the bend in the road seems treacherous, as it did for Dr. Hovey, we can smile and look right past it. We can lift our eyes above that bend and take in the beautiful hills outlined against the horizon. Then we can cast our gaze beyond even those, past the horizon and into the face of our Father. We know He loves us and watches over us, over the entire journey here and in the next world.

No matter what the future holds, no matter what may lie around the next corner, our help comes from the Lord who loves us. Nothing can keep us from His love. Parkinson's disease can't do it. Cancer can't do it. No matter what it is you're facing, whichever way your road bends—whatever obstacle looms before you in your road, that obstacle can't do it either.

> For I am persuaded that neither death nor life,
> nor angels nor principalities nor powers,
> nor things present nor things to come,
> nor height nor depth, nor any other created thing,
> shall be able to separate us from the love of God
> which is in Christ Jesus our Lord.
> —Romans 8:38–39

Psalm 13

To the chief musician. A Psalm of David.

1 How long, O LORD? Will You forget me forever?
   How long will You hide Your face from me?
2 How long shall I take counsel in my soul,
   Having sorrow in my heart daily?
   How long will my enemy be exalted over me?
3 Consider and hear me, O LORD my God;
   Enlighten my eyes, lest I sleep the sleep of death;
4 Lest my enemy say,
   "I have prevailed against him";
   Lest those who trouble me rejoice when I am moved.
5 But I have trusted in Your mercy;
   My heart shall rejoice in Your salvation.
6 I will sing to the LORD,
   Because He has dealt bountifully with me.

4

When God Delays

When peace like a river attendeth my way,
When sorrows like sea billows roll—
Whatever my lot, Thou hast taught me to say
It is well, it is well with my soul.

—HORATIO G. SPAFFORD,
"IT IS WELL WITH MY SOUL"

You and I live in an aging society. Of course, that's a statement that would be true of any time and place, wouldn't it? I know of no "land that time forgot." Everyone everywhere is a day older each morning they rise from bed.

But there's a particular crisis of aging in our culture. People who belong to that huge segment of society born between the end of the Second World War and the mid-1960s are finding their hair turning gray. They are worrying about being replaced by younger workers. The Pepsi Generation is quickly becoming the Geritol Gang. Many among us are coping for the first time with chronic illness, relentless pain, daily medication, and an exhausting and demoralizing battle against the time limits of the human frame.

Some of the illnesses have newly coined titles; others are old and familiar. Perhaps none is more heartbreaking than mental illness. Like any illness, the struggle against mental illness is difficult and depressing. But in the case of fighting against the loss of the human mind itself, there are unique and particularly devastating sorrows. Sharon Paul, a family friend, gives us an accurate idea of living and coping with a challenge of that magnitude in the following passage.

—

You can't judge a book by its cover—nor can you tell what's inside someone by his or her outside appearance.

If you could see me, you'd agree that my appearance is fairly ordinary. I've been married for eighteen years, about one or two of which could be described by the word *normal*—at least as the world defines that concept. As the medical world defines things, I am mentally ill.

By the time such an official diagnosis could be made, it was actually something of a relief. Does that statement shock you? You see, I'd been told I had demons inside of me. A formal medical diagnosis was very helpful; it made it possible for me to be treated properly and to better understand the many facets of my condition.

I was hospitalized for many years. That period is over, but even now I must spend time in hospitals when I face a crisis. Sometimes people want to know how I can be a Christian and still have these conditions, particularly conditions that could lead people like me to harm themselves. But they don't understand the reality of depression as I do. I feel better about all of it when I think about people of great faith who faced depression like mine—people such as Jeremiah, David, and Elijah.

There were times in our country when people like me would have been put away somewhere, out of sight and out of mind. But we've made progress since then, and I can find freedom in talking about my depression and even reaching out to others who are coping with what I've been through.

On my good days, you're likely to find me chatty, loving, caring, and serving others. I can take responsibility for myself. I pray, read the Bible, and try to work through the darker memories from my past.

On my bad days, I can simply be thankful for those loving people who care enough to reach out to me. My world becomes black and unmanageable, and I become unwilling to look in the mirror or eat. I spend my time terrified, crying, hearing voices that I know aren't there, and longing to lose myself in the darkness or to embrace the final release of death.

I have days when I get lost and can't find my way home. This often makes me afraid to go out the front door or into the backyard. I have other days when I weep for hours for no apparent reason. Sometimes the stimulus of the world is so overwhelming that I can't cope, and my only response is either to flee to the safety of a stronger individual or simply to the comfort of darkness.

Those are simply the everyday details of life when you cope with depression.

For me to function on a daily basis, I need the help of my husband, my Christian therapist, my psychiatrist, my close friends, my medication, and my Lord Jesus.

That's the nature of the life I live.

And yet, I must tell you that even on my darkest days—even when life is a deep tunnel with no light visible to me—I can still say I've seen Jesus. I've seen Him with the eyes of my spirit, even if the eyes of my mind and heart are blinded. I can feel His presence, even if I can't feel anything else but pain and panic. I'm so grateful that He is my Savior, for without Him, I'm very certain I would be dead.

In every life, at some time, a person finds himself in that dark tunnel where no light is visible. You weep and you cry out in frustration and you plead, "Lord, I can't take any more! I have no more patience and no more strength to hold out; I must hear from You *today*. If You don't resolve this issue, I don't know what I am going to do. Can't You see that I'm desperate? *Why don't You help me?*"

Most of us have been there. How about you? It may have been because of a long, drawn-out sickness. It may have been a long-term financial problem. It may have been a struggle with grief. It may have been an alcoholic spouse or an unsaved loved one or a dysfunction in the family. Or perhaps you've suffered through a problem at work: a demanding, unreasonable boss or a jealous, spiteful fellow worker whom you have to cope with every day, with no resolution in sight. Or maybe, like Sharon Paul, you've spent a lifetime sparring with mental illness.

Before you know it, you find yourself in David's shoes and can understand his heartfelt words and emotions. This man is a hero and a man of God—the favorite son and sweet singer of Israel. He is a man after God's own heart, yet he is a man of anguish and suffering, one given to depths of depression who cries out to God, "How long?"

David's boyhood had been that of a shepherd boy, just one of several sons in a large family. But what a fateful turn that life had taken. From the moment David killed the giant Goliath, he himself became a hunted man. One moment he was the toast of the nation; the next he was a young man hiding out in caves. The king, the insecure and temperamental Saul, was bitterly jealous. His stock had plummeted as that of the shepherd boy had skyrocketed. The women of Israel celebrated the victory of David over Goliath by singing a song which is recorded for us in 1 Samuel 18:7: "Saul has slain his thousands, and David his ten thousands." If you were the king, would you like to hear such a melody echoing through your streets?

It was an intolerable situation for a jealous and egotistical monarch. In 1 Samuel 18:8–9 we read his predictable response: "Saul was very angry, and the saying displeased him; and he said, 'They have ascribed to David ten thousands, and to me they have ascribed but thousands. Now what more can he have but the kingdom?' So Saul eyed David from that day forward."

He *eyed* him. Have you got a good mental image of that? Have you ever gotten that kind of treatment from a coworker or a fellow student or even a member of your church? Saul gave David the evil eye. He saw him through the blurry green lens of jealousy, which had become an obsession. First Samuel 18:29 tells us that Saul made an enemy out of the young man because he feared him. Fear is often the root of our great mistakes in life.

That is a story you may already be quite familiar with. But we often forget that David was a fugitive for eight or nine years. We forget that he lived a life on the run in the very country where he was a national hero. Furthermore, his life and plight were complicated by all kinds of personal entanglements. For instance, Saul, David's ultimate enemy, the same ruthless king whose life was dedicated to hunting him down and murdering him, was also the father of a son who was David's dear-

There are some favors that the Almighty does not grant either the first, or the second, or the third time you ask Him, because He wishes you to pray for a long time and often He wills this delay to keep you in a state of humility—and to make you realize the value of His grace.

—Jean Eudes

est friend and a daughter who had stolen David's heart. Can you imagine a more complicated personal scenario than that?

During these eight or nine years, David had to remain constantly on the move. He lived in the fields and in the forests, in the caves and in the deserts. Finally he was chased out of the land of Israel and into the very midst of the Philistines, the enemies whose hero he had slain. David ended up in a city called Gath, but the locals identified him quickly. The only way he could think of to escape was to act as if he'd lost his mind. The Scripture says that in order to get away from Achish, the king of Gath, David dribbled in his beard, scratched his hands on the doors, and gave the most convincing impression he could of insanity.

Later, David had the protection of six hundred of his faithful men. He settled in a place called Ziklag, where he managed to live peaceably for sixteen months. But one day he left on a military mission. When he returned home, the city of Ziklag had been burned to the ground. All the wives and the children whom the soldiers had left behind had been carried away—including David's own family.

David's men were not merely grief-stricken, but filled with fury. They turned their anger on David and threatened to stone him to death. It was all David's fault—that's the way they saw it. As far as they were concerned, David, their leader, had cost them their wives and their children. First Samuel 30 tells of David's deep distress. He had lost his own family and was blamed for the loss of hundreds of other women and children. And now he faced death by stoning.

He had killed a giant and become a hero—but he had to live a life of a fugitive. He was an anointed king—but he had to live like a beast of the fields. Now he faced a violent death at the hands of the men he trusted. David was desperate. Out of the pain in his heart, he cried out to the Lord. And out of that furnace of his desperation came the incredible words of Psalm 13:

> How long, O LORD? Will You forget me forever? How long will You hide Your face from me? How long shall I take counsel in my soul, having sorrow in my heart daily? How long will my enemy be exalted over me? Consider and hear me, O LORD my God; enlighten my eyes, lest I sleep the sleep of death; lest my enemy say, 'I have prevailed against him'; lest those who trouble me rejoice when I am moved. But I have trusted in Your mercy; my heart shall rejoice in Your salvation. I will sing to the LORD, because He has dealt bountifully with me.

F. B. Meyer, one of the great writers of biblical commentaries, said, "Saul's persecutions lasted for eight or nine years; and no hope of termination appeared. David was a man who spends five hundred days passing through a forest. The tangled over-growth hides the sun; and he begins to despair of ever emerging."[1]

David wrote this psalm when he was physically exhausted and emotionally depressed. His troubles with King Saul had gone on year after year, and he was dispirited and discouraged. This psalm was wrung out of the extremity of his soul. He simply could not go on, not for another day, not for another hour, not even for another minute.[2]

As we relate to God, we're so much like small children. You have a better perspective for appreciating this fact if you've ever been a parent. You're driving your family to a vacation at the beach far away. Those little voices come from the backseat, saying over and over, "How much longer? How much farther?" And of course, "Are we there yet?" You've said it as a child yourself or heard it as a parent. And from the backseat of life, we call out the same questions to God: "How much longer, Lord? How much farther? Are we there yet?"

We can see and feel that impatience and desperation in the words of David. I'm glad he put his deepest feelings into writing. It reassures me to know that someone we hold as a spiritual hero, someone whom God has honored, had the courage to say the kinds of things that we often feel ashamed of saying. In so many ways, David is one more child in the backseat of a long, hot journey. Aren't we all?

Our Struggle When God Delays

On those occasions when you struggle with God's timing, it's good to know these feelings didn't originate with you. Not only did David express the feelings you've had, but he did so repeatedly. Read through the psalms, and you'll find a number of them like the one we're exploring in this chapter. So many of them begin with a sigh and end with a song. But in life, you can't take in the song without letting out the sigh.

Just as a song has a refrain, this psalm's sigh has one—a recurring phrase that always comes back around. This time, the chorus or refrain is repeated four times: *How long?* That's right, David is singing the blues. He's overwhelmed with a sense of the permanence of trouble. Trouble springs up when we want it least, seems to have no solution, seems to mock our most diligent efforts to lead a happy and peaceful life, and finally consumes our last ounce of patience. And David, much like you, finally lifts his eyes to heaven in exasperation and says, "How much longer, O God? How much longer?" It's David's blues chorus.

Aren't you grateful for the psalms that are such remarkable illustrations of honest prayer? I don't always pray with total honesty, and allow me to venture a guess that you don't, either. Your friend at work brushes by you at the copy machine. "How's it going?" he smiles. And you say, "I'm doing fine," or you might even say, "Couldn't be better."

But wait a minute! Didn't you have an argument with your spouse this morning? Didn't you just now catch a lecture from your boss? So you just told your friend a whopper, and you don't even think about it. How many times have you and I both done that?

Well, doing that causes little damage to relationships with your friends, because they have no idea what is really going on in your life. But we have much less success posturing before God. He is with you during the argument with your spouse; He is saddened by the confrontation with your boss. And when you force a smile into your prayers and say, "I couldn't be better, Lord!" He is again saddened. He knows what you're going through, and He has been looking forward to talking it over with you. He'd be much happier with an exasperated "How long, Lord!" than with your forced smile.

When God Delays, We Feel Forgotten

You will come to the point of believing God has forgotten you. Don't worry—it's a common experience. We all pass through a dark stage of feeling that God either isn't there at all, or at the very least, He has forgotten us. Perhaps our problems aren't important to Him, we imagine. The psalmist encounters just those very doubts. In Psalm 10:1 he

---

It is not under the sharpest, but the longest trials,
that we are most in danger of fainting.

—Andrew Fuller

---

cries out, "Why do You stand afar off, O LORD? Why do You hide yourself in times of trouble?"

Maybe these cynical words have slithered through your mind: "God is always around when I don't need Him. But just wait until trouble comes around, when I go looking for Him. Just try to find Him then— He goes into hiding." If we stop and think about it, we haven't been too eager to find God when things were going well or when the smaller problems came up. Even the larger trials can be handled up to a point. We can take a certain amount with our faith intact. But the longer we go without God's peace and perspective in the midst of bad times, the more our faith begins to weaken.

Consider Job, the wise and godly man of the Old Testament. He lost his children, his animals, and his servants—virtually everything he had—all in one mind-bending period of tragedy. These were great losses, not garden-variety trials. But Job handled them all with patience and deep inner strength. Times did not improve for him. The devil extended his lease on Job's life, and the suffering servant of God began to realize that he was in for a long-term battle. That's when he began to come apart at the seams.

Everyone has a point somewhere in the geography of their souls marking the limits of their faith. It is the point at which faith begins to unravel. For younger Christians, that point may be just around the corner; seasoned believers can travel much farther before reaching it. Only we ourselves know where the point lies, and we find out during a season of testing. A trial will build to a crescendo in your life. You attempt to handle it, and you pray about it. But life will not cooperate. As the days turn to weeks, then weeks to months, and even months to years, you reach that personal point, somewhere in the scheme of your suffering, when you begin to give up on God.

What you believe is that He has given up on you. You may even be feeling that way right now. If so, please allow me to remind you that what you're contemplating is a simple impossibility. God never gives up on you; He never ceases to care about you, and He will not abandon His work on you—of which your trial is a part. I love the poignant words in Isaiah 49:15–16: "Can a woman forget her nursing child, and not have compassion on the son of her womb? Surely they may forget, yet I will not forget you. See, I have inscribed you on the palms of My hands; your walls are continually before Me."

The word picture is a revealing one, isn't it? Try to suggest a relationship more intimate than that between a mother and her nursing child. God wants us to realize that even if that woman could somehow forget the precious child at her breast, He would never forget you. He even says, "Your name is written on the palms of My hands." That image instantly snaps into focus in your mind—your very name tattooed on the palms of His hands. That means it is engraved there; it cannot be removed.

Such is God's concern for you. He cannot forget you. No matter what storm you're weathering now, you have never left God's mind or heart.

When God Delays, We Feel Forsaken

"How long will You hide Your face from me?" (v. 1). We can feel the frustration and despair in David's words. It seems as if God has forgotten him, yes, but even worse: It feels as if God has purposely averted His eyes from David, so as not to be bothered by the troubles of His suffering child. Perhaps he knows better, but David feels as if God simply doesn't care. David feels forsaken.

Forgotten is one thing, but *forsaken* is another matter entirely. We very innocently forget people—people we love and care about. That can happen in the hectic pace of things. But the act of forsaking is very intentional—*premeditated forgetfulness*. David said to himself, "Here I am at this place in my lifelong relationship with God, a relationship I was given to believe was a very special one; I've spent my days fleeing for my life, hiding, fighting battles, and losing families, finding myself farther than ever from that throne I was promised so long ago; and I cannot get beyond the conviction that God has forgotten and even forsaken me. He has led me through all these trials to abandon me."

That is how David feels; that is how you have felt: *My God, why have You forsaken me?*

You might recognize those words. Jesus said them in His anguish on the cross. Do you know where Jesus got those words? He pulled them from Psalm 22. If you study that psalm, you'll find that the same man, David, has repeated Psalm 13 almost exactly: "My God, My God, why have You forsaken Me? Why are You so far from helping

Me, and from the words of My groaning? O My God, I cry in the day-time, but You do not hear; and in the night season, and am not silent" (Ps. 22:1–2).

Here is the surprise that an in-depth study of the psalms will offer you. Psalm 22 has no historic place in the life of David as other ones do. This is what scholars call a Messianic psalm, looking ahead to Israel's long-promised hero and deliverer. It foretells the crucifixion of the Lord Jesus Christ, giving details of the torture and excruciating pain of crucifixion centuries before that method of execution was even invented. Old Testament people could read this psalm and look through a window to see the climactic event of the New Testament, as seen through the eyes of Christ.

And it all came full circle. In time, when the prophetic event came to pass, the Lord Jesus hung suffering on the cross and quoted the very words of Psalm 22 creating a window into the Old Testament. We read that "about the ninth hour Jesus cried out with a loud voice, saying, *'Eli, Eli, lama sabachthani?'* that is, 'My God, My God, why have You forsaken Me?'" (Matt. 27:46).

It's helpful to know that David suffered and felt forsaken. But it's life-changing to realize that even Jesus Himself—the Lord of heaven and earth, enclosed in flesh—experienced the same emotions. Please take in the full import of these words: The Lord Jesus Christ not only felt forsaken, *He was forsaken.* The Father turned His back on Jesus because He was a holy and just God who could not look upon the sin that Jesus carried to the cross—your sin and mine. The next time you feel forsaken and lift up your voice to pray to Almighty God, do this—go to a private place and spend significant time reflecting on the incredible truth that the One who hears your prayers has been there too. He knows exactly how you feel. He knows what it means to be forsaken.

"My God, My God," He cried out, "why have You forsaken Me?" He was forsaken indeed—but we are never forsaken. Here is the truth you must fully comprehend and stake your life upon if you remember no other words from this chapter: *He turned His back upon His Son so that He would never have to turn His back on you.* That was the excruciating price

He paid because He loves you that much. He lived and died and suffered on this earth so you wouldn't have to be forsaken.

When we cry out to Him in the midst of our trials, even when we can't sense it, God hears us. He'll never forsake us. That idea is pounded home in the clearest words possible in Hebrews 13:5: "For He himself has said, 'I will never leave you nor forsake you.'"

But that doesn't mean we'll never *feel* forsaken. Emotions will bring us to that point, and we can feel free to express our honest, naked feelings to God when that comes to pass.

When God Delays, We Feel Frustrated

Have you felt frustrated with God? If we're honest, we've all had times when we've said, or at least felt like saying, "God, I'm really upset. I've been praying about this for years, for months. It doesn't seem as if You're there." Listen to the words of the psalmist in the second verse of Psalm 13: "How long shall I take counsel in my soul, having sorrow in my heart daily? How long will my enemy be exalted over me?"

David is frustrated for two reasons.

1. He's frustrated because of his own emotions. He says, "Every day I go through this. Every day I must deal with this." Someone said that the problem with life is that it's so *daily*. Each morning we must rise and face our challenges—and the same ones are there every day, rain or shine, summer, winter, spring, or fall. Whatever we have to deal with, when we get up and "reboot" our minds, all the same crises take up right where they left off.

James Montgomery Boice, who has written a wonderful commentary on the Book of Psalms, says, "The third time David asks, 'How long?' he refers to a combination of what we would call dark thoughts and uncontrollable emotions. When we no longer sense that God is blessing us, we tend to ruminate on our failures and get into an emotional funk. And when our emotions take over it is always hard to get back onto a level course. That is because the best means of doing this—calm reflection and a review of past blessings—are being swept away. We discover that we cannot settle ourselves long enough to complete this exercise."[3] The problem begins to take over in our lives.

Have you ever experienced the frustration of something painful or negative or sad becoming your constant and daily companion? Of course, you know what to do—you've been taught to read your Bible, to pray, and to spend time with God's people. But you're no longer

---

David was talking about that knot in the stomach, the lead weight in the breast that makes the thought of food nauseating. . . . We can't sleep, can't eat, can't settle to anything. Every time we try to get our mind on something else, back it comes—that gnawing ache inside.

—John Phillips

---

dealing with a problem; the problem is dealing with *you*. It has taken over. It has gotten you into such an emotional bind that no matter how hard you try, you know you can't do the things you should do. It happened to David. He was frustrated by his emotions.

2. He was frustrated because of his enemy. David cried, "How long will my enemy be exalted over me?" (v. 2).

Try to take in this scenario. Imagine being told, early in life, that you would be the president of the United States, or perhaps that you would become the most powerful and successful business leader in the nation. And you were actually given that position, sworn in as president or appointed as CEO. Then, every possible harrowing event came to pass in your life. Imagine your frustration: You had visions of sitting in the Oval Office, or in an executive suite at the top of a towering skyscraper, changing the course of world events. Instead, you're running for your life and your friends have turned against you. The promises seem always to be deferred to some unspecified future time.

This was David's plight. He was the king in waiting; David had already been anointed by Samuel as the king of Israel, back in his days as a shepherd. Do you know how much time passed between David's anointing and the moment he actually became king? Fifteen years.

Jesse, David's father, had brought the boy to the prophet Samuel. Samuel had poured oil over David's head and had given him the wonderful news that he was the heir to the throne of Israel. Then David had gone back to the fields. He had slain a giant, and that's where all the plans seemed to go awry.

What was the meaning of all this? David shook his fist at the sky above him and cried out, "How long, Lord, is my enemy going to be exalted over me?" The king-in-perpetual-waiting evaluated his own resources (not too impressive as a desperate fugitive), and he evaluated the resources of Saul, a jealous, murderous, ungodly king. This bloodthirsty monarch had once sent thirty thousand men after the shepherd boy. Whose side was God on? If the answer was "David's," you could have fooled the young man. God seemed to give Saul everything and David nothing.

David, taking a stand with six hundred men against a kingdom, said, "Lord, what do You want from me? The monster in pursuit of me has a kingdom, and I have a cave. What on earth do You expect me to do?"

In his depression, it may well be that David decided God had taken on more than He could handle. Perhaps God had begun with all the best intentions for David. He had helped him kill the giant but wasn't prepared for all the chaos that followed. In other words, God had just gotten in over His head. So why should David keep resisting? He couldn't fight an evil empire. He had nothing but God, and God wasn't talking.

I doubt you'll ever face a hostile army or have a king put a price on your head. All the same, we have an enemy worse than any number of kings or assassins or regiments. The Bible tells us in 1 Peter 5:8 that we are to "be sober, be vigilant; because your adversary the devil walks about like a roaring lion, seeking whom he may devour."

I don't know if the enemy has ever pursued you, but he is relentless. You wonder, "Lord, how am I ever going to get victory over this sin, this problem, this addiction? I'm doing everything I know how to do, but it's just too much for me." David felt that way; he was frustrated and overwhelmed by his enemy to the point of giving in. Look carefully at the text, and you'll see how honestly he describes his feelings about being a fugitive and fleeing from the most powerful man on earth.

This is all very understandable and human. It's a comfort to know David had the kind of black days we do. But aren't you glad the psalm doesn't stop there? David may have thought he didn't have a prayer, but in fact, he was just where God wanted him.

Our Supplication When God Delays

Despite the desolation of his emotional state, at least David prayed. And what kind of prayer did he offer?

There is no textbook for genuine prayer. There is no professor who can teach it, no pastor who can make it happen for you. True prayer is a spontaneous outpouring of honesty and need from the soul's foundation. In calm times, we say a prayer. In desperate times, we truly *pray.*

"Lord," you cry, "I'm lost and helpless. I have nowhere else to turn." So, having come to the end of your own limited resources, you are desperate enough to try your last resort: You go to the Creator of the universe who loves you and made you and holds all the answers in His hand. That's when you pray.

The Foundation of Our Prayer

David repeats one little word three times in his prayer of desperation: the word *lest.* This is the kind of small, inconspicuous word on which the entire meaning of a Scripture passage can hinge. *Lest* is a conditional word. First, David says, "Lest I sleep the sleep of death." David was so worn out physically and emotionally that he fully expected to die. He seemed to have come to the last page, and since the book of his life story was about to close, it seemed like an appropriate time to pray.

Not only did he fear his own death, but he also feared his own defeat. He said, "Lest my enemy say, 'I have prevailed against him.'"

There is the word *lest* again. David is certain that Saul will come out the winner. David is preparing to surrender as a prisoner, and it seems like an appropriate time to pray.

Perhaps worst of all, David feared his own disgrace: "Lest those who trouble me rejoice when I am moved" (v. 4). Everyone in Israel knew that David was being pursued by Saul. When the enemy caught him, David would be humiliated, a subject of mockery. And the terrible thought of that for one who had been promised a kingdom made it seem like an appropriate time to pray.

Three great fears moved David to his knees. Quite frankly, he was not motivated to pray because he was a godly man, although we know that he was a man after God's own heart. David prayed in Psalm 13 because he was desperate. Through the years, I've often observed how God steers us into that emotional cul-de-sac. He likes to corral us into a corner where the only way out is up. We have nowhere else to turn, and that's when we get serious about praying.

If you're going through a time of trouble right now, as so many of us are, don't rail against God for what He has done to bring you to this place. Instead, ask Him how you can learn to be His trusting child and how you can hang on to the desperation that brings about sincere, heartfelt prayer. "O Lord God, I can't get through one day without You. I can't make it through these next hours without You."

When we become desperate, we cry out, "O Lord, help me!" And He always does.

The Form of Our Prayer

In his desperation, David prayed three prayers in verse 3. First He said, "Lord, consider me." The words actually mean, "Look on me." What he wanted to say was, "Lord, don't turn Your back on me anymore. Turn around and look at me and see me!"

His second prayer is, "Lord, hear me." David is pleading with God to answer his questions. "Lord, please hear what I'm saying."

And then there's a very interesting third request. He says, "Lord, enlighten my eyes." My first interpretation of that phrase was, "Lord, show me what You're doing." But that's not the meaning of the phrase. It really means, "Lord, put the light back in my eyes." Isn't that a fascinating thing to put in our prayers? *Put the light back in my eyes.*

You can easily spot a person suffering through depression. His face gives him away. Depression transforms one's countenance into a mask, empty and rigid. Most of all, the light in the person's eyes has been extinguished. David says, "O Lord, I have no hope. Please *see* me and *hear* me—and put the light back in my eyes." What a moving prayer this is.

But we come to a surprising place in David's prayer. If you read the chapter thoughtfully, you can't help but think, *Doesn't this portion belong somewhere else?* For we've heard the cries of a tortured man. We've heard his pleading and fears, and we've seen just how low a man can sink. And there in the depths of his despair come two verses in which despair is replaced by triumph. David is no longer the bitter, hopeless man who feels God can't or won't help him. He's suddenly a man filled with praise and a sense of victory, a man who has regained the light in his eyes.

The Focus of Our Prayer

David worked honestly through his darkest, most hopeless feelings. Then he turned his eyes away from his troubles and fixed his gaze on God. The focus of his prayer became "O Lord, my God." David called upon God; he called upon the power of God. In the midst of his prayer, in bringing his desperate plea to God, he began to look away from his problems and to see the One whom he had been addressing. He is suddenly conscious of an exalted and holy God, the Lord of the universe sitting enthroned in heaven. He addresses his Lord as *Jehovah Elohim*.

Jehovah reflects God's promises; *Elohim* reflects God's power. David says, "O God of power and promise, I appeal to You." In this moment of transformation, I believe David's mind must have gone back to the promise that was given him, the promise that he should ascend to the throne. I believe he had a resurgence of faith that he would sit on Israel's throne. God had promised him something, despite all that had transpired, and that meant something. It had to, he suddenly realized. David's heart suddenly returned to the conviction that the God who promises is the God who is powerful, who can stand behind His promises. David's faith rebounds and reasserts itself.

I always turn with joy to Jeremiah 20:11 when I'm facing difficulty: "The LORD is with me as a mighty, awesome one. Therefore my persecutors will stumble, and will not prevail. They will be greatly ashamed, for they will not prosper. Their everlasting confusion will never be forgotten."

A similar promise is found in Psalm 138:7–8: "Though I walk in the midst of trouble, You will revive me; You will stretch out Your hand against the wrath of my enemies, and Your right hand will save me. The LORD will perfect that which concerns me; Your mercy, O LORD, endures forever; do not forsake the works of Your hands."

We can find tremendous hope of victory in the midst of the deepest pits life can drop us into. But it's no simple process. There isn't a handy, guaranteed formula for hope in the midst of suffering. It takes absolute, fall-on-your-face humility and genuine, gut-wrenchingly honest prayer. We must come to the point where we hear ourselves saying, "Lord God, my life is devastated. I've been victimized by my emotions and overwhelmed by my problems. Life has thrown all it can at me, and I've caved in. I've experienced none of the victory; I haven't honored You. I am at the point of surrender. But O Lord God, in the midst of all of this, help me to see and know my Mighty Awesome One, *Jehovah Elohim*."

Only in the abject humility of such a prayer can we begin to catch the briefest glimmer of Him, and only then will our plummeting fortunes begin to reverse themselves.

There is a threefold progression in this psalm moving from tears to triumph. Right in the center lies the ultimate truth that makes the difference. That truth is that *Jehovah Elohim*—Almighty God—is in charge. No wonder David breaks into joyful song.

Our Song When God Delays

Our Song Is a Song of Triumph
"But I have trusted in Your mercy; my heart shall rejoice in Your salvation. I will sing to the LORD, because He has dealt bountifully with me" (vv. 5–6).

David's song is a song of triumph. And how did he reach that point? He began to see God.

Our troubles can cause us to avoid the places where we're most likely to see Him. I'm always puzzled when troubled people fall away from the church. They may be strong pillars of the local fellowship, but when trouble comes along, they disappear. Have you ever noticed that?

"We've missed you in church."

"Well, the truth is that we're having trouble in our marriage."

If that's true, get up early and go to both services! You need all the church you can get in such a time. Our faith isn't a luxury intended for periods of smooth sailing—neither is our fellowship. When trouble

---

The steadfast love of the LORD never ceases,

his mercies never come to an end;

they are new every morning;

great is your faithfulness.

—Lamentations 3:22 (NRSV)

---

comes along, that's when it's wonderful to be part of a faithful, Bible-believing body of people who will rally around you. They'll pray for you, support you with their resources, encourage you, and counsel you in the tough decisions. The devil is the only one whose opinion is that you should take a sabbatical from church in the hard times.

David says, "I have trusted in Your mercy; my heart shall rejoice in Your salvation." What does that word *salvation* mean to you? I hope you realize that it means more than being saved from judgment; it can also be about salvation from predicaments that occur in the here and now. God saves us in the big picture, but the Bible assures us that He saves us in the small ones too—when we ask Him.

You might question that conclusion, because you think about poor, beleaguered David. How exactly has God saved him in this situation? Saul is still coming after him. The armies are still on the march. Things look as hopeless as ever, on the face of things. What has really changed?

Nothing—except David's memory. He has recalled, as the spirit of prayer took hold of him and God counseled his hurting soul, that nothing has changed about *God*. Our Lord is changeless. He has been mighty in the past, and that has not changed. He has been loving and full of blessing, and that has not changed. He has had a plan for David, and that has not changed either. David has remembered these things, and he sings with joy, in words that simultaneously reflect past promises and future fulfillment: "God, You have delivered me!"

Has David been delivered from his plight? No, but in his heart and mind he has seen blessed deliverance, and he has claimed the promise of God. He proclaims—in advance, with the conviction of things hoped for and the evidence of things not seen—that "God has delivered me." David, the future king, has such faith in the future that he speaks of it in the past tense.

Our Song Is a Song of Thanksgiving

David writes, "I will sing to the LORD, because He has dealt bountifully with me" (v. 6). If you want to stay healthy as a Christian, you need to go back and remember what God has done for you in the past. You need to polish the monuments to the great victories in your life. That's among the wonderful reasons for keeping a journal. David consults the journal in his mind of his dealings with his Lord, and he realizes, "God has dealt bountifully with me."

How often David must have, in his quieter moments, thought back to that tumultuous day in the field, that day when he tried on the king's armor and couldn't fit into it. He must have recalled the intimidating size and fearsome demeanor of that giant whom he faced with only a sling and five smooth stones. God had dealt bountifully with him then, and that was an understatement. David must have reviewed it often.

David took out that nine-foot-six-inch giant with a single shot and, in doing so, preserved Israel. There was no way to experience such a thing and not realize it was God's work. David must have thought back even farther, to a time when God gave him incredible, superhuman strength and adrenaline to challenge wild animals that were threatening his flock of sheep. Why, a boy of his age couldn't have prevailed against a bear and a lion without God's presence. God clearly had a special purpose for him.

And it was undeniable that there had been times when Saul had been closing in for the kill. The game had seemed to be up. He was right in the very grasp of Saul and his sword, yet a miracle had always arrived.

We know from the psalms that David called upon his memory often to nurture and refresh his faith. When anxiety for the future built up—and it did time and again—David faced it with the testimony of the past. His life may not have been what he might have chosen, but it was a life that could never have lasted this long without God's intervention.

What a terrible danger it is for us to become trapped in the claustrophobia of the present during a crisis. That's our first impulse. The clear and present danger is so huge, so imposing, that it blocks our view behind us and ahead of us. We desperately need perspective. We can't change the future until it arrives, but we can gain wisdom from the past. It should hold for us an absolute conviction on the question of who God is and what He's done for us previously.

Make your list, and check it twice. Just what has God done for you? You lost your job, and you thought the world would end. What did God do? Your marriage was in terrible trouble, or perhaps you even faced the devastation of a divorce. What did God do? How about when one of your children broke your heart? Do you remember God's love for you then? Make a detailed inventory of His faithfulness in your life, and you'll be surprised at the length of it.

"I waited patiently for the LORD; and He inclined to me, and heard my cry. He also brought me up out of a horrible pit, out of the miry clay, and set my feet upon a rock, and established my steps. He has put a new song in my mouth—praise to our God; many will see it and fear, and will trust in the LORD" (Ps. 40:1–3).

Psalm 28:7 says it this way: "The LORD is my strength and my shield; my heart trusted in Him, and I am helped; therefore my heart greatly rejoices, and with my song I will praise Him."

Does it seem strange to you that Psalm 13, so filled with misery, builds to a final note of triumph, trust, and praise to the Almighty One? There's nothing strange about it. That's the way faith should work. We come to God honestly, pour our hearts out to Him, and experience renewed faith as He prods our memories and reaffirms His love.

In the Old Testament, there is a story of a prophet by the name of Habakkuk who lived at a time when the people of God lived in rebellion against His holy principles. Habakkuk was the prophet called to confront them in their wickedness, so he stood in their midst and cried out, "God, what are You going to do about this?"

The second verse of that prophet's book reminds us of Psalm 13. Habakkuk says, "O LORD, how long shall I cry, and You will not hear? Even cry out to You, 'Violence!' and You will not save."

God finally responded to Habakkuk's question in a veiled way. And once the prophet had worked over that answer and begun to grasp what it implied, he was shocked. It was the last answer he'd ever have imagined. For instance, in that same chapter, the Lord says to Habakkuk, "Look among the nations and watch—be utterly astounded! For I will work a work in your days which you would not believe, though it were told you'" (Hab. 1:5).

What kind of an answer is that? *What are You up to, Lord?* God is saying, "Take a good look around you and figure it out. If I tried to tell you, you wouldn't believe Me anyway."

God was absolutely right, I need not tell you. Habakkuk couldn't believe it. God had a plan to use the Chaldeans, a nation that was many times more evil and wicked than the people of Israel, to judge the people of Israel. I can just see this prophet of God putting his hands over his head and wailing, "O, Lord! The problem was terrible, and the answer is even worse!"

Habakkuk can't make any sense out of it at all. Why would God use those more evil than Israel as a means of punishing them? Where is justice or logic in such a thing? It made no sense. And the only sort of conclusion the prophet could ever come to in his perplexity was that God is God, and His ways are not our ways.

And yet Habakkuk finally does come to another conclusion: "Though the fig tree may not blossom, nor fruit be on the vines; though the labor of the olive may fail, and the fields yield no food; though the flock be cut off from the fold, and there be no herd in the stalls—yet I will rejoice in the LORD, I will joy in the God of my salvation. The LORD God is my strength; He will make my feet like deer's feet, and He will make me walk on my high hills" (Hab. 3:17–19).

Habakkuk, you see, made a choice. His country was in turmoil; his God had no answers that made sense. When there was no explanation for things that he could wrap his mind around, the prophet said, "I do have one option: I can praise God. The world around me may be in turmoil, yet though all of it falls apart, I will rejoice in the God of my salvation."

That same choice faces you. You can demand all the answers, neatly gift-wrapped. You can insist that God quickly resolve every trial and injustice in your life. You can hold out for the world, and your life within it, to become suddenly fair and rational, though they've never been so in the first place.

Or you can choose to lift up your eyes to the heavens, pour out your tears and grief and anger, and say in the very midst of them, "God, I have no clue what this turmoil is all about or where it is leading, but this is my resolution: I will put my trust in You, and I will praise You with all of my heart, unconditionally!"

The same God who has been there for you in the past is the God who is going to be there for you in the future. He will bring resolution in His own time, according to His own purposes. We become pre-occupied with our circumstances; God is preoccupied with our character. He will allow the tough times for the higher good of our character until He is finished with the great work that is invisible to our earthly eyes.

And yet, you can be encouraged. God never waits too long. He is never late, nor does He lose control. He makes no misjudgments or mistakes. Next time you're in that ceaseless tunnel, and there seems to be no light to lead you on, think of Sharon Paul's words: "Even on my darkest days, I can still say I've seen Jesus. I've seen Him with the eyes of my spirit, even if the eyes of my mind and heart are blinded. I'm so grateful that He is my Savior."

The writer of Psalm 13 concluded, "I will sing to the LORD, for he has been good to me" (NIV). I hope you've learned the joy of singing when God delays.

Psalm 138

A Psalm of David.

1 I will praise You with my whole heart;
   Before the gods I will sing praises to You.
2 I will worship toward Your holy temple,
   And praise Your name
   For Your lovingkindness and Your truth;
   For You have magnified Your word above all Your name.
3 In the day when I cried out, You answered me,
   And made me bold with strength in my soul.
4 All the kings of the earth shall praise You, O LORD,
   When they hear the words of Your mouth.
5 Yes, they shall sing of the ways of the LORD,
   For great is the glory of the LORD.
6 Though the LORD is on high,
   Yet He regards the lowly;
   But the proud He knows from afar.
7 Though I walk in the midst of trouble, You will revive me;
   You will stretch out Your hand
   Against the wrath of my enemies,
   And Your right hand will save me.
8 The LORD will perfect that which concerns me;
   Your mercy, O LORD, endures forever;
   Do not forsake the works of Your hands.

5

Worship in Times of Trouble

I found a Friend when life seemed not worth living
I found a Friend so tender and forgiving
I can't conceive how such a thing could be,
That Jesus cares for even me.
Each day, each year, my faith in Him is growing
He's ever near, His love is overflowing.
I have no fear, my worldly cares are few
I can depend on Him to see me through.
I found a Friend and He is your friend too.

—BARCLAY (RON) ALLEN

Carole Carlson was a good friend and a gifted writer. We collaborated on several projects before her death in late 1999, and her talents always shone brightly. Carole was a woman of character who understood bends in the road because she had made the trip herself. She knew what it was like to have a peaceful life suddenly disrupted by tragedy. A few years before she went home to be with her Lord, she sat down and wrote me a poignant account of her journey. She shared with me the nightmare she'd encountered and come to terms with. I felt the heart-wrenching emotions of her experiences, as I'm certain you will.

I believe Carole would have appreciated the topic of this book, and it pleases me that she can "collaborate" with me on it through these thoughts from her insightful pen. Her words live on and minister to you today, though Carole herself is no longer with us. Here is what she wrote.

—◂—

Kent left the house that Thursday with a smile and a bear hug from his mom. At eighteen, life for him was wonderful. He had graduated from high school with honors and had a good job working in a toy factory, and college was in his sights. The night before, he had gone to church and heard a message from two verses: "All things work together for good" (Rom. 8:28) and "In everything give thanks" (1 Thess. 5:18).

Kent was in a thankful mood, especially grateful for the airplane he and his dad had just purchased. His dream was to become a missionary pilot; the future gleamed with promise.

On Thursday night he called home and said, "Mom, I'm just going to go out and practice a few 'touch and goes.' Hold supper for me—I'll be home by nine."

Kent never came home.

In a clump of trees at the edge of a little country airport lay the crashed plane and the bodies of Kent and his buddy Rick. One moment in time changed our lives. On that warm June night, God chose to take one of our precious children.

How does a parent continue to *exist* beyond that moment? Will the knots in our insides ever leave?

In the weeks and months to follow, I learned more about God's love than I had in all my years of being a Christian. I learned that His Word speaks to our needs. "My grace is sufficient for you, for My strength is made perfect in weakness" (2 Cor. 12:9).

When I felt helpless to do even the small tasks of the day, I'd repeat, "I can do all things through Christ who strengthens me" (Phil. 4:13). Every time I saw a good-looking blond kid on the street and thought my heart would break, I remembered the verse Kent had underlined in his Bible: "But I do not want you to be ignorant, brethren, concerning those who have fallen asleep, lest you sorrow as others who have no hope" (1 Thess. 4:13).

When I began to indulge in self-pity, I'd embrace my husband, Ward, who was suffering as intensely as I was, and remember that God said, "Therefore comfort each other and edify one another, just as you also are doing" (1 Thess. 5:11).

In fact, we found strength in encouraging others. Kent's little brother didn't understand why his buddy didn't come home. His big sister had lost her pal and confidant. The friends in the youth group at church questioned God and the kids at school asked, "Why?" "Why?" "*Why?*"

The grace of God gave us comfort, but it also pierced us with the urgency to reach out to others. Ward and I grew closer together as we tried to console other parents who had suffered a loss. We developed an uncommon boldness to minister to those who were hurting.

I wish for no one the experience of losing a child. But a far greater tragedy is to lose the opportunity to know Jesus Christ intimately. How grateful we are that our children know and love Him. Life has meaning for us simply because we have the assurance, when this life is over, that we will all be reunited.

—

Life comes crashing down.

It happens for every one of us—not always with planes or automobiles or loss of family members or failed marriages. Somehow, all the same, life comes crashing down. The loss of one's own child may well be the most excruciating blow a loving parent can endure, but you can be certain that every other tragedy life dispenses offers its own unique form of suffering.

You're never prepared. That's the essence of the pain. Possibly for the first time in your life, you wonder whether there's any purpose in going on. For the first time, you wonder whether the gift of life on this earth—for *you*—is really a gift. For the first time, you seem to lack the strength even to rise from bed and perform the little rituals and have the little conversations that give daily life its color and rhythm. With a heart smashed in ten thousand pieces, you have no clue where to turn.

How wonderful, then, is that moment when you discover you can run into the arms of a Father who loves you and weeps with you. What an incredible moment when you fully comprehend that healing is possible. In Psalm 138:7, David wrote, "Though I walk in the midst of trouble, You will revive me."

He is ever faithful; He is ever present and attentive. One of the things we discover in the psalms is that we not only have a Lord God and a Savior when we face tragedy—even incomparable pain like the loss of a young, beloved child—but we have a wonderful Friend in the bargain.

Again and again, the psalms return to this beautiful, melodious theme. They burst out in song—for what other form than music could this book have ever taken?—over the amazing news that the high and holy God of creation is our Friend. They remind us that He knows every need we feel, every craving we experience. They assure us He is not a God who dwells in some distant, unapproachable realm, who paid a short call on this planet centuries ago—but that He is an always-present Father, who is totally immersed in the smallest details of our lives.

And when we come to Him in the midst of trouble, He hears us; He knows us. He loves us as we love our own children.

In Times of Present Trouble, the Lord Is to Be Worshiped

In Psalm 138, we find the song of "a man after God's own heart" who had traveled a long journey down the road of spiritual wisdom. He understood many deep truths about his relationship with God—one of which is brought home with clarity and passion here. David came to see that in times of trouble, the most clearly marked path to God is not the way of struggle and desperation. It is, instead, the path of worship. Psalm 138 speaks to us about worship in times of trouble.

Let Us Worship the Lord Thankfully

David opens this psalm by saying, "I will praise You." Who is the object of his praise? He doesn't say in the beginning, but he will go on to use the name of the Lord six times. The personal pronoun that refers to His name is found ten times in the first stanza. The words *You* and *Your* are everywhere. David is caught up in the majesty and presence of God.

As he writes, "I will praise You," the word he uses for "praise" deserves our attention. It gives a meaning to the sentence that might better be expressed as, "I will give thanks to You." Praise and thanksgiving are closely related. For David, this is a time of worship in a time of trouble, and he launches it by giving thanks to God. It takes a certain degree of wisdom and maturity for you and I to reach such a level. When difficulties burden us, we must struggle to remember our reasons for gratitude to God. This won't happen if we imprison ourselves within self-pity and preoccupation with loss. It requires the fortitude to open our eyes and see that, whatever seems to have been taken from us, we have received so much more that should move us toward gratitude.

In a spirit of thanksgiving, David has found the starting line that makes the difference. Scripture tells us elsewhere that we are to "come before His presence with thanksgiving" (Ps. 95:2).

Psalm 100:4 offers the same strategy. We are to "enter into His gates with thanksgiving, and into His courts with praise. Be thankful to Him, and bless His name." Gratitude is a doorway that admits us into the courts of godliness. Focusing inward on our misery traps us in our own private dungeon, and we lock ourselves away from those richer interiors that provide the healing and wisdom we need.

Gratitude is the key. You and I too often enter the Lord's courts driving a truck, don't we? We back it up to the courtyard, pull the lever, and unload everything we've been carrying. During the long nights, those supplies of tears and resentment and self-absorption have been building up. We can't enter into His presence without dumping all of it all over the steps of His holy courts. There is certainly a time for casting all our burdens upon the Lord—but perhaps not right there at the front gate. The psalms challenge us to come into His presence with thanksgiving. We worship the Lord God with a grateful heart in times of pain and crisis.

Is that a difficult lesson to learn? The next one is even tougher!

Let Us Worship the Lord Wholeheartedly

As you work through the life and writings of David over a lifetime, you'll come to this conclusion about him: Notwithstanding the blemishes and failings of his humanity, David was a man who offered himself wholeheartedly to God. Notice how he begins this psalm with the words: "I will praise You . . . I will sing praises to You" (v. 1); "I will worship . . . and praise Your name" (v. 2). These are variations on a theme—his heart formulates and reformulates new expressions for the worship and praise that is spontaneously flowing from him.

Worship for David, you see, was no matter for pews and passivity. He threw his entire heart and soul and mind into the praise of God! What pursuits in your life claim your all?

Here is how God would answer that question: *you*. He gave His all for *you*.

The Lord God Almighty has taken note of us. He became one of us, and then He gave up His life out of love for us. That's no mild commitment. He gave Himself wholeheartedly for us, and He allows us to enter into His very presence. Meanwhile, we sit in our pews harboring the great fear that we might slip up and let our emotions show in our worship. What would those people in the pew behind us think?

As long as those people sitting behind us are claiming any part of our concern, we're not giving ourselves wholeheartedly to the worship of the Lord God. It's worth stopping to examine which owns the greater portion of our heart: God or our public image. The answer could be a disturbing one.

Psalm 119 is the Bible's longest chapter. It's devoted to the power and glory and study of the Word of God. Read that psalm in its entirety sometime. What you'll find is that salted all through those verses, again and again, are the phrases "wholehearted" and "with a whole heart."

- "Blessed are those who keep His testimonies, who seek Him with the whole heart!" (v. 2).
- "With my whole heart I have sought You; oh, let me not wander from Your commandments!" (v. 10).
- "Give me understanding, and I shall keep Your law; indeed, I shall observe it with my whole heart" (v. 34).
- "I entreated Your favor with my whole heart" (v. 58).

The message could be no clearer. When you approach God, you must do so with an undivided heart. How do you come to the Lord with your worship? How do you approach Him in times of trouble? In times of blessing? Perhaps you're like me; in terms of approaching

---

We know not what the future holds
But take each day as it unfolds
The bitter with the sweet God blends.
We wisely take what 'ere He sends.
His dealings are in wisdom made,
The warming sun or chilling shade.
On mountain top in the dell
Our Father doeth all things well.

—David B. Stewart

God wholeheartedly, I've found it's often easier in times of need than times of abundance. When life is smooth and calm, that's when I'm tempted to hold back a part of my heart. I tend to relax, as if I have everything under control. But I won't be relaxing for too long. God sends the storm to force us to look for Christ walking on the waves. The thunder gets our attention, and when we're humbled in fear, we're far more likely to approach Him with our entire being.

Let Us Worship the Lord Courageously

David is determined that nothing should come between him and the worship of God.

In the opening refrain of Psalm 138, he writes, "Before the gods I will sing praises to You" (v. 1). The word *gods* refers to the pagan deities and leaders of the nations surrounding Judah. Our modern world is filled with false gods, and so was David's. He is showing a bit of godly arrogance here. In effect, he is saying, "Some people I know will fall silent while they're surrounded by pagan statues. But I intend to walk right up and worship You in the very midst of them all! I'm not ashamed of my Lord and my God." He didn't care what others thought. As for him and his house, they would serve the Lord.

Do you feel cultural pressure? The heat is rising for Christians in our society. There is more and more outright hostility for those who would claim Christian allegiances. I can remember when it was much more common to see families in restaurants joining hands around the table to thank and praise God before eating. Our family still does this—how about yours? It's wonderful to sit in a restaurant and see a family boldly praying together at another table. I try to encourage such families as I see them. We all need that encouragement in a world that ridicules us for trusting and obeying our Lord.

David said, "I couldn't care less what they think! I plan to praise my God in front of the pagan gods. I plan to speak of my God even to those who deny Him." David praised God *courageously*—with his heart, his soul, and his mind.

Let Us Worship the Lord Intelligently

Sometimes we come to the worship of God and don't know where to begin. What do we say? How can we praise? Anything we do with excellence must be done with intelligence, and there are intelligent ways to worship God. Here is how to praise Him:

Praise Him for His mercy and truth. David said he would praise

God's name for His lovingkindness and truth (v. 2). The word *lov-ingkindness* is the Hebrew word *hessed*, which is actually the word for *mercy*. Have you ever noticed how often mercy and truth are found together in the same passage? These two traits are twins in the Old Testament. In the psalms especially, we repeatedly see mercy and truth wedded together in the same text. For instance, Psalm 25:10 says, "All the paths of the LORD are *mercy and truth*." In Psalm 57:3 we read, "God shall send forth His *mercy and His truth*." And Psalm 85:10 says, "*Mercy and truth* have met together" (emphasis added on all).

Here's the big question: Why would the two qualities of mercy and truth be consistently paired together in Scripture? To find the answer, we need only take one good look in the mirror and another good look at the people around us. It's interesting to see that there are some people who are gifted in mercy and others who place a high premium on truth—but they're not often the same people. The high-on-mercy, low-on-truth advocate ends up practicing injustice. He issues mercy as a free pass without accountability or standards. And you know this person's opposite: The high-on-truth, low-on-mercy fellow is a self-righteous, modern-day Pharisee who will use the truth as a blunt weapon to injure people.

But our Lord perfectly balances mercy and truth. His mercy is poured out in the light of absolute truth, and His truth is saturated by infinite mercy. Neither is compromised in any way. When you come before Him in trouble, you know that He hears the very deepest cry of your heart even as He deals with you according to His divine standard. And because He is both merciful and truthful, when He gives you His Word, you can count on its being fulfilled.

Jesus embodied perfect truth and perfect mercy, and He is our model for doing the same.

Praise Him for His magnified Word. There are ideas and concepts I accept without completely understanding them. One of these is that God values His integrity so much that He has elevated it higher than His own name. Let me explain what I mean. When you study the Word of God, you can know He'll be with you—and why He has elevated His Word higher than anything in the universe. The Word of

God carries an authority matching that of the very name of God. Now, that's no insignificant item; it means that we can absolutely, fundamentally place our trust in the integrity of God. His Word is trustworthy, for He is trustworthy. He will always balance mercy and truth, and He can be relied upon to keep His Word—and to provide for us.

Praise Him for His mighty provision. Think about these words: "In the day when I cried out, You answered me, and made me bold with strength in my soul" (v. 3). I love this psalm! Why? Because every word is important. First of all, God doesn't delay in answering us when we come to Him. We may think He delays because we have our own timetable in mind, but God hears us the instant we cry out.

God will always be there when we're in trouble. Whatever He chooses to do about our circumstances, and whenever He chooses to do it, He will strengthen us for the battle. When David cried out to

---

When trouble comes . . .

Sometimes God takes us through it,

Sometimes He helps us in it,

Sometimes He keeps us from it.

---

the Lord, he always received an infusion of renewed vitality to face the problems ahead of him. "O Lord God," David often cries out in victory, "I called for Your help and You gave me power to stand in the midst of my enemies and my crises."

Let me be very clear that I'm not putting in a request for any more trouble in my life. I've had all I need for a while. Just the same, I can say that my darkest days have almost been worthwhile just for the experience of seeing God keep His promise to provide strength and endurance. I predict that I may be speaking for you too.

In Times of Future Triumph, the Lord Is to Be Worshiped

Crisis psalms nearly always lead to visible transformation. We see the psalmist in his pain, desperation, and supplication—then we see God transform him and fill him with renewed faith and resolution. In the fourth verse of this psalm, David forgets his crisis and gazes prophetically into the future. He says, in effect, "When it seems as if my life is caving in, I can still choose to praise God. But how humble are my troubled words of worship compared to the praise that will echo and resound around the world one day—the day His name is lifted up! The world will be joined together in praise and exaltation of His glories."

Thus David becomes a prophet. Would you like to hear about the future world he sees?

All Kings of the Earth Will Praise the Lord

Every knee shall bow; that will be the scenario.

Every king, president, premier, and prime minister across the expanse of the globe will bow before King Jesus and give Him the glory. The Bible tells us that "the kingdoms of this world have become the kingdoms of our Lord and of His Christ, and He shall reign forever and ever!" (Rev. 11:15). All people groups and all cultures will acknowledge that Jesus Christ is Lord. And Paul adds that "at the name of Jesus every knee should bow, of those in heaven, and of those on earth, and of those under the earth, and that every tongue should confess that Jesus Christ is Lord, to the glory of God the Father" (Phil. 2:10–11). So we can see that John caught a glimpse of that breathtaking new world, and Paul was allowed a hint of it too.

Before either of them lived, God revealed the same future vision to David. "All the kings of the earth shall praise You, O LORD," he wrote. And God gave him this glimpse in the midst of his worldly problems. "Now I praise You in my solitary suffering," he said. "Someday we will all be praising You in Your glory."

There was a commercial on television that used the catchline, "You can pay me now or pay me later." I don't remember what the product was, but I remember the line: *Pay me now or pay me later.* David's words in the psalm bring that commercial back to my mind, for God is saying, "Praise Me now or praise Me later. But you will praise Me someday, for every knee will bow and every tongue will confess that Christ is Lord."

Kings and commoners alike will worship God. The lofty will bow low, as the lowly are lifted up.

All Kinds of People Will Be Acknowledged by the Lord

God doesn't make distinctions about our place on earth. David divides people into two groups—the lofty and the lowly—but God seeks love and reconciliation with them all.

The Lord has always sided with the lowly. I think about this as I visit New York's inner city and see the people living in filth and poverty. No matter what devastating circumstances these people have experienced, no matter how low their lives have sunk or how far they've been pushed away from God, I sense a special relationship between God and the lowly. Jesus exemplified God's heart for the poor. They reach out to Him too. He relates in a special way to the victims of life—people who have been brought so low they can hardly lift their heads.

Isaiah 57:15 says, "Thus says the High and Lofty One who inhabits eternity, whose name is Holy: 'I dwell in the high and holy place, with him who has a contrite and humble spirit, to revive the spirit of the humble, and to revive the heart of the contrite ones.'" Some have suggested that God thinks the most highly of people who don't think highly of themselves. He hears their prayers and reaches out to them.

The church is the body of Christ who made Himself lowly. The church is not characterized by the high and lofty for the most part. Christian prosperity is the exception more than the rule. The church has historically been composed of people who wander together in their lowliness and their need for a Savior. We have been people who would be of little account in the world, but who understand that God is no respecter of persons, and that the ground is level at the foot of the cross. The church is a celebration party for people too lowly for parties—the broken and needy and contrite. They're God's people.

God has another kind of relationship with the lofty—those proud and arrogant enough to have declared independence from God. What is this relationship? David says the Lord resists the lofty. "The proud He knows from afar" (Ps. 138:6). Remember that God always reverses the human equation so that the first in worldly values become last, and the last become first. For the humble, who with hearts of desperation come with heads bowed seeking God's forgiveness, He shelters. He puts robes around their shoulders and rings on their fingers. For the proud and independent, He continues to wait by the side of the road. He knows them from afar.

The Bible tells us we must bow in humble recognition of who we are and who God is. And if we can't do that, there's no hope for us. In His presence, there is no proud and distinguished individual. The wealthiest ruler in the history of this planet stands as a beggar in rags in the presence of an omnipotent, glorious Creator. Those distinctions we set among ourselves mean absolutely nothing in the context of His majesty. So we can only kneel to acknowledge the truth of our condition. If we cannot see ourselves as heaven sees us, we cannot see ourselves.

In Times of Uncertainty, the Lord Is to Be Worshiped

David writes in verse 7, "Though I walk in the midst of trouble, You will revive me; You will stretch out Your hand against the wrath of my enemies, and Your right hand will save me."

It's one thing to be in trouble. You can have trouble on a nice day. You can have trouble with your children or your coworkers, but these are usually little troubles you know you can rise above. It's another thing to be *in the midst of trouble*. The appropriate word would be *stuck*. You find yourself in a crisis with no immediate resolution. You know this thing isn't going away. You know that when you wake up tomorrow morning, and the morning after that, this matter will leap to the forefront of your mind as soon as you wipe the sleep from your eyes. Some problem has risen up like a great tidal wave from the depths, and it dominates your landscape.

But if you're like David, there is something behind that wave—or perhaps it is between you and the wave—and that thing is called *hope*.

The Lord Continues to Protect Us

If such a thing as an honorary doctorate in Crises and Catastrophes had existed, David would have been awarded one. Although he was a man after God's own heart, his life was one long procession of problems. As we've seen, he spent years fleeing the wrath of a king—living as a fugitive, hiding, and sleeping in caves. When he finally did become king, he immediately had to deal with geopolitical crises on every front. His nation of Israel was at war with everyone in sight.

David coped. He calmed the waters the best he could, and when everything had settled down on the political front, that's when the domestic front exploded. He was like a man whose career finally begins to look promising, who gets the big promotion—and suddenly he has marital trouble and his sons get into trouble with the police. David's own sons were in open rebellion against him. The house of David was crumbling; there were cracks in the foundation.

Would you agree that David walked in the midst of trouble? If you're having a problem in your family or on the job, I challenge you to read the life of David. Maybe you'll feel a little better. David walked in the midst of trouble—he made terrible, fateful mistakes— yet he always remained one of God's favorite children.

God had promised to protect His child, and neither party to that promise ever forgot it. Think about nearly everyone's favorite chapter of Scripture, Psalm 23. When David so movingly paints us a picture of the Good Shepherd watching over His sheep, we see again David's faith and trust in a protecting God. David sang, "He restores my soul; He leads me in the paths of righteousness for His name's sake. Yea, though I walk through the valley of the shadow of death, I will fear no evil; for You are with me; Your rod and Your staff, they comfort me" (Ps. 23:3–4).

> *When you pass through the waters, I will be with you;*
> *And through the rivers, they shall not overflow you.*
> *When you walk through the fire, you shall not be burned,*
> *Nor shall the flame scorch you,*
> *For I am the LORD your God,*
> *The Holy One of Israel, your Savior.*
> —Isaiah 43:2–3

Every believer knows that when we walk through the valley of tears, God walks beside us; when we pass through the fire, He draws close to deflect the flames; when we wade through the flood, He is nearby to keep our heads up. In the storm or in the earthquake or in the midst of any disaster threatening to engulf us—that's the time we feel the presence of the Lord as we've never felt Him before. Other so-called friends may disappear. Their words may falter and their support may vanish. But God is closest in the crises, surrounding us with His presence. He promised us He would do it, and our Lord is always as good as His word.

David, recipient of the honorary degree in Crises and Catastrophes, bears testimony to that fact. His acceptance speech for such a degree would sound much like one of these psalms: thanks and praise to God Almighty, who keeps His promises. But at the end of the speech, David would add one more startling idea. He would assure you that the Lord will not only protect you, but *He will perfect you*.

The Lord Continues to Perfect Us

He is perfecting us. That means He is bringing to completion everything in the world that surrounds and defines us.

What happens when we go through troubles and lose our perspective? We begin to think that God has forgotten us. He must have discarded that plan He had for this life; He must have scratched us from His divine daily planner. It's a terrible feeling to have the sense that God has put you aside.

And of course, it's never true. When we navigate troubled waters, God is the Master of not only the waves, but also the ship. He never abandons His plans or His people. He will see the voyage through to its final destination.

But we're stubborn creatures who struggle to learn. And we learn the least when the sun is shining and the winds are crisp and life feels good. Peace and prosperity have never provided effective classrooms. Crisis and catastrophe, on the other hand, offer master's degrees. By the way, that accreditation makes you a Master of Disaster.

The truth etches itself into your mind and heart when you find yourself forced into a one-on-one relationship of dependency upon God. It's the "school of hard knocks," to be certain, but there's one momentous consolation: All the while, even while the bruises ache and the scars are fresh, He is still working all things together for our good and for His. It's essential that we cling to His promise of continuous perfection. He is our only hope, our only asset, our only possibility, and as we look into His eyes, we realize that from the very beginning life has always been like that. We just wouldn't learn it, for we're stubborn creatures.

During the difficult days, what is He doing? I call Psalm 138:8 the "Philippians 1:6 of the Old Testament." Sometimes there are church members or radio friends who ask me to sign my name in their Bibles. I often jot "Philippians 1:6" beside my name, because it says this: "Being confident of this very thing, that He who has begun a good work in you will complete it until the day of Jesus Christ."

No matter what, you must never forget that when you're deep in the midst of trouble, God is still busy at work in you, though He may be doing so out of your sight. Street workers are out of sight too. As you walk through a busy city avenue, you'll see an open manhole marked by a sign that says "Men at Work." You can't see them, but you can be sure they labor on in the dark underside of the city. Just mentally place a "God at Work" sign into that scar where your troubles have taken their toll. He's involved in very expensive renovation. You may be paying the bill right now, but you're going to like the beautiful new design and furnishings of your life.

He is perfecting you. He's working on the new design. It's true that you don't remember signing the papers for the design. Our God, the Landlord of our lives, doesn't ask our permission. But He is eager to show us how well He can protect us, so that He might demonstrate in the process how wonderfully He can perfect us. Then, when the noise and the dust of it all are gone, the dross will have been burned off. What is left will be all the gold of a lifetime of God's ongoing project of perfection in us.

What a wonderful God! When we begin to look at our difficulties from the perspective of the psalms, our depression fades. Our hope increases. Our love for God is intensified.

David's Final Appeal: "Do Not Forsake the Work of Your Hands!"

David asks the Lord to keep up the good work. "Do not forsake the works of Your hands," he says (v. 8). This is a man who has become aware of the work of the Sculptor who has been chipping away the raw stone of his life for years. He finally comprehends that at the end of all the painful chiseling, something smoother and elegant—a finer work of art—truly emerges.

The works of Your hands. David has felt the expert work of those skilled fingers, and he knows those hands hold his life in their secure grip. He is saying, "Lord, You started this work on me. Your art project began a lifetime ago with a small shepherd boy. It was inaugurated when Samuel poured the oil over my head to establish a new identity for me—a royal identity. He poured the oil, but You've poured on the wisdom, like burning oil, in the course of a lifetime. And You've continued to bring the king from the stone. Continue what You've begun, O Lord. Pour it on!"

Have you ever imagined yourself literally in the hands of the Lord? It's a wonderful thought. Those hands that created the universe, that hurled the stars out into space and crafted the mountains and seashores, and then molded Adam from the dust of the earth; those hands that took the nails and reached out in pain across the wooden beams to embrace all of humanity—*those* hands now hold and caress you with gentle love.

You and I stand beside David to say, "Lord, lift me up in those powerful hands. And let them continue their work, even when it causes the pain of authentic discipline."

Learning to Walk

Ron Mehl lives the life of a leukemia victim—not that it stops him from being a popular and productive pastor. He goes about his daily work in the Northwest, serving his congregation and preaching his sermons, always in the knowledge that he'll never truly be free of his disease. He even manages to travel across the country, preaching triumphantly and radiating the love of Christ, because Ron Mehl is a champion.

Ron had a friend who had recently become a grandfather for the first time. He invited Ron to come to his home for dinner and see his precious new granddaughter. She was learning to walk, and Ron's friend couldn't wait to show off his precocious little grandchild. He was like any new grandparent—bursting with pride he couldn't contain.

"Bumpa" was his designated grandparent name. Bumpa lifted the little girl and placed her beside the sofa so she could lean against it for balance. But it was clear to Ron that her chubby little legs were very tentative and unsteady. Even leaning against the sofa, she seemed certain to fall. But the proud grandfather was determined that the little girl would show her stuff. He walked across the room and sat in his chair. "Come on, little darling!" he called. "Come see ol' Bumpa."

The little girl really wanted to go to ol' Bumpa. Her heart was in it, and her spirit was game. She stepped out in a faith that exceeded her wobbly legs and collapsed in a little pile on the soft carpet. Ron teased his friend. He said, "Maybe she's just had a hard day."

But ol' Bumpa was determined his granddaughter could make the journey across the living room. So again she was propped up, and again she was exhorted to move forward. And one more time there was a heap of a ten-month-old little girl on the floor. Perhaps she landed a bit harder this time, or perhaps she was frustrated by the weakness of her young legs. In any case, she began to cry.

Then Ron's friend did a wonderful thing.

He could have allowed the little girl to crawl away in whimpering defeat, but instead he reached down with his big, work-hardened hands and took hold of her chubby little fingers. He lifted her up, turned her around, and set her tiny feet on top of his own. As he lifted his left foot, hers lifted with it. When he lifted his right foot, she took a step too.

And so Bumpa and his granddaughter walked across the floor. A huge smile chased the tears off her face, because, after all, she was walking!

"That was a sight I never forgot," Ron said. Ron knows what it's like to live in the limitations of a body that can't measure up to the heart's aspirations; he knows what it's like to have great hands reach down to bolster him and propel him forward.

How often have you tried to move forward in your own feeble power and ended up in a heap on the floor? You think you can do it, and God allows you to try. Proving to yourself and everybody around that you're simply not up to the task, you give up or give in. And just then, He reaches down with those loving hands and lifts you up to walk you through the barriers of your life—in His limitless strength.

That's the promise. He gave it to you and to me, and He stands behind His Word.

He stands behind *you* too. He may allow you to fall, but He'll never allow you to be defeated. That's an idea to set securely into your heart. Don't let life's commotion shake it away from you, because it carries hope. Whatever you may be facing today, don't give up or give in. Wait for those marvelous, loving hands to cover your own—and be ready to laugh with delight as He walks you, in His power, to places you never thought you could reach.

Psalm 63

A Psalm of David when he was in the wilderness of Judah.

1 O God, You are my God;
Early will I seek You;
My soul thirsts for You;
My flesh longs for You
In a dry and thirsty land
Where there is no water.

2 So I have looked for You in the sanctuary,
To see Your power and Your glory.

3 Because Your lovingkindness is better than life,
My lips shall praise You.

4 Thus I will bless You while I live;
I will lift up my hands in Your name.

5 My soul shall be satisfied as with marrow and fatness,
And my mouth shall praise You with joyful lips.

6 When I remember You on my bed,
I meditate on You in the night watches.

7 Because You have been my help,
Therefore in the shadow of Your wings I will rejoice.

8 My soul follows close behind You;
Your right hand upholds me.

9 But those who seek my life, to destroy it,
Shall go into the lower parts of the earth.

10 They shall fall by the sword;
They shall be a portion for jackals.

11 But the king shall rejoice in God;
Everyone who swears by Him shall glory;
But the mouth of those who speak lies shall be stopped.

6

A Desert Psalm

Listen carefully to the story of Steve Garrison. But before you listen, know that he was a thriving real-estate developer in California—among the best in the nation in his line of work. His prospects were soaring, and there seemed to be nothing but blue sky ahead of him.

Know also that he was a dedicated leader in his church and his local Christian Businessmen's Fellowship. Materially and spiritually, the path of Steve's life was a journey of joy—until the day his world fell apart. Here is how Steve tells the story.

⌣

My company was doing well. Sure, America was mired in a recession, but for a while we were hopeful of missing the worst of it in Southern California. We were invincible—at least that's how it seemed. The way we were building, selling, and profiting, why should we have worried?

But as you know, we didn't quite make it through. When the recession made it to the West Coast, its impact was that of a sledgehammer.

The slowdown in commercial real estate began late in 1990. By the end of the next financial quarter, construction was at a standstill; buildings sat half-finished, suspended in time, just like our careers. Boom times were over.

During the two previous years, my company had built thirty-six buildings to sell or lease in five industrial parks. We had accumulated some resources. But now it was early in 1991, and I was left with nine new commercial and industrial buildings on my hands. They stood tenantless with no buyers in sight. We'd kept our hands busy while the California sun was shining, and all our assets were tied up in the properties; the cash reserves vanished like water-mirages on a desert highway. My wife and I reluctantly cashed in our IRAs to meet our financial obligations, and in April of 1991, I had to release my last few employees. The doors to Garrison Development were shut and locked for the last time.

I was extremely fortunate to find employment as a commercial real-estate consultant. But even that drifted out of my grasp—within six months, the recession had cut me off and left me unemployed once again. All of this happened within a year. I'd owned my own company, with a career seemingly blessed by God; then I'd lost that and the job that followed.

I knew where I stood: My faith was going to be tested. It had been eighteen years since I had accepted Christ as my Lord and Savior, and I had trusted Him with my life and my family and all my prospects. I knew that I worshiped a sovereign God who is absolutely in control of everything. I knew I shouldn't keep my eyes on my unpleasant circumstances, but on His guidance. I knew I had to keep on trusting and obeying, hard times or not. So I kept my faith in Him—I had no other choice.

I'd come to my bend in the road. And just around my bend I found myself in a spiritual desert, arid and dry. I began to see that my walk with Him had gradually eroded during years of fruitfulness. With the blinders removed from my eyes, I was seeing myself in an unattractive new light; God was showing me hard truths about myself that I didn't want to see. Such things as my reputation, the esteem of my colleagues, and my net worth and assets had become pagan idols in my life. I'd had no idea that I'd lifted those things to such a level.

I saw my relationships honestly too. I hadn't always dispensed grace to those who worked with me. I'd been critical and impatient with my employees, rather than letting my relationship with Christ soak into that part of my life.

These things all came as a shock, because I'd thought I had it all together. God was "lovingly beating me up," as I've described it since then. These were difficult lessons to learn, but I sat at His feet and listened to His Word. And in the midst of the discipline, I came to love Him more than I had in the past—much more.

But there was still my livelihood to worry about. I stayed on the lookout for opportunities to make a new start in business life. In time, God led me to launch my own real-estate consulting business. That was the right move, because the Lord is the One who established it. Today I work with companies that are either relocating or expanding their facilities. The California economy has recovered and rebounded, though it has never matched the heyday of the late 1980s. My business has matched that trend—it's not as lucrative as it was in the "good old days," but I think my work life is just where God wants it to be.

These years have built my faith like nothing else could have done. I've learned the incredible power of praising God in the midst of adversity. I've discovered how to step back and look at my life and concerns from an eternal perspective, and it's been wonderful to find how many anxieties simply fade away when I do that.

—◦—

Steve Garrison's story is repeated a thousand times every day somewhere in our world. The details may vary, but the path is the same. But I'm not telling you anything you don't already know. Nobody expects to sail through life without a little rain and a few choppy waves. We expect the poor weather, but we have certain ideas about how the storm front will move in.

We expect we'll run into an occasional setback at appropriate times.

There's naturally going to be an inconvenience during our time in school, or a misadventure in the raising of a family. We have our mental calendars marked for the occasional midlife crisis or the messy business decision. As we figure it, we'll dispense with these inconveniences without losing more than a step or two along the path of life. We expect bumps, more than bends, in our roads—after which we can settle in and enjoy health, wealth, and happiness until the sun sets. Most of us envision an early retirement in that dream house, with the dream grandchildren and the dream retirement pension to allow us to see the world and partake of the American Dream.

That's the plan, anyway.

But the best laid plans often come to naught. Just ask Steve Garrison if his life moved in precisely the spiral he had charted in his mind. We never know what lies in the road ahead, and we never know when our world will fall apart. It may be when the journey has barely begun. It may come in the active middle years. Or perhaps in the quiet of those mature years, when we long to rest and enjoy the fruits of a lifetime, a terrible surprise will disrupt all we've hoped and arranged.

King David faced this variety of bitter disappointment—not that his life had been easy and carefree up to this point. We've seen the physical, personal, and political dangers he faced from the time the prophet Samuel came to visit his family when David was a young man. But the "man after God's own heart" had passed every grueling test. He had prevailed; Israel had thrived. The kingdom had grown to unprecedented heights of power and respectability. David looked toward a time when a temple might be built to house the ark of the covenant and enshrine God's law for generations.

But things didn't work out that way. His family was ripped by tragedy, bloodshed, and bitterness. It would have been enough to break the heart of many a middle-aged man less sensitive than David.

In an earlier chapter, we mentioned David's strained relationship with his son Absalom. We know this about Absalom: He was a physically handsome man, one of the few whose outward appearance is described in the Bible. And he must have had impressive charisma, because he succeeded in building a personal power base among the people of Israel. Right under the nose of his father, the king, Absalom convinced a strong coalition of citizens that the son should take the place of the father in the palace of Jerusalem. Absalom had set his heart on taking that place of power—by whatever means necessary.

He was very shrewd in public relations, understanding the importance of "grass-roots" politics. Absalom spent much of his time at the city gates, where the streets were filled with people entering and leaving the city. As they gathered, he worked the crowd. He made friends, listened to problems, and told how he thought they should be solved. David's boy was drawing crowds. The whispers inevitably began circulating: "We could use a change—here's the kind of fresh leadership we need." "The old man has lost a step—he ought to step aside and let the boy have his turn."

Absalom did something else: He nurtured and encouraged bitterness. The Scriptures tell us that as the citizens of Israel were bringing lawsuits to the king to settle, Absalom intercepted them and said, "It's a shame there's no one in the palace interested in settling this legal dispute you have here. I'm afraid we simply don't have a king in place to care about you—the one we have isn't interested in your problems. I know if *I* were king, I'd be right on top of a lawsuit such as this one, and I'd certainly get results—you can count on that. But of course, I'm not the king, am I?" And the Bible tells us that Absalom even began to hug the people there at the gate, reaching out, touching, embracing. He did everything we see politicians do today during campaign season. He was working the crowd in the best political tradition. As the Scriptures summarize it, "Absalom stole the hearts of the men of Israel" (2 Sam. 15:6).

The crowd at the gate began to evolve from a group of casual passersby to something like a political bloc. And quicker than you can say "insurgent," King David was receiving the startling news that a coup d'état was underway within his own court.

Keep in mind that we're talking about David, the people's choice—king by popular demand as well as divine appointment. This was the hero who had slain the giant, outlasted the tyrant, and multiplied the kingdom! The very idea of a coup was in itself unthinkable, a poison-tipped sword to his heart. But this rumor that the source of a coup was his own precious son—well, that was enough to send a father to an early death by broken heart. He loved Absalom deeply. And Absalom was set on destroying everything that David had fought and survived and perspired to build.

That wasn't all; things were even worse. Ahithophel, his favorite counselor and friend, was identified as one of the conspirators. Amasa, his nephew, was also in on the plot. How had the house become divided against itself? David must have been tortured by recriminating doubts. Maybe his son was right; maybe he'd "lost a step." At this moment of decision, with the fate of a nation in the balance, the king hesitated. In the midst of a no-win proposition, the king couldn't decide how to act, and every moment of delay solidified the strength of Absalom's battalion.

Absalom set up his bureaucracy, establishing headquarters in Hebron, which was a few miles from Jerusalem. And he spread the word throughout the kingdom that at the sound of the trumpet, everyone who cared about a new government for Jerusalem should rally to the side of the "new sheriff in town."

David heard this too, of course. And he knew he had missed his opportunity to put down the rebellion. The price of delay was that his life—along with those of his loyal circle—was seriously in danger. There was no recourse but flight from the palace and even from the city. What a tragic moment for a leader of historic significance! The man who need not fear stepping into the very presence of God had to flee for fear of his own son, his own flesh and blood.

As always, a few were courageous enough to stand firm with David even when his prospects were low. He took these followers and retreated from Jerusalem across the Kidron Valley and into the desert of Judah. He only hoped for a safe refuge where he could sort out the terrible mess he had somehow allowed his kingdom to slip into.

What goes through the mind of a seasoned and deeply spiritual king at such a moment? We know the answer, because David opened the pages of his blood-smeared, tear-drenched old journal and inscribed the immortal words of Psalm 63. Thousands of years later, we can look over his sad, sagging shoulders and peer into his journal and into his very soul.

How can we identify with an extraordinary life like that of David? You've probably never lived a life on the run because of an angry king, but an angry boss may have kept you on the run. You may never have been the object of a political coup, but you may have felt the pinch of younger coworkers pushing you off the corporate ladder. You may never have fled your home to protect yourself from your own child, but you may have felt the heartbreak of children who failed to honor their father and mother as they grew older.

In moments like those, you've found yourself in deserts that had no sand, deserts of personal desolation, spiritual despondency, and emotional depression. And as Steve Garrison discovered, when that moment of ordeal arrives, we're almost never prepared in body, mind, or spirit.

David's Hunger for God

Psalm 63 begins with its narrator, David, isolated in the desert. His first impulse is to call out for God to come and comfort him. The king in exile feels a gaping hole in his heart that only God can fill. His family has deserted him, his subjects have rejected him, and he has come to a place where his only refuge, his sole consolation, is his Creator.

One commentator, evoking the image of David in the desert, offers this observation: "We may imagine the psalmist in the wilderness. It is night, and he stands at his tent door. The light of moon and stars sprawls on a sandy waste, stretching into dimness and mystery. He is lonely and sad, and the emptiness all around and the memory of better times breeds this great longing in his soul."[1]

You and I get the picture. We know what it's like to feel emotionally bankrupt. There in the desert, David looks across the parched wasteland and sees it as a mirror of his own soul. And what can he offer in such a situation other than the response of any child who has stumbled and injured himself? David cries out to his Father to come, pick him up, and care for his hurts.

First of all, we see his desire for God. The first phrase in verse 1 is interesting. The original words of the Hebrew language are *Elohim Eli*. In our language it reads, "O Creator God, my God." The barrenness of his personal desert of the soul is swallowing him up. He cries out to the Creator of deserts and oases, "O Creator God, You are my God." The Lord of the desert is also the Lord of deliverance from it; David reaches for the comfort of that connection.

Then he uses three expressions to describe his hunger and thirst for intimacy with his God. The first phrase is, "Early will I seek You." Don't brush by those words too quickly! Come, let us reason together about what it really means to "seek God."

Seeking for God

The expression "to seek," in the Hebrew, is related to the Hebrew word for *dawn*. Do you find that curious? Here's the connection: Nothing can precede dawn in a day. As David awakes, he is seeking God. Nothing can come before that. It's the dawn of his daily life.

This phrase "early will I seek You" has such an impact upon this psalm that the Armenian and Greek Orthodox churches often refer to this chapter as the "Morning Psalm." In their liturgy they sing, "Early will I seek You."

Thirsting for God

David surveys the foreboding landscape around him: nothing but sand and heat, and no wells of cool, life-giving water. It strikes him that his life is little different. He thirsts for water to drink, but he also thirsts for the kind of spiritual water only God can provide. "Blessed are those who hunger and thirst for righteousness," Jesus says to us in Matthew 5:6. David himself has already sung in Psalm 42:2, "My soul thirsts for God, for the living God." Thirst is identified all through the Scriptures as the best metaphor to understand the deep spiritual yearning that each of us finds implanted within us.

But what has intensified David's thirst? This is a man who has sought after God all his life, but the great heartbreaks of life have

---

Say to those who are fearful-hearted,

"Be strong, do not fear!

Behold, your God will come with vengeance,

With the recompense of God;

He will come and save you."

Then the eyes of the blind shall be opened,

And the ears of the deaf shall be unstopped.

Then the lame shall leap like a deer,

And the tongue of the dumb sing.

For waters shall burst forth in the wilderness,

And streams in the desert.

—Isaiah 35:4–6

---

always driven him to seek God with a deeper thirst, a more powerful sorrow, and a more desperate knowledge of the terrible, hopeless plight of trying to live without his Master.

Longing for God

The words are so powerful, so evocative, and so passionate: "My flesh longs for You in a dry and thirsty land where there is no water" (Ps. 63:1).

When David speaks of longing, he uses words that are actually connected to fainting. The idea he has in mind is that of *weakness*. He is saying, "O Lord God, I've collapsed in every way! The strength has drained out of my body, and I've fainted. I'm desperate to be revived in the way only You can restore me to life and breath."

David points us to the fact that body, mind, and spirit are inter-dependent. When the spirit is ill, the body will be affected. His long-ing for refreshment and revival and recovery are physical and spiritual. David speaks of body and soul almost interchangeably in the psalms. He feels the pain of spiritual and emotional distress in every ligament and nerve of his body, and that pain seeks a spiritual solu-tion—it drives him to long for God in his soul.

Desiring, Deciding, Delighting in God

C. S. Lewis gave us a wonderful book called *Reflections on the Psalms.* If you enjoy reading the psalms, you'll be delighted with his book. Lewis wrote about the psalms more eloquently than anyone else I know. For example, listen to Lewis on the topic of David's hunger for God: "The poets in David's day knew far less reason than we do for loving God. They did not know that He offered them eternal joy. Still less that He would die to win it for them. Yet they express a longing for God, for His mere presence, which comes only to Christians in their best mo-ments."[2]

How right he is! We have so much more reason to seek God. We can know Him so much better. Yet how seldom we exhibit the ur-gency and desperation of the psalmist. But when the road bends into the dry desert of life and we find ourselves in arid desolation, our cry for God becomes the very focus of our existence.

What a vivid picture the psalmist paints for us in the early verses of Psalm 63. The dry and thirsty land that surrounds him physically is the picture of his soul without God. He realizes that the world itself can be a desert; indeed, the most luxurious palaces of kings can be dry and desolate wastelands. Only God can bring refreshment and rejuve-nated life. We can be surrounded by those things we've identified as pleasures and yet find no joy in them.

Someone has said that Satan knows nothing at all about pleasure;

his specialty is amusement. Only God knows genuine pleasure. About
fifteen years ago, author Neil Postman wrote an indicting study of our
modern culture; he called his book *Amusing Ourselves to Death.* That title
nicely captures the danger of chasing after pleasure, as our culture

---

You will show me the path of life;

In Your presence is fullness of joy;

At Your right hand are pleasures forevermore.

—Psalm 16:11

---

does, and capturing it, only to find it empty and joyless. We've actually found nothing more than amusement, at great cost to our souls.
Genuine pleasure is ordained by God and intended for our deep joy
and delight. It can only be captured by knowing God, realizing He
knows us, and being at rest in His presence.

Verse 2 brings us to an interesting decision by David regarding God's
presence. But we can't truly appreciate this verse without filling in the
blank—that is, learning a little more about what the author was thinking as he fled from the treachery of his son. Here is the background.

David was leaving the city. There was a group of loyal priests who
were evacuating the city with the royal delegation. Two of these were
Abiathar—David's personal chaplain—and the priest who served by
his side, Zadok. David wasn't aware that these two men, before leaving the city of Jerusalem, had crept back into the sanctuary where the
ark of the covenant was kept. The ark had always been carried by the
use of two iron bars, which fit through rings on the side of the great
structure. Priests would then lift and carry the ark by these bars. Abiathar and Zadok inserted the bars and raised the ark of the covenant to
their shoulders. Then they carried this sacred shrine of the Law outside the city. They had forgotten one crucial factor—they hadn't
asked for David's approval.

As they left Jerusalem and crossed the Kidron Valley, David discovered what the two men had done. They had brought the holy ark of

the covenant into the peril of the open country where David and his followers had fled. The ark symbolized the visible, practically tangible presence of God among the people of Israel. It was the most sacred material object in existence. The temple would be built one generation later for no other reason than to provide a worthy vessel to house it. The ark of the covenant was the physical symbol of God's presence. You or I might have been eager to carry it along to represent the spirit of God among those fleeing for their lives. But David didn't feel that way at all.

We read in 2 Samuel 15:24–25 that "there was Zadok also, and all the Levites with him, bearing the ark of the covenant of God. And they set down the ark of God, and Abiathar went up until all the people had finished crossing over from the city. Then the king said to Zadok, 'Carry the ark of God back into the city. If I find favor in the eyes of the LORD, He will bring me back and show me both it and His habitation.'" Pick up the story four verses later: "Therefore Zadok and Abiathar carried the ark of God back to Jerusalem. And they remained there."

We simply must conclude that David didn't think and act in the way you or I might have. He sent the ark back to the city. In his view, the sacred vessel belonged there, period, case closed. More importantly, David needed something more than a *symbol* of God's presence; he needed the *reality* of God's presence. This was the thinking behind his words to the two priests: "This isn't about the ark of the covenant and the work of priests. This is about *the very presence and guidance* of Almighty God Himself. If He goes with me, I'll see Jerusalem and my home once again, and the ark will be waiting for me there. If God has rejected me, all of the holy vessels in the world will do me no good."

David wasn't interested in relics and symbols of divinity. He insisted on the authentic presence of God Himself. There could be no substitutes. Now we understand David's words in the second verse: "So I have looked for You in the sanctuary, to see Your power and Your glory."

David *desired* the true God; he *decided* based on the true God. Finally, we can see in the third verse how he *delighted* in God. He said, "Because

Your lovingkindness is better than life, my lips shall praise You." His life was hanging in the balance, yet he realized that true life can only be found in the true God. He is saying an amazing thing. In essence he says, "Lord God, the way that You love me is more precious to me than life itself."

You'd better believe life is precious! The only alternative I can think of is death. So why is God's lovingkindness better than life? The answer is simple: God's love is eternal. Earthly life is not. As Paul wrote to the Corinthians, nearly everything else passes away, but the love of God, like His Word, is one of those things that resounds beyond the confines of this brief life in this bounded space. His love is greater than life!

Worshiping with God's People

The view inside David's heart always makes for a fascinating picture. He was by no means, from any perspective, a perfect man. His failures are as legendary as his accomplishments. He was a great leader who happened to be a member of that struggling, stumbling band known as the human race. Yet the final record of his life testifies to a consistent pattern—when the heat and pressure were ratcheted up a few levels, he seized hold of his relationship with God, gripping it with both hands and every ounce of his strength and every beat of his heart. David wasn't mouthing words of piety as an act of last-resort desperation. He sincerely, urgently yearned to be in God's presence. He craved the unique experience of worshiping with the people of God.

During my illness there were certain "frequently asked questions" I became accustomed to hearing. One of these was, "Are you afraid?" Here is my answer to that question: *Afraid, no. I am scared to death!*

Another question: "Have you cried?" My impulsive answer: *None of your business!* I didn't say this, of course; it's not a godly response to loving, concerned friends. For an extended period of time, the true answer was: *No, I have not.* I knew what was set out before me, and God prepared me for it. But the day came when the tears were shaken loose. I wept deeply. Please understand this is a difficult subject for me—as I remarked above, my first impulse is to be very private with my tears. But there's a significant point I wish to share with you, and that point requires transparency on my part.

It was Easter Sunday. Donna and I were in a hotel in Del Mar, California, near the outpatient stem cell transplant program at Scripps Clinic. The nightmarish adventure of the cancer experience had reached its blackest point in our lives. Our spirits were as low as they could possibly have been. And yet it was Easter Sunday; I rose early and made my way out to the hotel room's little living area. My thought was to escape the awful mood that had come over me. I would turn on the television set and find something to give me hope, something to set my mind on things eternal.

I may have been misguided in my efforts. There are better places to seek encouragement than Sunday morning television. But I had little spirit for any other endeavor, so I channel-surfed. I made the rounds of all the stations on the hotel television until I came across a broadcast from a large church. I found Easter music, church pageantry, and worship—just what I was looking for. I sat back and soaked in all the trappings of the people gathered for praise, and I lost myself for a few moments. I lowered my guard. And without any clue to what was about to happen, I suddenly began to sob convulsively. I completely lost my composure and nearly flooded the sofa and the living area with sloppy tears.

I was so embarrassed.

Donna rounded the corner, hurrying from the next room. Her eyes were great ovals. "Are you all right?" she asked.

"No, I'm not," I replied. "I want to be in church. I don't want to be here; I don't belong here. *I belong in church.*" It was a startling moment of discovery for me—realizing just how deep was my craving to be among the people of God on His day. There was no place else on earth for me to be but within the walls of the special kind of place set apart for the worship and magnification of God—a place happily filled with my brothers and sisters in faith.

I know you're smiling, nodding, and saying, "Of course, Pastor Jeremiah! You're the preacher—that's where preachers like to be!"

But it runs a bit deeper than that. It's not about preaching, but the experience of genuine, godly worship in the context of the living, celebrating body of Christ. Can you experience God outside the bricks and mortar of a steeple-topped building? Absolutely. But, dear reader, there's something holy and essential and irreplaceable about the Spirit of God manifest among His people, *especially* on Easter Sunday. In that lonely hotel room I suddenly felt a deep, burning exile from the only place where I can live and thrive and breathe the cool air of true fellowship.

I made a deep, serious vow in my heart that I *would* improve. I would be among my brothers and my sisters again, praising God.

And I meant business.

If you can understand what I felt, you can understand what David was feeling in his exile in the desert. There he stood, looking back across the barren desert sands to the horizon beyond which Jerusalem, the city of God, sat without him. There the people of God went about their lives and worshiped God together. He remembered the great feast days with their singing and pageantry. As he squinted at the horizon and felt so keenly his separation from God's people, he cried out in the pain of the gaping empty place in his heart. David ached for communion with God and the community of God.

In the next few verses, David helps us understand what we can expect when our path leads us through the desert's open, merciless spaces. He shows us how, when we feel we're walking alone through life's wasteland, we can make the journey in the comforting presence of our Lord.

What David Did

Do you associate praise with discipline? Most of us think of praise as positive and spontaneous, while we think of discipline as negative and forced. But that's the crucial point of this section of David's psalm.

There are those times when we walk through the desert, and our throats fill with dry dust. We feel thirsty, but the last thing we would think of to do would be to lift our voices and sing a song of victory.

Discipline is the act of inducing pain and stress
in one's life in order to grow into greater toughness, capacity,
endurance, or strength. So spiritual discipline is that effort of pressing
the soul so that it will enlarge its capacity to hear God speak and,
as a result, to generate inner force that will guide
and empower one's mind and outer life.

—Gordon MacDonald

But that's exactly the thing that will give us strength and endurance. In the hard times, praise is an act of obedience and discipline. It may not be spontaneous, but when we manage to praise God in the midst of pain, the results can be dramatic.

David praised God. We find ourselves in deserts or dungeons. Our friends would give us all kinds of advice, but the last thing they might counsel us to do would be to praise God. When Job lay suffering with every earthly pleasure stripped away, his wife advised him to "curse God and die." But such an attitude is in itself a form of death. It's spiritual suicide.

Genuine praise, offered stubbornly in the face of adversity, makes no sense by any worldly calculation. That's fine. There are deeper truths that don't "make sense" on the surface of things. The great Christian mathematician Blaise Pascal once said that "the heart has its reasons which the reason does not know." God's rules fly in the face of our logic. When we begin to praise God, not in response to prosperity, but in defiance of misfortune, we align ourselves with the deepest truths of the universe, the place where God dispenses deep wisdom and spiritual maturity. We unleash His victorious power in the world of pain and suffering. We create the environment where miracles occur.

And the first miracle occurs inside the mind of the afflicted.

Psalm 63 from first to last is a psalm about David praising God. It's not a psalm about being happy or about changing circumstances. We almost feel, in reading between the lines, that David anticipates the end of his life approaching. We can almost hear him saying, "Lord, I don't know how many days You have allotted for me. There could be seven remaining, or seven thousand. And I cannot know what those days might hold, joy or sorrow. But I do know I intend to spend them exalting Your blessed name."

Listen to the echoes of this sentiment in Psalm 104:33: "I will sing to the LORD as long as I live; I will sing praise to my God while I have my being." *Whatever breath You give me, Lord, easy or labored, I will give back to You in singing praise.*

As we move through this psalm, we find a variety of ways to praise the Lord. The first six verses of Psalm 63 offer seven different approaches, and each one is a precious jewel. Let's take in each facet of the psalm's diamond:

- *We praise Him with our lips.* "My lips shall praise You" (v. 3).
- *We praise Him with our tongues.* "Thus I will bless You" (v. 4).
- *We praise Him with our hands.* "I will lift up my hands in Your name" (v. 4).
- *We praise Him with our wills.* "My soul shall be satisfied" (v. 5).
- *We praise Him with our mouths.* "My mouth shall praise You" (v. 5).
- *We praise Him with our memories.* "When I remember You on my bed" (v. 6).
- *We praise Him with our intellects.* " I meditate on You in the night watches" (v. 6).

Think of that—praising God with your lips, your tongue, your hands, your will, your mouth, your memory, and your intellect. Our Father has issued us a full armory of weapons for use in the world. We fill them with the wrong ammunition. When the enemy closes in, we'll never defeat him using his own weapons. Instead, we load the weapons of our lips, our tongues, our hands, our wills, our mouths, our memories, and our intellects with the most powerful gunpowder that has ever been discharged on earth—worship and praise.

In the midst of the lonely desert road, what are you to do? Praise God with every part of your body, mind, and spirit. Learn to praise God regardless of your personal circumstances, and you'll see miracles occur. Your heart and mind will be renewed. Your perspective will widen panoramically. And your attitude toward God will never be the same.

David pictured God. Yes, David praised God, though his entire life was unraveling. He praised God in the desert. But he didn't stop there. His wise move is found in verses 6 and 7: He began to *picture* God.

Please don't misunderstand—this isn't about the trendy, New Age version of visualization. Take a close look at David's words in verses 6 and 7: "When I remember You on my bed, I meditate on You in the night watches. Because You have been my help, therefore in the shadow of Your wings I will rejoice."

David was not the kind of man to toss and turn in the night, fretting over circumstances beyond his control. He was in a mess, to be sure. But when insomnia cut him off from the sleep his body needed, he had one certain remedy—he meditated upon the Person of God.

We've all lost sleep over our anxieties. Maybe your child has left your home after a heated dispute or your financial health is in jeopardy. Maybe the future of your employment is no more than a question mark. Or perhaps your marriage is on the rocks. As for me, it was personal illness; I don't believe I ever lost a night of sleep until my health took a disastrous turn.

David tossed and turned in his bed too. But he had a prescription for sleeplessness, and it didn't involve the pills that too often grow into dependencies for people today. When David found himself sleepless, his thoughts drifted heavenward. He found God in the night watches. What a liberating lesson for those who labor miserably under insomnia! Our response is often to give in to increasing

desperation, which, needless to say, pushes the goal of sleep even farther away. Our thoughts entangle themselves in negative emotions.

Instead, we can find a placid spirit by turning the wheels of our
minds to the things of God. What has He done in your life? What is
He up to at the present? Why not spend time counting those blessings—naming them one by one—and offering praise to the King?
Sleep will come softly to a contented mind, and it will be deep and refreshing. That's a promise.

Lewis Smedes has written a wonderful book about hope that includes this striking insight: "A person who has the habit of hope also
has the habit of remembering. Hope needs memories the way a
writer needs notes. This is partly because hope depends so much on
imagination. Our images of the future are sweepings from our re-
membrances of things past. If we expect to keep hope alive, we need
to keep memory alive. Happy memories of good things we hoped
for that were fulfilled, and grateful memories of bad things we survived."[3]

When treading through life's desert, it helps to remember God's
help in ages past. We gain a wise perspective by realizing that nothing
that can be happening now is a surprise to Him. Our memories are
spiritual investments; they reap dividends when we consult them and
discover once again the perpetual faithfulness of God.

As I've studied the life of David, I've thought about the great king of
Israel tossing and turning in his bedchamber. I can imagine the loom-
ing giant of despair haunting him in the night and keeping him from
sleep, and I know how David responded. He thought of another
giant, one who loomed before him so many years ago. Here was a
nine-foot-six warrior, facing off with a young man with no weapon in
reach but a slingshot and five smooth stones—four more stones than
he actually needed. The world would not have given promising odds
to the challenger in that match. But David knew that if God is for us,
it's simply irrelevant who is against us. Height measurements are beside the point. Jesus said that invisible faith comparable in size to a
nearly microscopic mustard seed will prevail against a mountain, for
the faith is aligned with the will of a sovereign God.

David knew that—as a young shepherd and as a seasoned monarch. Nearly any anxiety can cast a long and menacing shadow during the night watch. Any minor worry can become Goliath when lights are low. But in the shining light of God's presence, the details of this life find their true size. "I am the Lord," we hear Him say. "Is there anything too great for Me?" David may have reflected that at one time a giant seemed invincible for an unarmored shepherd boy; surely there was no reason to give in to fear now, after so many years of the Father's faithfulness.

The shadows of the night were deep and mysterious. But David found refuge in more comforting shadows; he said to his Lord, "Because You have been my help, therefore in the shadow of Your wings I will rejoice" (v. 7).

David prayed to God. What did David do? He praised God to dispel the darkness; he pictured God to find encouragement. And finally, he prayed to his God. He wrote, "My soul follows close behind You; Your right hand upholds me" (v. 8).

Here is the closest translation of that first phrase: "My soul clings to You, God." That's something we do quite naturally in a crisis if our emotional wiring is functioning—we reach for God and hang on tight. We don't know what else to do. Sometimes a trauma is required to draw us as close to God as we should have been all along.

I'd like to share with you an experience that might clarify this point.

Fear of Fireworks

I'm afraid we committed a serious miscalculation with our grandson not too long ago. We took him to a San Diego Padres baseball game the night of a huge fireworks display. The idea was mine. I envisioned our little family group, with my grandson David Todd at the center, taking in the thrill of a nighttime sky canvas splashed with the breathtaking colors of summer fireworks. It was such an innocent notion. It never occurred to me that the thundering explosions of such a show were capable of terrifying a small boy.

I took the family to the game with smiling anticipation. David Todd sat on Poppy's lap (that's me), and his eyes were wide as he interacted with all the wonderful new sights and sounds as the major lea-

---

Helplessness is the real secret and the impelling power of prayer ...
For it is only when we are helpless that we open our hearts to Jesus
and let Him help us in our distress, according to His grace and mercy.

—O. H. Hallesby

---

guers played their nine innings. We were having great fun. But then came the fireworks—and that was the end of the party.

When the explosions suddenly jolted the stadium, little David Todd scrambled out of my lap and into his daddy's arms. You've never seen a child move so fast. And as I watched with alarm and crashing disappointment, I'll never forget what I saw. The little boy buried his head deeply in his daddy's shoulder and clung to him for dear life, with every terrified bit of strength he had. And I noticed that his dad had a mutually tight grip on his child.

King David's calm and fruitful life had also suddenly given way to deafening explosions. He scrambled from the comforts of the throne into the arms of his true Father, and he desperately buried his head in the Lord's loving shoulder. That's what you and I do so reflexively and so spontaneously, and it's absolutely the right response. How many times have you heard it from a friend or a relative? "It was such a terrible, frightening experience, but I never sensed the presence of God more than I did during those dark days."

Needless to say, God calmed the troubled waters of David's soul. He dealt with his enemies and gave His child a victory. And even while David endured his exile, he knew God would not fail him. You'll see this in the psalms: a kind of godly premonition He offers David—and He offers you and me—that things are going to be all right; the storm is going to pass. You feel some small light glimmer in your heart, and it pulses with a tiny but undeniable hope: *God will not fail me.*

David received that from God. And history confirms his assurance: One day, the armies of Absalom ventured forth to face the armies of David, and the forces of the father prevailed against those of the son. Have you heard the denouement? It features the indelible image of the handsome young Absalom, riding a mule toward his destiny as his great head of hair danced in the breeze. Passing beneath a terebinth tree, his hair caught in the branches. The Scriptures tell us rather ironically that "he was left hanging between heaven and earth" (2 Sam. 18:9). There he hung until Joab, David's general, came along and took Absalom's life—against the wishes of Absalom's grieving father. The political crisis was dispelled. David was left with a broken heart, but he was free to return to the throne of Israel with impunity. His shortcomings as a father had exacted the price of a son, but God had brought him through and preserved him just the same.

David had made his desert journey, just as all of us must travel that same road. Steve Garrison made the journey. I did. How about you?

I may not know you by name, but I'm certain that if you're not treading through the dust of despair at this very moment, the time is certain to come. But when that day arrives, you will not face it un-armed. The Bible, sharper than any two-edged sword, stands ready for combat. It contains desert psalms that can become your battle plans. The ammunition of praise is ready for discharge. And close by your side will be a faithful, powerful God filled with lovingkindness and plans for you, plans that lead to spiritual victory and personal fulfill-ment.

When your day comes, you'll no doubt be surprised. Just remember that nothing surprises God. He has prepared every detail for the dis-ciplinary adventure that will lead to your wisdom, strength, and matu-rity. He knows that the quietness of the desert is a place for you to get to know Him better, with so much more depth and fulfillment. He doesn't exult in your pain, but He delights in your tighter embrace. He has so much to show you and share with you.

And He knows the way through the wilderness to the hills of joy and laughter. Take His hand, little one, and follow.

Psalm 30

A Psalm. A Song at the dedication of the house of David.

¹ I will extol You, O LORD, for You have lifted me up,
 And have not let my foes rejoice over me.
² O LORD my God, I cried out to You,
 And You have healed me.
³ O LORD, You have brought my soul up from the grave;
 You have kept me alive, that I should not go down to the pit.
⁴ Sing praise to the LORD, You saints of His,
 And give thanks at the remembrance of His holy name.
⁵ For His anger is but for a moment,
 His favor is for life;
 Weeping may endure for a night,
 But joy comes in the morning.
⁶ Now in my prosperity I said,
 "I shall never be moved."
⁷ LORD, by Your favor You have made my mountain stand strong;
 You hid Your face, and I was troubled.
⁸ I cried out to You, O LORD;
 And to the LORD I made supplication:
⁹ "What profit is there in my blood,
 When I go down to the pit?
 Will the dust praise You?
 Will it declare Your truth?
¹⁰ Hear, O LORD, and have mercy on me;
 LORD, be my helper!"
¹¹ You have turned for me my mourning into dancing;
 You have put off my sackcloth and clothed me with gladness,
¹² To the end that my glory may sing praise to You and not be silent.
 O LORD my God, I will give thanks to You forever.

7

Life's Ups and Downs

I Arise Today

Through God's strength to pilot me:
God's might to uphold me,
God's wisdom to guide me,
God's eye to look before me,
God's ear to hear me,
God's word to speak for me,
God's hand to guard me,
God's way to lie before me,
God's shield to protect me.

—SAINT PATRICK

Your world falling apart?

The truth is that some crises are more like a flash of lightning and a crash of thunder, shattering a pleasant journey. We're knocked violently from our feet, and we lie there stunned and confused. We're incapable of climbing to our feet to resume the journey.

That's how Helen Barnhart felt.

Helen works faithfully for our television and radio ministry in the *Turning Point* office. She's one of those persons who would prefer to work quietly in the background. However, I've prevailed on her to tell you about the day when her worst nightmare broke in upon her. Here is that story, in Helen's own words.

I'm quite accustomed to the ringing of the phone at my office. I hear it three or four dozen times daily, bringing a wide assortment of messages, most of them mundane. But it was the sound of the telephone a few months ago that transformed my life forever. That was the day I was told my son had been removed from my home.

It didn't sink in at first. Someone I didn't know was trying to tell me terrible, unthinkable things about my husband. Could they possibly be true? Could they be talking about the man with whom I had lived for twenty-six years? The father of our children and the head of our household—our primary provider? My husband stood accused of unspeakable crimes. I'll never forget the feeling of those cold, merciless words sliding from the phone into my ear. This came only a few months ago, so please understand that my life still hasn't fully recovered. It's extremely difficult for me to discuss any of these things.

The youngest of our three children was in high school and living at home. He had to be taken away—that's how severe the accusations against my husband were. He was placed in the custody of his married sisters.

It was Christmastime when these things happened.

I found I had become the sole occupant of an empty, silent house. I spent the holiday season alone within its walls as the legal machinery worked through its customary functions. A court date had yet to be determined, so the law required that I could have no contact with my son and, by extension, with my daughters because they were his caregivers. I didn't even have the luxury of work to keep my hands busy and my mind occupied, because our office was closed for the holidays. I was a prisoner of grief in my own home.

I had one great prayer request, and I prayed it constantly. I asked God to reveal to everyone that the whole nightmarish crisis was simply a mistake, that my husband was innocent, that nothing had really happened. With God, all things are possible. So I prayed fervently, passionately, unceasingly for God to simply *change everything back*—to turn my world right-side up again in the cozy order that I had found so comfortable for so long. But it became clear I wasn't going to be granted that prayer request. The situation was genuine. The changes weren't going away, and sooner or later I was going to have to face facts.

The comforting cushion of the initial shock was wearing off. Through a slowly encroaching, terribly agonizing process, I began to confront the stark new realities of my life. I watched all my hopes and dreams for the future drain away during endless empty nights, and the loss of those cherished dreams left a void deep in my soul.

My husband's prison term might as well have been a life sentence. As for my son, the court system was considering not returning him to my shattered home. That meant a sentence of my own. How could I endure all this? How could I face the loss of my life partner and be deprived of the comfort of my own child? How could I explain the situation to my family and friends? What would be the effect on our son—on *all* of our children? On *their* children?

I was familiar with all the comfortable platitudes that are offered as substitutes for true comfort. I read through the psalms again and again, seeking any stray shred of relief. I told myself, "The clue will turn up here in the Scriptures. This will be the moment when God works His magic and shows me that *everything's going to be all right.*"

That didn't happen. Everything *wasn't* all right. And everything hasn't become all right since. And yet . . .

God never left—not for a moment. He's been with me all along, and I can truly say that, in the midst of the worst I could have ever imagined life dishing out, the Lord's presence was powerful. The picture of Shadrach, Meshach, and Abed-Nego in a fiery furnace came to my mind many times during those days. Someone was walking with them in the flames, and they weren't burned. And I knew that same Someone was with me, not for personal comfort, but for protection and grace.

Christian friends came, not with platitudes, but with practical help with the details of life that don't brake for crises. A new judge was assigned to my son's case and completely reversed the court's position. Praise God, my son came home! While the harsh reality of my husband's situation never stopped being real, I could see and feel the Lord in my life. Again and again circumstances took a turn, help was provided, and developments materialized to show evidence of God walking with me through the darkness.

I will never leave you nor forsake you. Those words of Jesus have a very personal meaning for me now. The end of my strength and wisdom are merely the beginning of His provision and grace.

—

The seminary professor was out of patience. His student had turned in a sermon with a dull, uninspired title. The professor knew the young man was capable of better things, so he stayed after him to keep working. "The title is crucial," he barked. "It must build interest in your listeners, and it must be intriguing and relevant and powerful. That's why you're going to take this sermon back to your room, right this moment, and you're going to return it to me tomorrow with a new title—one that will grab hold of your listeners and engage their attention. Do you understand?"

The young man was at a loss; he wasn't much good with fancy words and labels. "How do I come up with a catchy title?" he shrugged.

The professor sighed and replied, "It's not so terribly hard, son. I want you to picture your sermon title in great, bold letters on the signboard on the front lawn of your church. It's Sunday morning, and here comes a bus filled with people, just passing by. Son, you want a sermon title so powerful, so compelling, so intriguing that everyone on that Greyhound will come pouring down the steps of the bus. They can't resist the compelling bait of the words in that title. Got that image? I'm sure you can improve on your title, my boy."

The student thought about what his professor had said. He got the mental image fixed in his mind and thought of the words that would most stimulate and engage those bus passengers. The next day he bounded into the classroom with a new title page for the professor. It read, "There's a Bomb on Your Bus!"

When I hear a story like Helen Barnhart's, I think, *There's a bomb on the bus.* We're bumping along in life, all together on a wonderful pleasure trip, and suddenly something explodes. Everybody off the bus! The journey is suspended; how can we go on? After the explosion, we're no longer even certain where the bus is heading, and whether it will ever arrive. The meaning of things has fled, and we feel we'll never again have hearts filled with joy, only fear. Helen's home exploded;

I praise Thee while my days go on;

I love Thee while my days go on:

Through dark and dearth, through fire and frost,

With emptied arms and treasure lost,

I thank Thee while my days go on.

—Elizabeth Barrett Browning

---

in my life, it was my health. Perhaps your life, too, has been ripped apart by lightning on the road, shattered by a bomb on the bus.

But the road goes on, and it will rise to many more peaks and plummet to the bottom of many valleys. It will cross bridges into new lands you've never imagined. Fellow passengers will offer you deep friendships, and you will laugh together and weep together. Not even for the deepest, most devoted Christian will the journey be carefree. Depth and wisdom can only come from shadowy valleys of tears, sickness, loss, disappointment, and broken dreams.

Those deep valleys are places of spiritual dryness and conflict with God—things David faced and chronicled for us in Psalm 30.

A Psalm of Commemoration

Beneath the title of Psalm 30, your Bible will tell you that you've come across "a Song at the dedication of the house of David." What is the background?

Scholars have researched and debated that question, and their consensus is that this psalm is connected to events arising from the day David returned the ark of the covenant to Jerusalem. We're not referring to the period later in David's life (detailed in the previous chapter) when two priests fled an uprising with David and carried the ark out of the city. This is an earlier day when David at long last be-came Israel's king. After waiting so many difficult years for the culmi-nation of Samuel's promise, the crown finally rested upon David's head. His first royal initiative was to establish the ark in the city, where it would enshrine the idea of worshiping and trusting God. The culmination of that, of course, would come in the time of David's heir, Solomon, who would build the great temple.

The ark of the covenant, as we learned in the last chapter, repre-sented the presence of Almighty God. In the Old Testament system of worship, the ark was associated with the Shekhinah glory of God. Do you remember what happened when the Philistines took possession of the ark of the covenant? They paraded it throughout their own land to celebrate publicly their victory over the Israelites. But everywhere they stopped, terrible problems cropped up. There seemed to be a curse on the Philistines who had defiled the sacred vessel, and in time they gave up and sent away the source of their problems.

Time passed. During King Saul's administration, the ark was nearly forgotten. The king didn't spare it a thought, and the people reflected his lack of spiritual awareness. But David understood the true signifi-cance of the ark; he knew it merited placement in a central, visible lo-cation in Jerusalem as a reminder of the glory and power of God.

David made one mistake, however. When he sent for the ark, he as-signed the project to a group of men who weren't exactly well-versed in Old Testament law. Maybe you've relocated to a new home and used reckless moving men. Imagine relocating the most sacred object on the face of the earth. The movers ignored the precise and critical instructions from the Book of Numbers, where dealings with the holy ark of the covenant are set forth. These were apparently that breed of men who hate to read the directions. They talked it over and decided the most convenient way to move the great golden box was to drop it into a common oxcart.

They thought that should do the trick, but the whole misadventure resulted in a few tricks they hadn't anticipated. At one point along the route, they came to a threshing floor, and the cart began to wobble. A man named Uzzah reached out without thinking and grasped the ark to steady it. It was a forbidden thing for human hands to do, and God struck Uzzah dead on the spot for carelessly handling holy artifacts. The touch of the ark simply consumed him.

David's eyes were wide; the Bible tells us he was both angry and afraid. If you'd seen a man removed from the ranks of the living simply by touching a golden box, you might have been in awe too. He suddenly realized the enormous gravity of his responsibility. David remarked, "How can the ark of the LORD come to me?" (2 Sam. 6:9).

The newly nervous king didn't dare to move the ark even one more dangerous step, so he had it put aside in the home of a man named Obed-Edom the Gittite for three months. During that period, while the ark of the covenant was present in their household, the family was blessed in remarkable ways. David's view was, "Let's just keep the thing in storage. I'd rather not tamper with anything that dangerous while I have a kingdom to establish. I'll get around to moving the thing into Jerusalem one of these days." And he turned his attention elsewhere.

But after the ark of the covenant had been in the Gittite's house for about three months, word trickled back to Jerusalem that Obed-Edom had become a kind of King Midas—everything he touched seemed to turn to gold. His every endeavor was crowned with success. The presence of the ark meant blessing and goodness for his family. And David took another look. He began to revise his thinking about the box—it was dangerous, but it was wonderful as well.

The king dug into the Old Testament law, reviewed it carefully, and gave great attention to the strict commands for moving the ark. He then proceeded to bring the ark carefully from the home where it rested. After the movers took six paces, they halted and offered a great sacrifice of oxen and sheep. And David worshiped the Lord with great joy and intensity, even dancing before the Lord "with all his might" (2 Sam. 6:14). David had always looked to this day, but after his personal observations of the great powers of God's law—for blessing the benevolent or cursing the careless—his feelings about the ark of the law were even deeper. And it was at this point, many scholars believe, that David channeled his heartfelt gratitude into the song we now know as Psalm 30.

David's entire life, as we have seen, was an emotional and spiritual roller coaster. Even in this one story, we see David moving from anger to fear to joyful dancing. On the one hand he saw the damage caused by the mishandling of God's law, and on the other he saw the power for blessing when that law is properly respected.

We ride that roller coaster ourselves: the upward surges of joy and the deep plunges into depression. The higher the roller car races, the deeper and faster it will plunge. The psalm we'll be exploring together offers five contrasting experiences connected to life's ebb and flow. The psalmist begins in the first four verses—and picks up with verses 8–10—with the climbing, cresting, plunging cycle that moves from hurting to healing.

From Hurting to Healing

Before anything else, there is a profoundly moving theme of healing in this psalm. We can't be specifically certain what healing David might have required. We do know the story of bringing the ark to Jerusalem, but there may have been other issues and challenges in the life of the new king at this particular time. It may have been that he experienced some kind of illness. We do find clues, spread through other psalms, that David had to cope with physical health problems at times. Here in Psalm 30:8, we read David's prayer to move from hurting to healing.

Prayer for Healing

As David prays in his sickness, he argues with God. In more contemporary language, we can hear David saying, "Lord, allow me to plead my case with You for a moment. Why do You keep me ill? Why must I hover near death? What good could I possibly be to You as a dead man? Will my dust praise Your name? I believe I can worship You better in a state of life, dear Father."

Let's say this for David: His argument isn't totally self-serving. He's quite sincere in his concern for God's glory—if a bit calculated. He is saying, "If You'll save me, O God, You'll have one more worshiper in this world to bring honor and glory to Your name." We often approach God with the same agenda: *Don't You want to bless me, Lord, so I can serve You better?*

But finally, David realizes his inadequacy in negotiating with the Creator of the universe. He puts all that behind him and simply pleads to God for mercy. In verse 10 he says, "Hear, O LORD, and have mercy on me; LORD, be my helper!" No bargaining; no "Here's what I can do for You, Lord"; no rationalization; simply a heartfelt plea for mercy. And isn't that where we all end up? If you've ever been seriously ill, here are the words that finally find their way to your lips. You'll surely pass through the stages of deal-making and angry protest. But the time comes when you find yourself at the bottom line of hope or despair, and you become a small, frightened child approaching his father.

And you say, "Lord, I need Your mercy. Please, please help me!"

Praise for Healing

So David prays for healing. Then in the next four verses he offers up praise for healing. He's had a narrow escape with death, and he says, "I will extol You, O LORD, for You have lifted me up." The phrase "lifted up" from the Hebrew language is the same expression that is used for dipping a bucket down into a well and drawing water. David has this picture in his mind: "Lord God, You reached down to the darkest depths and pulled me right out of the grave. I was almost gone."

Or think of it this way: "I lift *You* up, O Lord, because You lifted *me* up."

This is a thought that comes naturally in the aftermath of a brush with the grave. When you know that you'll see the sun rise again, just when it looked as if you were facing the night of death, you begin to wake every morning thanking and praising God. You thank Him for the morning. You thank Him for sunlight, and for the simple but profound privilege of taking another breath of oxygen in this world. You need no reminders to thank God and worship Him, for you see everything in deeper colors and brighter lights. You hear the music of God's wonderful lovingkindness, and you wonder how you missed hearing such a lovely melody before. This is the joy you feel, and this is the joy David felt as he wrote this psalm.

That joyful, thankful perspective is essential to a positive life. The reason you are reading this book with the strength to turn its pages and the eyes to take in the light that illuminates it is that God has a purpose for you. He loves you, and He keeps you alive. He gives you life and strength and breath. Could it be that in those times in which you nearly died on the freeway or had some other brush with death that God reached out and preserved you—as He did with David? As He did in granting me the opportunity to write this book?

Absolutely! You and I are here on the good pleasure and indulgence of Almighty God. Shouldn't that make you see things through different eyes when you rise tomorrow? Shouldn't you begin the day on your knees with a great smile spread across your face—and maybe a tear on your cheek—as you whisper, "Lord God, thank You for keeping me alive through another day; thank You for preserving me through another night. I lift up my voice and my hands to You in praise for Your goodness. Now let me lift up my life today in service for Your purposes!"

Purpose for Healing

David moves from hurting to healing. Then he reflects upon the purpose for his healing. In verse 4, he says, "Sing praise to the LORD, you saints of His, and give thanks at the remembrance of His holy name."

Yes, healing has a purpose. We don't often get far enough to take that in, for too often we're like little children taking the candy from the hands of a parent. We scamper off without even saying thanks. But the truth is that when God answers a prayer and provides healing, He

---

Sweet are the uses of adversity,

Which, like the toad, ugly and venomous,

Wears yet a precious jewel in his head;

And this our life, exempt from public haunt,

Finds tongues in trees, books in the running brooks

Sermons in stone, and good in everything.

—William Shakespeare

---

has revealed something about His purposes—a precious clue about His wonderful workings in this world. He has intervened for a good reason, and we now have the same responsibility to offer praise as the responsibility we had when we prayed for healing. We prayed, "O Lord God, heal me and I will praise Your name." When the wonderful thing has come to pass, we cannot and must not forget our heartfelt promises.

So David exhorts the people: "Now let's all praise God—I'm talking to all of you who are His saints! Offer your gratitude and remember His name! Never, never forget what He has done for us on this day."

From Weeping to Joy

Psalm 30 can be seen as a study in contrasts. The first one David cites takes us from hurting to healing. Next he takes us from weeping to joy. We come to a beloved verse in which David says, "For His anger is but for a moment, His favor *is* for life; weeping may endure for a night, but joy comes in the morning" (v. 5).

In the general sense, weeping and joy don't accompany each other.

There are exceptions, of course—I know some people who cry when they're happy. But normally we associate weeping with sadness and laughter with joy. And David speaks of the great gulf that exists between the height of the peak and the depth of the valley. And yet we can experience both of those things in a brief span of time. We can be filled with joy one moment and find ourselves in tears the next, because the road can bend just that quickly.

But we can look at the inevitable movement from tears to joy from two perspectives.

This Is an Everyday Truth

The fact is, we understand the roller-coaster ups and downs of life simply through the lens of experience. Whether you're a believer or not, when someone you know is going through a difficult thing, you're likely to say to that person, "You know what, my friend? It's not going to be like this forever. Just hang in there and wait for your life to take a turn for the better. Don't give up! You'll get through this."

I heard about a wry individual who was asked to name his favorite verse in the Bible. He quickly replied, "And it came to pass." It didn't come to *stay*; it came to *pass*. I realize the man misinterpreted the familiar words, but I rather like his misinterpretation, don't you? It says something about the way life really is. Pain is so painful partly due to its feeling of permanence; it seems wrapped in the eternalness of hellfire. But as we open to the midsection of our Bibles, there is our old friend David, who puts his great bruised hand on our shoulder and comforts us. "Grief and misery come creeping up in the blackness of night," he tells us in this verse, "but hold on tight, for joy comes in the morning."

I see proof of David's words nearly every day as a pastor. We gather at the graveside on a somber afternoon to pay tribute to someone we've loved and lost. I stand before the grieving family, observing the deep sadness in their faces, and I think, "It will never, ever be the same for these dear people." But a year passes; I watch the family closely, and I can see that somehow God has brought them back from the depths. He has restored a measure of joy and gladness in the morning.

Our children are perhaps capable of bringing us the deepest grief of all. I know a pastor and his wife who have lived through the truth of that, enduring tragedy with one of their children. I'll never forget the words of that pastor's wife. She quietly said to her husband, "I wonder if we'll ever smile again." That's exactly how we all feel as the storm rages: *This is forever. I'll never be the same.* We can't remember what the sky looked like when it was blue, and we can't imagine the sun will ever break through the clouds again. But God has given us a far more powerful capacity for healing than we can possibly realize, and His powers of comfort and strengthening and revival are unlimited. The morning will come again, and with it, joy.

This Is an Eternal Truth

It's an everyday truth, but it's also an eternal one.

In the Old Testament account of creation, we find words that raise an eyebrow if we're listening closely. After describing God's creative work, the Bible says this: "So the evening and the morning were the first day" (Gen. 1:5). That pattern is repeated for each of the days of creation, with evening always preceding morning. Isn't that a backward statement of things? Doesn't the morning come first?

This brings us to a valuable little principle you should seize in your daily life—one of those treasures of common sense that can bless you immeasurably.

Begin your day *before* the morning comes. Begin it on the preceding evening with prayer, planning, pondering, and preparation, and the next day will be far more successful and effective for you. Instead of weighing your spirit down with the late news or the banalities of a talk show on television, lift them with a visit to God's Word. Inject the power of His wisdom into your mind before you rest your head on the pillow. Apply His Word to your plans, ready yourself for the day to come, and ask God to bless the day that will soon follow.

You'll be amazed at how well you'll sleep, as your Father takes what you have just offered Him and organizes and renews your mind, doing all the daily mental maintenance work that makes you the kind of servant He needs. When the sun rises, you'll be startled to discover how much confidence will fill your spirit, and how energetic and effective you'll be in the workings of your daily life. The evening and the morning will be your day.

We hear much about seeking God in the earliest hours. Maybe we should be seeking Him even earlier. Give it a try.

But the concept of the evening and the morning penetrates even deeper into the meaning of life. You and I are living in the evening of creation at present. The sun may shine, but our world is darkened by sin and rebellion. The Bible assures us that a morning will dawn bright and glorious someday. All the sorrow and sadness and difficulty we've known in the darkened skies of life will vanish. The Lord will return for us at the daybreak of eternity, and there will be no more weeping, no more pain or suffering, no more broken hearts. There will be no more valleys plunging away from the peaks.

He will dry every tear, and there will be joy in that great morning.

From Prosperity to Poverty

In the sixth and seventh verses of this psalm of contrasts, David takes us once again to the highest reaches and lowest depths. He says, "Now in my prosperity I said, 'I shall never be moved.' LORD, by Your favor You have made my mountain stand strong; You hid Your face, and I was troubled."

Those are the words of the New King James Version. Let's take a more contemporary look at what he really means. David is confiding a painful truth to us, something he has learned the hard way. He says, "I thought back on my life to the time when I had everything I'd ever dreamed. And I said to myself, 'I'm set for life—and set in stone. I've got it made! I'm a bigger man than anything life can throw at me.'"

These are the thoughts of a king who had everything going for him as he looked out from his throne of worldly power. Like Dr. Seuss's Yertle the Turtle, he says, "I am the king of all I can see!" But painful experience has taught him differently. He has realized the great danger of prosperity—that of confusing "invaluable" with "invulnerable" or ultimate wealth with permanent strength. As Yertle learned, how quickly it can all come tumbling down!

You and I see David's bitter lesson and initially feel a bit smug. We say to ourselves, "Worldly power is an illusion? Well, I could have told him that! What a fool that David was!" But can we be certain we wouldn't have slipped if we'd been in his place? Wealthy and powerful people are victimized by the Grand Illusion every day. They feel that they've discovered how to master and exploit so many things in life— money and power and fame and people—that they assume they've mastered it *all*. They're the kings of all they can see, but what about the things they can't see? There are more things in heaven and earth, as Shakespeare said, than they've dreamed of in their philosophies.

"Therefore let him who thinks he stands take heed lest he fall" (1 Cor. 10:12). Pride indeed goes before a fall. A simple ringing phone, combined with a single sentence from the doctor or the lawyer or even a stranger, and all our earthly security goes up in flames. It's a fine thing to have the fruits of our labor in life, as the writer of Ecclesiastes tells us; and it's important to secure our finances and have sturdy locks on our doors. But ultimate security cannot be purchased by any of these things. Worldly life is fragile. Eternal life is a gift from God, free and yet not for sale at any price.

The Old Testament tells us the story of a man who got it all wrong. His name was Nebuchadnezzar, and he was the king of all he could see in the great empire of the Babylonians. Daniel, who knew the king well, tells us of the bright and cheerful day when King Nebuchadnezzar was strolling through the palace in Babylon, admiring everything he'd established and the kingdom in his power. Listen to what he said: "Is not this great Babylon, that I have built for a royal dwelling by my mighty power and for the honor of my majesty?" (Dan. 4:30). He was thinking, *Not a bad spread I've built here, if I do say so myself.*

But the Bible tells us that "while the word was still in the king's mouth, a voice fell from heaven: 'King Nebuchadnezzar, to you it is spoken: the kingdom has departed from you!'" (v. 31).

But God wasn't finished with Nebuchadnezzar. No, He still needed the poor misguided king for several purposes, one of which was to provide an illustration for you and me, and a fairly interesting illustration, as you're about to discover. You may not believe the following story, but just open your Bible to the Book of Daniel if you're incredulous, and read for yourself. God's Word tells us that Nebuchadnezzar became arguably history's first recorded werewolf. He spent the next seven years eating grass out in the field like a beast, whether or not a full moon was out. In fact he was quite an odd exhibit for any zoo, for "his hair had grown like eagles' feathers and his nails like birds' claws" (v. 33). How the mighty had fallen!

We can only assume the king learned his lesson—the hard way, as usual. His belly filled with grass, and having endured a molting season or two, he was restored at the end of seven years. Daniel 4:37 shows us a king who is no longer foolishly proclaiming his own power and majesty: "Now I, Nebuchadnezzar, praise and extol and honor the King of heaven, all of whose works are truth, and His ways justice. And those who walk in pride He is able to abase."

That last sentence was something the king could heartily testify to from firsthand experience. Eat enough grass, and your world-view will change. Nebuchadnezzar finally realized that when you're flying high, filled with your own prosperity, God is more than able to burst your bubble.

From Mourning to Dancing

Prosperity to poverty may seem like a negative transition, but it can be positive indeed—it can if it brings us back to God. Whatever it takes to get us there, once we come to our senses and find our way back to Him, then we can identify with David's words: "You have turned for me my mourning into dancing; You have put off my sackcloth and clothed me with gladness" (v. 11).

This is the verse that provides scholars with their primary clue that
Psalm 30 is the companion chapter to 2 Samuel 6. The reference to
dancing binds the two passages together. Do you remember the rest
of the story?

Here is King David, entering his city with the ark of the covenant
carried by the priests. It's a victory parade, the kind when everyone

---

Remove falsehood and lies far from me;

Give me neither poverty nor riches—

Feed me with the food You prescribe for me;

Lest I be full and deny You,

And say, "Who is the LORD?"

Or lest I be poor and steal,

And profane the name of my God.

—Proverbs 30:8–9

---

turns out with ticker tape to honor the dignitaries. The band is playing, and the people are cheering. The king is decked out in his clerical
robe, wearing his linen ephod, the godly apparel of the priest. And
David dances with all of his might before the Lord (2 Samuel 6:14).
Certain pastors and Bible readers avert their eyes with decorum when
they come to this verse. Dancing! That's usually not on the program
for a joyful church celebration these days.

But there's no way to explain away this account from God's Word. It
means what it says. Keep in mind that we're not talking about ball-
room dancing, break dancing, or disco. This was godly dancing—a
physical expression of abounding excitement for God's mighty deeds.
The ark was among the people, and this was no time for somber, quiet
assemblies. There are times when we can best express our emotions
toward God and His faithfulness by having a godly party! David simply couldn't contain his joy, and we should have times when we feel
that same way.

God turned mourning into dancing and sackcloth into ephod. Life before Him is a study in contrasts, in ups and downs.

From Silence to Singing

The final verse of Psalm 30 leaves us with one last profound truth. The message is that we should never keep silent in light of God's blessings: ". . . to the end that *my* glory may sing praise to You and not be silent. O LORD my God, I will give thanks to You forever."

Please don't leave the thirtieth psalm without this firm understanding. If your life is filled with joy, give thanks to God; if you're enduring pain and tears, give thanks to God. In all things, offer your praise. Life's ups and the downs are only yard markers on the playing field of circumstances. Joy and sadness are temporary conditions, but praise and thanksgiving are permanent expressions.

When we finally come to understand that truth and begin to praise God in the midst of *all* things, we often find that circumstances themselves change in our favor. Godly faith changes the world around it, for we can live triumphantly, knowing that the pain is temporary and the end has been predetermined; it's an ending of reunion with the Father and an eternity in His loving presence. Why react in any other way than to lift your voice in praise?

Knocked Down, but for Good Reason

I must confess that one particular animal fascinates me. I consider this creature among the oddest God ever created. He's called a giraffe. He is a strange and homely creature in appearance; his movements seem awkward and peculiar. And then there's the matter of giraffe childbirth. What? You say you haven't read many books on giraffe childbirth? Well, I'm here to enlighten you. Gary Richmond wrote an article on giraffe calves that caught my attention, and I hope you'll indulge me as I pass on some facts from it.

Gary had been invited to a zoo where a captive giraffe was about to give birth. He said, "The moment we had anticipated was not a disappointment. A calf, a plucky male, hurled forth, falling ten feet and

---

I would willingly endure all the sufferings
of this world . . . to possess the smallest increase
of the knowledge of God's greatness.

—Teresa of Avila

---

landing on his back. The mother giraffe gives birth to its young standing up, and the distance from the birth canal to the ground is about ten feet."

Are you still reading? Think of this—ten feet is approximately the appropriate height for dunking a basketball, *plus* about four extra inches. So the calf fell out of its mother ten feet above ground, and landed on its back. It lay there for a few moments, and then, according to the story, it scrambled over to get its legs underneath it so that it could take a look around and check out the world it had just entered.

Gary Richmond continued his account. The mother lowered her head to see the baby, then she moved until she was towering directly above the calf. About a minute passed, then came the shocking surprise. The mother giraffe swung her great, long leg outward and booted her baby through the air. The calf sprawled head over heels across the ground, puzzled and protesting.

Gary was astounded to witness that display. He turned to the zoologist and said, "What's that all about?"

The zoologist replied, "She wants him to get up—and if he doesn't get up, she's going to do it again."

Gary continues, "Sure enough, the process was repeated again and again. And the struggle to rise was momentous, and as the baby grew tired of trying, the mother would again stimulate its effort with a hearty kick. Amidst the cheers of the animal care staff, the calf stood up finally for the first time. Wobbly, for sure; but there it stood on its little spindly legs. Then we were struck silent when the mother kicked it off its feet again."

Gary's zoologist friend was the only person present who wasn't astonished by the mother's brutal treatment of her newborn calf.

"She wants it to remember how it got up," he explained. "That's why she knocked it down again."[1]

To remember how it got up. Doesn't God nurture us in just the same rough way sometimes? And if we're ignorant as to His methods and purposes, the actions can seem cold and even cruel. We finally struggle to our feet, and it seems as if we're kicked again. But our heavenly Father knows that love must be tough—and it must take the long view. God knows the world will fall apart, and we must be sturdy travelers to stay on our feet. We must not forget how we got to where we are.

Have you ever felt that God kicked you when you were down? Perhaps, like Helen Barnhart, you've received one blow after another, and you've wondered if you should even try to get up again. One of the reasons for some of the challenges in our lives is that God is toughening us up, preparing us for warfare against forces intent on destroying us. I wouldn't be honest if I didn't admit to feeling kicked and abused at times, all the while hearing the voice that says, "Get up. Get moving. Get with it! And don't forget how you got up."

Our God created the principle of rigorous discipline. I hope that by now you can understand why it's necessary. I hope you will face your next great disappointment with a new perspective—that the next time things look down, you'll look up. I hope you'll gird up your heart, reach for renewed strength, and say, "Lord, I've been taken by surprise. Life has thrown me a curve, and it's a hard thing for me to cope with. Even so, I praise Your blessed name. Whatever comes my way, joy or sorrow, I will stubbornly and confidently praise Your name. No matter how circumstances may appear, I will praise Your name.

"For I know You are wise and loving, and that no mere circumstance can change that. Whether this current road leads to exhilarating peaks or gloomy canyons, I praise You and I thank You. You are my Father, and You love me enough to train me and remake me, and only You can turn my mourning into dancing."

Psalm 142

A Contemplation of David. A Prayer when he was in the cave.

1 I cry out to the LORD with my voice;
   With my voice to the LORD I make my supplication.
2 I pour out my complaint before Him;
   I declare before Him my trouble.
3 When my spirit was overwhelmed within me,
   Then You knew my path.
   In the way in which I walk
   They have secretly set a snare for me.
4 Look on my right hand and see,
   For there is no one who acknowledges me;
   Refuge has failed me;
   No one cares for my soul.
5 I cried out to You, O LORD:
   I said, "You are my refuge,
   My portion in the land of the living.
6 Attend to my cry,
   For I am brought very low;
   Deliver me from my persecutors,
   For they are stronger than I.
7 Bring my soul out of prison,
   That I may praise Your name;
   The righteous shall surround me,
   For You shall deal bountifully with me."

8

Praying under Pressure

Be not dismayed whate'er betide,
Beneath His wings of love abide,
God will take care of you,
Through every day, o'er all the way,
He will take care of you,
God will take care of you.

—CIVILLA D. MARTIN,
"GOD WILL TAKE CARE OF YOU"

Achilles, the great warrior of Greek mythology, was 99 percent invincible in battle. His armor was immaculate. But he had one area of vulnerability: his heel. Today we speak of a person's "Achilles heel" as being his or her obvious weak spot, the place among all his or her defenses that is most open to attack. For a significant number of us, our Achilles heel is found in our precious offspring. We would be willing to endure any personal injury if we could take their place in enduring it. We would gladly die for them, so deep-rooted is our parental love.

Glenda Palmer had that particular Achilles heel.

Glenda had a son named Kent who was in the prime of youth. He radiated all the infectious joy and energy of any twenty-two-year-old. Kent was an active, healthy young man, and his mother adored him.

When her son's life-threatening tumor came along, she never saw it coming. She recounts for us the story of her world falling apart.

⁓

Those who know me well will quickly tell you I've always been a crier. I cry during happy weddings and sad movies. I cry at church when we sing "How Great Thou Art." It really doesn't take much to coax tears from me.

But that particular year—the year of turmoil, the year of our son's cancer—I didn't cry very often. I believe there are sorrows and agonies that penetrate to depths within us where tears are simply insufficient.

Our year of turmoil began when Kent began to complain about his back. It wasn't like him to worry about sore muscles or aching bones, because little injuries here and there were commonplace to him— something to shrug off. He worked in construction and stayed active in sports competition. Still, I didn't particularly worry. Finally one day Kent said, "My back hurts so bad, I don't think I can surf." So I called for a doctor's appointment. I figured my son had probably pulled some minor muscle on a recent ski trip.

The doctor performed a few tests, then he called me on the phone. The surgeon wanted to admit Kent immediately for an operation. "It looks like a large tumor," he said. "It may be malignant."

I hung up the phone and sat silently, trying to take in the terrible medical words I had just heard. I closed my eyes and began to plead before God. "Dear Lord," I wept, "please, oh please, don't take my baby away from me."

But there were no more tears after that. I didn't cry after the surgery, as the doctor stood before us using the words I had prayed with all my might not to hear—words such as *disappointed* and *chemotherapy* and *nine-pound tumor*. Nine-pound tumor? I remembered that Kent had weighed only six pounds at his birth.

During the next months, Kent, his brother, Scott, my husband, and

I simply did what we had to do. We stood firm as best we could and focused on getting through the crisis. Oddly enough, we laughed a lot.
We didn't shed tears, but we laughed. During my darker moments in
the past, when I'd contemplated the unthinkable possibility of losing a
child, I'd imagined that I would weep continuously. But that didn't turn
out to be the case for me. We bottled up our grief and occasionally released it through laughter together.

I turned to my Bible and dug deeply into its wisdom and consolation
early each morning. The words I found there became my rock in the
storm as well as my marching orders for the day. I used hymns and
songs of praise as a channel for hearing God's voice, as well as lifting
my voice and my feelings to Him. And the Lord sent people—special
people He used as His angels. They ministered to me and prayed without ceasing for Kent. As terrible as the time was, it was also filled with
irrefutable evidence of the presence and grace of God.

Yes, His grace was sufficient! I had heard it in countless sermons, but
now I knew it was really true. I had a fresh certainty that, whatever the
outcome, my Lord would be with me and His strength would be
enough.

Kent checked into the hospital five times for chemotherapy—one
week in, one week out. He lost all his hair. Each treatment was more
and more painful and filled him with unbearable anguish. I suffered
with him.

I shed a few tears during those days, but only a few.

During the cycle of into-the-hospital and out-of-the-hospital, Kent
took classes to become a real-estate agent. He kept his eyes on the future, not on death or morbid thoughts, but on life and on hope. I admired his attitude.

The season of chemotherapy came to an end, but two small tumors
remained on his aortic artery. Kent's doctor suggested a surgeon in Indianapolis who specialized in that kind of intricate cancer surgery.
This was a crucial turning point, so I began praying and fasting. We
prepared ourselves for the next battle in the war against the elements
for our son's life.

Six weeks before our trip to Indianapolis, I lost my mother. This was a moment we'd known was inevitable, for she suffered from an extended illness. Daddy asked me to read Psalm 23 to her, and those rich words of David were on my lips as she left this life: *Yea, though I walk through the valley of the shadow of death, I will fear no evil, for You are with me.* The words had a deeper meaning for me than ever before. Mother was my best friend in this world.

But I didn't cry very much.

We went to Indianapolis. The surgeon stood before us, and we couldn't believe our ears. Was it a dream? "I removed the tumors," he said. "They aren't malignant." Almost before he could finish the sentence, I was hugging him and weeping freely.

The tears finally came. But I couldn't cry for long, for there was a long list of people to call. They needed to hear about our great and mighty God whose grace is sufficient.

All of that was ten years ago. I feel great joy in telling you that Kent is alive and well, with the tumors only a distant memory. He is happily married, and he works as a mortgage lender. God has been so good.

I find that I'm able to cry again—oh, yes! I cry at weddings and during sentimental movies. But most of all, I cry when I sing "How Great Thou Art."

David was a man of faith. That much is perfectly clear from all we know about him in the Scriptures. He was a man of vision, a wise military and governmental leader, and even a man gifted in music and poetry and dancing, but like many people who love and trust God— people like Glenda Palmer—he was also a man who struggled with discouragement and depression.

David coped with a plethora of turbulent emotions during his fugitive years. He had to flee for his life from the wrath of King Saul. He had to bolster strength and courage through devastating days and fear-laden hours. Facing many of these things alone, he turned for solace to music and worship, as well as the comforts of writing about his feelings. In fact, students of the psalms believe that David wrote at least eight different psalms during his season of flight.

The superscription beneath the heading of Psalm 142 tells us we've

---

Fits of depression come over most of us.

Usually cheerful as we may be, we must at intervals be cast down.

The strong are not always vigorous,

the wise not always ready,

the brave not always courageous,

and the joyous not always happy.

There may be here and there men of iron . . .

but surely the rust frets even these.

—Charles Haddon Spurgeon

---

come to "A Contemplation of David. A Prayer when he was in the cave." In this chapter we'll also briefly consider Psalm 57, a song arising from the same historical setting. Its superscription reads like this: "A Michtam [that is, a teaching psalm] of David when he fled from Saul into the cave."

We already know that David was running away from the most powerful man in his world, nearly always outnumbered, and without the support of anything close to the armament of his enemy. As we look in on this episode of his life, David has finally stumbled across a refuge where he can find sanctuary. In the midst of the wilderness, he has come to a place where he can lay low, pour out his heart to God, and sort out the shattered fragments of his life. He has found a cave. And he has entered the darkness of the cave of despair.

Many of us have descended into the cold, darkened reaches of the cave of despair. Glenda Palmer was there during her son's illness. You and I have paid our own visits. The cave has its own twists and hidden

passages, and we can feel lost. We begin to imagine that God has forgotten us, that His comfort doesn't extend to these dark passages. Or
perhaps we feel in our honest moments He just doesn't care.

It helps us to follow David's story. If nothing else, we can discover
that we aren't the only ones who have experienced discouragement.
One of the reasons we wear out the pages of the psalms is that it helps
us simply to know that somebody has gone before us—even thousands of years before us. We find comfort in recognizing the emotions
we're feeling here and now displayed in a man who lived so long ago.
And we can't read the psalms without finding words somewhere along
the way that fit the situation directly before us.

What a treasure we have in our hands. David preserved all these
honest emotions and wise prescriptions. He maintained an invaluable
journal that has never lost its power or its richness. We should begin
to realize the value of keeping our own journals. I feel very strongly
about that particular spiritual discipline, and I will discuss this more in
depth later in this chapter. As a matter of fact, I intend to share ex-
cerpts from my own journals in the last two chapters of this book. I
hope you're taking time to regularly record your thoughts and your
prayers before God. Journals are precious.

David went beyond simple journaling. He went beyond simply
recording for us the events of his life. He wrote out his prayers to
God, then kept an account of God's workings. Here in our Bibles, we
can actually chart the course of David's life as he moves through his
series of crises and emerges victorious on the other side.

David is now seeking solace in a cave named Adullam. We need to
clarify the point that this is one of two caves in the young man's life;
the other is the cave of En Gedi, the place where David cut off the
skirt of Saul's robe. You can find that account in 1 Samuel 24.

It's interesting to place the psalms and the historical books side
by side to seek the full context of the psalms. We can discover, for example, how Psalm 142 seems to flow from the life of David:

David therefore departed from there and escaped to the cave of Adullam. And when his brothers and all his father's house heard it, they

went down there to him. And everyone who was in distress, everyone who was in debt, and everyone who was discontented gathered to him. So he became captain over them. And there were about four hundred men with him. (1 Sam. 22:1–2)

What was happening? Most scholars believe King Saul had levied a heavy tax on the people of Israel. It would then be clear that people were flocking to this cave of Adullam to be with David in their anger and rebellion over the unfair taxation. They were poor and had very little, and many of them were the very people who had insisted before God that they needed a king. Be careful what you pray for—Saul was that king.

Many others of the four hundred were, no doubt, old friends of David who gathered to lend their support. Goliath's conqueror was still admired by most citizens of the nation of Israel. As word leaked out concerning their hero's flight, more and more of them decided to join David in his hiding place. In fact, in the next chapter of 1 Samuel, we discover that the number grew from four hundred to six hundred. Needless to say, this cave was no foxhole on the side of the hill. It was a huge cavern with a forty-foot opening.

So we have David, fleeing his problems, fleeing Saul, fleeing life. Finally he has come across a place of respite, and suddenly there are great crowds of people flowing toward him from every direction. What kind of people are these? Not exactly the best or the brightest. These are the debtors, the troublemakers, and the discontented who are flocking to the side of David. How do you think he feels about all this company? Keep in mind that David is sick and discouraged. I believe he sought a cave not only for safety, but also for solitude. The fact is that misery doesn't always love company. The last people we want to be with in our despair are those with problems to match our own.

That's why I can't imagine what this massive social call must have been like for David. He is struggling just to cope with his own turbulent emotions, and now all the outcasts of Israel are straggling to his side in the cave of Adullam.

Some commentators cast David as the Robin Hood of his day. W. Graham Scroggie, an Old Testament commentator, has this to say about the men who resorted to David: "What a crew! The three d's have formed many an assembly since then [the debtors, the distressed, and the discontented], but such are ill to get on with, and a man like David would feel lonely among such!"[1]

Thus David, having entered a cave to be alone, finds himself surrounded by the most distressed citizens of Israel. I imagine he has taken a hard look at his life and his place among the people of Israel before coming to his journal to write this psalm. David is introspective. He is emotional and very transparent with those emotions. His feelings flow out in psalms and music and praise and tears.

Do you feel that Christians shouldn't show emotions? Some believers seem to have adopted that very peculiar notion. "Christian deportment," according to the grim stereotype, is a calm, plain-vanilla demeanor characterized by a pleasant smile that never wavers even when the lions are chasing us around the Roman arena. Supposedly putting on a "happy faith" is the visual proof of godliness. But David, a man after God's own heart, vented his emotions in violent colors and operatic crescendos. We wince when we read some of his work! You need only take a close look at the psalm before us. The journal entry never denies honest emotion; there can be little doubt that the author is a man whose very soul is in distress.

The Discouragement of David

Let's take a closer look at the discouragement of David.

David Feels Disoriented

David confesses to us in Psalm 142:3 that his spirit within is "overwhelmed." The Hebrew words literally mean "the muffling of my spirit." What vivid terminology—have you ever felt a muffled spirit?

David has come to a place where he has begun to distrust his powers of judgment. He is no longer certain where to turn or what course to take. Life has become a great flood rushing in upon him, and he struggles to stand firm against the current.

David's muffled spirit is a picture of disorientation. He is pursued by two armies, one made of soldiers and the other of sufferers. His life is entangled in a knot of problems—which thread should be loosened first? If you read his story, you discover that he has recently made a serious mistake; his entanglement has distracted him from the will of God for a period of time—with tragic results. As punishment for harboring his prey, Saul slaughtered the village of Nob, which cared for David during his prodigal journey from God's will. David realizes that he is spiritually responsible for the mass slaying of an entire village, and he is nearly driven insane with guilt. He has entered the darkened depths of the cave to better contemplate the darkened depths of his soul, but the crowd will prevent the solitude his grief now craves.

I have often imagined David slumped within the silence of the cave, his head in his hands, reflecting on the place to which his life has brought him. Shadows flicker at the edge of his vision, and he hears the approaching echo of voices. His gaze travels to the passage of the cavern. There, a rough assortment of people is beginning to swell the passageway. They are shouting about taxes and family problems and a thousand other worries.

David closes his eyes with a sinking heart. He puts his head farther down in his hands and whispers, "O Lord God, what now? What would You have me do?" He feels lost, disoriented. But that's not the only emotion he's feeling.

David Feels Deserted

We come to the fourth verse of our psalm. In my estimation, it's one of the saddest verses in the Bible. David writes, "Look on my right hand and see, for there is no one who acknowledges me; refuge has failed me; no one cares for my soul." Can you imagine any words more desolate and despairing?

This is the same David who wrote in Psalm 16:8, "I have set the LORD always before me; because He is at my right hand I shall not be moved." There had been a time when he felt the Lord God always at his right hand. If God was for him, who could be against him? Life was rewarding and victorious; no matter where he was or what he was doing, the Lord was always there.

But the pit into which his soul has plunged is a dark one. He sits in the one most appropriate, most symbolic place for his mood—a cold, foreboding cave. And even with a mob of "supporters" closing in, he is more convinced than ever that nobody really cares about him. They care about what he does for them, for the defeating of giants and the fighting of battles; but they don't care about *him*. He has turned to his right hand, and there is nothing but the wind.

He is alone in terms of people too. Have you ever felt alone in a crowd of four hundred? It may seem a contradiction in terms, but anyone who has ever been lonely will confirm that the greater the number of people present, the more intense can be the feeling of loneliness. This is why large, thriving cities are pockets of despair and alienation. A cave filled with the echoes of demanding voices can be lonely too. The psalm suggests to us that David saw the friendly mob and felt the fundamental difference between them and himself. Suddenly his sense of isolation was a knife in his heart. No one knew the depth of his emotions; no one cared what he felt or how he suffered.

Have you ever visited such a cave?

Problems tend to isolate us. I am the kind of individual who is certain to turn inward when the problems come. Like a turtle, my head snaps quietly back into the thick, protective shell. I want to sort it all out for myself without outside interference. I think this is a particularly strong tendency for those of us who are male. We seek the nearest cave that might offer protection from the world and its questions. We believe no one else has ever experienced such a problem as the

present one, and even our wives and children are unlikely to understand—or such is our feeling. So we bury ourselves in a cave.

Scripture commentator Alexander MacLaren offers this description
of the process: "The soul that has to wade through deep waters has always to do it alone. . . .We have companions in joy, but sorrow we
have to face by ourselves. . . . Unless we have Jesus with us in the
darkness, we have no one."[2]

Laugh and the world laughs with you, weep, and you weep alone

—Ella Wheeler Wilcox

It matters not how many people are around; you may be in the center of a crowd of thousands, but you'll believe you're hopelessly isolated. Elijah suffered from this misconception. It was he against the
world; he was firmly convinced that he was the only prophet left who
believed in God. It took the Lord to remind him that He, the Creator,
was still in control—and that there were a few thousand more soldiers
in God's army, than the prophet had calculated.

Problems encourage isolation, and isolation nurtures misconception.

David Feels Depressed

In the sixth verse, David says, "I am brought very low." Isn't that what
the condition of depression is all about?

We've come to a very sensitive topic for contemporary Christianity.
I've actually heard preachers claim that if you're in a state of depression,
then you can't be a Christian. *Real* Christians, they say, don't experience
depression. My first question for these preachers is whether they've
read all of the Word of God. How are we supposed to approach Elijah,
who was depressed? How are we supposed to understand Jonah, who
was depressed? And what about Moses? He, too, faced depression.
Then we come to the matter of King David, a man deeply loved by

God, a man of profound spiritual experience and wisdom, who also grappled with depression throughout his life. The word that David uses for *depression*, interestingly enough, is the word for *indentation*. He applies that condition to his soul. Therefore David is saying, "I'm suffering from an indentation in my soul. I am depressed."

As a pastor, I've occasionally counseled believers in the midst of depression, and I know what a heavy burden it is for people to be "brought very low." I've known people who have suffered such intense depression that they eventually ended their own lives. They looked into the future and saw nothing but emptiness and hopelessness and despair. Heartfelt expressions of hope or encouragement were no longer enough to reach them. Life simply didn't seem worth living anymore, and they chose to forfeit the precious gift of life.

David felt a depression that may have approached such a zone of desperation. All of his hope and joy were gone; his thoughts had turned inward. At one time, the problem had been a simple one—the king was hunting him down to kill him. But now David's plight was something more abstract, something considerably more complex, something whose source was David's own heart. He had allowed his circumstances to drive him inward instead of upward. He had come to fall back on his own resources, and those resources were now spent; the well had run dry. There was nowhere else for David to turn. He no longer sensed the presence of God in his life.

But did this mean David was no longer a child of God? Of course not. Believers do indeed enter the dark cave of depression at times, and this is particularly true of godly leaders. These are men and women who dwell in the world of momentous expectations and great, ponderous burdens of responsibility. They wear the mantle of greatness with unease. And quite naturally, great expectations can lead to great depression.

David Feels Defeated

In the grip of his low spirits, David cries out to the Lord, "Deliver me from my persecutors, for they are stronger than I" (v. 6). He turns his focus to his enemies.

David is in a place where he can see nothing but grim prospects. He is wearing dark glasses that tint the entire world in shades from gray to black. He does what most of us do when we're feeling low. He sits within his cave with a yellow legal pad and proceeds to take inventory of his life, placing each element in one of two columns

---

Man's despair is not despair of God at all,
but despair of all that is not God.
Beyond that certain despair lies Christian hope,
the certainty that God alone is enough for man.

—William McNamara

---

marked *good news* and *bad news*. When he gets to the bottom line, he takes a look and concludes, "I've got some bad news and some more bad news." Nothing good seems to be visible through dark glasses in a dim cave. The assets are zero, and the liabilities are endless. One of those itemized listings would have read, "My enemies are stronger than I am," and you can be sure that's a man's depression talking. David would like to be counting his blessings, if only he knew where they all went.

Depression is certainly not the best venue for formulating objective conclusions. Sober reasoning is impossible. David goes on to compare himself to a man in prison in verse 7. And so he is; he is a prisoner of his own perspective. He has locked himself into the dungeon of despair and thrown away the key. We can only be thankful to God that he made his escape.

The Defeat of David's Discouragement

There can be no doubt that discouragement defeated David. There had been a time when he had sent a stone into a giant's head; now he had encountered a giant that could get into his own head. But for the people of God, there is never a pit too deep to escape. There is never a cave too dark for His light to illuminate. And finally, as the Scriptures attest, David defeated discouragement.

David traveled a path to liberation from the imprisonment of his mind, and he left a map for all of us to follow when we feel hopelessly lost in our despair. We simply need to listen to the Word of God.

David Verbalized His Problems to God

Have you ever asked the following question? *Why should I tell God my problems? If He knows everything, why should I bother to go into all the details?*

All I have to offer you is the biblical answer to that question, and I believe it is sufficient for us. We tell God about our problems because He has commanded us to do so. That certainly seems reason enough for me; how about you?

Even so, I can think of a few other reasons to open up before God. One of these can be found at the beginning of this psalm. Let David spell it out for you—not once, but three times:

- "I cry out to the LORD with my voice" (v. 1).
- "I cried out to You, O LORD" (v. 5).
- "Attend to my cry" (v. 6).

Perhaps David is a man after God's own heart because he is willing to share his own heart with God. He pours it all out before his Father, doesn't he? When David feels that he'd really love to see his enemies all die violently, that's exactly what he says. When he feels terribly sorry for himself, he shares exactly that. If you or I wrote a book of psalms, just how accurate a map of our souls would we lay out? Our map of the geography of David's heart, after thousands of years, is precise down to the smallest detail.

Prayer should be a time of no-holds-barred, straight-ahead communication with God. We cut to the root of the problem, and we're not afraid to name names. And when that happens, we feel a tremendous sense of unburdening ourselves before the most intimate Friend imaginable. He is listening, He cares, He responds, and we can tell Him anything at all.

Yet we have this lingering impression that God, as the CEO of the universe, is too busy and industrious to take time for our problems. We can't talk to the president, we can't talk to the governor, and maybe not even the mayor. Our calls will be screened by a small army of support personnel. So why should we expect the God of creation to take a call from us? Why should He care about our little problems? When we think along those lines, we're likely to sink deeper and deeper into depression.

Cast human logic and bureaucratic conventions aside. God has said we are to cast all our cares upon Him—period. If we hold back any burden, we short-circuit the healing process that He is so eager to bring about within us. We also shield ourselves from truths that we need to face honestly—truths that will suddenly become bright and clear the moment we bring them into the light of God's presence.

I found an enthusiastic endorsement of that truth in an unlikely place, an airline magazine. During a recent flight, I was thumbing through the usual pages of advertisements when I came across a little article on a topic that interested me: journaling. I went on to read the following:

> Battling illness and pain with pen and paper may be unorthodox, but it may also spell relief. "People who write for twenty minutes a day about traumatic events reduce their doctor visits, improve their immune systems and, among arthritis sufferers, use less medication and have greater mobility," says James W. Pennebaker, Ph.D., a professor at the University of Texas at Austin, who has conducted studies on the topic. . . . Why the relief? Suppressing negative emotions can weaken the immune system and arouse your fight-or-flight system, churning up blood pressure and heart rate. . . . Writing about conflict or trauma helps organize the experience. The net effect is that people can move beyond the stressful event.

The author quotes another Ph.D. Mark A. Lumley an associate professor of psychology at Wayne State University in Detroit. This scholar theorizes that the positive results of journaling have something to do with the nature of pain. "Writing . . . about stressful events relieves the emotional part of pain. That's when the patient says, 'I can still feel it, but it doesn't bother me as much.'"[3]

It is interesting to me that as science stumbles along in the modern world, it tends to come across truths that we've had for thousands of years in the Word of God. This particular article concluded that it's important for us to honestly express the issues of our lives. *Amen.* That's what the Lord has been trying to tell us all along.

If a candid journal can be a healthy thing, how much more can an honest prayerful expression be, when we bring our concerns before the Lord? Insert Almighty God into the equation of that magazine article, with all its research experts, and the effectiveness of what they're prescribing is elevated far beyond anything a psychologist can possibly imagine.

When you find yourself within the dark, cold walls of the cave, feeling isolated and depressed, aren't you glad we have the kind of God whose patience has no limits, whose love cannot be exhausted, and whose tender mercies never come to an end? Aren't you glad you can write down your thoughts then lift your voice and say, "Lord, here, I've expressed it! This is exactly what I'm feeling. And I know I can offer it to You without fear or shame."

When you do that, God begins the process of recovery.

David Recognized His Presence before God

David says, "When my spirit was overwhelmed within me, then You knew my path" (v. 3). David has verbalized his problems before God. He has unrolled them as if they were a great scroll holding all the secrets of his mind and heart. Suddenly he makes a startling realization: All this time he has been pouring out his heart, God was already at work with David on his discouragement. Every moment David felt overwhelmed by problems, God was busy dealing with them. Every second David despaired over the lack of God's presence, God was right there, as close as ever.

A friend of mine asked his little granddaughter, "What did you learn in Sunday school about God?"

She said, "What I learned is that God never says, 'Oops!'"

We laugh because we feel it's a charming little story. Then we realize it's a profound theological truth in disguise. God makes no mistakes. You never find yourself in a place that's not exactly where God

---

At times when we feel forsaken, may we know
the presence of the Holy Spirit who brings comfort to all human
hearts when we are willing to surrender ourselves.
May we be convinced that even before we reach
up to Thee, Thou art reaching down to us.

—Peter Marshall

---

expected you to be. David could never find a cave where God wasn't waiting for him, just as Jonah could never charter a boat capable of cruising outside the Lord's jurisdiction.

God knew about David and his depression and every single problem he'd ever had or would have in the future. God knows. Our term for that is *omniscient*. It means He knows every detail of your life and your feelings. Isn't that a comfort?

David Realized His Provision in God

He says, "You are my refuge, my portion in the land of the living" (v. 5). David has remembered he is praying to the Creator of heaven and earth. And now he begins to rejoice in the provision that God has made for him. An old African-American preacher once commented unforgettably on this verse: "There's no living in the land of the living like living in the living God!"

The land of the living is not a reference to eternity or heaven. It is a reference to living *right now*. Aren't you glad the Bible has been writ-

---

There has to be a song—
To make our burdens bearable,
To make our hopes believable,
To transform our successes into praise,
To release the chains of past defeats,
Somewhere—down deep in a forgotten
corner of each man's heart—
There has to be a song.

—Robert Benson

---

ten for people who are living in the land of the living? It's about so much more than "pie in the sky in the sweet by and by." The Bible is written for the rough realities of life, the nitty-gritty of the here and now. It is intended to help those of us who rise every morning, drive to work, and punch the clock to face genuine challenges. Its pages are filled with real-life solutions for real-life problems.

David Resumed His Praise to God

David writes, "Bring my soul out of prison, that I may praise Your name; the righteous shall surround me, for You shall deal bountifully with me" (v. 7). David has moved from the depths to the heights in these few verses, and he is ready to praise God again. Prayer will do that for us. We can pray our way right through the pressure. We can pray our way right through the sickness. We can pray our way right through the crises and the losses and the fears. If we will only come before Him honestly, He'll meet the needs in our lives—every one of them.

David has traveled from prison to praise. He recorded the journey in his masterpiece known as Psalm 142. And I like to imagine that he wrote a sequel. I enjoy picturing him recording the final word of Psalm 142, then turning the page of his journal to begin Psalm 57— another psalm written in that cave.

This piece is "a [teaching psalm] of David when he fled from Saul into the cave." Most scholars believe that Psalm 57 was written at the same time or in the same setting as Psalm 142. But this one is much more like a song. It's closer to the hymns we sing in joyful worship of God. It's structured in two verses and one chorus. The two verses play out, and after each verse, the chorus can be sung.

Be merciful to me, O God, be merciful to me! For my soul trusts in You; and in the shadow of Your wings I will make my refuge, until these calamities have passed by. I will cry out to God Most High, to God who performs all things for me. He shall send from heaven and save me; He reproaches the one who would swallow me up. Selah. God shall send forth His mercy and His truth. My soul is among lions; I lie among the sons of men who are set on fire, whose teeth are spears and arrows, and their tongue a sharp sword.

Now here is the chorus:

Be exalted, O God, above the heavens; Let Your glory be above all the earth.

Then David starts to sing verse 2:

They have prepared a net for my steps; my soul is bowed down; they have dug a pit before me; into the midst of it they themselves have fallen. Selah. My heart is steadfast, O God, my heart is steadfast; I will sing and give praise. Awake, my glory! Awake, lute and harp! I will awaken the dawn. I will praise You, O Lord, among the peoples; I will sing to You among the nations. For Your mercy reaches unto the heavens, and Your truth unto the clouds.

And then the chorus comes around again. Why not read it out loud?

Be exalted, O God, above the heavens; let Your glory be above all the earth.

Next time you read Psalm 142, continue on to the rich music of Psalm 57. It makes a fitting doxology to the honest emotional journey of the first cave psalm. We can just imagine David's beautiful singing voice, the first voice to sing so many of these immortal psalms, echoing through the cold, stony walls of the cavern—a beautiful melody dispersing the darkness. In an echo chamber, it doesn't take a loud voice to be heard for many miles:

"Be exalted, O God, above the heavens . . ."

Imagine the setting. The voice is clear and beautiful, soulful as befits a singer who has known years of deep turmoil. Nothing but the one voice can be heard in those rocky corridors. Then, suddenly, a rough, untrained voice joins him in unlikely harmony. The duet continues along. And just like that, one by one, a choir of four hundred ragged, rejected, and unloved singers is lifting one mighty choral voice together. Debtors and derelicts are making beautiful melody, accompanying a king in exile. There has never been such a concert, and there may never be another, unless it will occur in a Roman coliseum or a German prison camp—in a place where music and hope and laughter were thought to have been cast out forever. It is the music of the miraculous.

Tears and melody are now mingled without shame in a purity that is revealed whenever believers sing against all worldly expectation, when, for example, Glenda Palmer weeps through her chorus of

"How Great Thou Art." In a cave of exile, David and his choir pour out a song of praise. Their concert hall is a natural geological sound chamber, one whose acoustics were designed by God long ago, for this very earthshaking, despair-breaking moment.

The people sing on, praising God, their voices penetrate the massive stone of the natural ceiling to drift to the very portals of heaven, and perhaps even the angels stop to listen.

"Be exalted, O God, above the heavens . . ."

Psalm 107

1 Oh, give thanks to the LORD, for He is good!
  For His mercy endures forever.
2 Let the redeemed of the LORD say so,
  Whom He has redeemed from the hand of the enemy,
3 And gathered out of the lands,
  From the east and from the west,
  From the north and from the south.
4 They wandered in the wilderness in a desolate way;
  They found no city to dwell in.
5 Hungry and thirsty,
  Their soul fainted in them.
6 Then they cried out to the LORD in their trouble,
  And He delivered them out of their distresses.
7 And He led them forth by the right way,
  That they might go to a city for habitation.
8 Oh, that men would give thanks to the LORD for His goodness,
  And for His wonderful works to the children of men!
9 For He satisfies the longing soul,
  And fills the hungry soul with goodness.
10 Those who sat in darkness and in the shadow of death,
   Bound in affliction and irons—
11 Because they rebelled against the words of God,
   And despised the counsel of the Most High,
12 Therefore He brought down their heart with labor;
   They fell down, and there was none to help.
13 Then they cried out to the LORD in their trouble,
   And He saved them out of their distresses.
14 He brought them out of darkness and the shadow of death,
   And broke their chains in pieces.

15 Oh, that men would give thanks to the LORD for His goodness,
And for His wonderful works to the children of men!

16 For He has broken the gates of bronze,
And cut the bars of iron in two.

17 Fools, because of their transgression,
And because of their iniquities, were afflicted.

18 Their soul abhorred all manner of food,
And they drew near to the gates of death.

19 Then they cried out to the LORD in their trouble,
And He saved them out of their distresses.

20 He sent His word and healed them,
And delivered them from their destructions.

21 Oh, that men would give thanks to the LORD for His goodness,
And for His wonderful works to the children of men!

22 Let them sacrifice the sacrifices of thanksgiving,
And declare His works with rejoicing.

23 Those who go down to the sea in ships,
Who do business on great waters,

24 They see the works of the LORD,
And His wonders in the deep.

25 For He commands and raises the stormy wind,
Which lifts up the waves of the sea.

26 They mount up to the heavens,
They go down again to the depths;
Their soul melts because of trouble.

27 They reel to and fro, and stagger like a drunken man,
And are at their wits' end.

28 Then they cry out to the LORD in their trouble,
And He brings them out of their distresses.

29 He calms the storm,
So that its waves are still.

30 Then they are glad because they are quiet;
So He guides them to their desired haven.

31 Oh, that men would give thanks to the LORD for His goodness,
And for His wonderful works to the children of men!

³² Let them exalt Him also in the congregation of the people,
And praise Him in the assembly of the elders.

³³ He turns rivers into a wilderness,
And the watersprings into dry ground;

³⁴ A fruitful land into barrenness,
For the wickedness of those who dwell in it.

³⁵ He turns a wilderness into pools of water,
And dry land into watersprings.

³⁶ There He makes the hungry dwell,
That they may establish a city for habitation,

³⁷ And sow fields and plant vineyards,
That they may yield a fruitful harvest.

³⁸ He also blesses them, and they multiply greatly;
And He does not let their cattle decrease.

³⁹ When they are diminished and brought low
Through oppression, affliction and sorrow,

⁴⁰ He pours contempt on princes,
And causes them to wander in the wilderness where there is no way;

⁴¹ Yet He sets the poor on high, far from affliction,
And makes their families like a flock.

⁴² The righteous see it and rejoice,
And all iniquity stops its mouth.

⁴³ Whoever is wise will observe these things,
And they will understand the lovingkindness of the LORD.

9

When You Are at Your Wits' End

The Lord's our rock, in Him we hide,
Secure whatever ill betide
A shelter in the time of storm

The raging storms may round us beat
We'll never leave our safe retreat,
A shelter in the time of storm.

—IRA SANKEY

When I was first diagnosed with cancer, I went to certain special people for counsel and comfort. One of these was Dr. Marv Eastlund of Fort Wayne, Indiana. I knew he was a man who would fill three critical roles: first, as a close, trusted friend of many years; second, as a career physician of excellence; third, as a fellow struggler who had grappled with serious illness in his own life. I leaned on his support, advice, and brotherly encouragement; I'll never forget his ministry to me.

Dr. Eastlund's bend in the road was a pancreatic disorder. I've asked him to tell you about the medical misadventure that landed him flat on his back for several weeks at the Mayo Clinic.

There are certain kinds of change none of us ask for, and none of us receive with open arms. In my life, pancreatitis was an uninvited visitor—

the last item that would ever have appeared on my agenda. I was thoroughly miserable when the doctors broke the news to me about it.

The dreadful disease moved into my life like a tornado, demolishing my control over my life, my career, and all my plans for the future. My first reaction was intense anger, to be honest. I resisted this outrageous medical intrusion and fought it with all the energy I could muster. One of my main weapons was denial. I insisted on keeping my usual schedule and simply ignoring the pain.

That was a losing battle, as I'm sure you can imagine. The pancreatitis won. I soon reached my pain threshold, and I could no longer pretend that my body was fine and healthy. I was filled with anger. Who could I blame? I could find no scapegoat, so I blamed myself. Anger gave way to discouragement and self-pity. I wallowed in my own misery for extended periods of time, fully realizing that I was sick—really sick—and that my life would never again be the same. What response was there for me but despair and gloom? I became consumed with my own problems. And if there was any small thread of hope left within me, the repeated hospitalizations snuffed it out.

Discouragement gave way to depression. There were days I could do nothing but sit and stare. My family tried desperately to encourage me, but I made certain they didn't succeed. I was investing a good bit of energy in my negative emotions, and I didn't want to cheer up. Life was unfair. The future was hopeless.

And yet deep within me, there was the nagging question of my faith. I couldn't give up the life commitment I had made to God. He meant too much for me to simply turn away from Him. So I was being torn by great spiritual conflict: How could a believer experience the thoughts and emotions I was feeling? Why had God let me sink into anger, discouragement, and depression? If my faith was as strong as I'd always thought it was, why, then—how, then—could I now be questioning His very existence? Where was He? Why didn't He answer my pleas?

My faith was on very rocky ground indeed. Physically, mentally, and spiritually, I had come to my wits' end. I had nowhere to turn. So I lay down on my back one day, sighed deeply, and stared up at the ceiling. And as I did that, I realized that my eyes were fixed in the right direction—up. I was looking toward heaven. *Up* was the only direction a bed patient could look. And with new resolution, I realized I had to be faithful to Him and keep trusting Him. I could not turn

---

From this side of glory we see the tapestry from underneath, and it is full of knots and twisted threads and frayed ends that lack meaning and beauty. From God's perspective, it is all under control.

—Charles Swindoll

---

away. As distant as He seemed at times, I realized that my pain and despair only served to draw me closer to Him than health and happiness could ever have brought me.

Through the pain, I began to know Him better. I found a friend in God, a *genuine* Friend I had never known before.

I see my problems differently now. When life closes in, I know that the only way out is the way up.

God is a genuine friend—Dr. Eastlund found that out, and the psalms repeat that rich theme over and over.

Pictures of Helplessness

Psalm 107 celebrates the friendship and the faithfulness of God. It's a beloved hymn of thanksgiving for His deliverance. We can find, in the section spanning verses 4 through 32, four word pictures of circumstances faced by God's people along their journey. These four separate pictures have a common overlapping theme: the human feeling of helplessness.

We'll be taking a close look at these fine pictures. As we do so, I invite you to imagine you and me walking through the Bible's great gallery of art. It is a fabulous museum, filled with inspiring portraits and fantastic renderings in every corner. We've begun with the beautiful landscapes of the tranquillity of the Garden of Eden, the towering summit of Sinai, and the pastoral beauty of Canaan. We've seen portraits of prophets, priests, and patriarchs. Finally, as we enter the building known as the Book of Psalms, we come to Room 107. It's a thought-provoking gallery. We'll need to spend some time here in contemplation.

Here are four paintings carefully rendered by the artist whose goal is to portray four great challenges of life. I'll be serving as your tour guide for this particular room, and I ask you to keep up with the group and, please—no flashbulbs! As we study the paintings, I will pause briefly at the first three to make some general comments. Then we'll engage in an in-depth exploration of the fourth and final painting. This one is the culmination of the other three, a masterpiece filled with emotion and symbolism that will astonish you. We will spend the majority of our time there, and I predict you'll be coming back to gaze at the painting on your own time and again.

But let's begin our tour, shall we?

Painting #1: The Desert

The first painting is a landscape, but it's not one you're likely to see from the brush of your typical painter. This landscape happens to be a desert.

We might call this one "Wanderers in the Wilderness." The title would draw its inspiration from a description found in verses 4 through 9 of Psalm 107. There we read about the experience of being lost in the desert. Of course, we realize that not all deserts are composed of sand, and we can be lost without losing our physical bearings. Listen to the word picture painted by the psalmist: "They wandered in the wilderness in a desolate way; they found no city to dwell in. Hungry and thirsty, their soul fainted in them." We grow thirsty just hearing these words.

Many have lost their way in a dry wilderness, devoid of meaning and purpose. For some, the desert is loneliness. Others are lost in a cycle of routine futility. Still others become dislocated in a desert of affluence, which turns out to be a drier and thirstier land than they ever expected. The wanderers trudge through the sand without hope or help, seeking the true spiritual home that always eludes them.

As we move to the next portico, we find a different scenario.

Painting #2: The Prison

The desert may have seemed an odd subject for a painting, but verse 10 offers one even less likely. It is a group portrait of prisoners, "those who sat in darkness and in the shadow of death, bound in affliction and irons."

Leonard Griffith writes, "People are like prisoners, trapped in the dungeon of their own moral folly, the victims of evil rather than the doers of it. They started out with freedom of choice, but they continued to choose the wrong thing." But that freedom will be fleeting when we choose evil. The wrong choices become patterns of behavior that finally master those who made the choices. "The drug addict would give anything to be set free from the chains of his habit, but it has him hooked and he knows that the end of it will be his death. . . . In his sober moments, the alcoholic hates himself for the hell that he creates in his own home, but his bottle is like a chain, and he knows that he cannot break loose from it."[1]

So there are prisons of addiction—gambling, drugs, and alcohol—but there are also prisons of abuse or of improper relationships. People are taken prisoner by their own conduct.

Not all prisons are of our own making, however. Some of us are trapped by difficult circumstances from which there seems little hope of escape. These prisons might have been constructed by other people's evil, by persecution, or by matters over which they have no control. We don't have to be at fault to become hopeless captives. Our painting shows the desolation of imprisonment, and it saddens us to look upon this canvas. We take one more look, and we move on.

Painting #3: The Hospital

Now we come to the portrayal of a familiar but forbidding setting, that of a hospital. In verses 17 through 22, we find something not too different from an ICU. Are you surprised to find that in the Bible?

In me there is darkness, but with Thee there is light.

I am lonely but Thou leavest me not.

I am feeble in heart, but Thou leavest me not.

I am restless, but with Thee there is peace.

In me there is bitterness, but with Thee there is patience;

Thy ways are past understanding,

but Thou knowest the way for me.

—Dietrich Bonhoeffer

Look closely at the picture painted for us in these verses: "Fools, because of their transgression, and because of their iniquities, were afflicted. Their soul abhorred all manner of food, and they drew near to the gates of death" (vv. 17–18). This is a ward of illness and affliction, and it serves as a corridor that opens into the darkness of death.

Not every illness, of course, is caused by sin. But the people here have poisoned themselves with their own transgressions. They are suffering, ready for the release brought only by death. There in the ward they lie, waiting only for their final moments on this earth. That's the story laid out for us in the third of the four paintings. We take in its gloomy canvas and move to the last picture. This one is larger than the others, and it captures our full attention.

Painting #4: The Storm

The picture causes us to catch our breath. It captures perfectly the power of nature in all its unleashed fury. As our eyes move across the canvas, we know what it means to be clinging to the deck of a ship that is caught in a terrible storm. We take the forces of nature for granted—until we become their helpless prey.

We know how the disciples felt, violently tossed in the nighttime waves and fearing death before Jesus came. We know how the passengers of the *Titanic* felt on a far calmer night—but one in which the greatest ship ever built was no match for a stray block of ice. We're gazing at the portrait of a furious tempest:

> Those who go down to the sea in ships, who do business on great waters, they see the works of the LORD, and His wonders in the deep. For He commands and raises the stormy wind, which lifts up the waves of the sea. They mount up to the heavens, they go down again to the depths; their soul melts because of trouble. They reel to and fro, and stagger like a drunken man, and are at their wits' end. Then they cry out to the LORD in their trouble, and He brings them out of their distresses. He calms the storm, so that its waves are still. Then they are glad because they are quiet; so He guides them to their desired haven. Oh, that men would give thanks to the LORD for His goodness, and for His wonderful works to the children of men! Let them exalt Him also in the congregation of the people, and praise Him in the assembly of the elders. (Ps. 107:23–32)

A Closer Look at the Storm

The Place of the Storm

These sailors realize their small stature, their seeming insignificance, out on the open sea. There is no land in sight. There is no one to rescue those in peril on the sea.

You may never have crossed the ocean on a large ship, but the picture will remain just as powerful for you—for we all know what it's like to be caught in one of life's many storms. You realize immediately that towering waves and billowing storms can come in many forms.

When I've encountered the storms of my own life, I've taken encouragement from this psalm. It has always been when I've ventured out onto the open sea, when I've been taking a great step of faith and moving beyond the borders of safety, that I've been caught by the treacherous winds. I feel certain that I'm pursuing the will of God for my life, but my faith is sternly tested by the wind and the rain. That's when I have thought about the assurances of Psalm 107. At the end of this chapter, I'll tell you how this psalm became permanently etched on my soul.

For now, let's consider Jesus and the small circle of men around Him. They understood the terror of the tempest. They also understood the mystery of deep waters. We know this from Luke 5:4–6, when Jesus commanded Simon Peter to "launch out into the deep and let down your nets for a catch." Simon grumbled a little about this, reminding the carpenter from Nazareth that the professionals—men who knew their trade—had been fishing all night, and they hadn't caught a thing. Nevertheless, Simon said, if that's what Jesus wanted, the boys would take one more shot. And you know the rest. After one more trip, the nets were overflowing, literally bursting with fish.

The message? Great works are done in deep waters. If you're diving for pearls, you have to move out of the shallow end. Many of us never learn that lesson; fear restricts us to the comfort zone, where we miss out on untold adventures. But Jesus tells us to launch out into the deep—in risk taking, in the pursuit of excellence, and in the knowledge of Him. We walk to the edge of all our light, and that next step into the blackness holds the destiny God has for us. But it also holds whatever dangers lie in the darkness. We know that, we realize the risks, and perhaps we'll never take that one terrifying step that makes the miracle possible.

It's not simply biblical sense—it's common sense as well. If you're in the business world, you realize that. Play it safe, and you'll never build a business. Launching a new firm is launching out into the deep. The storms are certain to come, and the winds will howl. You'll be out on the edge, all by yourself in an unsteady boat. Perhaps your business will fail despite all your best efforts and intentions. But you'll never know unless you cast the net.

No one ever said it would be easy out in the deep waters. No one ever guaranteed fair weather and smooth sailing. It's your choice—stay along the shore and you'll always be safe from drowning and disaster. But you'll also never know the blessings of the deep things of God.

The Producer of the Storm

What's wrong with this picture? What seems unusual about the storm depicted in this psalm?

"For He commands and raises the stormy wind, which lifts up the waves of the sea" (v. 25). The pronoun *He* is capitalized. Now we realize the striking thing about this storm. As great as the power of the wind and the waves may be, there is something—Someone—more powerful in the background, behind it all. It is God—the God who sends the rains.

Did you step back from the canvas when you realized that detail? Are you shocked? We're much more comfortable crediting God with calming storms than with causing them. And yet we must take the Scripture at its word. The Bible teaches us that He is Lord of all—and that includes the storms that serve His purposes along with everything else.

Let's take care before blaming God for every storm, however. Sometimes we've done just fine on our own bringing on those dark clouds. We make the mistakes, and God's place is simply to let us discover how deeply we need Him when we're just about to go under the waves. So we're not referring to those self-induced tempests. We're talking about storms brought about expressly by divine intention. And those do exist.

Job understood that. He had a disciplined understanding that character is a function of trial, and even trials were deeply tied to His friendship and faith in God. He said, "He knows the way that I take;

when He has tested me, I shall come forth as gold" (Job 23:10). *He knows.* Job found strength in the knowledge that God knew him intimately, and he set out with the understanding that tests would deepen that friendship. When the storms came, he was prepared. Even during the most excruciating pain, Job knew God was in control of his problems. He knew that pain had a purpose.

Listen to this expression of the same understanding in Psalm 66: "You brought us into the net; you laid affliction on our backs. You have caused men to ride over our heads; we went through fire and through water; but You brought us out to rich fulfillment" (vv. 11–12). Have you felt people "riding over your head" at your workplace recently? Have you been through fire and water in family problems? A devoted believer will pray for God's deliverance from problems, but a wiser one will pray for God's use of them.

Even Jonah—rebellious, dispassionate Jonah—knew Who was behind the storms. When God sent him on a mission, he booked passage on a ship and headed in the opposite direction as quickly as he could. The belief that he could run away demonstrated an appallingly limited view of God. His God was too small! But the ensuing tempest enlarged his perspective. Here was a God who could trouble the sea. Job realized that he could run, but he couldn't hide. The Lord sent the storm just as He sent Jonah. Jonah was God's messenger to the Ninevites, but the storm was God's message to Jonah.

Why did He send the storm in your life? Is it intended to cut off your flight from God, as in the case of Jonah? Is it to draw you closer, as in Job's life? If you're weathering a storm, you can be certain the winds are no random weather front. They blow for a clear purpose. As you're caught up in a tempest, ask God to help you be caught up in His purposes.

The Peril of the Storm

"They mount up to the heavens, they go down again to the depths; their soul melts because of trouble. They reel to and fro, and stagger like a drunken man, and are at their wits' end" (Ps. 107:26–27). What an image God paints on the canvas of our minds here!

In his masterful paraphrase, *The Message*, Eugene Peterson rewords the passage like this: "You shot high in the sky, then the bottom dropped out; your hearts were stuck in your throats. You were spun like a top, you reeled like a drunk, you didn't know which way was

---

Usually prayer is a question of groaning rather than speaking,

tears rather than words. For He sets our tears in His sight,

and our groaning is not hidden from Him

Who made all things by His Word

and does not ask for words of man.

—Augustine of Hippo

---

up." This is a riot of mixed metaphors, of course, in the service of a strong point—the "you" in this passage is spinning wildly out of control! Have you ever lost control of an automobile on an icy highway? If so, you know this feeling well. These passengers of the rocking ship are at their wits' end.

By the way, did you know where the expression "at your wits' end" came from? Right here in the psalms. These people have been outwitted. They've come to the end of all their ideas and strategies. The tempest has mastered their vessel. The ship has set off to navigate the winds and the waters, but that's all been turned upside down. The wind and the waters are now navigating the ship. The passengers can do little but watch—and pray.

The Prayer in the Storm

Unfortunately, prayer seems to be our last port in a storm. It should be the first. But the people of this passage do turn to God in verse 28: "Then they cry out to the LORD in their trouble, and He brings them out of their distresses." Have you ever noticed the inverse relationship between depth of crisis and length of prayer? You could almost create a mathematical formula to demonstrate that the calmer things are, the lengthier and more eloquent our prayers tend to be. But the greater the storm, the shorter and simpler we pray—starting with this classic prayer adopted by many devout and troubled believers over the centuries: "Help!"

When we were living in Fort Wayne, Indiana, the driveway of our little house emptied out into a busy highway. For us, a simple trip to buy groceries was a guaranteed adventure. One day, I was sitting in the passenger seat while Donna backed out into traffic—and never saw the approaching car. But I did, right at the last moment. I looked up, anticipated the collision, and blurted out, "Lord—help!" Yes, the car hit us; but it barely missed the side of the car where I was seated, and I escaped a serious injury. I assure you I have several prayers more inspiring and articulate than "Lord—help!" But it was just the thing for that occasion—precisely the right length.

The seafarers of the psalm may have called out the same words, and probably more than once. Their circumstances have certain similarities to the characters in the other paintings. Let's look at the first picture again. The desert wanderers, hopelessly lost, "cried out to the LORD in their trouble, and He delivered them out of their distresses" (v. 6).

How about those prisoners in their cell? What are they saying? "Then they cried out to the LORD in their trouble, and He saved them out of their distresses" (v. 13).

Meanwhile, back in the sterile, deathlike hospital ward, what are the patients saying? "Then they cried out to the LORD in their trouble, and He saved them out of their distresses" (v. 19).

In the storms, in the wilderness, in captivity, and in illness, people desperately seek an escape. And Dr. Marv Eastlund has said it for all of us: The only way *out* is the way *up*. No matter what the problem may be, no matter what trouble may ensnare us, there is only one path to safety. The only hope is to reach beyond ourselves to Someone stronger than we are, and stronger than the shackles that bind us. Only One can fill that requirement. And even the proverbial atheist in the foxhole realizes it in the depths of his heart. Even the most thoroughgoing skeptic will finally come to that point of absolute desperation and look up to the heavens to cry, "Lord—help!"

God's part in the storm is a sensitive topic for us right now—it hits a little too close to home, for many of us are being tossed around by ill winds at this very moment. We fear that if we stopped to consider that God may be the Author of the storm, we might be overcome with anger at God. And yet I imagine arriving in heaven when my day comes, and hearing my Lord admit that He has used storms quite frequently to drive me to my knees. I'll be capable of handling the knowledge of it then, and He'll smile and say, "That one was a real corker, wasn't it, David? That crisis you went through that particular year? I really had you going! But now you can see that it brought you back into My camp at just the right time. You weren't paying as much attention to Me in those days, remember? You were drifting, and where might you have finally ended up if I hadn't stepped in and done something to get your attention? Remember how it all paid off? I'm sure you never realized how that whole crisis prepared you for the good things to follow!" And for the first time, I'll be able to laugh about some sore spot or other; we'll laugh together, but in a joyful way.

God certainly hates everything that causes us pain, whether it may be imprisonment or illness or a storm of some kind. But He knows that lesser pain is a necessary part of avoiding far deeper pain later. It hurts to pull out a thorn, but the pain of leaving it would cause the deeper agony of infection. God knows that He has to pull out a few thorns occasionally, and we'll cry out in pain and even anger at Him. But it's all for a purpose.

God knows, even if we don't, that we're not self-sufficient. He loves to bring us to our knees in fresh dependence on Him. If only peacetime prayers carried the intensity of storm-tossed prayers! If only we could seek Him with the passion that possesses us when we feel trapped and desperate. God hears those passionate prayers. And He provides the peace that can be found nowhere else.

The Peace in the Storm

"He calms the storm, so that its waves are still. Then they are glad because they are quiet" (vv. 29–30).

Have you ever noticed the wonderful purity of silence after a prolonged cacophony of noise? The tyranny of sound suddenly loses its hold on us, and the ensuing quiet seems to liberate the spirit. It's truly a peace that passes understanding. We refer to this phenomenon as "the calm after the storm." It's about comfort and relief. Deep inside us, we realize that the Bringer of the storm is also the Master of it; He can take it away in the blink of an eye. When we realize He is great enough to send and remove storms, we fall down in worship.

When the people of the psalm were being battered by the storm, they cried out in fear and helplessness. And God responded. He calmed the storm and stilled the waves. And that idea quickly reminds us of the stories of Jesus. The events played out in Psalm 107 foreshadow the remarkable episodes we find in the Gospels. The disciples, having chosen to pursue the Teacher and the adventure He called them for, found themselves in the middle of turbulent experiences, challenges for which they must have felt ill-prepared. We can read these accounts and realize the Lord was allowing the storms to break loose because He wanted them to learn lessons that would serve them well later. They would face persecution. They would face hostility and terrible odds against an intimidating goal. They could not learn the lessons and build the strength in any other classroom than the stormy seas.

On one occasion, the disciples climbed into a boat to travel across the Sea of Galilee. Jesus boarded with them, crawled into the back, found a nice spot, and went to sleep. As they traveled far out to sea, suddenly the weather changed. A storm front quickly rolled in, and it looked like a serious one. Here were the disciples, hopelessly far from safety; surely they were going to die together. According to Matthew 8, Jesus awoke, took a good look around, and asked why His friends were so worked up. He also dropped in a stinging remark about the weakness of their faith. Then he stood in the boat, rebuked the winds and the sea, and watched the calm settle as far as the eye could see.

That's Matthew's story. But it's rewarding to discover what Luke adds to the picture. Always the astute observer of human emotions, he shows us the dimension of fear the disciples experienced. It is in Luke's account that we find out how some of the men came to Jesus and jostled Him awake, gasping, "Master, Master, we are perishing!" (Luke 8:24).

These fishermen and tax collectors and assorted commoners were shaking the arm of the Lord of glory, the One who created the winds and the waves and the sea that had them so frightened. If they had realized the full import of this, they wouldn't have demonstrated so much panic in the way they roused Him. They might even have been looking forward to the show Jesus was capable of putting on as He stilled the storm. But they were fully expecting to die. I've always been impressed by this story, and years ago I scribbled a little note next to it in the margin of my Bible. My note reads, "We are far more secure in the storm with Jesus in our boat than we will ever be on the shore without Him."

And I still believe that. If you've opted to pursue the adventure of following Jesus, you've already discovered that the journey doesn't occur in a luxury limousine. He will lead you to and through some rough places. It may be that you've found yourself in the "old gospel ship," rocked by the waves and thrashed by the downpour as lightning and thunder boomed all around you. The moment may come when you say, "I didn't sign up for this! I know I sang, 'Wherever He leads, I'll go,' but can't we at least check the weather report first? How could He lead me into a storm like this one?"

Just cling to the knowledge that you could be in no safer place than a storm of His making. You are safer and more secure in the tempest with Jesus than you could ever be in the calmest place without Him. That calm, you'll come to realize, is an illusion; and the storm is for a good purpose and a short duration.

Speaking of storms, my friend Ron Mehl tells about a woman who was caught in a frightening storm in the middle of the Atlantic Ocean. She was aboard a luxury liner carrying a large number of children. The woman saw that everyone else was panicking, running to and fro through all the passages. All this was upsetting the children, so she gathered them together and began telling them Bible stories to keep them calm. The children became quiet, captivated by the wonderful stories.

The ship made it through, safe and sound. As the captain made his rounds, he saw the woman laughing and talking with the children. She had stayed calm through the storm, and she was calm now. He was puzzled. "How did you keep your cool when everyone else was falling to pieces?" he asked her. "Have you been through something like this before?"

"It's simple," said the woman. "I have two daughters. One of them lives in New York and the other one lives in heaven. I knew I would see one or the other of them in a few hours and it didn't make any difference to me which one."

Does that story seem a trifle sentimental and unrealistic to you? It shouldn't. It simply describes the mind-set of the serious believer—the follower who takes Jesus at His Word. If you feel such a story is simply sentimental, you may feel the same way about heaven and the concept that God is in control. Grace through the storm is a function of believing that the Creator of the storm is also the Deliverer from it. He is also the One who can bring us peace and strength when all those around us are falling to pieces.

He is our Deliverer, and that fact is gloriously portrayed in living color in every canvas of the eternal gallery known as Psalm 107. The first painting shows desert wanderers—those who can't find the path. "And He led them forth by the right way, that they might go to a city for habitation" (v. 7). *A city for a habitation*—the very words that define hope and peace when you've been lost in the desert.

Then we revisit the darkened prison. What happens to the captives? Someone comes to unlock their cell and show them the sunlight again. "He brought them out of darkness and the shadow of death, and broke their chains in pieces" (v. 14).

Over in the hospital, patients hover near death—only to be healed miraculously. "He sent His word and healed them, and delivered them from their destructions" (v. 20).

Downpour or desert, dungeon or disease—the specific facts of the crisis ultimately don't matter. For God is in control. Wherever we are, whatever we may be up against, when we cry out to God in our trouble, He will hear us. He will calm the waters. And the time may come when He will even let us know the reasons He unleashed them.

The Purpose of the Storm

"So He guides them to their desired haven" (v. 30).

The Lord didn't stop at delivering the people from the storm. He took them where they needed to go. There's only one twist: The storm may change our idea of a destination. Crises never leave us the same as they found us. Those of us who love and trust God through the worst times—those of us who are receptive to what He might be trying to teach us—find that our hearts have changed by the time the stillness replaces the storminess. We will be far more in tune with His desires. Our goals will have moved closer to His own.

If you doubt that point, you might want to ask Jonah a few questions. Was he a different man after the whale spit him up onto the shore? Were his purposes closer to God's purposes after he discovered what can be wrought from disobedience? He came out of the belly of a whale and hit the ground running. There were no roads that could deliver him to Nineveh fast enough.

God changes our *want-to* in the midst of His storms.

The Praise after the Storm

What is there for us in that time when the calm returns but to praise our God? And how we wish everyone we know, and all men and women on the face of the earth, would join us in worship and exaltation. He is greater than any of the forces of nature.

"Oh, that men would give thanks to the LORD for His goodness, and for His wonderful works to the children of men! Let them exalt

Him also in the congregation of the people, and praise Him in the assembly of the elders" (vv. 31–32).

We've been hopelessly lost in the barren wilderness, and suddenly we find ourselves in an oasis. What do we do? We give thanks. "Oh, that men would give thanks to the LORD for His goodness, and for His wonderful works to the children of men! For He satisfies the longing soul, and fills the hungry soul with goodness" (vv. 8–9).

We've been imprisoned by addiction or abuse or past memories or another cruel master—when we discover a Master who is loving and who frees us. What do we do? We give thanks. "Oh, that men would give thanks to the LORD for His goodness, and for His wonderful works to the children of men! For He has broken the gates of bronze, and cut the bars of iron in two" (vv. 15–16).

In the first two word-pictures in Psalm 107, we offer thanksgiving to the Lord for what He has done. But in the last two pictures, the image changes.

We've been desperately ill, waiting only for death. How do we respond to healing? We come together for worship. "Oh, that men would give thanks to the LORD for His goodness, and for His wonderful works to the children of men! Let them sacrifice the sacrifices of thanksgiving, and declare His works with rejoicing" (vv. 21–22).

And finally, we make it through the storm. God brings us through, and what do we do? We assemble for thanksgiving, praise, and worship. "Oh, that men would give thanks to the LORD for His goodness, and for His wonderful works to the children of men! Let them exalt Him also in the congregation of the people, and praise Him in the assembly of the elders" (vv. 31–32).

Is it really important to include other people in this celebration? Shouldn't it be enough simply to thank God quietly, in the privacy and sincerity of our own hearts?

I hear that sentiment more and more frequently these days. "I don't really need to worship God in a church," people say. "I can worship Him just as well by myself, working in my garden on a Sunday morning, or up at my lake cottage."

It sounds convenient, but it's not very biblical. We're told all through Scripture to come together in the assembly for the exaltation of God together. "In the presence of the elders," that is, of the leaders, we give praise to God. Together we become something greater than we could ever be individually. Together we offer an entirely different brand of worship than we offer in solitude. Together we are the living body of Christ.

From Raging Storm to Rejoicing

I have turned to Psalm 107 in my Bible through the years, and its meaning for me grows as I advance in age. This psalm, I feel, has my name written on it. I've felt that way ever since something that happened early in my ministry at our current church.

Almighty God, Father of all mercies, we, Your unworthy servants, give You humble thanks for all Your goodness and loving-kindness to us and to all men. We bless You for our creation, preservation, and all the blessings of this life; but above all for Your incomparable love in redemption of the world by our Lord Jesus Christ; for the means of grace, and for the hope of glory. And, we pray, give us such an awareness of Your mercies, that with truly thankful hearts we may make known Your praise, not only with our lips, but in our lives, by giving up ourselves to Your service, and by walking before You in holiness and righteousness all our days through Jesus Christ our Lord, to whom, with You and the Holy Spirit, be all honor and glory through all ages, Amen.

*—A General Thanksgiving,
Book of Common Prayer*

I've been pastor at Shadow Mountain Community Church for more than nineteen years. But in the early years of my time here, I held two jobs. I accepted a call not only to pastor the church, but also to become the president of Christian Heritage College. I had a strong feeling of God's leading in holding both positions. But I never saw the storm front that was moving in. Eight years ago, the college was seriously ill, hanging on by a thread.

During one particular summer we had run out of resources, the tuition money was gone, and existing funds were insufficient to carry us through to the fall. The church had underwritten us, but now those resources were no longer available. The church had simply given all it could give. Nearly every week, I attended meetings in which we agonized over what to do. Slowly but surely, we were edging toward the idea of simply closing the doors of the college. We even met with another Christian college to explore the possibility of a merger. I remember wondering if this was what God had in mind—but I could feel no peace about it.

One day I was filled with a sense of the storm. I felt like the waves were crashing over us, and that we were drowning in the waves. I didn't know what to do. I gathered our senior staff, and we all traveled to a local Christian camp called Pine Valley. It was vacant, and the caretakers allowed us to use one of their conference rooms. Our group gathered around the table to pray, but I still felt a deep sense of despair and hopelessness. No options were appearing; our prayers weren't being answered, or so it seemed. We'd tried everything we could think of trying.

And then I came to Psalm 107.

It was the storm. My feeling of enduring a storm reminded me of the imagery in the psalm. So as we sat there in the conference room at Pine Valley, I opened my Bible and I read this passage to the group. I told the senior staff, "There is one crucial thing we can never forget. Together we have chosen to do business in the great waters—deep waters. Not many churches have schools, but we have several. We have a preschool, three elementary schools, a junior high school, a high school, and a college. We've pursued these out of obedience to

God's leadership. It's not supposed to be easy. We've launched out into the deep, and we shouldn't be surprised to find ourselves caught in the storm."

We talked about the challenge at hand, and I returned to the theme of the psalm. "What we have to do is to *cry out to the Lord*. We have to ask God to move into the midst of this situation and do something that only He can do."

I've experienced few events like that one, and I'll never forget what followed. We began to pray around the table with very intense, heart-felt emotion. It was one of those powerful, spiritually charged atmospheres that come about when needy Christians get serious about seeking God's deliverance. There were tears; there was pleading. There was a knock at the door.

It was the proprietor of the camp. She motioned for me to come out into the hall, where she told me, "You need to call your office."

I found a pay phone and called Glenda at the church office. She said, "Are you sitting down?"

I said, "Glenda, I'm in a phone booth."

"Well if you can't sit down, hang on," she began. And this is what she told me. She said the women down in the college mailroom had been routinely opening mail. They came across a strange envelope— it contained no letter. No letter at all, but it did have a check inside— *a check for half a million dollars.*

I went back into the meeting with my eyes filled with tears, and everyone was anxious. They wanted me to tell them who had died. I said, "No one has died! Let me tell you what has happened. We've been sitting here in this room, in the midst of a storm. We've been crying out to God for His help, and He heard our pleas. He reached out to us in our trouble and brought us into a place of peace."

To say that we began to praise God would be an understatement. When you come out of a storm in which all had seemed lost, and God does something magnificent, the worship is unforgettable!

That's known as a happy ending. Do you still have doubts that your story will have one? Perhaps the storm is raging for you as you read these words. Perhaps you're lost in a wilderness of shattered hope, or shut away in a prison of debt. Perhaps you face a hospital ward of health concerns, or family problems are rocking your boat and you feel you'll be lost forever.

Wherever you are, whatever the crisis may be, there is an important principle at work. If you feel helpless, you've become eligible for the assistance of God. You need only cry out for His salvation. He will do the rest in His time, *and He'll do it well.*

When the storm is over, you'll be a new creature—wiser, stronger, and ready to serve Him. The sea will be calm, the breeze will be soft, and the silence will present itself as a sanctuary for you to exalt His name and sing His glorious praises. If He can control the storm, what other wonderful works might He bring to pass in your life?

With that exciting thought, you'll cast off and launch out into the deep waters.

Psalm 46

1 God is our refuge and strength,
A very present help in trouble.

2 Therefore we will not fear,
Though the earth be removed,
And though the mountains be carried into the midst of the sea;

3 Though its waters roar and be troubled,
Though the mountains shake with its swelling. Selah

4 There is a river whose streams shall make glad the city of God,
The holy place of the tabernacle of the Most High.

5 God is in the midst of her, she shall not be moved;
God shall help her, just at the break of dawn.

6 The nations raged, the kingdoms were moved;
He uttered His voice, the earth melted.

7 The LORD of hosts is with us;
The God of Jacob is our refuge. Selah

8 Come, behold the works of the LORD,
Who has made desolations in the earth.

9 He makes wars cease to the end of the earth;
He breaks the bow and cuts the spear in two;
He burns the chariot in the fire.

10 Be still, and know that I am God;
I will be exalted among the nations,
I will be exalted in the earth!

11 The LORD of hosts is with us;
the God of Jacob is our refuge. Selah.

10

Triumph over Trouble

A mighty fortress is our God
A bulwark never failing,
Our helper He amid the flood
Of mortal ills prevailing.

—MARTIN LUTHER,

"A MIGHTY FORTRESS IS OUR GOD"

It was October 1998. I was on my way to Charlotte, North Carolina, where I'd been invited to preach for a prayer ministry. I have a friend in that city, Pastor Page, who has struggled with a very rare variety of leukemia. We've compared notes over the last couple of years, sharing back and forth about my cancer and his leukemia.

By the time I arrived in Charlotte, I was quite weary. Cross-country flights have that effect. But the schedule was tight, and there was no time to catch my breath. In little more than the blink of an eye, I was sitting at a banquet, talking with the pastor and his wife about stem cell transplants. Pastor Page has endured two rounds of that procedure, and he and his wife cataloged all the highlights for me. But there was a strange feeling in the back of my mind. Have you ever had the odd impression that you should listen closely to someone—that this person's words could very likely become important to you in the future? I felt this distinctly. It wasn't a pleasant thought, but I wondered if I was being prepared for something that lay in my future.

The evening, however, was a fine one. My preaching time was well received, and afterward I lingered to meet and mingle with the friendly people. All of this happened on a Friday night at the end of a busy autumn week. But I had miles to go before I could sleep. I still had to drive to Boone, North Carolina. I looked forward to attending my son's college football game there on Saturday.

By the time I found my way to the condo where I was to stay the night, I didn't want to think about how late it was. I believe it was at least 2:00 A.M., following a full day of packing, flying, speaking, and driving. The Appalachian air had a bite to it, so I climbed wearily into bed and coiled myself into blankets and bedding, more than ready to sleep like a rock.

But it didn't happen that way.

It was in the middle of the night when I awoke. Perspiration was flowing and my bedclothes were drenched. It was as if I'd just come in from the rain, and I had to get out of bed and change into something else. This was a completely new experience for me, but I had no doubt about the meaning. The doctors, you see, had been preparing me for this possibility. Every time I'd been in for a checkup, I'd heard the stern question, "Have you had any night sweats?" While my answer had always been no, I'd learned that this was one of the sure symptoms of lymphoma.

Through the night and early morning, I lay alone in a condominium thousands of miles from home, knowing my earthly body had lost one more crucial battle with the armies of disease. All my fears were revived, and I knew for certain that drifting back to sleep was out of the question. So I sat up and began to pray, pouring out my anxious heart to God. I talked over every aspect of my condition with Him. It was really the only option I had, wrapped in blankets in that North Carolina condominium.

Somehow I managed to get up and get myself to the football stadium the next day. College games, of course, are loud and spirited and require plenty of energy. I flew home Saturday night in order to be there to preach my regular Sunday schedule. Now if there's any day in which it's difficult for a pastor to rest, it's Sunday. The marathon went on and on—and brought me the next day to the office of my chiropractor, whom I told about the pain I had begun to experience in my left shoulder. He gave me the gift of yet another appointment, sending me to my oncologist. It was his opinion that something was amiss in my left collarbone area.

I made the appointment to see my oncologist, but getting an answer would have to wait. The oncologist wanted to get a biopsy of the swelling, and that surgery would have to be scheduled for the future. A week and a half had passed since I'd first realized something was wrong. I was tired both physically and emotionally, and the demands on my body and my soul seemed never to reach an end.

While I waited for the surgery to be done, I returned to North Carolina to see my son play another game. But I had another purpose for making this jaunt across the country. I have a friend in that area, Dr. Furman, who is among the finest doctors in his field. He is a tho-

---

From My Journal

Lord, I cannot rid myself of this nagging fear. Deep in my heart, I know the disease has crept back in. I can feel it stealthily going about its work of destruction in my body. Please help me to do whatever I can to nurture my immune system. Show me how I can rebuild the strength that has drained away from my weary vessel.

Today I've been tired and listless. I simply can't continue feeling that way. Please lift my dying spirits, Lord—You are the only true Healer and I put my trust entirely in You. I await Your loving hand, nursing me back to strength and service.

---

racic surgeon, but his general knowledge of medicine is quite broad. Dr. Furman was good enough to take a look at my weary body. It was his opinion that the swelling in my collarbone was nothing for me to worry about. That was the good news.

The bad news was the swollen nodule Dr. Furman found in my neck. And it really was bad news, for in all likelihood it meant a recurrence of the cancer I had fought off before.

I knew Dr. Furman had the correct diagnosis. My cancer was back, with a vengeance, and that was nearly impossible for me to accept. I had celebrated a victory over the dread disease. I had put it behind me, assigning it to the closed files of my unhappy memories. I had determined to live happily ever after. But the road had come to another bend—if anything, an even crueler one. It felt almost like a mockery to my sense of gratitude to God for bringing me through it before. My mood went black. Could I survive another weary bout with the giant? What was the meaning of being forced into the battle again? Wasn't once enough?

It was the darkest night of my soul, a nightmare with no hope of waking. I can't even begin to tell you.

The psalms are dotted and drenched with more tear stains than any other part of the Bible. Music is a direct portal to the soul, and the Book of Psalms is the hymnal of the Old Testament. Every conceivable emotion from ecstasy to anger to despair can be found in these pages. Many of the most beautiful verses ever written are gathered in this collection of the hymns and poems of the kingdom of Israel. What Paris's Louvre museum might be to art, the Book of Psalms is to poetry.

If there is a single great message here, it is that our pain is real, but God's presence is just as real. The psalms bear witness to the fact that we aren't the first to walk down the difficult roads of disappointment and persecution and bitterness. Here we find hope in the time of storm, even when the thunder and lightning cause us to run for shelter. As we read the Book of Psalms, we feel as if our story has been recorded before we have lived it. And if the problems have been there before us, the solutions must be there for us too. There can be no more powerful healing balm than the wisdom we find in this book positioned strategically in the center of the Bible.

Whenever I have suffered, the psalms have provided my medicine. When I have been wounded, they have bandaged me and pointed me toward healing. When I've most needed these verses, no commentaries or scholarly notes have been necessary. The simple and heartfelt words I've found here have always been enough. I've drunk deeply of them, bathed in them, and let them wash over me until I've felt the dust of the world cleansed away by the hope and peace of God's presence in the music of the psalms.

But at other times, I've yearned to swim to deeper depths in these verses. I've wanted to go farther beneath the surface to understand something of the writers and the context and the problems that inspired these songs. It's no different than I've felt about the classic Christian hymns. I have in my library four or five volumes that chronicle the stories behind the great hymns. What inspired the composer? From the setting of what life encounter was he writing? As I read how these timeless melodies came into existence, I can never sing them thoughtlessly again.

It's just the same with the psalms. We get a "backstage pass" and discover what was happening in David's life or what Israel was enduring when a psalm came to be written. And the words and the music of these pieces seem to come alive with new meaning.

I think you'll be interested in how Psalm 46 came about.

The year is 701 B.C. The king of Assyria is a man whose name strikes terror in the hearts of those in the Mediterranean world—Sennacherib. He is obsessively intent on expanding his kingdom, which has rapidly risen to dominance. He has led his army on a ruthless

---

From My Journal

I've been thinking lately—wondering if I'll ever feel one hundred percent well again. I'm sure it's quite normal for me to feel this way, but I also realize I've been learning one of the toughest of truths: "When I am weak, then I am strong." Help me not to forget the lessons of the bend in the road.

---

march throughout the Mediterranean world, heading south now toward Judah. Like a swarm of locusts, the Assyrians have consumed and conquered everything in their path. Among the rising and falling dynasties of the ancient world, this empire is a cruel and mighty one, merciless in its drive toward conquest.

In his great journey of capture and enslavement, Sennacherib the conqueror has come across a curious little kingdom called Judah. This kingdom revolves around the hub of a city the people call Jerusalem. And Sennacherib's military intelligence tells him that Judah is ruled by a man by the name of Hezekiah. They say he is a godly man who came to the throne when he was young.

Judah shows signs of having been through great unrest and civil discord. Many of the previous rulers, it is said, ruled foolishly and weakened a once proud and powerful state. But Hezekiah is different. Hezekiah has shown the same regard for reform and spiritual rule as Sennacherib has shown for conquest and domination.

For example, these people have an ancient tradition they call the Passover. Under past rulers, the ancient practice has been virtually discarded and forgotten, but Hezekiah has reclaimed it and lifted it to its original place of prominence and spiritual significance. He has pointed his people back to the temple and the work of the priests and of godly sacrifice. He has been absolutely intolerant toward idols and pagan practices inconsistent with his God, and the shrines and statues have been toppled and smashed during his regime.

The historians will record this description of Hezekiah:

> He did what was right in the sight of the LORD, according to all that his father David had done. . . . He trusted in the LORD God of Israel, so that after him was none like him among all the kings of Judah, nor any who were before him. For he held fast to the LORD; he did not depart from following Him, but kept His commandments, which the LORD had commanded Moses. The LORD was with him; he prospered wherever he went. (2 Kings 18:35–7)

An interesting man, this King Hezekiah; he is a foe Sennacherib cannot take for granted. The Assyrian monarch has already conquered Israel, the kingdom to the north that was once part of a unified nation that included the province of Judah. The inhabitants of Israel have been conquered, shackled, and marched off in captivity to spend the rest of their lives as slaves. And word of this has spread southward like wildfire. The people of Judah realize the ravaging, merciless forces of Sennacherib are marching toward Egypt at this very moment, and Judah lies squarely in their path. Confrontation is a certainty—and destruction is almost as sure.

Soon, Assyrian troops surround the walls of the city. Their foreign voices can be heard outside the gates, hurling ridicule and threats. "We've heard about the God you serve," they taunt. "We're here to find out how special He is. Why don't you send Him out to defend you? We've destroyed many tribes, and none of their gods put up a fight."

They also attempt a shrewd and deadly maneuver.

> Thus says the king: "Do not let Hezekiah deceive you, for he shall not be able to deliver you from his hand; nor let Hezekiah make you trust in the LORD, saying, 'The LORD will surely deliver us; this city shall not be given into the hand of the king of Assyria.'" Do not listen to Hezekiah; for thus says the king of Assyria: "Make peace with me by a present and come out to me." (2 Kings 18:29–31)

"Never mind what your leader says," they're saying. It's a line as old as the snake in the garden and as new as a bumper sticker that reads, "Question authority." *Ignore your leader. Do what is right in your own eyes. Have we got a deal for you!*

The Assyrians especially target Hezekiah's idea that God should be trusted and obeyed. "Come on out now with a nice gift for your new boss, Sennacherib," they're saying. "Hezekiah and his naive faith are finished." All this time, the policy of King Hezekiah is not to deal with terrorists—to ignore the taunting outside the gate.

But this city has something else interesting about it: prophets. And at present, there happen to be two effective ones named Micah and Isaiah. King Hezekiah leans on them, and he is now given a word of encouragement through Isaiah. Here's a paraphrase of the message:

"Relax. God says that everything is under control, and you're doing the right thing in ignoring the challenges of Sennacherib's men. Don't worry about him, for he has blasphemed the name of God, and he will be dealt with. Sennacherib will hear rumors that turn him homeward, and there he'll die by his own sword."

The bottom line? "It may look bad, King Hezekiah; you may see your city surrounded. But seeing is not believing—believing is *seeing*. See what your God is doing. See that He is still in control." The blasphemy of Sennacherib is this: He has mixed the name of the one true God with the names of all the false ones in that part of the world. He has broken one of the highest and holiest of commandments—defaming the name that is above every other name. His own mouth has sealed his fate.

A few days later, messengers come running in to Hezekiah holding a letter from Sennacherib. It's not a very polite letter. It's filled with ugly threats and details about how the people of Judah will soon be destroyed. And the king of Judah does something very interesting. He carries the letter with him to the temple, and he spreads the letter out before him and before God. "Read this, Lord!" he is saying.

You and I have felt exactly like that, haven't we? The problem is so great and terrifying that all we can do is run to God, lay it all out before Him, and say, "Look! Just look what I'm facing!"

Hezekiah spreads the menacing letter before God. "Well, Lord?" he says. But his prayer is much more eloquent than that. It's recorded in 2 Kings 19. He concludes, "Now therefore, O LORD our God, I pray, save us from his hand, that all the kingdoms of the earth may know that You are the LORD God, You alone" (v. 19). Hezekiah realizes the true issue—that the power and sovereignty of God have been challenged.

The king leaves it all with God. He walks back to his palace, passing by the walls beyond which foreign soldiers are still hurling ridicule and dark warnings. And he waits. It is all the king of Judah can do, wait and pray and have faith. He knows that at midnight, the attack will come. The ominous moments tick by.

You can read the climax in 2 Kings 19:35. The angel of the Lord comes by night, and he executes 185,000 Assyrians. When the break of day comes, the men of Judah return to their posts and can't believe what is laid out before them—acres of Assyrian soldiers, no longer

---

From My Journal

Look at me, Lord! You know me so well, and You know how terrified I am about the idea of enduring another cycle of chemical treatments. You know I can't face the idea of losing all my progress toward the five-year cure I've been counting on. But, Lord, You know me so well. I lay this before You and trust Your will for me. I need Your help as never before. My strength is as weak as it's ever been. You give above and beyond all that we ask or think, and I know I can trust You with this challenge. I also know that my fears are a waste of precious mental energy.

---

ridiculing, no longer frightening or imposing. It's a landscape of death. Listen to the exact words of Scripture: "There were the corpses—all dead."

The Lord God has taken up the challenge of Sennacherib and his men.

Many people would have laughed at the seeming folly of Hezekiah, hurrying to the temple to show God a threatening letter. But this leader lays out his burdens before the Lord, and the Lord lays out His response outside the gates. It's just that simple. All the citizens of Judah quickly realize that this day will be forever celebrated in the history of their nation. It is a red-letter day, and a red-letter psalm is penned to commemorate it: Psalm 46. This, one of the most famous of all psalms, is actually a song of celebration written after the invaders were put down.

But who actually wrote the unforgettable words of the psalm? One candidate for that distinction is Hezekiah himself. Some scholars point to the king, who would obviously have led the worship and celebration. But others point to Isaiah, a poet of unsurpassed eloquence.

The author might well have been an anonymous scribe whose name is lost to the ages, but the occasion for Psalm 46 is crystal-clear: the rout of the Assyrians by the angel of the Lord.

If you've never before known the story behind this great hymn of victory, how do you feel about it now? Psalm 46 towers over us as a biblical monument to the awesome and limitless power of God. Like all monuments, it has the function of helping us to remember something precious and sustaining—in this case, that no barrier is too great for God to overcome. A city surrounded by an entrenched enemy, inches from destruction by a mighty army, cannot be of any great concern for the God who has set the galaxies in space, the God who created and continues to sustain the earth. Kings and armies seem like juggernauts from our limited perspective, but they're nothing in the great scheme of God's hold on history. The Greeks, the Romans, the Assyrians, and the Babylonians all seemed invincible for a brief time. They are now no more than colorful characters from ancient history, and God's strength has not waned.

That's why this hymn and the story behind it have always offered me such comfort and assurance. Psalm 46 radically realigns my per-

---

God is our hiding place; He is our power.
Providing in trouble, He's there every hour.
And fear will not find us, though earth be in motion,
And mountains fall into the heart of the ocean,
Or tidal waves roar and the flood waters pour;
No, the mountains themselves cannot shake His devotion.

—Psalm 46, from Ron Suggs, My Rhyming Bible

---

spective. It shows me that with God, all things are possible. It persuades me that victory is always within reach for anyone who is willing to spread out their concerns before God. It is not the might of the enemy but the strength of God's power that wins the day.

When Trouble Comes, Retreat to Your Refuge

Psalm 46 divides neatly into three sections, each of them punctuated by one word: *Selah*. Each stanza is built around a powerful, godly concept that will strengthen and reassure us in times of trouble. We have so many treasures to unlock from the wealth of this chapter.

The first three verses set the tone for the psalm.

Our God Is an Awesome Refuge

The first and most dominant image from Psalm 46 is the picture of a hiding place: "God is our refuge and our strength." The Hebrew word for *refuge* invokes a quiet place to go for protection. Hezekiah finds refuge in the temple. And it's not a place for leaving his problems outside—the king brings them in to spread before Almighty God, revealing every detail.

This idea is sprinkled throughout the Old Testament. Listen, for instance, to Deuteronomy 33:27: "The eternal God is your refuge, and underneath are the everlasting arms." We are placing ourselves in His comforting hands and our hope in His powerful arms.

Psalm 91:2 says, "I will say of the LORD, 'He is my refuge and my fortress; my God, in Him I will trust.'"

Psalm 18:2 offers us, "The LORD is my rock and my fortress and my deliverer; my God, my strength, in whom I will trust."

I hope you've learned through experience, as I have, that God is your guaranteed refuge. We try many other alternatives. At the first sign of trouble, we rely on our own resources. Then, when we fail to solve the problem, perhaps we'll call on family or a close friend. Friends, of course, are notoriously unreliable in giving the right advice or dependable support. They can even aggravate the problem. We may go see a godly counselor or, if worse comes to worse, even a minister. The ultimate answer is not to be found in any of these options, some of which can provide a Band-Aid or a cup of cold water. The answer is in the midst of us. Our Lord is our refuge, a very present help in trouble.

October 31, 1517, is often called the Fourth of July of Protestantism. On that day there were the first tremors of a spiritual earthquake of worldwide proportions when a quiet, obscure monk named Martin Luther nailed a parchment to the door of the University of Wittenberg in eastern Germany. His document contained ninety-five theses, or points for debate. He raised questions that ignited an ecclesiastical revolution. The great idea at the center was salvation by faith, not by works; being a good church member is insufficient to pay the price of our sins. The movement launched by Luther also reestablished that we have direct access to God through Christ, our high priest.

But there were other wonderful ideas that rose out of the Protestant Reformation. One of these was the rediscovery of congregational singing. Luther had strong convictions about the power of sacred music, and he expressed his convictions in a number of statements. For instance, he wrote, "If any man despises music, as all fanatics do, for him I have no liking; for music is a gift and grace of God, not an invention of men. Thus it drives out the devil and makes people cheerful." *If you dislike music, you're a fanatic.* I didn't say that—Martin Luther did.

He also declared, "The devil, the originator of sorrowful anxieties and restless troubles, flees before the sound of music almost as much as before the Word of God." And since I'm a preacher and I love music so much, I gravitated toward this quotation: "I would allow no man to preach or teach God's people without a proper knowledge of the use and power of sacred song."[1]

It's clear that Luther, who helped to redefine modern, faith-based Christianity, carried a high opinion of the place of music in worship. And which hymn was most central to the Reformation? That one's easy—"A Mighty Fortress Is Our God," a song Luther wrote based upon Psalm 46. This hymn became the battle cry of God's people during the Reformation, a great source of strength and inspiration, especially among those who were martyred for their convictions. This hymn has been translated into almost every language, and there are more than sixty different English translations of the text itself.

When difficulty or discouragement came upon Martin Luther and his friend Philipp Melanchthon, the two key architects of the Reformation, sometimes Luther would say, "Philipp, come, let us sing the Forty-sixth psalm." The two of them would bring out the metric version Luther had written, and they'd sing the words together. If you travel to Germany and visit the place where Luther is buried, you'll find the first line of the psalm engraved on the great man's tomb.

A mighty and awesome refuge is our God—for our time, for Luther's time, for any time.

Our God Is an Accessible Refuge

Our God is "a very present help in trouble" (v. 1).

Trouble—that's a word that needs no introduction. As used here, the more precise meaning would be "in tight places." Have you been in tight places recently? We speak of being stuck between a rock and a hard place. We have no room to maneuver. The words *very present* convey the idea that God is easy to find. He is as real and as much there with you as He could possibly be. Some of our friends run out when trouble rolls in, but God isn't like that. He moves in closer, putting His great arms around us. When we're in tight places, He draws us tighter.

In Exodus 33:14, God's word to Moses was, "My Presence will go with you, and I will give you rest." That's exactly what He does for us all. He is very present.

Our God Is an Ageless Refuge

Our refuge is not only accessible, but ageless. "Therefore we will not fear, though the earth be removed, and though the mountains be carried into the midst of the sea; though its waters roar and be troubled, though the mountains shake with its swelling" (vv. 2–3).

The psalmist comes to this section and asks himself, "What would be the greatest natural catastrophe imaginable?" And he invokes a flood that could wash away mountains and remove the earth itself. The earth is the most ageless thing available to our senses. It is basically the same earth that Moses and David and Jesus and Paul walked upon. But what if even the earth were to crumble? Even in all this, he says, we'd have no reason for anxiety. The world may be *ancient*, but God is *ageless*—and that's a different matter entirely. We feel as if there's no more time for God to act, but what is time to God? He created it. He is ageless.

When trouble comes, we can retreat to our refuge, who is awesome, available, and ageless. No problem is any match for Him.

Knowing these liberating truths about God our refuge strengthens us and fills us with courage. Then what should we do to face the task at hand?

When Trouble Comes, Rediscover Your Strength

The challenge forces us into the waiting arms of God. When we realize that He is in control, we're overjoyed and immensely comforted.

From My Journal

Lord, never let me forget that my mind must be fixed on You. I think of You so much more now than the time before my cancer arrived. I have become more sensitive now to Your will and to the process of becoming holy. I want my life to honor You. I want to live for You. I want to serve You wholeheartedly.

In these days when I face an uncertain future, my heart would be troubled; help me to remember that "You will keep him in perfect peace, whose mind is stayed on You."

But our overriding impulse, once within the stout walls of God our refuge, is simply to faint from exhaustion. We've been weakened by the anxiety, fear, and commotion of all that has befallen us. We've been functioning on sheer adrenaline, and in the sudden realization of safety, our last ounce of strength seems to flee. Our resources are spent.

Now is the time when we learn that God is more than a refuge. He is also our strength.

We Have a Secret Power Within

In ancient times, the sentries of a city would bring news of approaching invaders. The city walls would quickly be fortified, and everyone would seek safety inside. What do you think the greatest fear would be in such a situation? It wasn't catapults or rocks or flaming spears. The people most feared being cut off from supplies of food or water. The invaders may not be able to come inside, but they could stop you from getting the things you needed from the outside.

In advance of the arrival of the Assyrians at Jerusalem, Hezekiah had time to prepare his defenses. In the Kidron Valley outside of Jerusalem bubbled a deep spring called Gihon. It provided the water supply for Jerusalem, so it was of enormous strategic importance. Hezekiah knew that above all costs it must be protected, so he redirected the spring through a conduit that was 1,777 feet long, hewn of solid rock. He brought the spring waters beneath the walls of Jerusalem into a reservoir in the middle of the city. Then he covered up all traces of the spring in such a way that Sennacherib would have no idea where the water supply was. If the angel of the Lord hadn't destroyed the Assyrians that night, the people of Judah would still have had fresh water for a lengthy period of time. Hezekiah had planned well.

There is a suggestion of this incident in the psalm. "There is a river whose streams shall make glad the city of God, the holy place of the tabernacle of the Most High" (v. 4).

The meaning and symbolism of water in the Bible run deep—no pun intended. God's Spirit is ever present in our midst to refresh us, cleanse us, and strengthen us for the journey. He is the eternal spring that never runs dry. Jesus sat by a well one day and said, "Whoever drinks of this water will thirst again, but whoever drinks of the water that I shall give him will never thirst. But the water that I shall give him will become in him a fountain of water springing up unto everlasting life" (John 4:13–14).

Soon after that, Jesus said, "If anyone thirsts, let him come to Me and drink. He who believes in Me, as the Scripture has said, out of his heart will flow rivers of living water" (John 7:37–38).

The Holy Spirit of God living within you is a secret fountain of life-giving water. People don't realize the depth of God's Spirit in residence within your soul. Through the Holy Spirit, God has come to live inside you. There's no way to overstate the powerful implications of that startling truth. Why should we look outside for help when trouble comes? Almighty God is among us and within us. He is the source of living water, springing up into eternal life.

We Have a Secret Person Within

"God is in the midst of her, she shall not be moved; God shall help her, just at the break of dawn. The nations raged, the kingdoms were moved; He uttered His voice, the earth melted. The LORD of hosts is with us; the God of Jacob is our refuge" (Ps. 46:5–7).

"Just at the break of dawn," as we read here, God certainly did help her! That's when the angel of the Lord dealt with the Assyrians. The armies of Judah may have been outnumbered and out-armored, but there was one Warrior who tilted the scales toward a rout of the Assyrians.

The Lord stepped into time and space like that mysterious fourth silhouette in Nebuchadnezzar's furnace, as recorded in the Book of Daniel. Shadrach, Meshach, and Abed-Nego—a clear and simple total of three—were marched into the furnace to await the flames. Who was this fourth shape in the fire, "like the Son of God"? The Lord occupied the fire with His children. In tight places, He holds us even tighter. We're safer in raging flames sheltered in His arms than in the coolest and calmest climate without Him.

That same truth applied to the besieged walls of Jerusalem.

When Trouble Comes, Redirect Your Thoughts

In times of trouble, God's advice to us is not abstract, but pragmatic. He offers not empty philosophies, but sound battle plans.

The Lord reminds us that the mind is a powerful element in our armory—both weapon and shield. Our thought patterns are crucial in the midst of our difficulties. Any soldier would tell you that the moment the enemy can be demoralized, he is beaten. Competitive athletes and even combative politicians will confirm the pragmatism of this concept. In the spiritual realm, we must go into battle with our thoughts fixed on Him.

A sanctified mind can stand against any worldly foe. How can we offer our thinking to God when we're facing a crisis?

Review the Works of the Lord

"Come, behold the works of the LORD, who has made desolations in the earth. He makes wars cease to the end of the earth; He breaks the

---

From My Journal

Our faith is being stretched, Lord—how true that is. I may not enjoy it, but I know You have a loving purpose in this. Keep us trusting You with each day and with each new twist in the uncharted road we're traveling. Lord, I know that the times allotted to me are determined by Your eternal plan—and You will surely accomplish above and beyond all that I can even ask or think.

I trust You, even when I am afraid.

---

bow and cuts the spear in two; He burns the chariot in the fire" (Ps. 46:8–9).

The God of today is the God of yesterday. If we want to know what to expect from Him, we need only to review His record. How it helps us to put our minds to the task of remembering God's works! The same God who sustained you in the past, who brought you victoriously through every previous crisis, is the God who stands with you here and now, in the midst of this fresh testing of your spirit.

That's why God's salvation of Judah during the crisis of Sennacherib was infinitely precious to God's people—it created a milestone for them. The dramatic mass destruction of the enemy became a kind of "memory monument" so tall it would never be forgotten. Parents would tell their children, children would tell their grandchildren, and of course the event was memorialized in God's Word to astound and inspire countless generations to come. The people of God could always look back, even from bondage, and say, "Remember how the angel of the Lord slew the Assyrians? Surely He is among us, and surely He will protect us." The power of memory—for good or for evil—is formidable indeed.

This is a good place to put in yet another request for you to start keeping a journal—and now you can see a good reason for doing so. Journaling memorializes the blessings of God. My mind will often wonder, "What was going on in my life on this day in 1994?" The pages of my journal sit open and ready to fill in the details. After I read and refresh myself, I'll nearly always smile and say, "Amazing! I'd forgotten all about that. God did a wonderful thing for me, and I had let it pass from my mind." Your journal provides spiritual fuel, made up of the ingredients of your past, to add power and hope to your life.

Time is the loving creation of our God. That's why the great enemy of time and memory is the devil. Satan loves to trap our minds within the present calamity, where the problem can expand to massive proportions, stripped of the context of God's purposes. Our Lord would use time and crises to mold us in wisdom and maturity to the image of Christ. But the evil one prefers that you not dwell on that fact. Doesn't he whisper in your ear that this new bend is the end of the world? Doesn't he tell you that God has forgotten you, that you're all alone against the wheels of fate, and that none of this has any meaning other than to break you against that wheel? If those sentiments sound familiar, just remember who it is that whispers them to you. Satan has managed to impress that philosophy upon the majority of our writers, filmmakers, and cultural minds. Your life is being lived in a lonely, meaningless vacuum, according to that tragic mind-set.

But from the victorious perspective of heaven, today's trouble is a blip on the eternal horizon—a "wisdom upgrade" to boost you toward the place where you ultimately want to be. And when you come to doubt the stated philosophy of that view, it will help you to take a look at the record. You need your Bible. You need your journal. You need those sanctified memories that convince you that God is in control. Gird yourself against the foe with the weapon of memory, by reviewing the mighty works of the Lord.

Reclaim the Words of the Lord

Have you heard these golden words before, this timeless call to worship? "Be still, and know that I am God; I will be exalted among the nations, I will be exalted in the earth! The LORD of hosts is with us; the God of Jacob is our refuge" (Ps. 46:10–11).

"Be still!" If we stripped them from their present context, you'd identify those two words as an exasperated admonition to your young children. "Stop that! Be still!" And don't you think God sees us as rambunctious children sometimes? Can't you imagine Him leaning over the banister of heaven and calling down, "Be still!"

He is calling some important message to us, as everything from the lips of God is important. But we can't hear Him. We're too busy squabbling and playing games and doing everything but listening. So He cries out for us to slow down, silence our voices, and listen.

A refuge, after all, is a place of quietness. When we seek safety, silence is our friend; it hides us from the enemy, allows us to listen for important information, and affords us the opportunity to regather our strength. It allows us to be still and know that He is God.

This is the closing message of this immortal psalm. We're enjoined to be silent that we may become aware of His presence and His purposes. Whatever their specifics may be when translated into our lives, they all converge in the ultimate one: that He should be exalted among the nations and exalted in the earth. The nations begin with the people as individuals, so we can be certain that He will be exalted in our personal circumstances—if only we will be still and know that He is God.

For the second time, the psalmist says, "The LORD of hosts is with us." We have a tendency to let our eyes hurry over such phrases as if they were so much conventional religious jargon. But in fact, they're crucial to the meaning of this section of the psalm. Read them and take them in, for the author has seen fit to speak them twice. "The LORD of hosts is with us; the God of Jacob is our refuge."

Who is the Lord of hosts? In the Hebrew it is *the Lord of Sabaoth*: the Lord of the angels, the Lord of the hosts of heaven. Why is this worthy of consideration? Think about the story from 2 Kings. The angel of the Lord—*one* angel of the Lord—was dispatched from heaven to defend the city of Jerusalem. That angel destroyed 185,000 Assyrians who were bent on the destruction of God's people.

The people of Judah needed only one angel, but the Scriptures promise us we're not limited to one angel. We have the Lord of them all with us.

Keep that in mind the next time you hear one of those trendy angel stories—you've noticed how angels have been all the rage in contemporary culture lately. We hear of angels at dangerous intersections, angels in hospital wards, even angels helping you find a good parking spot. We'd have to conclude the angels have gotten very busy lately, and they're now more involved in highway safety than in defending the walls of Jerusalem and 185,000 invading soldiers. Perhaps this is so. I've personally not been the recipient of any obvious, visible angelic encounters—but I do believe we have angels watching over us.

Perhaps guardian angels are provided for us. But would you rather have your own angel than the Lord of Sabaoth as your God? He is the One who created and empowers the angels. And that same mighty God lives within our hearts. Perhaps when our hearts are troubled, we should spend less time looking for angels and more time speaking to the awesome God within our hearts, telling Him, "O Lord, God of creation, I know You are present with me. Give me strength and power to face this moment."

There is a wonderful word in the Old Testament. It is *emanu*, which simply means, "with me." Perhaps the most astounding fact of all astounding facts about our great God is that He is "with me." There can be no greater geometric line than the one defined by the distance between those two points—my lowliness and His omnipotent perfection. And yet He is "with me."

That word *emanu*—"with me"—travels through time and becomes something deeper and wiser, just as all of us hopefully do. *Emanu* ultimately gives birth to a new word, *Emmanuel*: "God with us." And He will be called Emmanuel, for God is with us.

Hannah Whitall Smith was one of our greatest writers of devotional literature. Many of her works of spiritual depth came from the crucible of terrible emotional pain from the loss of children, the infidelities of her husband, and the loss of many of her close friends. One of her greatest works is called *Living Confidently in God's Love*. When she wrote it, she had been experiencing terrible pain and unanswered questions. She didn't know where to turn or whom to seek for counsel. It seemed to her, just as it seems to you and me, that no one had ever been on the path she was traveling. No one could possibly understand what she was experiencing. Here are the words she used to describe her feelings:

> There happened to be staying near me just then for a few weeks a lady who was considered to be a deeply spiritual Christian, and to whom I had been told I should go for additional help to get through my trouble. So I summoned up my courage, and one afternoon I went to see her. I poured out my troubles before her, and I expected, of course, that she would take a deep interest in me and would be at great pains to do

all she could to help me. She listened patiently, did not interrupt me, but when I finished my story, and I paused, expecting her to respond in sympathy and consideration, she simply said, "Yes, all you say may be very true, but then in spite of it all, there is God."

I waited a few minutes for her to say something else. But nothing came, and my friend the teacher had the air of having said all that was necessary, and I knew she was done. But I continued, "You don't understand how very serious and perplexing my difficulties are."

"Oh, yes, I did," replied my friend. "But then, as I tell you, there is God."

I could not induce her to make one other answer. It seemed to me most disappointing and unsatisfactory. I felt that my peculiar and really harrowing experiences could not be met by anything so simple and so mere as the statement, "Yes, but there is God."

[But] . . . from wondering, I came gradually to believe that being my Creator and Redeemer, He must be enough. And at last, a conviction burst upon me that He really was enough. My eyes were opened to the fact of the absolute and utter all-sufficiency of almighty God.[2]

What do we mean when we say, "God is enough"? Let's be honest and agree that it sounds suspiciously like the language of piety and self-righteousness, just a tired cliché.

But in reality, those three words are so much more than jargon. God *must* be enough, in fact, for if He isn't, where do we find ourselves?

From My Journal

I believe that You and You alone are the answer, O Lord. My doctors are merely tools You will use. Lord, it is to You alone that I look for healing. You are Jehovah Rophe, and You can heal according to Your will.

Where do we go for Plan B? If the God of heaven and earth, who is mightier than all the world's armies, who can cause the earth to melt into the sea, who is "with us"—if that God is not Lord of your crisis, you're in deep trouble, and so are the rest of us.

Praise His name that we need not worry about that possibility. The fact is that God *is* sufficient. Our God is in control. He holds the destiny of the galaxies in His hands, all the while knowing the precise number of hairs on your head. He has preserved His people time and again, performed miracles on battlefields and in cattle fields, among prophets and priests and plumbers. Above all else, He loves you and chose to measure that love out not in words, but in blood. He loves you enough to give you the greatest gift conceivable. Would such a love allow you to suffer without a purpose? Would such a love neglect to have a wonderfully happy ending lying in wait for you?

God has never run away from you, so you must never run away from Him. Run into His waiting arms, for that's what He most desires. He is your refuge—your city wall, your cool and refreshing stream, and your impenetrable defense from the enemy. He is a very present help in times of trouble.

Psalm 16

A Michtam of David.

1 Preserve me, O God, for in You I put my trust.
2 O my soul, you have said to the LORD,
    "You are my Lord,
    My goodness is nothing apart from You"—
3 And to the saints who are on the earth,
    "They are the excellent ones, in whom is all my delight."
4 Their sorrows shall be multiplied who hasten after another god;
    Their drink offerings of blood I will not offer,
    Nor take up their names on my lips.
5 You, O LORD are the portion of my inheritance and my cup;
    You maintain my lot.
6 The lines have fallen to me in pleasant places;
    Yes, I have a good inheritance.
7 I will bless the LORD who has given me counsel;
    My heart also instructs me in the night seasons.
8 I have set the LORD always before me;
    Because He is at my right hand I shall not be moved.
9 Therefore my heart is glad, and my glory rejoices;
    My flesh also will rest in hope.
10 For You will not leave my soul in Sheol,
    Nor will You allow Your Holy One to see corruption.
11 You will show me the path of life;
    In Your presence is fullness of joy;
    At Your right hand are pleasures forevermore.

11

The Best Is Yet to Come

> While we walk the pilgrim pathway,
> Clouds will overspread the sky;
> But when trav'ling days are over,
> Not a shadow, not a sigh!
> Let us then be true and faithful,
> Trusting, serving ev'ry day.
> Just one glimpse of Him in glory
> Will the toils of life repay.
>
> —E.E.HEWITT

The worst is behind me, I thought. What a relief!

I had survived the greatest trial and most paralyzing fear of my life, and my faith had stood firm. And it wasn't merely intact, but deeper and more resonant. For I felt that I had a tight handle on just what was occurring spiritually in my life. God was using my serious illness to draw me into a deeper knowledge of Himself. I was grateful for what I had learned and for the rewarding new insights I had into His ways. Best of all, the crisis was over!

Then the nodule was discovered.

So much for having all the answers; my bubble was burst. I was despondent.

That was late in 1998. I checked into the hospital and had the nodule surgically removed from the base of my neck. The doctors sent it away for pathology studies, and I had to wait and brood over the freshly revived question of my mortality. When I returned to see my oncologist, Dr. Saven, he confirmed what I already knew—I was facing a recurrence of lymphoma. The only good news was that the lymphoma was still in the quadrant of my body in which the cancer had originally appeared. It had been contained and prevented from spreading.

Then the doctor told me I was a candidate for a stem cell transplant. "Stem cell therapy may not be what you had in mind for the months ahead," he said, "but it's the best opportunity we're going to have to drive out this disease once and for all."

I thought of my conversations with Pastor Page, detailed in the previous chapter. He had been through two rounds of stem cell transplants, and his experiences suddenly became very relevant. Now I understood why I had been led to take such a great interest in his medical history. I realized that God had prepared me for this crisis by providing me with a friend who had walked down this road ahead of me.

I was soon to meet Dr. Mason, who heads up the stem cell transplant department at Scripps Clinic. Dr. Mason is a leader in the field of outpatient stem cell transplant. His research has helped to shape what we know and can expect in this new medical frontier. And I was grateful, because I entered this new experience with many qualms. I had the impression that a stem cell transplant had frightening side effects. I had heard that the white blood cell count plummets, and you're open to every kind of infection and illness. I pictured myself quarantined in the hospital, unable to see visitors, wearing a mask on my infrequent visits to the outside world, and desperately playing defense against the normal germs of the air.

Dr. Mason painted quite a different picture of what was ahead for me. He explained that patients living within twenty minutes of the hospital have the advantage of living at home throughout the procedure. Only those from distant addresses had to check in and stay.

I learned that, before anything else, I had to qualify for the treatment. I had to receive more standard chemotherapy to determine whether the tumors would shrink. In other words, as the doctor put it,

"If the little hammer doesn't work, the big hammer's not going to work either." So it was up to my body to demonstrate that it was still sensitive to the chemicals in question. The tests took several weeks and, by this time, Christmas had come and gone. We were into the year 1999.

Needless to say, "happy holidays" weren't operative for me in 1998. I felt very burdened by the new tests and the procedures that lay ahead. There was also a speaking tour on a cruise to the Bahamas scheduled for January 1999. Was I taking a risk by heading for the other coast for a cruise and extended biblical teaching responsibilities? Dr. Mason smiled and urged me to carry on my life as it should be lived. He counseled me to do everything I normally would do, even though I was taking chemotherapy and my hair was beginning to come out.

The success of the stem cell transplant could also be boosted if I built up my strength by taking daily exercise. That was just the kind of thing I was eager to find—a rare opportunity to take my prospects into my own hands, at least in a small way. I immediately immersed myself in a program of one hour per day on the treadmill. By the time I entered the hospital in March, I could count no more than four or five days when I hadn't walked 4.2 miles on the treadmill. Even on the cruise ship sailing in the Bahamas, I logged my hours in the exercise room and kept up my program. That treadmill was my road to wellness, and I was hurrying down it daily.

If there was anything I could do—anything at all—to increase my chances of success in the ordeal that lay ahead, I was determined to give it my very best shot.

March 22, 1999.

The day had a great, red, nervous circle scribbled around it on our family calendar. After arriving at the hospital, I was taken through all the pretransplant procedures. I had already provided many stem cells during my first episode of chemotherapy. There were eighteen bags of stem cells in cold storage waiting for me.

During the procedure I was attached to a Groschond catheter. This was placed in my chest during a surgical procedure, to provide access to my veins both for blood testing and injecting of the chemotherapy.

After that procedure, the medical team began the flow of toxic chemicals. They selected four of the most powerful toxins ever injected into the human body.

It was a long and demanding day, and I was able to rest during the following one. But the stem cell transplant began. During this process,

---

So much depends on me, yet all I have for this task is whatever health and energy You give me.... I eat carefully, rest, exercise, and think positive thoughts, and still this wretched lump of clay fails me. You have Creator's rights on my body. You formed every miraculous part. What You take away is Your business. I will do what I can with whatever capability You give me. It's Yours....

The days end as the years end, with never enough time for all the good that could be done, only just enough for Your priorities, if I get them right. You created time, and it does not limit You. But I do not have a thousand years today, God. I have only now.

So this day is Yours; I am Yours; these people are Yours; the resources are Yours. The challenges we face are Yours, as is anything we hope to accomplish.

It's Yours, God. It's not mine.

— **Richard Kriegbaum, Leadership Prayers**

---

the toxic chemicals bring the white count down to the lowest possible number by which your body can survive. In such conditions, as I'd been told, there is no defense against infection or disease. The body simply doesn't have the resources to fight back.

The doctors then reintroduced the white cells from the stem cell collection back into my body—in my case, about eighteen bags of stem cells were returned to my system. At this point, the toxic chemicals began to take their toll, and I became gravely ill. The toxicity of the chemicals ate the lining away from my throat, all the way down my esophagus to my stomach. I couldn't swallow my own saliva. I couldn't eat. If I had not been on morphine, I wouldn't have been able to sleep. It was an excruciatingly painful time to be alive. I had been forewarned, but I had never dreamed that any procedure in modern science could be so miserable and uncompromising.

I'll never forget Easter Sunday. I was back in my hotel room after having blood work done at the hospital, and I was beginning to feel truly uneasy about what lay ahead—and whether I had run out of options. I knew that the wonderful people at church, buoyed by the hope of the resurrection, were pouring out their intercessory prayers for my health and well-being. My white blood cell count had yet to begin its rebound.

But we were in for a shock. The day after Easter, I went to the hospital with an anxious heart, preparing myself for the latest results. I couldn't believe my ears. The incredulous doctors told me that on Sunday, my white count had soared from two hundred to twenty-eight thousand! This was in the realm of the miraculous. With a heart filled to bursting with joy and relief, I thought about the prayers of God's people on Resurrection Sunday. What power they had unleashed! How wonderful to know that on the day of celebration for Christ's defiance and defeat of death, my body had seen a resurrection of its own.

I had come through the night season—just like David, the psalmist, sufferer, and singer. David knew about the night seasons, and Psalm 16 is our evidence of that.

Once again, by the words beneath the title, we know that we've come to one of David's very special psalms. Scholars suggest this one may have been written during a brief interlude of peace—a welcome respite in the hectic world of David, who was suddenly granted a vacation from fearing for his life. David had found himself holding the life of Saul at the point of a spear. A quick thrust and a twist, and his problems would have been over.

But the anointed slayer of Goliath refused to exploit the opportunity before him—and Saul, in the light of such mercy, didn't have the heart to keep hunting the one who had pardoned him. The whole story is played out on the pages of 1 Samuel 26.

Saul and three thousand of his best soldiers were hot in pursuit of David. They had camped for the night in the Wilderness of Ziph, without having any idea of the proximity of their prey. For David was in the immediate area. He came to the place where the army of Saul was encamped, and he could see they had settled in for the night. They had relaxed their guard. David decided to embark on a spontaneous fact-finding mission, joined by Abishai, who was the brother of Joab, the general of his army.

David and Abishai crept up to Saul's camp in the dark of night. They could see Saul himself, sleeping soundly with his spear embedded in the ground beside his head. This was the ultimate in vulnerability—a resting warrior's greatest nightmare. Abner and all of Saul's finest were in close reach. It could be a rout—a slaughter. That's the way Abishai saw it. He put his mouth near David's ear and whispered, "Why not kill him now and get it over with? We'll never have to run or hide again!"

Here is David's reply: "Do not destroy him; for who can stretch out his hand against the LORD'S anointed, and be guiltless?" (1 Sam. 26:9)

David saw what lay before him in terms greater than his own self-serving options. He looked at things as God would see them, and he realized that he wasn't in a spiritual position to remove from this earth the one God had anointed. Instead, he did something very clever. He took hold of Saul's spear, protruding from the ground by the king's head, as well as a bottle of water lying nearby. He walked away with both items. This was calculated to cause more than a bit of concern in Saul's camp. How would you feel if the spear that guards your life was within easy grasp, and you woke to find it removed? As it happened, however, nobody awoke because God had placed the whole camp into a deep sleep.

The second half of 1 Samuel 26 tells the whole story. David and Abishai made their way out of that clearing and across the valley. Once he found himself at a safe distance, David stood atop a hill and shouted toward Saul's encampment. David's character is consistently fascinating. Here was a man who has been godly enough to do the right thing when he had the opportunity to take the life of his tormentor, yet he was human enough to have a little fun with the situation. He couldn't resist toying with Abner, Saul's right-hand man—letting Abner know about his brush with death.

Here's what David, in so many words, was saying: "Hey, Abner! Looks to me as if you're not a very good bodyguard! I was standing right beside your king a few minutes ago, and I could have taken him

---

To seek aid in time of distress from a supernatural Being is an instinct of human nature. I believe in the truthfulness of this instinct, and that man prays because there is something in prayer. As when the Creator gives His creature the power of thirst, it is because water exists to meet its thirst; and as when He creates hunger there is food to correspond to the appetite; so when He inclines men to pray it is because prayer has a corresponding blessing connected with it.

—C. H. Spurgeon

---

out in the blink of an eye while you were snoring. Next time you might want to watch your back, and your king's too!"

Saul was startled to hear David's voice, and he called out, "David, is that you?"

David basically replied, "Yes, it's me. King Saul, why do you insist on tracking me down? What have I ever done to you? Please listen closely to what I'm about to say. If God has led you to do all this, then praise God—let's lift up an offering to Him. But if it's a matter of people polluting your heart with all this plotting and conspiracy, those people are cursed in the Lord's eyes. I have an inheritance from God, and these people have tried to push me out of the picture and force me into the service of false gods. My king, I ask you not to spill my blood, as God is our witness. Think about it—you, the king of Israel, mobilizing your forces against a mere flea."

Saul was clearly moved by this speech. His words in verse 21 can be paraphrased in this way: "You're right—I have sinned. Come home,

David, my son. Today you spared me and counted my life as precious, and it's time for me to return the favor. I've played the fool—I can see that now. And I'm ashamed of myself."

The phrases we find in 1 Samuel 26:19–20 offer the clue that unlocks the connection with Psalm 16. The wording almost precisely matches the wording in Psalm 16:4–6. That psalm reaches across history to us today, reminding us in our crises to reflect on the goodness of God. We may feel our world is coming to an end. We may feel so tightly entangled in the problems of this world that there's no escape. But when we pause to reflect on the power and majesty and love of God, everything begins to change. There's an awesome power unleashed by a simple action when you "count your many blessings, name them one by one."

I read a book recently that analyzes where modern counseling has gone wrong. The author was making the point that psychiatrists often urge us to dredge up any and every unhappy event from the past. These negative memories then receive all the blame for our problems. I've had people tell me that after taking the tour of every unhappy event in memory, they felt worse than they did before seeing the counselor.

The author I was reading had a countersuggestion. Instead of taking inventory of the negatives, why not total up the positives? What if the counselor said, "Let's take a few moments to review your life, and see if we can find eight or ten genuinely good things that have happened to you. Let's reflect, review, and accentuate the positive. See if that doesn't make you feel better."

Of course, that strategy is unworkable in the therapeutic community. Once put into practice, it would be so effective that people wouldn't need the expensive therapy! The cure would be bad for business.

Maybe that's too cynical a view of the psychiatric profession, but we can be certain of one thing: Celebrating the blessings of God is wonderful therapy for the spirit. The Word of God never ceases reminding us to review the mighty works of the Lord. Try these two examples:

"I will remember the works of the LORD; surely I will remember Your wonders of old. I will also meditate on all Your work, and talk of Your deeds" (Ps. 77:11–12).

"Bless the LORD, O my soul, and forget not all His benefits" (Ps. 103:2).

Never, never forget the things He has done.

But we do forget, don't we? Industry is the enemy of reflection—and we modern people are nothing if not industrious. We become so busy hustling to get things done, watching life become more and more complex, getting ourselves caught up in anxiety, that we simply forget all the good things God does on a daily and even momentary basis. You and I know people who are enormously blessed with health, wealth, beautiful families, remarkable talents, and exciting occupations. Blessings are breaking out all over them. Then we're not at all surprised to find those same people consumed with anxiety. They would stand out more in this world by displaying an attitude of gratitude than they would by needing a checkup from the neck up.

And that's during normal circumstances, when the waves are calm. When the storm comes, the winds are blowing, and the waves are high, we've lost our reference point with the blessings of God. We can't find our way back to Him, and the black clouds and high tides are more than we can handle. We've lost that invaluable perspective. For if we were to measure our lives against those of people in the rest of the world, we'd find ourselves crying out, "Thank You, Lord—I'm so blessed!"

David finds himself in a temporary oasis of tranquillity. He's not running for his life, and he's able to enjoy peace of mind. He takes the time to reflect upon all the good things he has received from the Lord. Psalm 16 is the record of his spiritual inventory.

Remembering Who God Is

"Preserve me, O God, for in You I put my trust." That's how David begins the psalm we'll be exploring in this chapter. "O my soul, you have said to the LORD, 'You are my Lord, my goodness is nothing apart from You.'"

There are psalms in which David comes around to remembering who God is, and we see his entire perspective transformed within a few verses. But in this chapter, we can say that David begins right at

---

There is no music in a rest, but there is the making of music in it. In our whole life-melody, the music is broken off here and there by "rests" and we foolishly think we have come to the end of the tune. God sends a time of forced leisure, sickness, disappointed plans, frustrated efforts, and makes a sudden pause in the choral hymn of our lives. . . . but how does the musician read the "rest"? See him beat the time with unvarying count, and catch up the next note true and steady, as if no breaking place had come between. Not without design does God write the music of our lives. Be it ours to learn the tune, and not be dismayed at the "rests." They are not to be slurred over, not to be omitted, not to destroy the melody, not to change the keynote. If we look up, God Himself will beat the time for us. With an eye on Him, we shall strike the next note full and clear.

—Mrs. Charles Cowman, Streams in the Desert

---

the beginning—by acknowledging who God really is. And he sees God in several profound dimensions. Let's examine them.

Seeing God in His Personal Presence

David turns his attention toward the presence of God in his personal life. In the first two verses we find three different names for God. If we were to read it directly from the original Hebrew language, it would go something like this: "Preserve me, *Elohim*, for in You I put my trust.

O my soul, you have said to *Jehovah*, 'You are my *Adonai*, my goodness is nothing apart from You.'"

David is fully aware of the magnificent and manifold presence of the awesome God. He sees the God of the covenant, who deals with His children with love and grace. He sees the powerful *Elohim*, who presides over all creation. He sees the personal *Jehovah* God who knows the most intimate details of our hearts and minds. He feels the perfect presence of *Adonai*, and he cannot help but be overwhelmed that the God who is all this and more would surround him with love, protection, wisdom, and strength.

God is with us. From the womb to the tomb, we are always in His presence and we're never apart. The distractions of the world will rob us of the full implications of this, and that's why we need to pause whenever and wherever possible to simply soak it in and allow it to transform us: We live in the presence of *Elohim*, *Jehovah*, *Adonai*.

At the end of the psalm, David looks within himself and gravely observes that he finds no goodness apart from God. That is no simple thing; it's actually among the most profound revelations that can ever come to us. Have you reflected seriously upon the fact that there is no good thing in your life—your family, your talents, your possessions, your friendships, your potential—that doesn't have a string leading back to the love and grace of God? There is no good thing within us or about us or connected to us that doesn't come from Him. "Every good gift and every perfect gift is from above, and comes down from the Father of lights, with whom there is no variation or shadow of turning" (James 1:17). Choose any good thing, large or small, and follow it back—follow it back as far as you can.

> *Back of the loaf is the snowy flour,*
> *And back of the flour, the mill*
> *And back of the mill is the field of wheat,*
> *The rain, and the Father's will.*[1]

You say, "I make my own bread." *Oh, is that right? Where did the flour come from?*

"Well, I got the flour at the mill." *Where did the mill get the flour?*

"They got it from the grain." *Where did the grain come from?*

"It came from the ground." *How did it grow?*

It grew because God allowed the sun to shine, and because He sent the rains to shower down upon the earth where the grain was planted. Every good and perfect gift is from the Father of lights—not *some* of the good gifts and *some* of the perfect gifts, but *every* one of them is a specially chosen, lovingly crafted gift from the Creator of all.

Romans 8:32 tells us that receiving the Lord Jesus Christ as our Savior makes us the recipient of even more than eternal salvation. He will bless us bountifully in every way. "He who did not spare His own Son, but delivered Him up for us all, how shall He not with Him also freely give us all things?" And Jesus said, "I have come that they may have life, and that they may have it more abundantly" (John 10:10). Why? Simply because He is a Father who adores His children, despite all their imperfections.

We are blessed by the presence of *Elohim*. Of *Jehovah*. Of *Adonai*.

Seeing God in His People

David's thinking first takes in the greatness of God, and then he moves to the subject of his friends, whom he calls "the saints who are on the earth." During his time on the run, David has been surrounded by dedicated friends who put their lives on the line to help protect him. And he is profoundly moved by the thought of it.

He says, "They are the excellent ones, in whom is all my delight." Do you ever stop to simply delight in your friends? Do you let them know they are "the excellent ones" in your life?

David may have had his wonderful, devoted friend Jonathan in mind. He may have been thinking about Abishai, who had stolen quietly into the camp with him that night and risked his own life just to help a friend. He may have been thinking about both these men and others as well. While David had been through more than a few harrowing experiences, God had never failed to provide a friend to go alongside him. David had never had to be alone.

That's an important spiritual principle. Do you go it alone when times are tough? God never intends you to do so. Read 1 John closely, and you'll see the premium placed by God upon our place in the family of God. John says it so simply and so eloquently: Loving people and loving God are closely related. In 1 John 3:14, the apostle writes that we know we have new life in Christ by the way we love our brothers and sisters in fellowship—and if we feel no love for others, it's a sure sign that we are abiding in death.

John goes on to say, "Beloved, let us love one another, for love is of God; and everyone who loves is born of God and knows God. He who does not love does not know God, for God is love" (1 John 4:7–8). John is writing a commentary that extends from what he had

---

**My friend Joe Ivey sent me this wonderful letter
after hearing of my sickness:**

I personally feel that God has you in a very specific place in your kingdom work here on earth. Just before writing you, I was meditating on Psalm 103:1–5: "Bless the LORD, O my soul; and all that is within me, bless His holy name! Bless the LORD, O my soul, and forget not all His benefits: who forgives all your iniquities, who heals all your diseases, who redeems your life from destruction, who crowns you with lovingkindness and tender mercies, who satisfies your mouth with good things, so that your youth is renewed like the eagle's."

I know this is a familiar passage to you, brother. It starts out in blessing the Lord but then continues with He "heals all [our] diseases." That is our prayer for you.

---

given us in John 3:16. For "if God so loved us, we also ought to love one another" (1 John 4:11).

He also gives us a warning in 1 John 4:20–21: "If someone says, 'I love God,' and hates his brother, he is a liar; for he who does not love his brother whom he has seen, how can he love God whom he has not seen? And this commandment we have from Him: that he who loves God must love his brother also."

Jesus said it first, in John 13:35: "By this all will know that you are My disciples, if you have love for one another."

Can the scriptural imperative be any clearer? You are not alone.

So David reflects upon his relationships with the people of God. Have you ever stopped for a moment when you are in the midst of difficult times and counted up the true, godly Christian friends that God has given to you? One of the best things about going through a little storm, or even a big one, is that all of a sudden the true nature of God's people becomes clear to you. You find out that God has given to you some fantastic, godly friends.

Seeing God in His Principles

In verse 4, David observes, "Their sorrows shall be multiplied who hasten after another god; their drink offerings of blood I will not offer, nor take up their names on my lips." Here David has moved from the roll call of beloved friends to the relationships that are a bit more troubled. David is always honest about the fact that there are a few flies in the ointment of his life.

During his frantic tour of the countryside, David has seen the idols of Moab and the idols in Philistia. He serves the true God and knows the competition. He is also aware, from the existing Scriptures, of the tragic idolatry in the history of his own people. He is thinking, *I know the goodness and love and majesty of God. And I've seen the alternative. How thankful I am that I have never fallen into idolatry, that I serve the one true God, and that He counts me as worthy to worship and serve Him.*

God does so many things for us. He blesses us coming and going, right and left, when we awaken and when we sleep. But if He never gave us any other blessing, He would be worthy of our constant praise just for His constant presence among us. To know God and to be known by Him—this is an indescribable blessing. It means that we need never be truly lonely. It means that we are never isolated. It means that we are significant, circled points on His map.

But David doesn't stop there. In the heart of this psalm, he takes a look at God and at what He is doing at the present time.

Rehearsing What God Is Doing

God never sleeps. Isn't that comforting?

He is always at work, always fine-tuning the minute details of our lives—not that He provides us with a detailed agenda. There are many times when we're puzzled about what He is up to. We look ahead and wonder if He hasn't forgotten us, because nothing seems to be happening in the way we expect.

Other times we become Monday morning quarterbacks, second-guessing His decisions and the directions He allows life to take. These are the symptoms of spiritual immaturity, as natural as they are for us. Rejoicing in what God is doing—whether we like it and understand it or not—is a way of worshiping Him. It is an act of obedience and a sacrifice of praise.

The Lord Is Our Completeness

"You, O LORD, are the portion of my inheritance and my cup" (v. 5). Old Testament language combines these Hebrew words, simply saying that the Lord is the One who makes us complete, who provides for us whatever we need. It is the answer to that part of the Lord's Prayer that says, "Give us this day our daily bread."

How blessed we are as God's people to know that few of us in the Western world have ever gone hungry. God has generously provided for us. When you bow at the table to thank God for your next meal, be sure you're thanking Him from your heart. Realize what a blessed privilege it is to be provided with the essentials of life. Know that He gives them to you to provide the strength you need to serve Him.

The Lord Is Our Certainty

"You maintain my lot," David says. What he means is that God takes care of his circumstances. And how can the psalmist doubt it? For years he has lived as a nomad, fleeing from hiding place to hiding place from a powerful king and an army bent on finding and destroying this one man. And he has lived to tell the tale.

David has lost nearly everything—his freedom, his home, his family, and his good name. Yet he is able to praise God in the midst of it all and say to God, "You maintain my lot. You provide for me in my time of need."

The Lord Is Our Contentment

The sixth verse offers us a beautiful statement of faith. David says that the Lord is his contentment: "The lines have fallen to me in pleasant places; yes, I have a good inheritance."

What are those "falling lines"? David is saying, "Lord, as I look back across the years, I realize that I've led a good life, and I have been given good things." Can you say that?

I can. I was born in a Christian family. I was reared on the gospel, nurtured on the milk of the Word of God, and educated in Christian schools and a Christian college. I was blessed with godly friends. I've been deeply influenced by people who stayed in our home and people who came along at certain times and in certain places to speak to me, mentor me, and bless me. I was given good friends capable of providing solid counsel when I needed it. I was divinely protected from the things that could have—and perhaps *should* have—happened to me when I was running wild as a young man.

I have no choice but to look back and say the lines have fallen to me in pleasant places. In no way do I deserve the blessings I've been given. The good things showered upon me would have been sufficient for 150 years, and I've received them in this brief lifetime. And that's exactly what David is saying in the sixth verse.

How is it that we come so often to feel just the opposite? How is it that we throw regular pity parties, with a guest list of one? We brood in solitude, thinking that we have the worst fortune; nothing ever goes our way, we never win the prize, and everyone else has it better. I have those moments just as you do. Self-pity throws everything out of perspective—upside down, to be precise. If we don't feel we're getting what we deserve, we should stop and think about what it is that we *do* deserve—after a moment's reflection, perhaps we won't want "justice" so much. If we think nothing ever goes our way, we need to check the record. If we think everyone else has it better, we need to think about some of those wealthy people and whether or not, in the truest sense of the word, they really "have it better." We need to clear up our vision.

We can clear it up by taking time to meditate on how greatly God has blessed us. We need to learn the joy of contentment in what we've already been given. The Word of God tells us how to do that (Phil. 4:11). Did you know that contentment is something we have to develop intentionally? It doesn't happen automatically. All babies are born discontented.

We learn contentment through conditioning our minds to dwell on our blessings, and to turn to expressions of gratitude. David, like Paul, learned to be content.

The Lord Is Our Counsel

"I will bless the LORD who has given me counsel; my heart also instructs me in the night seasons" (v. 7).

What a blessing it is to know our Creator and Sustainer on a first-name basis and to be able to approach Him night or day. The Word of God tells us that when we lack wisdom, we should simply go ask God for it (James 1:5). It never tells us that when we lack wisdom, we should go through the appropriate channels. It never tells us to call technical support and wait on "hold." It never tells us that we're on our own and should fend for ourselves. The Word of God says for us to go directly to the Source. We can fearlessly approach God, and He will be overjoyed to see us! He will pour out wisdom and blessings we never thought to request. He will urge us to come to His side again and again. No question is unwelcome.

God is always available. We may be deep in sleep, yet He is available—watching over us, gently handling our minds, dealing with the problems we've been facing. It is as if God does His holy maintenance work on our minds and hearts as we rest. You climb into bed at night

---

From My Journal

Dear Lord, I pray that this might be my final visit to this insidious disease. I pray that I might not ever have to undergo the trials of chemotherapy again. I ask that You would continue to give me good health as I strain to recover my strength and resume my life. I need You, Lord, and I pray that You would be the sole source of strength in my life. I love You for what You have already done for me!

---

thinking about the challenge weighing down your heart, and you lay it before God before drifting off. During the night, a quiet miracle comes to pass. You wake up feeling entirely differently about things. How could you have not seen it this way before? God has brought it all together in your mind and resolved yesterday's care.

I believe David had that experience. "My heart also instructs me in the night seasons," he tells us. The Lord is our completeness, our certainty, our contentment, and our counsel. But David isn't quite finished. He ends this little section by adding one more attribute to the magnificent collection.

The Lord Is Our Confidence

David reviews the blessings of God and says, "I have set the LORD always before me; because He is at my right hand I shall not be moved." What a powerful statement that is, declaring that with God in our sights, the world and all its forces can align against us, and we will be unstoppable. David, who has faced armies, has more than earned the right to tell us that.

David's agenda for Psalm 16 is becoming clear to us. First he has reviewed who God is. Next he has rehearsed what God does. And now he brings Psalm 16 to a joyful and victorious conclusion by rejoicing at what God is going to do. Before us we have one of the most spectacular portions of the Old Testament, because it provides a ringing demonstration of the supernatural quality of God's Word. Here is David, gazing into the future through the eyes of faith and seeing things he has no right to see. He comprehends things that have never been communicated to him, as far as the Scriptures tell us, except by the Holy Spirit.

And he lays out what he sees accurately—so accurately that when New Testament writers, far in the future, will discuss these events, they will prove their points by quoting the writings of David in Psalm 16.

Rejoicing in What God Will Do

We never cease to be astounded by the foresight of Old Testament writers revealing future events. How can anyone doubt the validity and authority of the Scriptures when they observe this trait? Prepare to be astonished by the prophecy of David.

Rejoicing in the Resurrection

First, *David rejoices in his own resurrection.* He says, "For You will not leave my soul in Sheol." You may recognize the ancient word *Sheol.* It was used to refer to the abode of the dead or the grave itself. David continues, "Nor will You allow Your Holy One to see corruption" (v. 10). In the text, the words *Holy One* are capitalized because they refer to the Lord Jesus. But we should be clear that before David foresaw the resurrection of Christ, he saw his own resurrection. While he doesn't understand completely what is going to happen, David has rehearsed for us all of the good things God has done for him, and is doing for him, in his life. He reflects on all these uplifting truths, and in his incredible spiritual insight he comes to the realization that surely such a loving and protective God will continue to care for him in his death and beyond.

David's view into the world of eternity is a startling one—it surpasses even the prophets. Allow me to give you an example. We all know, at some time or other, a family that loses a small child. People become deeply concerned about the eternal fate of an infant who dies. How does God deal with a soul too young to have had any chance to accept the gospel? Will a doomed infant be saved?

When someone brings that question to me, I always return to the story of the first child born from the union of David and Bathsheba. The Bible says that while this newborn was dying, David fasted and wore sackcloth. He mourned; he pleaded with God. But the baby died, and David rose and dressed, anointed his body, ended his fasting, and returned to normal life. Seeing the grief he had endured while the child was still alive, no one could understand his acceptance of the child's death. Some of the servants asked him to account for his behavior.

David explained it, and his answer has tremendous implications for us. "While the child was still alive," he said, "I fasted and wept; for I said, 'Who can tell whether the LORD will be gracious to me, that the child may live?' But now he is dead; why should I fast? Can I bring him back again? I shall go to him, but he shall not return to me" (2 Sam. 12:22–23).

Did you catch that last sentence? David knew he would see his child again one day. In other words, the infant would be in the place David knew he would someday go—into the arms of his loving Father. He knew what we know, that there is a place known as heaven; but he also knew that God cares for His helpless little ones. David had seen his own resurrection.

But, yes, he had also foreseen the resurrection of the Messiah.

David rejoices in Christ's resurrection. David has said, "For You will not leave my soul in Sheol, nor will You allow Your Holy One to see corruption" (v. 10). One phrase stands out here, and it takes this verse to a whole new level—one that becomes one of the great, victorious peaks of the Old Testament. While David has been talking about his own death, he finds himself thinking in deeper terms—supernatural terms that wander far beyond the reality of himself, his time, and his place.

David would never refer to himself as "the Holy One." It's totally out of character with the David of the rest of the psalms—the David known for a deep humility and a sense of his own unworthiness before God. Never does he even approach claiming for himself holiness of any kind. But as he speaks of victory over the grave, the Holy Spirit lifts a corner of the curtain and gives him a glimpse into the future and the cornerstone of human history—and the first Christians were quick to notice it.

The amazing, farseeing words in verse 10 are carefully selected and quoted on two occasions in the New Testament. The first of these came when Peter was preaching on the Day of Pentecost—without a doubt one of the most amazing, Spirit-empowered sermons ever preached. Three thousand souls entered the kingdom of heaven and the fellowship of Christ in the wake of that lightning bolt of a sermon. In the grip of true inspiration, Peter describes Jesus:

. . . whom God raised up, having loosed the pains of death, because it was not possible that He should be held by it. For David says concerning Him: "I foresaw the LORD always before my face, for He is at my right hand, that I may not be shaken; therefore my heart rejoiced, and my tongue was glad; moreover my flesh will also rest in hope, because You will not leave my soul in Hades, nor will You allow Your Holy One to see corruption. You have made known to me the ways of life; You will make me full of joy in Your presence." (Acts 2:24–28)

Empowered by God's Spirit, Peter confirms that David had been speaking of Christ's resurrection. Even so soon after Christ's ascension, His followers realize the full implications of David's written words so long ago. Did David himself know whereof he spoke? As journalists say today, just what did he know and when did he know it? We can't be certain David grasped the full meaning of the events to which he was pointing; the important thing is that he spoke the truth. He validated his inspiration by accurately foretelling Christ, and Paul added the Holy Spirit's affirmation that Psalm 16 looks forward to Jesus.

But these verses come into play in another New Testament context. You'll find it in Acts 13; the place is Antioch and the agent is Paul. He, too, is delivering an inspired sermon when he explains, "Therefore [David] also says in another Psalm: 'You will not allow Your Holy One to see corruption.' For David, after he had served his own generation by the will of God, fell asleep, and was buried with his fathers, and saw corruption; but He whom God raised up saw no corruption" (Acts 13:35–37).

Paul is very clear on this: David talked about seeing no corruption, but he himself certainly returned to the earth, ashes to ashes and dust to dust. "He whom God raised up," on the other hand, overcame the terrible power of the grave. He ascended to heaven in the body. David, Paul attests, was speaking of Christ. Peter knew it, Paul knew it, and it must have been common knowledge among those first believers who knew their Hebrew Scriptures.

With perhaps the limitations of his understanding, from the vantage point of his particular spot in history, David may have been unable to fathom the full implications of what he was writing. But we, with the advantage of knowing and embracing the Gospels, can see what David might not have seen. Praise God, we need never endure the corruption of the grave. Christ has written the last word. He has saved us from eternal death.

Rejoicing in the Rapture

We come finally to a beautiful ending for our psalm. Try to imagine a more powerfully positive—and positively powerful—bottom line than this one: "You will show me the path of life; in Your presence is fullness of joy; at Your right hand are pleasures forevermore" (v. 11).

Once again, David is seeing into the future, to a time when there will be the possibility of a perfectly intimate relationship with our Lord. Yes, David has attested that the Lord will emerge from a guarded tomb and confirm His status as the Chosen One. But David, who has looked down the road through time all the way to the Easter event, now looks even farther and sees a certain path—the "path of life," as he calls it. This path leads through all the troubles and cares of the world and right into the holy presence of God. "I'll walk down that path one day," David says. "And I'll be in a land where joy is made full, and pleasure can be found at God's right hand."

David can sense the hope that will be made real in Christ. The ultimate pleasure is to be found in the realization of dwelling in the presence of our all-wise, all-knowing, all-loving Creator. And to realize we can spend all of eternity in the perfection of that presence is to feel true hope and joy indeed.

Do you know how to enter that presence? I know only two ways you can accomplish that. The first way, if you are a child of God, is simply to die. As Paul said, "For to me, to live is Christ, and to die is gain" (Phil. 1:21). Even death is positive if it brings us near Him.

Paul teaches in 2 Corinthians 5:8 that we will be well pleased to be absent from the body and present with the Lord. At the very instant of death, we will find ourselves in a new world—the world of being right at His side. We no longer see in a mirror dimly, but face to face. And we need never worry or shed a tear again, for our joy will be made complete.

I see that and my heart surges with joy. What a glorious day it will be to be reunited with Christ. But Paul also said, "To live is Christ." This earth need not be a place to simply escape someday. I'm hoping my years on this planet will stretch out a bit longer. I've looked cancer in the face, and I'll be honest enough to tell you my desire is to beat the rap.

I want to be here for the rapture of the church. Paul tells us, in 1 Thessalonians 4:16–17, that Christ will appear from heaven with a shout. I wouldn't mind being around to witness that event. I want to hear the trumpet Paul has foretold, and I want to see those graves open up and give forth their dead, who will joyfully race through the skies to rejoin their Creator and Redeemer. Then, as Paul says, "we who are alive and remain" (I'm counting on numbering myself among that group) will be caught up with Christ as well. It will be quite a spectacle!

And that, my friend, would be the second way to come into God's presence. Burial or rapture—we can travel to His side by land or by air.

If I had to die today, I know I would have the thrill of being immediately in the presence of my precious Lord. But if I stubbornly push this earthly vessel of my body a few more miles, and if I continue to fight the good fight against cancer and live on—well, there are the considerable consolations of living for Christ in this wonderful world: enjoying my loving wife and counseling my children in adulthood, seeing how God nurtures and develops my grandkids, enjoying the many pleasures of fellowship in the body of Christ and the simple joys of daily living.

Death or life? I agree with Paul—it's a win-win proposition, wouldn't you agree? I agree with David as well, as I realize the fullness of these things and begin to sing God's praises. I have so much to be thankful for. God is everything for me, as I hope He is for you—counselor, friend, provider, and loving Father. He has prepared a mansion for all of us—an appointed room for you, and one for me.

We are going to know joy as it is meant to be known and pleasure as we have never known it.

I want to tell you about a woman who was a staunch and faithful church member. She was ravaged by illness, and no one expected her to live much more than another week or two.

She knew her day was approaching, and she called the pastor and asked him to come help her plan the funeral. So he joined her at her

---

No one experiences complete sanctification without going through a "white funeral" — the burial of the old life. If there has never been this crucial moment of change through death, sanctification will never be more than an elusive dream. There must be a "white funeral," a death with only one resurrection—a resurrection into the life of Jesus Christ. Nothing can defeat a life like this. It has oneness with God for only one purpose—to be a witness for Him.

—Oswald Chambers

---

deathbed, and they began making arrangements. The ailing woman listed for him all the hymns she wanted sung, all the Scripture verses she wanted read, and those she preferred as the soloists.

Then she said, "Pastor, there's one thing I want you to do. You may feel this is strange, but I want you to promise me today that you'll fulfill my wishes anyway."

The pastor frowned mildly. "What's that?" he asked.

She said, "I want to be buried with a fork in my right hand."

The pastor's frown became deeper. This was quite an odd request. "That's a request I've never heard," he said kindly, "but perhaps if you try to help me understand your reasons, I can feel better about carrying out your request."

She said, "Pastor, I've been a member of our church for most of my life. And one of the great joys for me has been the potluck dinners we have. I don't think I've missed one dinner in my life. In the old days, we had them on a weekly basis. And what I remember best is how, after the first course was served, one of the hosts would always stand up and say, 'Save your fork. The best is yet to come!' So, pastor, I'm counting on you to bury me with a fork in my hand. When my loved ones pass by the casket and look at me, I want you to be standing nearby. Those people will ask you why I'm holding an eating utensil, and you'll smile and tell them that for me, *the best is yet to come."*

Can you believe that? Can you look beyond the bend in your road and trust that, even though you can't see where the road winds, the best is yet to come?

Can you look beyond the terrible frustrations of poor health, and believe that God is preparing a sumptuous feast for you? Can you stand in the midst of family trauma, or a crisis in business, or whatever your trial might be, and praise the name of your Father, because you know He is your rock and your salvation?

David could do that, and countless souls throughout the ages have joined with him in joy that flies in the face of rational explanation— pursued as they have been by the giants of life, the jealous kings of daily experience, the limitations of relationships, and the disappointment of hopes and dreams. They have found that these very times of discouragement have not been defined by the absence of God, but somehow, by the miraculous, closer presence of Him. They have stared at the emptiness of death and realized that it held the fullness of a feast.

They have clung to Him, found His love and peace and wisdom, and joined with the great throng who sit at that banquet table. The dessert hasn't arrived, but the anticipation of it is already in the air. Perhaps in one way this is the best moment of all, the moment of anticipation—the moment when we realize the best is yet to come.

Epilogue
Resuming the Journey

When through fiery trials thy pathway shall lie,
My grace all-sufficient will be thy supply,
The flame shall not hurt thee, I only design
Thy dross to consume and thy gold to refine.

In the end, the doctors gave me the thumbs-up.

They told me the stem cell transplant couldn't have proceeded more smoothly, that this body of mine came through the ordeal better than we had any right to expect.

I remembered another day, in what seemed like another lifetime, when I saw the doctors smiling and giving me that same seal of approval. I had been at Scripps Clinic, breezing through a battery of tests on my physical exam. How confident I had been—how unsuspecting of what was lurking in wait for me, to be revealed on that black afternoon. What would I have thought of the endless trials, treatments, chemotherapy episodes, renewed hopes, and shattered dreams that were to dominate my life in the months and years ahead?

That day in September of 1994 seemed a lifetime ago indeed. Now, I'd made it through the stem cell transplant. I'd love to take all the credit for having done so well. After all, hadn't I exercised fanatically every single day, running for my life on a treadmill?

Or maybe I was blessed with exceptionally excellent doctors. Certainly their expertise had played a role, and I thank God for gifted medical practitioners every day. I placed my life in their hands, and they surely hadn't failed me.

But from my vantage point, there was one powerful factor that went the farthest to explain the success of my ordeal. I attribute my healing to the faithful prayers of the people of God—so many of them in scattered places. There were Christians interceding for me before God's throne around the clock. I know I felt fresh spiritual vitality from their prayers, just as I felt fresh physical vitality from my 4.2 daily miles on a treadmill. Never underestimate the power of prayer. Walking on a treadmill is refreshing, but walking with God is transforming.

Today, I live in remission. My life can be characterized as the sweet calm after the storm.

I suppose the storm passed with the stem cell transplant. I stayed briefly in the hospital to get through those first critical hours and days of recovery. Then I was sent home to begin my journey toward recuperation, and hopefully a restored, healthy life. I rested at home for several weeks during which I read, slept, and enjoyed a few visits with the people in this world who are dearest to me. Then, on Mother's Day of 1999, I returned to Shadow Mountain Community Church to preach for the first time since March.

The feeling of walking into that packed auditorium is something I'll never forget for as long as I live. Here was the throng to whom I owed so much, the loving people who had spent countless hours lifting me up before God. I honestly believe everybody who had ever attended our church was present in that sanctuary to welcome me back. And they all rose from their seats to applaud as I entered the room.

How would you have kept your composure in such a situation? One moment such as that is worth a lifetime of struggle. I was emotionally overwhelmed by the outpouring of love and acceptance. I silently thanked God from the very depth of my being, trying to maintain my composure—but I can tell you it was quite a challenge to do so, for my heart was as full, and as electrified, as the church sanctuary. What a blessed man I was—and still am.

More than anything else, today I'm grateful to God. I continue to pray that the doctors got rid of all they were looking for this time, that my days of excruciating treatments are finally at an end. But I also know that cancer is not a battle; it's a war. And I can only be thankful for battles won and land retaken in the name of Christ. I feel thoroughly undeserving of the depths of His mercy, the deep well of His strength and His infinite compassion poured out upon me. I trust you can say much the same thing.

That's why you and I face the road ahead with lighter hearts and lesser burdens. The bending path can seem like a lonely one, but we all must walk it. I hope the true stories that have been shared—mine and those of several of my good friends—will somehow serve to fortify you for the battles, conflicts, and struggles of your own life.

Even more, I hope that God's Word, as we've explored it through the wisdom of the psalms, will be your beacon in those dark times you may well be facing at the present. Never forget that He has offered us a storehouse of guidance in the field of adversity. We have the answers for how God's people can face their trials with courage, faith, and hope. That storehouse can be found between the covers of your Bible.

Let's you and I hold that Word close to our hearts and turn our eyes to the bends that lie ahead. I'm thankful that I can still walk down it with you in this body that has been through so many struggles.

This life is a remission for both you and me, don't you agree? Jesus, the Great Physician, has performed our treatment with His skilled hands, and He "got it all"! Death has been defeated. We've come through the ordeal with hearts filled with gladness and gratitude. But on earth, the skirmishes continue even after the war has been won. We continue to fight daily battles with the forces of sin, which want so badly to infiltrate our lives and spread so insidiously.

But now we know what we're up against. We set our eyes on the One who gave us our marching orders, and we march ever onward.

We travel this road for the days that God has ordained for us, taking the difficult curves, but also seeing the wonderful scenery along the way. The journey is rewarding, and the destination is the only one worth the traveling. Let's walk it with joy—together.

The Irish poet traditionally blessed the traveler with the words, "May the road rise up to meet you." Allow me to rephrase it this way as my parting words of encouragement for you:

> *May you rise up to meet the road,*
> *and all its snares and hazards,*
> *in the grace and wisdom*
> *and wonderful sufficiency of God.*
>
> *Amen.*

Notes

Chapter 1: A Bend in the Road

1. Gordon MacDonald, *The Life God Blesses* (Nashville: Thomas Nelson, 1994), 25.
2. Ibid., 28.
3. Source unknown.
4. MacDonald, *The Life God Blesses*, 25–26.
5. Laura A. Barter Snow, "This Thing Is from Me," (Grand Rapids: Faith, Prayer and Tract League, n.d.
6. Ron Mehl, *Surprise Endings* (Sisters, Oreg.: Multnomah, 1993), 60.
7. MacDonald, *The Life God Blesses*, 42.
8. Mehl, *Surprise Endings*, 60.

Chapter 2: Psalm for a Dark Night

1. "Luck Rivals Worst of Sick Jokes: 'There's Hope,' New Yorker Says," *Los Angeles Times*, 19 March 1995, A28.
2. Source unknown.

Chapter 3: I Need Your Help, Lord

1. Lloyd John Ogilvie, *Falling into Greatness* (Minneapolis: Gregson, 1984), 191.
2. William Barclay, *The Daily Study Bible: The Gospel of Luke* (Philadelphia: Westminster Press, 1975).
3. Eugene Peterson, *A Long Obedience in the Same Direction* (Downers Grove, Ill.: InterVarsity, 1980), 40–41.

Chapter 4: When God Delays

1. F. B. Meyer, *Choice Notes on the Psalms* (Grand Rapids: Kregel, 1984), 23.

2. Adapted from John Phillips, *Exploring the Psalms*, vol. 1, *Psalms 1–88* (Neptune, N.J.: Loizeaux Brothers, 1988), 99.

3. James Montgomery Boice, *Psalms: An Expositional Commentary*, vol. 1, *Psalms 1–41* (Grand Rapids: Baker, 1994), 109.

Chapter 6: A Desert Psalm

1. H.D.M. Spence et al., *The Pulpit Commentary*, vol. 2 (Chicago: Wilcox & Follett Co., n.d.), 25.

2. C. S. Lewis, *Reflections on the Psalms* (New York: Harcourt, Brace & World, 1958), 50–51.

3. Lewis Smedes, *Standing on the Promises* (Nashville: Thomas Nelson, 1998), 91.

Chapter 7: Life's Ups and Downs

1. Gary Richmond, *A View from the Zoo*, out of print.

Chapter 8: Praying under Pressure

1. W. Graham Scroggie, *A Guide to the Psalms*, vol. 4 (Grand Rapids: Kregel, 1995), 79.

2. Alexander MaClaren, *The Psalms*, vol. 3, *Psalms 90–150* (New York: A. C. Armstrong & Son, 1894), 408.

3. Dorothy Foltz-Gray, "Words of Comfort," *American Way*, July 1999, 36.

Chapter 9: When You Are at Your Wits' End

1. Leonard Griffith, *God in Man's Experience* (Waco, Tex.: Word, 1968), 108.

Chapter 10: Triumph over Trouble

1. Source unknown.

2. Hannah Whitall Smith, *Living Confidently in God's Love* (Springdale, Penn.: Whitaker House, 1984), 278–80.

Chapter 11: The Best Is Yet to Come

1. Ray C. Stedman, *Jesus Teaches on Prayer* (Waco, Tex.: Word, 1975), 72.

About the Author

DR. DAVID JEREMIAH is the senior pastor of Shadow Mountain Community Church in El Cajon, California. He is the author of several best-selling books, and his popular syndicated radio and television Bible-teaching program, *Turning Point*, is broadcast internationally. David and his wife, Donna, have four children and ten grandchildren.

NEW YORK TIMES BESTSELLER

New York Times Best-Selling Author

WHAT IN THE WORLD IS GOING ON?

DR. DAVID JEREMIAH

10 Prophetic Clues
You Cannot
Afford to Ignore

The Bible prophecy prequel to
Living with Confidence in a Chaotic World
by Dr. David Jeremiah

IS THE TURBULENT ECONOMIC & POLITICAL STATE OF THIS WORLD ACTUALLY PROPHESIED IN THE BIBLE?

If so, what are we to do about it? It is hard to piece together all this information in a way that gives a comprehensive picture of what the End Times will look like. That's why so many theories abound. And that's why Dr. David Jeremiah has written *What in the World Is Going On?*, a unique book that cuts through the hundreds of books and numerous theories to identify the ten essential biblical prophecies that are affecting our world today.

There is no other book like this. You'll find it is the ultimate study tool for understanding the future. You'll have a greater sense of comfort that, even in these turbulent times, God is indeed in control. If Bible prophecy has always been a mystery to you, Dr. Jeremiah's book will help you solve the mystery. At last, Bible prophecy can make sense, and make a difference. It's never been more important. *What in the World Is Going On?* is shocking and eye-opening but essential reading in these turbulent days.

WHAT IN THE WORLD IS GOING ON? BRINGS BIBLE PROPHECY TO LIGHT ON:
- The oil crisis
- The resurgence of Russia
- The new axis of evil
- The importance of Israel
- The new powers of the European Union

WHAT IN THE WORLD IS GOING ON?

is available in fine bookstores everywhere and through Turning Point where you will also find a correlating study guide, ten message CD album, DVD presentations, and small group curriculum of this book.

VISIT DAVIDJEREMIAH.ORG TO ORDER

FURTHER
YOUR STUDY

INCORPORATE THESE CORRELATING
STUDY MATERIALS
BY AUTHOR DR. DAVID JEREMIAH

STUDY GUIDE
This 128-page study guide correlates with the *Living with Confidence in a Chaotic World* messages by Dr. David Jeremiah. Each lesson provides an outline, overview, and application study questions for each chapter.

AUDIO MESSAGE ALBUM
10 AUDIO MESSAGES
The material found in this book originated from messages preached by Dr. David Jeremiah at Shadow Mountain Community Church where he serves as Senior Pastor. These ten messages are conveniently packaged in one audio album.

DVD MESSAGE PRESENTATIONS
10 DVD MESSAGES
Watch Dr. Jeremiah deliver the ten *Living with Confidence in a Chaotic World* original messages in the special DVD collection.

SMALL GROUP STUDY CURRICULUM
The *Living with Confidence in a Chaotic World* DVD-Based Small Group Kit will take your small group or Sunday school class through ten weeks of Dr. Jeremiah's teaching for living with certain hope in our uncertain times.

ORDER THESE *LIVING WITH CONFIDENCE IN A CHAOTIC WORLD* RESOURCE PRODUCTS FROM DAVIDJEREMIAH.ORG

OTHER TITLES
BY DR. DAVID JEREMIAH

CAPTURED BY GRACE *A NEW YORK TIMES* BEST-SELLER!

By following the dramatic story of the "Amazing Grace" hymnwriter, John Newton, and the apostle Paul's own encounter with the God of grace, David Jeremiah helps readers understand the liberating power of permanent forgiveness and mercy.

LIFE WIDE OPEN

In this energizing book, Dr. David Jeremiah opens our eyes to how we can live a life that exudes an attitude of hope and enthusiasm . . . a life of passion . . . a LIFE WIDE OPEN! *Life Wide Open* offers a vision, both spiritual and practical, of what our life can be when we allow the power of passion to permeate our souls.

SIGNS OF LIFE *A NEW YORK TIMES* BEST-SELLER!

How does the world recognize us as God's ambassadors? In *Signs of Life* you will take a journey that will lead you to a fuller understanding of the marks that identify you as a Christian, signs that will advertise your faith and impact souls for eternity.

MY HEART'S DESIRE

How would you answer a pollster who appeared at your church asking for a definition of worship? Is it really a sin to worship without sacrifice? When you finish studying *My Heart's Desire*, you'll have not just an answer, but the biblical answer to that all-important question.

SEARCHING FOR HEAVEN ON EARTH

Join Dr. Jeremiah as he traces Solomon's path through the futility of:
• The search for wisdom and knowledge
• Wild living and the pursuit of pleasure
• Burying oneself in work
• Acquiring as much wealth as possible
Dr. Jeremiah takes readers on a discovery to find out what really matters in life, the secret to enjoying "heaven on earth."

WHEN YOUR WORLD FALLS APART

When Your World Falls Apart recounts Dr. Jeremiah's battle against cancer and the real-life stories of others who have struggled with tragedy. Highlighting ten Psalms of encouragement, each chapter is a beacon of light in those moments when life seems hopeless.

SLAYING THE GIANTS IN YOUR LIFE

Loneliness. Discouragement. Worry. Anger. Procrastination. Doubt. Fear. Guilt. Temptation. Resentment. Failure. Jealousy. Have these giants infiltrated your life? Do you need the tools to slay these daunting foes? With practical appeal and personal warmth, Dr. Jeremiah's book, *Slaying the Giants in Your Life* will become your very own giant-slaying manual.

TURNING POINTS & SANCTUARY

These 365-day devotionals by Dr. Jeremiah will equip you to live with God's perspective. These topically arranged devotionals enable you to relate biblical truths to the reality of everyday living—every day of the year. Perfect for yourself or your next gift-giving occasion, *Turning Points* and *Sanctuary* are beautifully packaged with a padded cover, original artwork throughout, and a ribbon page marker.

STAY CONNECTED

TO THE TEACHING OF DR. DAVID JEREMIAH

Take advantage of two great ways to let Dr. David Jeremiah give you
spiritual direction everyday! Both are absolutely FREE!

TURNING POINTS MAGAZINE AND DEVOTIONAL

Receive Dr. David Jeremiah's monthly
magazine, *Turning Points* each month:

- Monthly Study Focus
- 48 pages of life-changing reading
- Relevant Articles
- Special Features
- Humor Section
- Family Section
- Daily devotional readings for each
  day of the month
- Bible study resource offers
- Live Event Schedule
- Radio & Television Information

YOUR DAILY TURNING POINT E-DEVOTIONAL

Start your day off right! Find words of inspiration
and spiritual motivation waiting for you on your
computer every morning! You can receive a daily
e-devotion communication from David Jeremiah
that will strengthen your walk with God and
encourage you to live the authentic Christian life.

Sign up for these two **free** services by visiting
us online at www.DavidJeremiah.org and clicking
on MAGAZINE to sign up for your monthly copy
of *Turning Points* and your Daily Turning Point.

MAXIMUM CHURCH

READY! SET! GROWTH!
LET DR. JEREMIAH'S MAXIMUM CHURCH TAKE YOUR CHURCH THERE.

With a united vision to strengthen the Body of Christ and reach the community, your church can experience spiritual and fiscal growth through creative and compelling campaigns.

With over forty years of ministry experience, founder Dr. David Jeremiah now shares his passion for pulpit teaching and church leadership by offering solid Bible teaching campaigns designed to stimulate the spiritual and fiscal growth of local churches. Maximum Church campaigns are created for full-spectrum ministry including preaching, teaching, drama, small group Bible curriculum, and suggested Sunday school material—all supported by electronic, print, and audio visual files.

SIGNS OF LIFE

Lead your church to become one of Christ-like influence in your community as you take the five Life Signs discussed in this book and apply them to the lives of your congregation.

This campaign is based on Dr. David Jeremiah's best-selling book *Signs of Life*.

CAPTURED BY GRACE

Based on the best-selling book *Captured by Grace* by David Jeremiah, this ministry growth campaign will help your church and community discover the depths of God's unrelenting love and grace.

For more information on Maximum Church,
VISIT WWW.MAXIMUMCHURCH.COM